ASSASSIN OF YOUTH

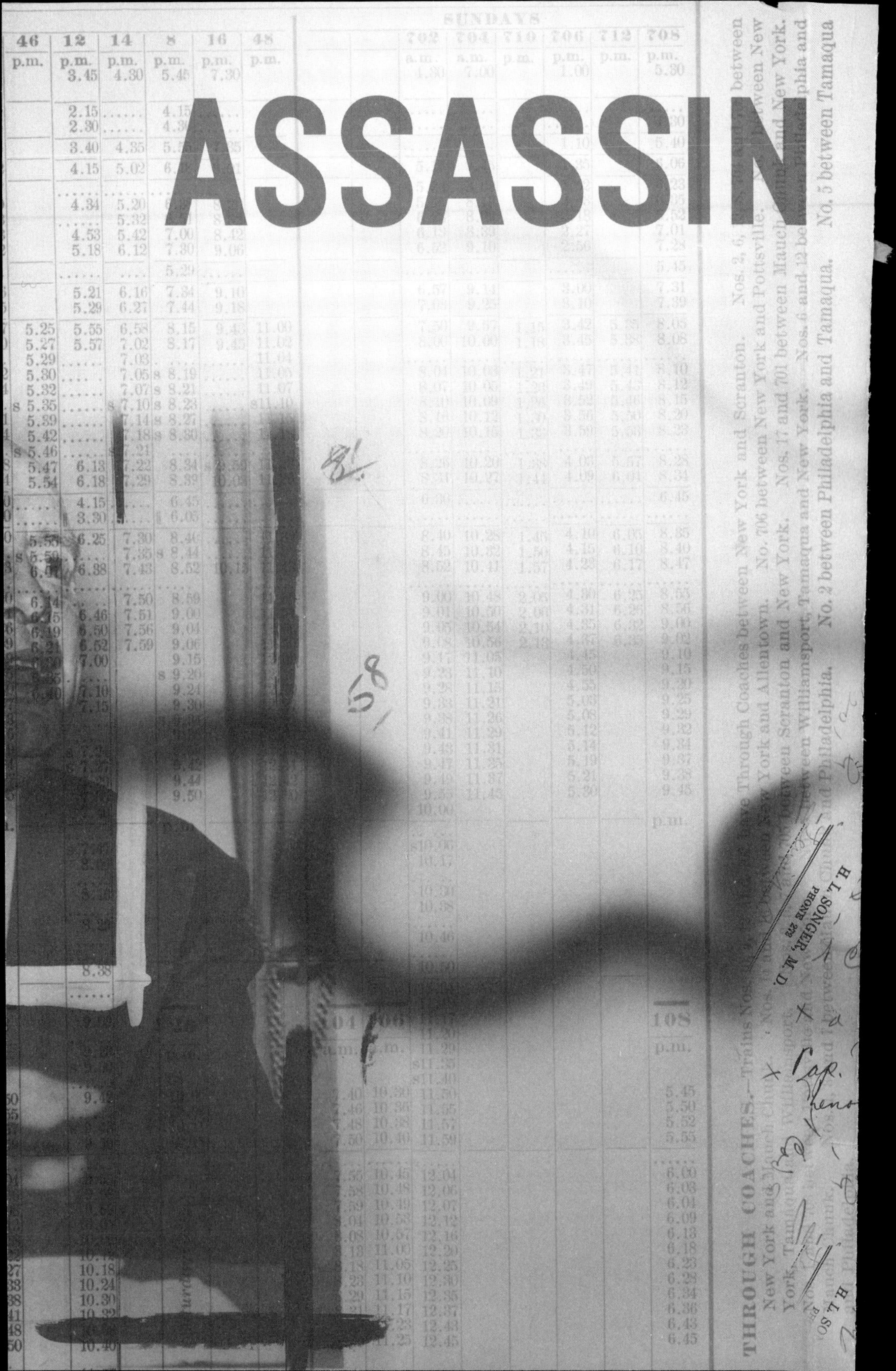
ASSASSIN

OF YOUTH

A Kaleidoscopic History of Harry J. Anslinger's War on Drugs

ALEXANDRA CHASIN

THE UNIVERSITY OF CHICAGO PRESS · CHICAGO AND LONDON

Publication of this book has been aided by a grant from the Neil Harris Endowment Fund, which honors the innovative scholarship of Neil Harris, the Preston and Sterling Morton Professor Emeritus of History at the University of Chicago. The Fund is supported by contributions from students, colleagues, and friends of Neil Harris.

The University of Chicago Press, Chicago 60637
The University of Chicago Press, Ltd., London
© 2016 by Alexandra Chasin
All rights reserved. Published 2016.
Printed in the United States of America

25 24 23 22 21 20 19 18 17 16   1 2 3 4 5

ISBN-13: 978-0-226-27697-7 (cloth)
ISBN-13: 978-0-226-27702-8 (e-book)
DOI: 10.7208/chicago/9780226277028.001.0001

Portions of this book previously appeared in *Denver Quarterly*, vol. 49, no. 3 (2015) and *Fence* (Summer 2014). Used with permission.

LIBRARY OF CONGRESS CATALOGING-IN-PUBLICATION DATA

Names: Chasin, Alexandra, author.
Title: Assassin of youth : a kaleidoscopic history of Harry J. Anslinger's war on drugs / Alexandra Chasin.
Description: Chicago : The University of Chicago Press, 2016. | Includes bibliographical references.
Identifiers: LCCN 2016011027 | ISBN 9780226276977 (cloth : alk. paper) | ISBN 9780226277028 (e-book)
Subjects: LCSH: Anslinger, H. J. (Harry Jacob), 1892–1975. | Drug enforcement agents—United States—Biography. | United States. Bureau of Narcotics—Officials and employees—Biography. | Drug control—United States—History—20th century.
Classification: LCC HV5805.A57 C43 2016 | DDC 363.45092—dc23 LC record available at http://lccn.loc.gov/2016011027

♾ This paper meets the requirements of ANSI/NISO Z39.48-1992 (Permanence of Paper).

Dedicated to the alpha and omega of my writing teachers,
Helen S. Chasin and David R. Jauss

CONTENTS

Prologue

MARTHA

EXTINC

Martha, the last survivor of the
American passenger pigeon species,
preserved and on display in 1967.
The last of the species died in 1914.
Smithsonian Institution Archives.
Image SIA2010-0612.

1   THE TROUBLE WITH HARRY

Kaleidoscope. A *kaleidoscope* is a plaything, an optical device that continuously juxtaposes elements in a mirrored chamber, generating constantly changing patterns according to the twist of the viewer. What if a kaleidoscope could point *out* on the world and its past, rather than in on a handful of triangles, marbles, or other baubles? What if that kaleidoscope set its sights on a handful of historical elements, a set of values and laws, a number of related events, a personage? What if we accept that all vision is distorted one way or another, and insist not on plain correction but on rich distortions? What a twisted way to look at history.

Blind Spot. Whereas it is commonly understood that drugs distort perception, the sober and sobering official treatment of drugs in the United States has been particularly blind to the realities of traffic and use. Rather than solving social problems, drug policy and law have, in effect, constructed criminality along identity lines, turning a criminal justice system into an administrative mechanism for racist and classist social control.

War on Drugs. At base, there is a penal code in which the severity of punishment corresponds with the classification of the drug in question. But the war on drugs also works through the following disciplinary principles: harsh penalties, compounded penalties for repeat offenders, and mandatory minimum sentencing. Imagined as deterrents, these mechanisms have nothing to do with drugs per se, so their ideological attachment to drugs had to be forged, through and for a "war"—a metaphor with material consequences. This war is a complex cluster of changing cultural values rendered in law and enforced by the state over time affecting the lived experience of millions of people, causing suffering in as many unique minds and in too many imprisoned bodies and their extended networks, disabling economic options at every scale, coloring community life, further segregating the polity, and giving the lie to any national claim to justice. And at the nodal point in that cluster, a man named Harry J. Anslinger.

Anslinger's War on Drugs.   Anslinger was the first drug czar. Commissioner of the Federal Bureau of Narcotics from its establishment in 1930 until his retirement in 1962, Anslinger was the chief architect of drug prohibition in this country, an elaborately disastrous set of policies and laws. Anslinger's war on drugs predated and preconditioned Nixon's War on Drugs and the Rockefeller Drug Laws of the 1970s. Anslinger's war on drugs is the reason those dominoes could go down; it is fear and hysteria, trading in same, in the guise of hardboiled and hyperrational traffic in truths and facts.

Here's to Your Knowledge.   At this point, a great deal is known about the costs of a drug war: the thriving global black market, the personal and collective effects of drug use, the dynamics of enforcement, including its ineffectiveness. But the best knowledge of multiple disciplines, the wisdom of lawmakers and judges, reliable statistics, medical research, psychological insight, and great bodies of literature have produced compartmentalized conclusions and partial understandings of the disaster and therefore no real solutions. What is already known did not prevent Sandra Bland from getting killed.

Sandra Bland.   In July 2015, having been pulled over for a failure to signal a lane change, Sandra Bland ended up dead after a three-day stint in jail in Waller County, Texas. Bland was an African American woman for whom public sympathies shifted after it was discovered that she had been high on pot when she was initially stopped and high again at the time of her death. Bland died—and was judged—in the nation Harry Anslinger wrought.

Mirror.   A kaleidoscope works by way of a mirror. What else should we have in there?

Whiteness. White middle-class readers may be able to get drugs easily, and may not live in fear of the police, but that does not mean that we are no longer living in Anslinger Nation.

Anslinger Nation. No proof is needed that the United States is a carceral society; our incarceration rate is a global embarrassment.[1] The bars of the jail cell—those literal straight lines that imprison people of color very disproportionally—are the perfect emblem of a system that tracks, administers, follows, stops, frisks, arrests, convicts, releases, and repeats with whole social groups. Rows and columns of attendant statistics, the rules of procedure, the panoptic organization of detainees and prisoners attest to organizational sophistication. If assembly-line automation seems bygone, consider the role of administration and management in a criminal justice system that processes so many human beings every year. Methods of social control have not declined in the last fifty or sixty years; by all measures, there is more policing activity than ever. Though it may look like the forces of sex, drugs, and rock 'n' roll have prevailed, the squares are not vanquished. A spectacular blur of commodities dazzles the eye, drawing it away from police and prison—even as policing and prisons themselves are commodified both as private enterprise and as entertainment. In both fiction and nonfiction, policing has produced systematic brutality, systematic damage to individuals and communities. "5 times as many Whites are using drugs as African Americans, yet African Americans are sent to prison for drug offenses at 10 times the rate of Whites" in Anslinger Nation.[2]

Anslinger. Harry J. Anslinger was born in Altoona, Pennsylvania, in 1892, a child of Swiss and German immigrants. He began his career with the Pennsylvania Railroad Company as a teenager, turning briefly to service in state government in Harrisburg before heading down to Washington, DC, and then rising through federal ranks, from attaché to commissioner.

Meanwhile. Meanwhile, during Anslinger's youth, cultural and legal tracks were laid for drug prohibition: time and space were subdividing; the Chinese method of consuming opium came under legal proscription; medical professions professionalized; immigrants immigrated; periodicals proliferated; the United States became an imperial character on the global stage, amassing military and financial superpower. Perhaps more than any other industry, railroads were central to legal capitalization in the nineteenth century. With its machine shops headquartered in Anslinger's Altoona, the Pennsylvania Railroad Company (PRR) employed over thirty thousand workers and controlled about $400 million in capital by 1880, at which point it loomed as the largest privately owned corporation in the nation if not the world. Next stop, drug prohibition.

Prohibition. Though the word is associated with the alcohol prohibition of the 1920s, prohibitionism refers to a strategy of total suppression—meaning that all production and trade in a given commodity is either specially licensed or illegal. This means, in turn, that anybody who produces or trades in that commodity without license to do so is subject to prosecution. The system of legal control of drug possession and trade known as drug prohibition has been the rule in the United States since the passage of the Harrison Act in 1915, and it has proved far more durable than the insanely expensive and counterproductive prohibition of alcohol while reproducing all of its worst tendencies: unregulated product, loss of revenue, heightened police corruption, and anemic public health frameworks. What can account for the continuity and popularity of a program that has constantly failed to achieve its own stated goals for over seventy years? Drug prohibition has been extremely effective at disempowering and disenfranchising young Black and Latino men, even if domestic policy was never an explicit conspiracy by a small powerful elite to do so. So prohibition must deliver and maintain some desired effect, some perceived social good, the fulfillment of some agenda for economic, social, and political power. Perhaps disempowerment and disenfranchisement are that good. And the isms do die hard.

Isms. On the one hand, this is a history of the emergence of drug prohibition: a national fantasy that derives from Puritanism, Federalism, Capitalism, Liberalism, Victorianism, Fundamentalism, Progressivism, Revivalism, Temperance, and Prohibition (of alcohol), among other things. Prohibition manifests in values like *abstinence* and policies like *suppression*, travels the circuit from high religion to biochemistry and back at the speed of culture, materializes in commodities and market practices, drives incarceration and corruption, often ignores or manipulates medical sciences, and stands in logical, social, economic, and political opposition to everything empirically true and commonsensical, from gravity to relativity. Prohibition denies social facts, ignoring, in particular, the will of capital—and its manifestations in narcotics and alcohol—to sneak around, to creep and seep into, and otherwise to exceed jurisdictional lines.

Tracking the Origins of Drug Prohibition. So how did the United States get hooked on drug prohibition in the first place? All possible answers, all approaches, all angles, all roads and rivulets through the history of drug prohibition in the United States lead to the overwhelming presence of Harry J. Anslinger, and back through him to the beliefs, like those above, that he ingested as a child, and others in which he trained in his first jobs at the PRR.

Biography. So is this a biography of Harry J. Anslinger? No, its subject is not a person. On the one hand, the subject of this book is the origins of drug prohibition. Yes, Anslinger is a significant part of the story, but this book seeks to entertain the broader cultural and historical context of Harry's war on drugs, concerning itself with everything from dominant belief systems to magazines and camels. In this light, Harry figures less as an extraordinary individual—the subject of a normal biography—and more as the sum of his functions, which naturally diminishes his humanity in favor of his utility as a carrier of cultural values. Such idiosyncrasies of his as can be found in the archive are used to make points rather than to inflate him as a quirky individual. Although I tend to see ordinary people as agents of historical change, I don't doubt that there are individuals whose qualities and impact exceed their time and place. I don't see Harry as one of those. He certainly had personal qualities, like cleverness and tenacity, that enabled a young man with his ambition to take advantage of opportunities that presented themselves, but I value him primarily as a vehicle for ideas—those in which he trafficked, and those in this book. The rest is contingency. And the question of what made Harry Harry.

On the Other Hand.   This is a story of the ingestion and transmission of values, the formation of mental habits, the skill set and circumstances that made Harry Anslinger a particular vehicle for drug prohibition. This is not a story about Harry's experience, much less his subjectivity—the closest it comes is his *persona*. But Harry's life and career are so integrally related to the development of drug policy in the United States that he is irresistibly the lead figure in that development, and the archive does indeed point to a figure with a coherent set of beliefs, a well-documented office, and a long and stable period of influence. As a character in this book, which will inevitably seem to be a narrative, Harry will inevitably seem to have a self.

Reproducing Harry.   But it is too late in history to treat Anslinger as a unified character walking through a plotted narrative—even in his own story. Furthermore, the self in question here—at least as preserved in the archive—is not that of a credible feeling person. Rather it is the carefully crafted persona of a public political figure who understood the power of rhetoric and narrative, definition and diagnosis.

Anslinger is perhaps most famous for his prowess as a propagandist, which he demonstrated in his first media campaign, against marijuana, in the 1930s. Anslinger was a spin doctor. He knew that control of narrative engendered other forms of social control. Harry understood that rhetoric was key to his work whether drafting law, crafting order forms, or writing instructions for how to fill them out. From his personal diary to a certain diplomatic achievement in the Caribbean to a curriculum for training agents, Harry J. Anslinger wrote his way to and through the position of commissioner of the Federal Bureau of Narcotics. The stories he told, which were both inherited and invented, the processes of inheritance and invention, and the causes and effects of the telling, are prime objects of this study.

Cause and Effect.   Exactly.

Toward a Poetics of Drug Policy: Review of the Literature.
Anslinger's record creates a powerful narrative that begs for investigation. Analyzing Harry's rhetoric (along with that of the Supreme Court, newspapers, and social scientists) requires attention to language. Of course, neither his language nor mine transparently purveys true knowledge: language is itself the problem. Thus, this book proposes poetic representations of an analysis of Anslinger's poetics, collapsing the distinction between poetic and analytical modes—as propaganda itself can do. Anslinger's rhetoric inflates a persona that goes hand in hand with principles of prohibition; in order to interrupt the lines of thought that produce prohibition, it is necessary to disrupt representations of Harry J. Anslinger's disciplinarian persona. This kind of life writing disrupts the semblance of narrative from between the lines.

This disruption takes many forms. For example, though it is chronologically ordered, this chronicle is complicated by synchrony and/or achronologic techniques, also by argument, meditation, imagery, and even extranarrative features. The prose style takes its time, juxtaposing as it goes. It meanders and doubles back. The language waxes lyrical. Lyricism for its own sake, I confess, pleasure as a reason for being—also, not incidentally, a motivating force for Lotus Eaters. Collecting the roots of three ancient Greek words in one, a *kaleidoscope* offers a *vision* of *beautiful forms*.

Apparently beginning as an origin story, this book attends to the tale of Harry's becoming, but it bogs down in the mid-1930s and again in the early 1950s, digresses wildly, savors the sonic properties of language, and periodically hands the narrative over to Lotus Eaters, who drink, shoot, snort, and smoke it to smithereens. The original Lotus Eaters are in Homer's *Odyssey*, the drugging natives who almost derail Odysseus's good men. But wherever they lurk, the Lotus Eaters—those literary figures and tropical bogeymen, those equatorial loiterers and dark idlers—are the antiheroes who throw the narrative train off the track, a critical maneuver in a war waged on aesthetic fronts no less than geopolitical ones. Their hyperlyrical tendencies challenge the very idea of progress. No page-turners, they. No, this book animates a set of characters whose mission is to interrupt the flow of narrative.

Martha and the Lotus Eaters. Throwing another wrench in the works of conventional history, this book experiments with speculation as an affirmative value, as a legitimate mode of knowing. In this text, imaginative techniques allowing for unreal characters like Martha, who stands for a speculative and alternative view of history, and Lotus Eaters, who stand for everything from id to inmate, are critical to surfacing repressed points of view. But who's Martha?

Marthas. Actually, there are multiple Marthas. You can spot them. Marthas know more than statistics, other than facts. They are many, historical personages and fictional characters, legends and keys, hiding in plain sight throughout. One of them is married to Harry. There's even a Martha named Ida.

Epistemological Experiments. Marthas occupy alternative historiographical perspectives and are thus in position for, and disposed toward, speculation. Peeking and sometimes speaking through the bars of the ruled page, Marthas mount a defense of speculative history, conjuring elsewheres, pointing to where the known leaves off, veering perilously close to fiction. But what if speculation did not simply reduce to fiction, and rather constituted a whole different way of knowing from accumulating verifiable facts and collating others' opinions?

If language were transparent, life writing might be a window on a self and its realization in history; we could know Harry. It isn't. Perhaps that is reason enough to explore the kinds of knowing associated with speculation, juxtaposition and metonymic associations, appropriation of bureaucratic forms, polemic, lyrical excess, and the opacity of language. I have not chosen these features randomly, and not just to stake a claim for poetic license, but rather because these formal elements counter the linguistic and disciplinary regime of Harry J. Anslinger. The almighty metrical, the train and other tracks, the bars, the many bars—of Anslinger's piano, of the prison, of the bottom line of his budget and all the little line items—the covert code for your own good. His statistical scientificity. His ramrod rectitude.

Between the lines lies the undoing of Harry, his underlining, his undermining by Lotus Eaters. From between the lines, the un- or inter-disciplined, the indolent and indigent, those adversely affected by generations of draconian drug laws, the hapless addict, the dissociated cartel operative, and the occasional Martha may make a break for it.

Rectilinearity. Recti-what?

If I had to sum up the trouble with Harry in one word, it would be "rectilinearity," to describe a kind of mental gridlock, graphed in train timetables and meeting flesh in emblematic, but nonetheless material, prison bars. My response is prose that is squirrelly, spirally, circular, and, in places, downright rococo—as a pushback against the requirements of linear argumentation. The prose here, where it goes curvilinear, rejects the rhetorical principles of administrative control, of discipline and punish, and leaks across lines of discipline and genre, with features a historian might find "creative," even "poetic." That would be correct. Now and again, unruly winds blow narratives and their heroes off course. Prolific prolixity pushes this text beyond the bounds of the page. The text enacts the opposite of mandatory minimum sentencing, exceeding the judgment and spilling, like drugs and capital, across boundaries. Interdiction is useless: discourse and its by-products leak across jurisfictional lines.

Document. See for yourself.

Documents. What kinds of knowledge do they call into play, these images that are no more windows on the *real past* than the language that surrounds them?

Kinds of Knowledge. The methodology—rather than the content—of the book disrupts the inherited accounts of Anslinger and drug policy. It's not news that Anslinger was a bad guy. It's not news that his expertise lay in bureaucracy, and in detecting, turning a blind eye to, and manufacturing conspiracy. Though the book relies heavily on standard historical research techniques, there are no revelations here about the extent of Anslinger's knowledge of or direct engagement with the CIA's nefarious experimentation on human subjects, or new anecdotes reconfirming his patent racism, no new insights into his relationship with maternal figures, no cache of previously undiscovered or even recently FOIAed memos.[3]

This book seeks to proliferate available logics for inquiring into history and culture—again, it does this in part through its form. The formal foils here are not only History and Biography but also disciplinarity more generally. Yet this book seeks to go beyond interdisciplinarity, aligning itself with that maligned thing: intergenre work. Can a mash-up of different and conflicting ways of knowing—creative and scholarly, say—produce legitimate, richer knowledge?

Creative Nonfiction. For the concerned reader, the notes patrol the border between fact and fiction. For the writer, facts have no material reality—they have expression in representational systems—so even the nonfictionest of writers slants the facts, if only by paraphrasing a received account. Therefore, my only choice is to choose my slant, which is political, and of course formal.

Patterns. Look for doubling, doppelganging, tripling, quadrupling, chiasmus, rhyming, chiming, alliteration, typos, tics, and other forms of repetition, up to and including history itself.

The History of Now. Following the one hundredth anniversary of the passage of the Harrison Act, it might look as though drug prohibition is losing its purchase. Marijuana, criminalized relatively late, in 1937, has been rehabilitated as a medication, and recognized as a recreational drug that poses less risk and costs less, individually and collectively, than alcohol. Bona fide research, though still difficult to procure funding and approval for, has begun to make inroads into a century's worth of misinformation. Revenues begin to trickle in. But full legalization of opiates, cocaine, and hallucinogens is not on the table and will not be any day soon.

Legalization policies in other countries indicate that it is less expensive and more effective to treat drugs as a matter of public health rather than criminal justice. Imagine that ideas, like drugs, could flow across national boundaries. They can, and do. Imagine ideas creeping up on the guards and the guards entertaining available modes of desertion. Never mind crossing that border, sit on it and smoke the peace pipe, scuff up the line in the sand with a friend from the other side. Invent the peace.

Meanwhile, we live in a regime of mass incarceration that literally decimates communities and disenfranchises particular, and very large, social cohorts, by means of drug laws—a perpetual motion mechanism producing a "criminal" class on a mass scale. Until drug laws are radically changed, and attendant ideology has withered away, there is no possibility of full democratic participation in civic and political and economic life in the United States.

As the Kaleidoscope Turns. Anslinger's war on drugs rages on. His campaign to demonize people of color as drug dealers and drug takers is ongoing after him. Odysseus's men keep running into and out on Lotus Eaters, without stopping to listen. There are still prison-houses to break out of, legally and culturally, materially and discursively. And it's a long journey home, even after the war is over.

Why examine such a serious social issue with a plaything? Why toy with the actual past? Anslinger Nation is stuck on certain ideas, or certain worldviews are particularly stubborn; backward commitments carry forward, persist. But pick up a kaleidoscope. With a twist of the wrist, you're a revisionist, unsticking history.

THE

PHARMACOPŒIA

OF THE

UNITED STATES OF AMERICA.

1820.

BY THE
AUTHORITY OF THE MEDICAL SOCIETIES AND COLLEGES.

MEDICATED VINEGARS.

VINEGAR OF OPIUM.

COMMONLY CALLED BLACK DROP.

Take of Opium, half a pound.
      Vinegar, three pints.
      Nutmeg, bruised, one ounce and a half.
      Saffron, half an ounce.

Boil them to a proper consistence, then add

      Sugar, four ounces.
      Yeast, one fluid ounce.

Digest for seven weeks, then place in the open air until it becomes a syrup; lastly, decant, filter, and bottle it up, adding a little sugar to each bottle.

From *The Pharmacopoeia of the United States of America*, 1820. Courtesy of the New York Public Library.

2   IN A WORD

> PREFACE. It is the object of a Pharmacopoeia to select from among substances which possess medicinal power, those, the utility of which is most fully established and best understood; and to form from them preparations and compositions, in which their powers may be exerted to the greatest advantage. It should likewise distinguish those articles by convenient and definite names, such as may prevent trouble or uncertainty in the intercourse of physicians and apothecaries.
>
> *The Pharmacopoeia of the United States of America* (1820)[1]

The *Pharmacopoeia* of 1820 offers a plausible if necessarily arbitrary place to begin to review the story of drug prohibition in the United States. A plan put forth in 1817 called on the authority of all the medical societies and schools in the United States for the collation of district pharmacopoeias into a book of greater scope. Over one hundred years before Harry J. Anslinger became the commissioner of the Federal Bureau of Narcotics, over seventy years before he was even born, this important book articulated the values of standardization, classification, enumeration, and professionalization with respect to an as yet unregulated drug market. If Anslinger prevailed with prohibitionist policy as the consummate drug bureaucrat of the twentieth century, he did so because of the way that market—*and those values*—had developed since the publication of the first national pharmacopoeia.

Drug making, an ancient and ubiquitous practice—older even than drug taking, if only by minutes—took many forms in the nineteenth-century United States of the *Pharmacopoeia*. Most drug manufacture, distribution, and consumption revolved around local and regional medical practices. Manufacturers, physicians, patients, and the wholesale and retail vendors who connected them were remotely located and diversely experienced, their common sources of knowledge few and old. Over the course of the century, those who worked with medicines in legal markets (soon to be *pharmaceuticals*) would join and create professional associations, like their peers in other fields. Generations before Harry J. Anslinger was born in the sleepy valley that was becoming Blair County, Pennsylvania, pharmacologists brought their profession into institutional, rule-writing, and standard-bearing being.

In 1820, existing state medical societies and schools formed national bodies with districts and delegates, conventions and elections, secretaries and dues. Professionalization included not only national organization but journal publication and the development of academic disciplines. With the founding of the College of Pharmacy at the University of Pennsylvania, in 1821, pharmacology was first named as a discipline. The Massachusetts College of Pharmacy followed in 1823, and similar programs were established in Maryland in 1840, Cincinnati in 1850, Chicago in 1859, and St. Louis in 1864. The *Journal of the Philadelphia College of Pharmacy* began printing in 1825 and *The Druggists Manual* came out the next year. A national organization of organizations, the American Pharmaceutical Association, formed in 1852. This level of coordination both called for and enabled the construction of standards for everything related to professional medical practice: standard nomenclature, standards for curricula and accreditation of educational institutions, standards for the licensing or certification of individuals, and, in the case of pharmacology, standards for the quality of ingredients, preparation of drugs, and proper applications thereof. These last standards called for a compendium, of which the 1820 *Pharmacopoeia* was the earliest attempt.

Along with these cultural shifts around plant-based medicines came a shift toward more widespread recreational use of certain plant-based substances, particularly opium and cocaine (derived from *Papaver somniferum* and *Erythroxylon coca*, respectively). While physicians in Europe and the United States experimented with the anesthetic effects of these substances, lay people experimented with their mood-altering effects, as Thomas De Quincey's 1822 *Confessions of an Opium Eater* illustrates. If it felt good not to feel the surgeon's knife as he gouged at an abscess or a boil, as he amputated against the gout or the gangrene, as he pulled out shrapnel, and if it felt good not to feel the apothecary's pliers as he extracted a tooth, it also felt good not to feel the humdrum daily down-in-the-mouth-ness of pushing a

2. IN A WORD | 17

plough, hauling water, working on the railroad, stoking the fire, milking a cow, shoveling bricks, spinning and weaving, or wondering what it's all about. In the common interest, then, chemists discovered ways to isolate alkaloids extracted from the poppy, yielding, among other things, morphine and heroin. Alcohol no longer held a monopoly on the party. Nitrous oxide, ether, and other gases found their patients and partiers as well.

To wit, in December 1844, a medical student named Gardner Quincy Colton advertised an entertainment that would commence with twelve young men demonstrating the inhalation of nitrous oxide; after which, the rest of forty gallons would be administered to anyone in the audience who desired it.

> **The effect of the Gas is to make those who inhale it either Laugh, Sing, Dance, Speak, or Fight, and so forth, according to the leading trait of their character. They seem to retain consciousness enough not to say or do that which they would have occasion to regret.... The object is to make the entertainment in every respect a genteel affair.** [2]

This dubiously genteel event speaks for the time just before the times into which Harry J. Anslinger was to be born, in another social class altogether. Colton's shenanigans engaged young men of native birth and high class merely dancing on the edge of disinhibition: "N.B.—The Gas will be administered only to gentlemen of the first respectability."[3] This 1844 notice indicates that social class is at stake in the distinction between good and bad drugs—which is often mapped as the difference between medical and recreational uses. The later distinctions between morphine and heroin, like those between powder cocaine and crack cocaine, derive from the moral overlay on social distinctions already in play before heroin had ever been synthesized. There were those who indulged, and then there were habitués; by the middle of the nineteenth century, there were already markets, and all kinds of parties to them. The First Opium War ended just before this event, so there was already a thriving, if violently contested, transnational opium market, but opium was not yet so big in the United States—and it was not yet illegal. At parties like Colton's, it would have been hard to see, through the wobbly gaseous effect, the future rise of an *illegal* drug market.

At the same time, a critical new method of drug delivery was in development. In use by 1845, the syringe enabled hypodermic injection. Attached to a hollow needle that formed a delicate bridge between the outside and inside of the body, the syringe revolutionized drug delivery, first to medical patients in pain and from there to people of all descriptions. Injection supplemented the age-old techniques of ingestion and topical application of analgesics but did not replace them, of course. Patients benefited, for example, from an improvement in topical painkilling that in 1855 the Scottish doctor Alexander Wood called a "new method of treating neuralgia by the direct application of opiates to the painful points."[4]

Other forms of painkilling, ingestion in particular, needed little improvement. In 1854, the Scottish novelist Timothy Shay Arthur published *Ten Nights in a Bar Room and What I Saw There*, a morality play in which a barkeep's innocent son is driven to parricide by whiskey. In the end, the bar hosts a local temperance campaign, the likes of which cropped up all over the eastern United States, collectively gathering momentum as a highly organized political movement in subsequent decades. As proponents of temperance began to heat up, intent on legislative solutions for epidemic levels of alcohol consumption, prohibition became a kind of utopian scheme, and though it bore on alcohol almost exclusively in the nineteenth century, it articulated an irreducible ideal, one with a potentially strong pull for a puritanical people. Abstinence, as an idea, would later attach to drugs in very much the same way. This is the spiritual, the moral, carryover from alcohol to drugs. The other carryover is more administrative: though prohibition of alcohol has offered lessons about the financial, medical, and social costs of a fruitless strategy of suppression, twenty-first-century drug policy has yet to recognize and incorporate them. Hindsight is 20/20, unlike Harry J. Anslinger's vision, lost in one eye in an accident when he was seventeen. A mysterious Martha had been preparing a compound to promote hindsight since at least 1820, but her recipe is not in that big book, and we will not meet her until later.

It was the object of the *Pharmacopoeia* to form preparations and compositions, to name names, to prevent the kind of trouble or uncertainty in the intercourse of physicians and apothecaries that results from lack of standards. It is the object of the present book to compose a concoction, propose a preparation, that definitely names Harry J. Anslinger, his powers exerted to the greatest advantage in an office most fully established to distinguish among substances and prevent uncertainty in the intercourse of parties to the drug discourses that produce and enforce prohibitionist policy and law. Harry J. Anslinger, first commissioner of the Federal Bureau of Narcotics, was the manifest alchemist of that policy. Like a tincture, the policy and its infinite repercussions on the body politic are murky business. It is difficult to distinguish their ingredients, yet these are the substances whose properties must be probed. People have been, and continue to be, adversely affected. Anslinger didn't cook up this deadly policy by himself, but he did, like a syringe, imbibe a thoroughly modern model of corporate organization from the petri dish of the Pennsylvania Railroad Company and shoot it into the executive arm of government. As criminals professionalized around him, Harry did bring that long and pockmarked arm of the law down hard on the line between medicine and recreation, legal and illegal markets, racial and social classes, this plant and that. To wax poetically. To take poetic, not medical, license from the *poeia* that suffixes the *Pharma* in the name of the big book that opens this one.

Blair County &c.

Deed Book B

Before the subscriber one of the Justices of the Peace in and for said County
personally came the above and within named Henry Noveen and Sarah his wife and acknowledged
the foregoing Indenture to be their act and deed, and desired the same might be recorded as such
the said Sarah Noveen being of lawful age by me examined, separate and apart from her said husband, and the contents of the said Indenture being by me fully made known to her she declared that she did of her own free will and accord sign, seal and as her act did deliver the same
without any coercion or compulsion of her said husband. In testimony whereof I have hereunto
set my hand and seal at Antes Township this second day of April one thousand eight hundred
and Fifty

James L. Gwin

Recorded on the 8th day of April A.D. 1850.

DEED

David Robison and wife
To
Archibald Wright

For a tract of land in Allegheny
Township, Blair County, containing 223 acres, 125 perches & all

Consideration $1100.—

This Indenture Made the twenty fourth day of April in
the year of our Lord one thousand eight hundred and forty nine. Between David Robison of the County of Blair and State of Pennsylvania and Susanna Robison his wife, of the one part and Archibald
Wright, of the City of Philadelphia and State aforesaid, of the other
part, Witnesseth, That the said David Robison and Susanna Robison
his wife, for and in consideration of the sum of Eleven hundred dollars lawful money of the United States of America, unto them well and
truly paid by the said Archibald Wright at and before the sealing
and delivery of these presents, the receipt whereof is hereby acknowledged, have granted, bargained, sold,
aliened, enfeoffed, released and confirmed, and by these presents do grant, bargain, sell, alien,
enfeoff, release and confirm unto the said Archibald Wright his Heirs and Assigns, a tract or
parcel of land, situate in Allegheny Township, in the county of Blair and State of Pennsylvania,
to wit, Beginning at a post near a small marked hickory, being the corner also of land late of
William Peterson, thence North forty one degrees East one hundred and thirty perches to a stone
heap, South forty six and a half degrees east two hundred and eighty nine perches to a hickory, South forty one degrees West one hundred and thirty one perches to a stone heap, North forty
one and a half degrees West twenty one perches to a stone heap, and North forty six and one fourth
degrees West two hundred and forty eight perches to the place of beginning. Containing two hundred and twenty three acres and one hundred and twenty five perches, and allowance, be the
same more or less. (Being part of the same tract of land surveyed for Baynton and Wharton
on a warrant dated the twenty eighth day of July A.D. 1785, and by virtue of sundry assurances in
law, vested in James Galbraith, who obtained a patent therefor dated the sixteenth day of February A.D. 1802, which said parcel of land (part thereof) was devised to Patrick Galbraith by the
last will and testament of the said James Galbraith, deceased, which was duly proved, and afterwards by virtue of process issued out of the Court of Common Pleas of Huntingdon County directed
to the Sheriff of said County against the said Patrick Galbraith, John Patton Esquire, then Sheriff
of as aforesaid by his deed Poll duly executed and acknowledged, and dated the thirtieth day
of November A.D. 1807, conveyed the same unto David McMurtrie, and the said David Mc-
Murtrie and Martha his wife by deed duly executed and acknowledged, and dated the
seventeenth day of May A.D. 1812, sold and conveyed the same unto Samuel Noble, who having
afterwards died intestate, the said land descended to and vested in his legal representatives, his
seven children (John Noble was one), And the said children and heirs of the said Samuel
Noble deceased, by deeds of release duly executed and acknowledged, released their respective
titles, interests and estates in the said parcel of land unto their brother the said John
Noble as by reference to the said Deeds more fully will appear, his now

Pennsylvania Railroad Company, deed, Hollidaysburg, Pennsylvania, 1849, Vol. B, p. 441. Courtesy of the Blair County Genealogical Society.

3 THE SQUARE LAST MENTIONED

The boundaries of the farm were about on the present lines of Eleventh street from Fourth to Fourteenth avenues on the northeast and Sixteenth Street between same avenues on the southwest, Fourth avenue from Eleventh to Sixteenth streets on the southeast and Fourteenth avenue between the same streets on the northwest. The first building erected after Altoona was laid out was made of rough board to be used as an office for the railroad contractor and a boarding house for the men; it also stood in the square last mentioned, near the old farm house.

A History of Blair County, Pennsylvania (1896)[1]

There that building stood at 40°31'7" N and 78°23'42" W, due east of Pittsburgh, west-northwest of Philadelphia, south of Buffalo, north of Charlottesville, bought for the purpose of running track, train, people, and property from one to the other to the next. There that building stood on a lot, X marking the spot around which a town would grow up and a railway run through it. The lot was bought for the purpose of locating the machine shops and mechanical headquarters of the largest corporation in the United States. With its purchase, the Pennsylvania Railroad Company put Altoona on the map.

Picture that patch of Pennsylvania at that hour: The flat dirt of cleared and graded land. Horse, manure, and machinery. Mud puddles and human garbage everywhere else, and beyond that, woods forever. Trees were felled, their trunks stripped bare and re-upped as telegraph poles, flagpoles, and switch poles, laid flat at right angles to each other one atop another, and joined at the corners of cabins, shacks, and sheds. The floors of the train shops, dirt inside and out, lay perpendicular to the telegraph poles that went up in 1856 situated at regular intervals in straight lines, their crossarms parallel to the flat earth. Yet more trees were felled and burned in the increasing number of fireplaces of Altoona, ashes to ashes.

The county seat of Blair County, Hollidaysburg, had, by the time of Altoona's incorporation, been pleasantly and picturesquely farmed. Almost one hundred years earlier, in 1768, the frontier area was claimed by a family of Irish immigrants who feared that if they settled any farther west, they would live "in constant dread of savages."[2] Fighting Indians and counterclaimants, the Hollidays named that stately little town after themselves. Today, large and unique houses are surrounded by spacious lawns and gardens; planted wildflowers proliferate. Hollidaysburg is an outpost of ease and near-urbanity, and may have figured as an exemplar, a beacon, an aspirational specter, to the denizens of the dense and dirty company town of Altoona immediately to the north. But the mud of Altoona was destined to be imprinted by the growth of the major industries, of giant robber barons stomping around Pennsylvania, valleys quaking as their giant footfalls fell and giant hands prodded, peeled, and poked into the mother-loded mountains with their gigantic pliant fingers. This is ex post speculation; at the time, iron, steel, coke, and coal lay quietly in wait for the speculum, for their futures as commodities, the stuff of manufacture and distribution, sale and purchase, consumption. These metals would become the distributed goods as well as the means of distribution themselves—the iron horse with its motive power of burning coal, exhausted in the run on the steel rails.

In the days of Harry's youth, you could get from Altoona to Hollidaysburg and back on the interurban streetcar line. But before its day of modern glory, before its founding, before the deed and the record of a certain rectangle of dirt around which it grew, Altoona the city derived its name "from the beautiful, liquid and expressive Cherokee word *Allatoona*, meaning 'high lands of great worth.'"[3] The Cherokee, by the reports of the sons of the worth seekers, shared their liquid words:

> high: ga-lv-la-di, ᏍᎬᎳᏗ
> land: ga-do-hi, ᏍᏙᎯ
> great: e-qua, ᎡᏆ
> value: tsu-gv-wa-lo-di, ᏧᎬᏩᎶᏗ

The Cherokee were right: the value of land in Altoona changed by virtue of the railroad's interest in the location. The Lenni Lenape, more recent and longer-term residents than the Cherokee, had been reduced in number by white settlement, aggression, and development in Blair County by the time the train-building worth seekers arrived in Altoona in the late 1840s. There, the railroad company found "only forest, sterile fields and one poor farm house."[4] That farmhouse belonged to one poor David Robeson and, with its 223 acres and 123 perches, "was not worth more than $2,500 for farming purposes." But Robeson was able to command $11,000 for it, in 1849, when the Pennsylvania Railroad Company set its sights on Altoona as the place to locate its mechanical shops.[5]

Over at Logan's Narrows, five miles west of Altoona, Horseshoe Curve still stands as one of the greatest feats of antebellum railway engineering and construction in the United States. In order to run a train line through the Alleghenies, engineers brought fill dirt in to support tracks across two ravines and shaved off Kittanning Point, the promontory that had formerly separated them. Completed in 1854, this line connected the eastern and western divisions of the Pennsylvania Railroad, which the mountains had formerly separated.[6] Horseshoe Curve, and other engineering achievements like it, would spell the end of the horse as a mode of transportation. New motive power replaced the animate horse, long after the Cherokee had flowed away to the south. Then, as now, the city and its ghosts rest at least 1,120 feet above sea level, though hills rise 100 to 150 feet higher. But now, Altoona has already peaked.

In the end, Altoona will degrade back into the mountain, which will return to swamp, which will turn, in turn, into eternal sea. In the end, Altoona will disintegrate into the minerals from which it emerged. But until then, the ghostly hammers still ring in the work yards while people and goods keep chugging their way around Horseshoe Curve. In the end, the prison doors will open, and the waste products of a century of prohibitionist drug policy and its enforcement—poverty, inequality, disenfranchisement, and stigma, to name a few—will flow freely through the gutters and down the drain. Already, Harry J. Anslinger, its architect and chief enforcer, wrought from the dirt of Altoona in 1892, is dust once more, resting

and remaining in peace in a sunny cemetery in Hollidaysburg, south
of Horseshoe Curve.

As a child, Harry lived just outside the original lot described in the
deed book of 1849, the one from which Altoona had grown up, at 506
Third Avenue, in a very small house on a straight and narrow street of
small houses very close together betwixt and between other straight
and narrow streets dotted with little houses with little space between
them. Housing for workers had cropped up to dot the grid that was
the town, the town a long and narrow rectangle. Harry would grow
up in the literal shadow of the Pennsylvania Railroad Company, cross
streets and avenues to walk one way to school, and then later on, walk
back the other way to work, to study at the knee of the ascendant
giant corporation. When Harry J. Anslinger left Altoona on his own
ticket, he would take the values of the town, or its company, with him.

4 MAYBE BORN IN BERN

In 1859, Robert John Anslinger, who was to be Harry's father, was born in Bern, or maybe Morat, Switzerland.[1] Then, in 1860, Rosa Christina Fladt, who was to be his mother, was born in Baden, in Germany, unbeknownst to Robert. Twenty years down the road, they would marry. In their old-country youths, they may have frolicked in lederhosen or dirndl, silken hair flapping in the fresh breezes of spring. Robert's and Rosa Christina's parents were not well-to-do but neither were they indigent. Robert was becoming a barber, not a bourgeois. It is not known how they met. Maybe Martha knows.

Be that as it may, when they were twenty-one and twenty, respectively, Mr. and Mrs. Anslinger began to build their own family, bearing Charlie in Switzerland in 1880 and Elsie in early 1882. Later that year, the Anslingers set out for the United States. After arriving at Ellis Island, they remained in New York City for a couple of years, Robert barbering. Then they migrated again before John was born on January

September 1, 1882, Castle Garden ship manifest for the *Saint Germain*, p. 8. Anslinger's father is passenger no. 417. Courtesy of the National Archives and Records Administration and Ancestry. com.

25, 1887, in Houtzdale, Pennsylvania, not yet the home of a medium-security prison.

The growing family lived there only briefly, moving one last time, in 1888, to Altoona. While the tendrils of the development of the criminal justice system intersect with a wave of German immigration west to the East Coast of the United States and then farther west toward the Great Lakes, whole subsections of the population land between here and there, settling down into mountains and mines en route to the Midwest. Migration includes migrants plunking down and having babies. The unborn Harry J. Anslinger has nearly nothing to do with the future Houtzdale facility, except that the population of future prisons will have everything to do with him. Trace him back and forth fast enough and you can see the conditions of his coemergence with prohibitionist drug policy and enforcement.

5 A WILLING AND CHEERFUL OBEDIENCE THERETO . . .

There were 339 such rules, 3 conditions, and 3 procedures applying to the conduct of enginemen, firemen, conductors in various departments, car masters and car inspectors, dispatchers, station agents, baggage masters, brakeshop clerks, foremen of machine shops and of road repairs, several kinds of watchmen and supervisors, and to the trains themselves. Also, to "special agents." These rules reflect an elaborately organized company with workers specializing in a wide range of types of labor. The organizational chart reveals that order itself is a core value as well as a practical necessity for the functioning of the company. A person who came up through the company as Harry did would be halfway to law and order, halfway to government, its divisions and subdivisions, drills and routines, and "special agents."

Growth, or expansion—the drive of both empire and capital—was already at work in the rise of professionalism and corporatism. Thus, as though naturally, local organizations linked with state,

7

RULES

OF THE

PENNSYLVANIA RAILROAD COMPANY.

GENERAL RULES.

1. The Rules and Regulations, Special Orders and Official Directions, issued from time to time, by the Transportation Department of the Pennsylvania Railroad Company, being designed for the security of the lives of Passengers, and of Property entrusted to the Company for transportation, as well as for the security of Employees engaged therein, and for the proper care and oversight of the property and interests of the Company entrusted to this Department of the service: every Employe is expected, and will be required, to yield a willing and cheerful obedience thereto. When an individual enters or remains in the service of the Company, it will be considered as in itself an expression of willingness to do so.

From *Rules and Regulations for the Government of the Transportation Department of the Pennsylvania Railroad*, 1857, p. 7. Reproduced by permission from the Pennsylvania Historical and Museum Commission, Pennsylvania State Archives; and The Pennsylvania Railroad Company.

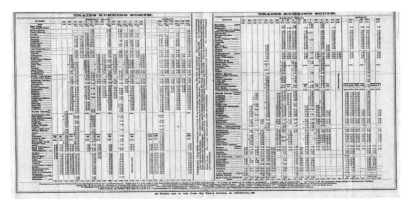

"Trains Running North" and "Trains Running South," Robert H. Coleman Collection, "Time Tables, 1886–91." From the collection of the Lebanon County Historical Society.

regional, and national ones over the course of the nineteenth century. Trains too linked locality to locality, and as the century wore on, train systems linked themselves together, bigger ones buying littler ones, joining in a national network dominated by fewer and fewer larger and larger train companies. Altoona, with its location and its body of labor, formed an essential node in the largest of these companies in the United States. By 1880, efficiency, departmentalization, standardization, economies of scale, a shrewd strategy of acquisitions, and an effective monopoly on long-distance train travel in the Northeast had made the PRR (a.k.a. "Pennsy") a transportation empire.

According to a textbook read by Altoonan elementary school students in the same period, the human body was a machine, "like a watch or a steam engine," meaning those students didn't just grow up *with* the Pennsylvania Railroad, they grew up *like* the railroad.[1] And the railroad grew up like them. Altoona grew up around them all, with an interurban streetcar system that connected it to Hollidaysburg like a miniature railroad, or like a capillary of the railroad that looked, conversely, like an interurban streetcar system writ large. From the northeastern seaboard—from Boston, Bedford, New London, New York—trains ran inland through all parts of Pennsylvania on tracks like veins across the land. And as they sped toward interior waterways—the Ohio and Monongahela Rivers and the

Great Lakes—they often ran into obstacles, such as horses stopping to water on tracks. Such obstacles held up trains, and held up work, wasting untold amounts of time. Control of the tracks came under debate, as stakeholders looked to waterways and roads for principles of control:

> The weight of popular opinion was in favor of the rules governing turnpike roads and adverse to centering the control of motive power on them either in the agents of the Commonwealth, individuals, firms, or corporations. Monopoly was the bugbear in the dreams of the people, whilst the greatest good to the country was expected to follow giving to each and every individual citizen the largest liberty to roam as a carrier over the railroad at such times and in such a way as would suit his own convenience. It required actual performance to educate the people and demonstrate the fact that good results could only be attained by intelligent administration and executive control of railroads being centered in a proper and absolute authority.[2]

That authority was to be the Pennsylvania Railroad, "with its tentacular reach, its supervised, graded, and uniformed army of workers, its mechanical precision of operation and monopolistic ambitions," which led the way for steel, oil, banking and finance, and insurance industries to adopt "the new bureaucratic form of the corporation."[3] Here, the corporation is a beast with a central nervous system, a beast capable of complex feats of organization. A leviathan with as many extremities as necessary, and a brain that can let one tentacle know what the others are doing, can coordinate labor and parts to purvey goods and services and consumers across space, can, indeed, coordinate their movement in time as well as space. Next stop, *E pluribus unum*.

As it was, and as it had been for ages, each locality ran on its own time, set by the motion of the sun, and synchronized locally by a large clock high up enough on a tower to be widely visible, or a gun shot at an appointed time, or some other kind of established signal. The trouble for trains was that local times varied, so that, for example, Philadelphia local time was "seven minutes faster than Harrisburg time, thirteen minutes faster than Altoona time, and nineteen minutes faster than Pittsburgh time."[4] Then, in 1869, Charles F. Dowd, the principal of Temple Grove Ladies Seminary in Saratoga Springs, addressed a committee of railway superintendents in New York, publishing that address as "A System of National Time for Railroads" in 1870. In Dowd's scheme, the continental United States would be divided into four zones, each differing from the adjacent zone by one hour. Dowd's baton was taken up by William F. Allen, managing editor of the *Official Guide to the Railways* and secretary of the General Time Convention, which approved the division of the continental United States into time zones in October 1883. On November 18, 1883, also known as the day with two noons, the United States Naval Observatory sent the telegraphic signal that coordinated the zones with one another in the United States, noon after noon after noon after noon.[5]

"Philadelphia and Reading R.R. Lebanon Valley and East Penna. Branches," Robert H. Coleman Collection, "Time Tables, 1886–91." From the collection of the Lebanon County Historical Society.

Then, in a great noncoincidence—rather, in close and logical sequence—the General Time Convention became the American Railway Association.

In this way, the railway industry called time zones into being, and not just domestically. One day, perhaps apocryphally, while Mr. and

Mrs. Robert Anslinger were starting their family, Sandford Fleming, the engineer-in-chief of the Canadian Pacific Railway, missed a train at Bandoran, also known as Bundoran, on the west coast of Ireland, because its departure time was listed as p.m. rather than a.m., or so the story goes.[6] So that no one else would miss another train for the same reason, Fleming proposed a twenty-four-hour clock to govern time globally. While local time zones would differ from one another, every time zone everywhere would maintain a consistent time difference from Greenwich Mean Time. Thus the standardization of time.

Before and during Harry's toddlerhood, the Pennsy bell was the bugle of its day, calling the preponderance of Altoonans who worked for the company to and fro, on and off, all day, six days a week. A half-size replica of the Liberty Bell (the original, cracked and out of commission over in Philadelphia), it was out of use by 1895. In March 1905, the *Technical World* explained the telling of time according to the US Naval Observatory, and the utility of chronometric regulation and coordination:

> **The original object of this time service was to furnish mariners in the seaboard cities with the means of regulating their chronometers; but, like many another governmental activity, its scope has gradually broadened until it has become of general usefulness. The electrical impulse which goes forth from the Observatory at noon each day, now sets or regulates automatically more than 70,000 clocks located in all parts of the United States, and also serves, in each of the larger cities of the country, to release a time-ball located on some lofty building of central location. The dropping of the time-ball—accompanied, at some points, with the simultaneous firing of a cannon—is the signal for the regulation by hand of hundreds of other clocks and watches in the vicinity.[7]**

By which point, the telegraphic system of synchronization was already obsolete; thereafter, time signals were transmitted by radio. Wireless telephony was already on the horizon.

In other words, to locate Altoona in time and space—then and there—is to hold off, but only for a little longer, the time-space

LEHIGH & LACKAWANNA R. R.

North Bound.		STATIONS.	South Bound.		
13	9		1	103	7
p.m. a.m.			a.m.	p.m.	p.m.
3.45	7.05	Leave.....New York, foot Liberty St.....Arrive.	10.55		9.25
3.30	7.50	....................Philadelphia { 3d and Berks........	10.45		8.55
4.15	9.00	{ 9th and Green........	10.00		8.23
5.57	10.12	Leave.............Easton.............Arrive.	8.30		6.55
5.35	10.52	........Bethlehem Junction........	8.11	4.50	6.05
6.36	10.58	..............Union Street..............	8.00	4.45	6.03
6.45	11.05	..................Shimer..................	9.00	4.24	5.54
6.50	11.05	...................Ritter...................	7.57	4.17	5.50
6.54	11.10	................Brodhead................	7.50	4.07	5.45
6.57	11.13	................Steuben................	7.49	4.05	5.39
7.01	11.18	...........Township Line...........	7.44	3.51	5.30
7.05	11.30	...................Clyde...................	7.42	3.45	5.21
7.06	11.32	..................Snyder..................	7.40	3.38	5.29
7.08	11.35	....................Bath....................	7.36	3.30	5.26
7.10	11.30	.........Chapman Quarries.........	7.34	3.30	5.23
7.17	11.34	.................Summit.................	7.26	3.42	5.18
7.19	11.36	...............Point Phillips............	7.26	3.45	5.16
7.22	11.39	............Bender Junction............	7.25	3.50	5.13
7.27	11.45	.................Kateline.................	7.18	2.50	5.06
7.32	11.47	...........Horn's Springs...........	7.14	2.30	5.04
7.37	11.52	.........Saylorsburg Junction.........	7.08	2.08	4.59
7.40	11.56	...............Wind Gap...............	7.05	2.06	4.57
7.48	12.04	...............Pen-Argyl...............	7.01	1.50	4.51
7.52	12.05	.............West Bangor.............	6.57		4.47
7.57	12.06	.........Bangor Junction.........	6.54		4.44
8.05	12.10	Arrive...........Bangor...........Leave.	6.50		4.40
p.m.	p.m.		a.m.	p.m.	p.m.

Connections.—At Bethlehem, trains Nos. 1 and 7 for Mauch Chunk, Tamaqua, Wilkesbarre, and Scranton.
Train No. 3 from White Haven, Mauch Chunk, and Tamaqua. Train No. 13 from Scranton, Wilkesbarre, Tamaqua, and Mauch Chunk.

EASTON AND PHILADELPHIA.

Sun.							Leave.	Arrive.						Sun.
a.m.	p.m.	p.m.	a.m.	a.m.	a.m.				a.m.	p.m.	p.m.	p.m.	p.m.	Sun.
9.10	6.15	4.15	9.00	6.15		Phila { 9th&Green	10.00	8.40	8.22	10.48	11.05			
8.50	6.05	3.50	7.50	5.50	4.15	{ 3d & Berks	10.45	3.11		8.55				
11.18	8.35	6.10	10.43	9.20	6.15	Ar } Bethlehem { Lv	8.25	12.20	4.30	6.30	9.00	9.10		
12.08	8.43	6.10	10.50	9.25	6.34	Lv } Junction. { Ar	8.22	11.31	4.05	6.19	8.40	9.03		
12.32	9.10	6.38	11.15	9.44	6.57	Ar.....Easton.....Lv.	7.55	11.12	3.40	5.57	8.17	8.00		
p.m.	p.m.	p.m.	a.m.	a.m.	a.m.		a.m.	a.m.	p.m.	p.m.	p.m.	p.m.		

UPPER LEHIGH BRANCH.

NORTH BOUND.					STATIONS.	SOUTH BOUND.				
92	4	10	60	90		13	3	5	7	9
p.m.	a.m.	a.m.	a.m.	a.m.	Leave.	p.m.	p.m.	p.m.	p.m.	p.m.
4.04	4.30				New York, ft. Liberty St.		2.52	6.15	9.25	
7.50	9.30				Philad'a { 3d and Berks.	3.11		8.55		
9.00	6.15				{ 9th and Green	3.28	5.89	8.22	10.49	
4.36	1.35	10.36	8.27	6.00	White Haven.	7.45	10.00	12.48	4.15	6.10
4.37	1.40	10.45	6.32	6.05	Upper Lehigh Junction.	7.40	9.55	12.40	4.10	6.05
4.46	1.57	11.00	8.47	6.30	...........Lookout...........	7.31	9.45	12.30	4.01	5.58
5.10	2.00	11.20	8.55	6.50	Pond Creek Junction.	7.25	9.36	12.23	3.55	5.45
5.21	2.35	11.41	9.06	7.00	........Soule Siding........	7.16	9.29	12.13	3.48	5.34
5.26	2.50	11.45	9.10	7.05	Ar...Upper Lehigh...Lve.	7.13	9.26	12.10	3.40	5.30
p.m.	p.m.	a.m.	a.m.	a.m.		a.m.	a.m.	p.m.	p.m.	p.m.

Trains Nos. 90, 10 and 92 run to Sandy Run, leaving Pond Creek Jc. at 6.90, 11.10 A.M. and 4.53 P. M.; returning, leave Sandy Run at 6.40, 11.30 A.M. and 5.00 P.M. Nos. 10, 4 and 92 connect at White Haven from Scranton and Wilkesbarre. Nos. 13, 5, 7 and 9 connect at White Haven for Wilkesbarre and Scranton.

"Lehigh and Lackawanna R.R.," Robert H. Coleman Collection, "Time Tables, 1886–91." From the collection of the Lebanon County Historical Society.

continuum that would soon relocate it in a field of relativity, and to return briefly to a world in which forward movement was defined by ever more precise and accurate measurement of ever smaller units of time and space, of labor, goods, and services. The rules of higher physics were an authority to which the railroad could not answer; train transportation would be outstripped again and again. The twentieth-century corporation would adjust, as would modes of communication, but trains would not. In the meantime, however, the Pennsylvania Railroad Company was the king of the corporations, capable of operating on unprecedented economies of scale, consuming and being consumed, and growing progressively larger, more organized, and more profitable throughout the rest of the nineteenth century.

To locate Harry's Altoona in time and space is to resubscribe, for a moment, to a worldview according to which rationality might yet triumph, and might be proof of Man's supremacy among animals, even his perfectibility (Man is himself a system). Harry so subscribed. The large-scale social systems in play, the profit motive, changes in motive power, the ever finer indices and institutionalizations of time and space, of labor, goods, and services, that surged together to get the trains moving—those systems were at once fully arbitrary and complexly overdetermined. For example, a globally synchronized time regime doesn't have to be centered in Greenwich, England, but uncountable historical contingencies nevertheless place the actual regime's center there. And until that centering took place, all was chaos and mayhem, and many a man missed his train.

"Strains at a Gnat and Swallows a Camel," *The Wasp*, January–June 1888, Chinese in California Collection, 2/18/88:8-9, The Bancroft Library, University of California, Berkeley.

6 TO PROHIBIT VICE IS NOT ORDINARILY CONSIDERED WITHIN THE POLICE POWER OF THE STATE

The bloom had already gone off the poppy in the wake of the Civil War. Morphine had come into service heralded as a "wonder drug," giving relief to sick and maimed soldiers on both sides. But its effects dragged on for decades, or as long as veterans suffered from addiction. "The Army Disease" left visible social traces and some circumspection about the drug. Meanwhile, as Robert and Rosa Christina Anslinger came of age on the east coast of western Europe, immigrants came from the Far East to the west coast of the United States of America to work on transcontinentalizing the railroads.

Picture those photographs of Asian immigrants, their black hair tied back in pigtails, under traditional hats fashioned from straw to shade their faces while they worked outside, coolies bent over and underselling their labor, thus making it harder for white men to find work. Or so went the story of the time. The story went on that the Chinese railroad workers brought opium with them from home: the opium that may have made stonecutting in China in cold weather, and chair bearing there in any weather, less unbearable may also have made heavy labor on the railroads in the United States less onerous. The opium also allowed the Chinese workers to induct white women into the evils of smoking it: "many women and young girls, as also young men of respectable family, were being induced to visit the [opium-smoking] dens, where they were ruined morally and otherwise."[1] This story ran in newspapers and magazines, in fiction and nonfiction books, and in debates about medical and legal practice and policy.

For one or more of these reasons—imagined, exaggerated, utterly

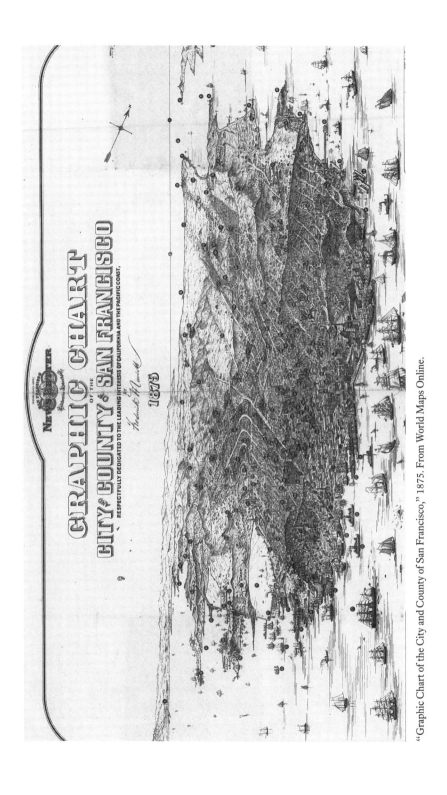

"Graphic Chart of the City and County of San Francisco," 1875. From World Maps Online.

real—opium dens were outlawed in San Francisco in 1875. Selling and possessing opium were still legal, as was private smoking. Opium could still be taken in liquid form, as in laudanum where it was mixed with alcohol. That was the white way, the more-likely-to-be-medicinal way, and a not-uncommon treatment for female complaints, like vapors, which were quite popular at the time. Whether they were as popular for females as they were for snake-oil salesmen, hucksters, and other unlicensed pharmacologists is a matter of speculation, and whether females, particularly white ones, also complained about being inducted into opium smoking is anyone's guess. In any case, the impulse to save those real or imagined girls may have prompted the first ordinance that prohibited any kind of drug-related activity in the United States.

Other cities and states adopted similar ordinances, which were similarly ineffective in slowing the flow of opium into white veins. Although it was already clear that previous measures had produced "clandestine" importation and smuggling, Congress intervened in 1883 by once more raising the tariff on opium prepared for smoking. Then, in 1887, Congress prohibited the importation of such opium altogether. The same legislation outlawed the importation of opium by any Chinese subject. But if there was a moral problem, its solution did not lie with the law; according to the California State Supreme Court: "To prohibit vice is not ordinarily considered within the police power of the state. . . . The object of the police power is to protect rights from the assaults of others, not to banish sin from the world or make men moral."[2] Here, opium is a medium of assault, a weapon in the war on Americans waged by Chinese others. In a sense, this decision merely compounds the Chinese Exclusion Act of 1882, which suppressed immigration by Chinese subjects for ten years.

In fact, as the secretary of the Treasury described it in 1888, these opium prohibitions served

> to stimulate smuggling, extensively practiced by systematic orga-
> nizations. Recently completed facilities for transcontinental trans-
> portation have enabled the opium smugglers to extend their illicit
> traffic to our Northern border. Although all possible efforts have

been made by this Department to suppress the traffic, it is found practically impossible to do so.[3]

Like the iron and steel and coke and coal, forged from the mountains as both commodities and the means for their own distribution, the railroads the Chinese workers forged became the medium of transcontinental drug traffic. Opium smugglers worked in systematic organizations that bested the Department of the Treasury and its suppression efforts. The parallel tracks of rising corporatism and recreational drug taking converged, along with laws and mores governing both, and they didn't need non-Euclidean geometry to do it.

Or what's a roundhouse for? Every track is ambidextrous. While one track here runs east–west, another a lot like it runs west–east. Soon, fruit companies in the north will grow large on the back of the south, while fruits of various vines run, or are run, from south to north. Tracks cover land from waterway to waterway, and they extend over bridges, which cross rivers, bays, and canals. Trains carry the goods across topographical and geopolitical boundaries, as syringe and needle do across bodily ones, carrying substances from one body of fluid to another. The same instrument both draws and injects, from the vial to the bodily canal; inside rushes out and outside rushes in. The Army Disease is practically contagious. The operation of the syringe is not unlike the official US dispensation toward Chinese workers: "a well known instrument, serving to imbibe or suck in a quantity of fluid, and to squirt or expel the same with violence."[4] By the late nineteenth century, lawmakers already knew that neither ordinance nor tariff nor exclusion could prevent drugs from circulating, and they associated this impossibility with Chinese railroad workers.

7 NOW BUILDING AT ALTOONA

While Congress tinkered with the tariffs on morphine and opium, Altoona went to work modernizing itself: "in 1888 the need of a complete and comprehensive sewer system was fully realized."[1] The same year, the Anslingers arrived in town, and the state fair that failed in Altoona fared better over in Hollidaysburg. Perhaps Altoona had simply bypassed the agricultural stage, going from woods to industrial zone in a century flat.

> **Thus in less than 100 years an uninhabited forest has been changed to a rich, populous and productive region, and a scarcely distinguishable trail, passable only on foot, has been superseded by a steel railroad over whose length, glide almost with the speed of light pondrous trains of cars bearing thousands of tons of freight or hundreds of travelers.**[2]

In 1891, yet more trees were felled to erect yet another set of poles, sixty-five-foot poles to post electric lights over the railyards, their heights and intervals determined by the imperative that the light not interfere with the train signals.

And then, on Friday, May 20, 1892, Harry J. Anslinger was born, the sixth of the nine children of Robert John Anslinger and Rosa Christina Anslinger, née Fladt. That day, the *Altoona Mirror* was rife with train news, from the opening of the Illinois Central to a little smashup on the Blue Line in Elizabeth, New Jersey, involving a mayor and a meat

Altoona Mirror, May 20, 1892, evening edition. Courtesy of the Blair County Genealogical Society.

car.[3] The relief organization of the Pennsylvania Railroad printed a synopsis of accident, sickness, death, and funeral benefits paid to its workers.

According to the *Mirror*, John Stewart, Harry's neighbor over on Fourth Avenue, was run down by a southbound freight train whose wheels caught his leg and almost ground off his foot, which led to its amputation. Also on the local tracks, a new "passenger coach, now building at Altoona, is being fitted with nickel plated window sides, with spring and oak strip. The innovation is an improvement in that it does away with the rattling of the sash, which, in the old style of sash fitting, is a source of annoyance to passengers. It also excludes dust and cinders." Harry was born in a cindered city at 506 Third Ave.

Altoonans reading the *Mirror* that day learned that "the Women's Christian Temperance union will hold a dime social this evening in the rooms over the post office. All are welcome." In the same vein but a little farther abroad, "six delegates and six alternates were today named to represent Montana in the National Prohibition in Cincinnati in June." But at the same time, in Chicago, "the directors of the whiskey trust have decided to manufacture spirits on a large scale by using the 'Jakamine' process. The Northern distillery at Peoria is to be used for that purpose hereafter." At the wax show in the Curio Hall and Theatre of the World's Museum on the Arcade Block of Altoona, "The Home of Temperance" was on display along with "The Home of Intemperance," all in lifelike figurines. The wets and the drys were scaling up, squaring off. "Martha Punished for Stealing the Gift of Sight."

Advertised miracle cures abounded and included Beecham's Pills, Dr. Fahrney's Teething Syrup, Dr. King's New Discovery, Dr. Miles' Nerve and Liver Pills, Dr. Miles' New Heart Cure, Hill's S.R. & S. Ointment, Kemp's Balsam, Krause's Headache Capsules, Lydia Pinkham's Vegetable Compound, Max Klein's Silver Age Whiskey, St. Patrick's Pills, and Syrup of Figs. These were purveyed, dispensed, sold, distributed, carried, and supplied by the town's drugstores: J. Mateer's, W. H. Irwin's, and O. F. Randolph's. Down on Eleventh Avenue, Dr. George promised that "none need die of disease" and instructed patients on "how to maintain good health, free from pain, and live one hundred years." Perhaps it was a "miracle," perhaps simply "unbelievable," to Mrs. Anslinger, as she delivered her sixth child, that "she can bend" if she buys certain stays: "The strength of posterity is regulated by the strength of the mother. The Equipoise Waist is sensible."

In other good news:

LITTLE NELLIE WILCOX NOT DEAD

Chestertown, MD, May 20—The reports that little Nellie Silcox [*sic*], who was assaulted by Jim Taylor, the colored man who was lynched Tuesday night had died, is false. As reported in these dispatches yesterday, the girl is improving and the physicians expect her to recover. The negroes have accepted the lynching of Taylor as an act of justice, and no trouble is feared [*sick*].

"Christ and the Erring Woman" held their pose in wax on the Arcade Block, and industry throve. The same edition of the paper projected that the Broad Top coal region—lying to the south and east of Blair County—would almost double its output in the coming year.

The back end of the kaleidoscope looks in on a baby whose dresses have been worn before, most likely by elder sister Bertha (just out of them herself), one who will pass them on again to Annie Lucinda in another two years. Perhaps more than most, Harry looked as a baby as he would look as an old man; in iconic photos Commissioner Anslinger sports a shiny bald pate. Maybe only mother's milk would soothe the crying infant; no peace in the home until Mrs. Anslinger finished her chores and established herself in the corner of the hair sofa, unlacing her garment and loosening her stays so she could bend over to pull baby Harry onto her lap and attach him to her breast. Though she was meticulous about her economies, she could not afford a soluble food like Carnrick's. Bertie could perhaps remember her own feedings, but brother John would be sent from the room, too old for such things now.

Looking backward, we see a time when men were men and women women, fathers fathers and mothers mothers. When time too doubled back on itself (as it does in any other age) even as it subdivided into smaller and smaller measurable units, ambidextrous as the track itself, though trains must run in one direction at a time—as time itself appears to—or collide. On Harry's first Independence Day, the Altoona and Logan Valley Electric Passenger Railway Company was formed. Later that summer, boll weevils entered Texas from Mexico and soon infested most of the cotton fields in the South, reminders of the porousness of national boundaries and the dangers of the inflow of others. In 1892, the year of Harry's birth, his father gave up barbering to go to work at the Pennsylvania Railroad. Robert Anslinger left his home in the middle of a grid of dirt streets and freshly macadamized avenues in the morning and returned to it at night. Everywhere he went—and the same could be said about any Altoonan, even little baby Harry—Robert was a point from which various tracks radiated out, and to which they radiated back, the interurban line to and from Hollidaysburg and the railroad that connected Altoona to both New York and Erie. Behind him, as Robert walked in his own tracks to work in the morning, the sun rose, and as he walked home in the late afternoon, it set behind him too. Both coming and going, he heard the diminishing reports of the whistle as the trains rounded Horseshoe Curve.

8 IN ALL CASES OF DOUBT OR UNCERTAINTY

As its employee, Harry's father was governed by the Pennsylvania Railroad's standards and codes of behavior:

> 15. **Strict propriety of conduct, and the avoidance of profane or indecent language in the presence of Passengers and in the transaction of business with others, and with one another, is required.**
> 16. **Smoking, and the use of intoxicating drinks, whilst on duty, is prohibited.**
> 17. **Persons known to be in the habitual use of intoxicating drinks, will not be retained in the service, and any employee known to have been intoxicated will be immediately dismissed.**[1]

Robert, raised in Switzerland, may have had a culturally based penchant for firm rules, or not, just as he may or may not have liked his nightly lager, or more. Robert was certainly unused to using English profanities and evidently possessed the self-control to avoid German oaths, or reserve them for his leisure time. If his cultural inheritance and/or the rage for rules that tore across Pennsylvania in the nineteenth century informed his parental style, he was likely a firm father, enforcing the domestic code of behavior, but maybe only when Mrs. Anslinger saw fit, when the graver childish infractions called for a distinctly paternal mode of discipline. Perhaps he was a distant father who was nevertheless utterly committed to providing for his large family, which may explain why he left off barbering and joined the Company when his sixth child was born. But I speculate. We can't be sure about Robert's motivations for, or experience while, working at Pennsy, so a good rule of thumb is

18. **In all cases of doubt or uncertainty take the safe course and run no risks.**[2]

This much is certain: the Altoona public schools at the turn of the century assumed a distinctly parental posture; their intention to function like substitute misters and missuses for a lot of little Harrys was articulated in yet another set of rules. The phrase "Rules and Regulations for the Government of" headed untold documents in the nineteenth century, setting forth, in listable performatives, the standards of public, private, and religious institutions, including the Pennsylvania Railroad and the Altoona school system. The *Rules and Regulations for the Government of the Public Schools of the City of Altoona* of 1894 articulates a particular species of in loco parentis that reflects official presumptions about proper parenting; these are among the "duties of teachers":

> **It shall be their duty to practice such discipline in their schools as would be exercised by a kind and judicious parent in his family, always firm and vigilant, but prudent. They shall endeavor to impress upon the minds of their pupils the principles of morality and a sacred regard for the truth, love of God and man, industry and frugality.**[3]

Toddlers of Harry's time enjoyed lining up the toy Civil War soldiers just so, only to knock them down again, and on and on, as toddlers did and still will do, industriously. Perhaps little Harry would have been too young to spot the Pinkerton agent infiltrating the Confederate ranks to gather intelligence and bring it back to the Union. Beginning well before the war, in 1850, the Pinkertons produced the profession of detection and forged its relation to policing, in ways that bordered, in cases like strike-busting, on the mercenary, like some kind of muscle for industrial giants. It was, in part, the railway industry that called forth the Pinkertons, who were mobilized during the Great Railroad Strike in 1877, a couple of years before Harry's parents were married. In 1892, as Harry purred and mewled, adults in Altoona would certainly have heard about the troubles over in Pittsburgh, where the Pinkertons had been called in to break the Homestead Strike. As Harry pulled

RULES AND REGULATIONS

FOR THE

GOVERNMENT

OF THE

PUBLIC SCHOOLS

OF THE

CITY OF ALTOONA,

TO WHICH IS ATTACHED A

GRADED COURSE OF INSTRUCTION.

PUBLISHED BY AUTHORITY OF THE BOARD OF DIRECTORS OF THE ALTOONA SCHOOL DISTRICT.

Adopted August, 1873.   Revised March, 1894.

ALTOONA, PA.,
DERN & PITCAIRN, PRINTERS,
1894.

Rules and Regulations for the Government of the Public Schools of the City of Altoona, 1894.

himself up by his baby bootstraps in 1893, Congress passed the Anti-Pinkerton Act to prevent the federal government from employing the private company as a militia. And a then-toddling Harry could not have known at the time that the Pinkertons operated on behalf of the railroad companies once again as they worked to break the Pullman boycott of 1894. But the Pinkertons would make a mark on Harry, as his career in detection would demonstrate; like them, Harry would figure as a nodal point between detection and policing. Meanwhile, large railroad companies would continue to grow, and tracks would proliferate, radiating out from an ever-growing number of also-growing urban centers, as Union Stations cropped up across the country.

When Harry was in diapers and his father began working at the railroad, the Liberty Bell replica rang out over all of Altoona at 6:00 to wake workers, at 6:50 to give them walking time to work, and at noon, 12:50, 1:00, and 5:00 to mark the starting and stopping of work throughout the day. When Harry got into long pants, he went to school in the district ruled and regulated as above. At home and in school, he was impressed, molded, with the righteous value of truth, and later, when he got his own first job, also with the Company, he would pursue truth vigorously, but that is jumping the gun. The Pennsy bell would have long since ceased to ring by the time Harry was twelve, becoming no more than a vague memory to him eventually. But the tintinnabulation of the company tympanum must have rung in his bones forevermore, or the sense of virtue associated with its discipline settled in there. In all cases of doubt or uncertainty, the resonance exceeds the rule.

9 ALCOHOL IS A POISON

Iplace Harry at Washington Elementary School because it was the public school closest to his house. All local public schools in Harry's district required students to undergo alcohol education. The superintendent's report lists Alfred F. Blaisdell's series of physiologies as the textbooks for children in physiology classes in the ward schools. Blaisdell wrote multiple textbooks, intended for children of varying ages, reprinted numerous times in the 1890s and 1900s, and widely distributed in the northeastern United States. Blaisdell's *The Child's Book of Health* was the physiology text geared toward elementary school students.

In this text, if not also at home under the tutelage of his firm but prudent parents, Harry would have imbibed instruction about muscles, bones, skin, the nervous system, the digestive and circulatory systems, and "how alcohol does harm" to some and "injures" the others. The "Few Facts about Alcoholic Liquors" section included "The evil nature

Washington Elementary School (*left*) and Lincoln Elementary School (*right*). Courtesy of the Altoona Area School District.

of these drinks is due to the alcohol which they all contain," and "Alcohol is a poison."[1]

As they occur in nature, apples are sweet, and grapes and their juices are good for us to eat, but when they turn, they turn very, very bad. Rye and rice and wheat and barley and other grains are good to eat, but alcohol derived from them is not food. By 1905, the health text for younger children included a warning that "children, and some grown people, have been suddenly killed by drinking liquors that contained much alcohol."[2]

In the text designed for Harry's older brother John's high school cohort, *Our Bodies and How We Live*, Sir Andrew Clark states that "alcohol is a poison. So is strychnine; so is arsenic; so is opium. It ranks with these agents." This is followed by the concurrence of Willard Parker, MD, that alcohol "answers to the description of a poison" and "has its place with arsenic, belladonna, prussic acid, opium, etc."[3] The temperance movement exercised significant control over the information in school textbooks, ensuring that science and health lessons treating alcohol would convey the moral message.

MORE ABOUT ALCOHOLIC LIQUORS   47

WRITING EXERCISES

Strong drink may make us want more of it.
Strong drink may make us say bad words and do bad things.
Strong drink keeps people from doing good work.
Strong drink does more harm than war, pestilence, and famine.
Strong drink may become a poison both to the mind and to the body.
A golden text for us all to remember: Never drink a drop of strong drink!

Harry, along with his classmates, rehearsed exercises like those found in *The Child's Book of Health*, each one taking a turn with his chalk, each child writing one sentence on the chalkboard at the front of the room, to improve his penmanship even as he drank in these draughts of ideology:

Now your own body, the house in which you live, is in many ways like a delicate machine, —like a watch or a steam engine for instance,—with many parts, both inside and outside, that need your best care. The Creator has given this most wonderful

I can imagine the future commissioner tugging on his trouser leg to straighten it out before sitting back down at his desk and placing his chalk in its proper place in the tiny ditch that ran parallel to the edge of his desk. And I can see him wiping his fingers clean of the white powder, looking up at the flag by mistake before finding the clock, and recalculating the number of minutes remaining before he could go outside to play.

Seen from the outside, the front, back, and sides of Washington Elementary School figured as four grids, each absolutely symmetrical around a central axis. On the front face of the school, that axis was the line from which the front doors of the building opened out, to take students in in the morning, to disgorge them in the afternoon. The only curves in sight: the high arched windows over the two side stairwells, themselves equidistant from the central exterior stairs up to the entrance. Outside, the only moving part in the picture, and only when there was a breeze, was the flag that waved back and forth across the pole that extended the vertical line between the two front doors heavenward. Inside the school, the wild yeast plants and ferments, those unruly poisons, threatened to wriggle off of page 43

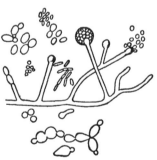

Wild Yeast Plants, or Ferments

Ferments are found upon the skin of grapes and are concerned in the fermentation of wine

of Harry's physiology textbook and into students' bodies, while the students tried to sit still.

Until the bell rang. Then Harry and his wriggling mates gathered up their satchels and pushed one another in a grand rush of children out the classroom door, down the hall, through the hall door, down the stairs, into the front hall, and finally out the front doors, bursting the seam of the school. From there, the children spilled down the front steps, fanning out, a large squirming mass becoming so many rays extending toward so many homes, shops, parks, and the nearest streetcar stop. If, at any point between school and home, Harry had stopped and lain down on the ground, his satchel by him—books full of warnings and squirming ferments, writing exercises and review questions shut up inside—he would have seen telegraph wires slicing the sky over Altoona into strips and quadrilaterals. The wires would have mirrored the streets, running above his own Third Avenue and every other avenue; the crisscrossing of the wires would have mimicked the crisscrossing of Third Avenue and Eighth Avenue and every other intersection; another set of wires would have hovered over the streetcar tracks to Hollidaysburg and back. Long before he went to work by the timetables in which towns and city stations met names of trains in arrays of hours and minutes, long before he donned that

48   THE CHILD'S BOOK OF HEALTH

REVIEW QUESTIONS

1. What is alcohol?
2. What will a little poison do to the health? What will more do?
3. Has any one ever been suddenly killed by drinking alcoholic liquors?
4. What can you say of those who have been injured, but not suddenly killed, by these liquors?
5. Where do we find the water which nature prepares for us to drink?
6. Do we find alcohol thus prepared for us by nature?
7. What is the juice of apples called when squeezed out?
8. What does new cider do when it has stood in warm air for a short time?
9. What causes it to do this? Describe ferments.
10. Where are ferments found?
11. When do they get into apple juice?
12. What do ferments do to good fruit juice?
13. Why is the juice of apples sweet?
14. What do ferments do to the sugar in apple juice?
15. What two new substances take the place of the sugar?
16. What becomes of the gas? What becomes of the alcohol?
17. Why, then, is cider a poisonous drink?
18. What is it the nature of alcohol to do to those who drink any liquor containing it?
19. Why is it more dangerous to drink liquors that have a little alcohol in them than to drink milk?

uniform and marched to the tune of the whistles in the yards nearby, on any sunny school day when he plunked himself down on the ground somewhere between home and school, landing at 40°31'5"N and 78°23'42"W, Harry and his arms and legs would have fallen like lines north-northeast–south-southwest, west-northwest–east-southeast, his head a warm-blooded roundhouse in which any idea he might have had would have expressed itself as a signal crossing and recrossing the closed circuitry of his growing brain.

Explain why you would or would not agree with the following statement:

> In its effect upon the living system, alcohol is first an irritant, and afterward, when it has entered the circulation, it becomes a narcotic. Were alcohol an irritant only, a man would as soon poison himself with arsenic. The narcotic element is the siren that leads him to ruin and death.[4]

10 THE NARCOTIC ELEMENT IS THE SIREN . . .

During those same days and nights, Harry kept on growing, like a microcompany, a body of working parts—blood, bones, muscles, organs, each with its own function, working in concert with the other parts for the viability and growth of the whole—with a big brain to count and calculate, to speculate and then make executive decisions, to assess safety and danger, the prospects of profitability and

12

SIGNALS.

18. Conductors, Enginemen, Firemen, Brakemen, Station Agents, Telegraph Operators, Foremen of Road Repairs, Switchmen, Road and Bridge Watchmen, and all other employes having to make Signals, are required to provide themselves with them, keep them on hand in good order, and always ready for immediate use.

19. **Red** signifies **Danger**, and is a Signal to **stop.**

20. **Green** signifies **Caution**, and is a Signal to **go slowly.**

21. **White** signifies **Safety**, and is a Signal to **go on.**

22. **Green-and-White** is a Signal to be used to stop Trains at **Flag Stations.**

23. **Blue** is a Signal to be used by **Car Inspectors.**

24. **Flags** of the proper color must be used by day, and **Lamps** of the proper color must be used at night, or in foggy weather. Red Flags or Red Lanterns, must never be used as Caution Signals, **they always signify Danger— stop.**

13

25. A Lantern swung across the Track, a Flag, Hat, or **any object** waved violently by **any person** on the Track, signifies **Danger**, and is a Signal to **stop.**

26. An **Exploding Cap or Torpedo** clamped to the top of the rail, is an **Extra Danger Signal**, to be used **in addition** to the regular Signals, at night, in foggy weather, and in cases of accident or emergency, when other Signals cannot be distinctly seen or relied upon.

The explosion of **one** of these Signals, is a warning **to stop the Train immediately:—** the explosion of **two** of these Signals, is a warning **to check the speed of the Train immediately**, and look out for the regular Danger Signal.

27. A **Fusee** is an **Extra Caution Signal**, to be lighted and thrown on the Track at frequent intervals, by the Flagman of Passenger Trains at night, whenever the Train is not making Schedule speed between Telegraph Stations.

A Train finding a Fusee burning upon the Track **must come to a full stop,** and not proceed until it is burned out.

2

From *Rules and Regulations for the Government of the Transportation Department of the Pennsylvania Railroad*, 1857, pp. 12–13. Reproduced by permission from the Pennsylvania Historical and Museum Commission, Pennsylvania State Archives; and The Pennsylvania Railroad Company.

loss associated with competition and cooperation relative to other growing bodies.

> **Admiration for the great mythical corporation grew because Americans assumed that at the center of the octopus was the single controlling brain—the greedy and ambitious, hard-working and independent, single American individual.**[1]

This octopus is the tentacled beast, its body singular and plural, whole and parts, centralizing executive functions while distributing goods and values. But it is a mythical beast, part human and part institution, or rather wholly human (made up of human beings and operating in the image of a human), and also wholly institutional (made up of departments and divisions and rules and regulations and operating according to financial and legal principles). Across the country, people, railroads, and courts played out an ambivalence and/or conflation about the similarity and differences between the person and the corporation.

After all, while corporations were not "natural persons," they were nevertheless legal persons, as the Supreme Court decided in *Santa Clara County v. Southern Pacific Railroad Company* (a case bound up with several similar cases, including the [presumably natural] *People of California v. Central Pacific Railroad*).[2] As the Central Pacific Railroad worked with the Southern Pacific Railroad to run a train line from the Missouri River to and through El Paso and on to the Pacific Ocean at San Diego, they ran into tax issues with county and state entities, which were finally resolved with the court's declaration that

> **the court does not wish to hear argument on the question whether the provision in the Fourteenth Amendment to the Constitution, which forbids a State to deny to any person within its jurisdiction the equal protection of the laws, applies to these corporations. We are all of the opinion that it does.**[3]

Though the personable Central Pacific Railroad may not have played well with the people of California, railroads all over the continent did play quite well with each other, doing what corporate persons do, which is incorporate. The phenomenal growth of the larger railroads in the nineteenth century depended largely on the acquisition of smaller ones. To incorporate is not only to form into a legal corporation, or form into a body, but also to admit a new member to an existing corporation, or assimilate others into such a body. To bring into the body. To eat, and even to drink.

The health of the individual body, the corporate body, and the body politic are bound up together. *The Child's Book of Health* asked students in Altoona in the 1890s to consider the hazards of incorporation:

REVIEW QUESTIONS

. . .

3. Has any one ever been suddenly killed by drinking alcoholic liquors?

4. What can you say of those who have been injured, but not suddenly killed, by these liquors?

. . .

18. What is it the nature of alcohol to do to those who drink any liquor containing it?

19. Why is it more dangerous to drink liquors that have a little alcohol in them than to drink milk?[4]

This text impressed upon children the dangers of the incorporation of alcohol. In compliance with the stated intentions of the superintendent, schoolteachers were expected to impress upon, nay, to inculcate in, students "the principles of morality and a sacred regard for the truth, love of God and man, industry and frugality."[5] Everywhere they turned, around the turn of the century, Altoonan children would have heard these ideals articulated. They were espoused at home, embodied by father and mother, as well as professed by teachers. But not all Altoonans lived in concert with them.

When he was twelve years old, Harry was deeply upset by an encounter in a house near his. He would later claim this as a defining moment in his memoir, *The Murderers*:

> Visiting in the house of a neighboring farmer, I heard the screaming of a woman on the second floor. I had never heard such cries of pain before. The woman, I learned later, was addicted, like

to the counter. The tinkle of the bell on the door brings the druggist to the counter a moment later. Harry's chest hurts; he feels like crying. Exploding cap. In a rush, Harry explains his mission. He watches the druggist reach up for the bottle on a narrow shelf and decant some of the solution into a smaller bottle, finish with a neat turn of the wrist, stopper both bottles, wrap the one in paper, and tie it with twine. As he watches, heart ticking, Harry feels a large Percussion Cap—Extra Danger Signal, to be used in cases of accident or emergency—secured by clamps to the top of his head, but he must not show it. If Harry takes pride or pleasure in this chapter, does it lie in his ability to hide his anxiety from the druggist and feign nonchalance, his power to stop the woman's suffering, or the confidence placed in him by his neighbors?

It is 1904. Harry hurries out of the drugstore and back out into the night with a package of morphine. He unties the horses and climbs into the cart. The horses know the way home; they need no lashing. A train shrieks. How must he hold morphine—he has never held it before—and where, under his coat or in his trouser pocket? Or does he set it beside him on the seat of the cart? He arrives in short order at the farmhouse. Harry hustles inside, the husband hurries up the stairs, and a hush falls over the house. Ah. Harry has brought an end to screaming and pain. She is fixed.

All of this he remembers, but still what he can't forget are her screams—and the unasked questions of the druggist who sold him the morphine. I have questions of my own. Like, did this happen? And if so, was this truly a formative experience, a kind of training, forging Harry as a warrior against the ravages of improperly distributed drugs, or did Harry retrieve this memory later in light of his having turned out, through a series of contingencies and demonstrated generic capacities, to become a high-ranking soldier in an army engaged in infinite battles against Others at home and abroad, against the Otherness itself that seems to fill the being of the self, which is nonetheless understood as a War on Drugs? Is addiction the trouble with women, or is his great sensitivity to, or his exploitation of, this moment the trouble with Harry? He pre-Company, preadolescent, preconscious, had not yet organized his own mind to later purposes. Perhaps he simply remembered and could not ever forget; and he could integrate

the memory into his account of himself as a developing commissioner. Yet Harry gives luminous, almost numinous, value to the episode
of the woman on the second floor—I don't say Martha, though she
might have been—which took place the same year that Franz Kafka
penned the following passage far from Altoona, far from the shadow
of the corporation in question.[9] I can't make out what she's saying,
but the ghostly siren sings from the second story and the flare of
history goes up:

> **For words are clumsy mountaineers and clumsy miners. Not for
> them to bring down treasures from the mountains' peaks, or up
> from the mountains' bowels.**
>
> **But there is a living mindfulness that has passed gently, like a
> stroking hand, over everything memorable. And when the flame
> shoots up out of these ashes, hot and glowing, strong and mighty,
> and you stare into it as though spellbound by its magic, then—**

11 LOTUS EATERS:
Whosoever

Whosoever Understands the Locomotive Force of Narrative

. . . but wave and current, and the northern wind, together beat me from my track away, as I was doubling back around, as I was doubling back around, and now I should have come to mine own country all unhurt, but the wave and the stream of the sea and the North Wind swept me from my course, driven thence by foul winds for a space of nine days, for nine whole days, and we'd have reached our native land unharmed and all unhurt, but the cloud-gatherers had other things in mind for us.[1] Nine days fierce winds drove me across the fish-filled seas, borne by ruinous winds over the teeming deep, and on the tenth we landed where the Lotus Eaters live and set foot on their land.

Here the narrative, such as it is, takes a station break, much as Odysseus did, more than once, on his long trip home to Ithaka. The engineer kills the engine and announces a ten-minute wait; the lights go out. Passengers are permitted to leave the car and walk out onto the platform or into the station. Here the

236   THE ODYSSEY.   Book IX.

Across the deep, wherein the sea fish play;   100
And on the tenth we touched upon the land
Of the Lotophagi, who feed on flowers :
We landed and drew water for our ships
And by their side my comrades took their meal.
When we were satisfied with food and drink,   105
I sent some of my comrades to enquire.
Who they might be who lived upon the land;
And two I chose, a herald was the third.
And soon they met with the Lotophagi :
They on my comrades schemed no ill design   110
But offered them the lotus flower to eat.
Whoe'er may taste its fruit so honey sweet,
Will never wish to bring a message back,
Or to return ; but ever wish to dwell
With these Lotophagi; and ever feed   115
On that weird plant, forgetful of his home.
But these I drove back weeping to their ships
Dragged them on board, and bound them in the
    holds :
And to my other much loved comrades all
I gave command to go on board their ships   120

From *The Odyssey of Homer, Rendered into English Verse*, trans., G. A. Schomberg, 1879–1882, p. 236. Image courtesy of the University of Michigan Library.

Lotus Eaters have their way and interrupt the very rule of narrative, its forward progress.

But what place is this?

Back we go to Africa; back is the only way to go to Africa anymore. The straight lines of the temperate zones go wavy in the heat of the tropics. Blown off his course by an unruly wind, tossing and turning on the currents and waves, Odysseus doubles back. His course goes screwy. Curvy. Scurvy. The straight line is the death drive, and the wavy lines land a man in the slow lane; he slows to a halt. Up and down the western coast of Italy, beautiful and selfish women bewitch Odysseus and his men, but in the tropics, the Achaeans find the indolent people, not working and not white, the temptations of torpor, listlessness, not-to-do lists, shiftlessness, idyllic idleness. If the fruit falls from the tree within an arm's length, why cultivate? If the cloud-gatherers gather no clouds, why build shelter? A man hangs with the lotus-loving do-nothings. Why wouldn't we want to ease back down the ladder of evolution, regress to a place where the men are softer than women and commerce has no truck? Go rudderless, without direction or speed, altogether without government. If the captain lets go and goes with the flow, if the captain ceases to govern the boat, civilization itself slides backward. But the wave and the stream of the sea, sea currents and the waves and the North Wind swept me from my course as I was doubling back around, fierce winds drove me away from there, across the fish-filled seas, thence for nine whole days was I borne by ruinous winds over the teeming deep, foul winds washed me up "probably near the Little Syrtis on the coast of Africa."[2]

We went ashore and carried water back. We had our food and drink, and then I sent forth certain of my company, some of my comrades, out to make search what manner of men they were who here live upon the earth by bread, learn about the men who ate the food the land grew here in this country. We landed in the country of the Lotus Eaters, who feed on flowers, eat a flowery food, and feed upon its flowery fruit, but meant us no harm, had no thought of destroying my companions or killing them, and devised not death for us. They on my comrades schemed no ill design but offered them the lotus flower to taste of and to eat, which was sweet and like honey. Certain of my company went among the Lotus Eaters who did them no hurt,

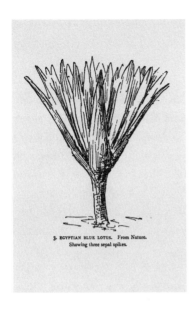

3. EGYPTIAN BLUE LOTUS. From Nature.
Showing three sepal spikes.

From William Goodyear, *The Grammar of the Lotus*, 1891, p. 27. Image courtesy of the Internet Archive (at archive.org) with funding from the Microsoft Corporation.

but gave them to eat of the lotus, which was so delicious that those who ate it left off. . . .

But what plant is this?

The year before Harry was born in Pennsylvania, British archaeologist William Goodyear had attempted to demystify the plant in *The Grammar of the Lotus*:

> Considering its deserts, the lotus has been a much-neglected plant, notwithstanding its fame. It has been recently mistaken for "garlic," for a "branch," for an "Assyrian tulip," for a "daisy," for a "pigtail," for "palm fronds," for a "fan-shaped flower," for "the branch of a tree," and for a "triad." Worse than all, it has been confounded with the lotus of the "lotus eaters," i.e. with the jujube tree.[3]

Goodyear's study dealt with decorative representations of the lotus as ancient, mostly Egyptian and Cypriot, design elements. Archaeologists were not the only ones to study the lotus; botanists, herbologists, horticulturalists—and philologists—had also been trying to identify, classify, taxonomize, and otherwise describe it.

The eleventh edition of the *Encyclopedia Britannica*, published in 1911, offers a brand-new entry:

> LOTUS, a popular name applied to several plants. The lotus fruits of the Greeks belonged to *Zizyphus Lotus*, a bush native in south Europe with fruits as large as sloes, containing a mealy substance which can be used for making bread and also a fermented drink.[4]

During the first decade of the twentieth century, as Harry J. Anslinger adolesced, encyclopedia editors had prepared the above entry, turning to the scholars of classical literature who debated the identity of the lotus as located in Homer's land of the Lotus Eaters, where Odysseus and his men landed after doubling back around:

> **There has been considerable discussion as to the identification of the Homeric lotus. Some have held that it is a prickly shrub, *Zizyphus Lotus*, which bears a sweet-tasting fruit, and still grows in the old home of the Lotophagi. It is eaten by the natives, who also make a kind of wine from the juice.**[5]

During and following the moment of Harry's violent awakening to the evils of morphine, debate continued about the identity of the lotus eaten by Odysseus's men:

> **P. Champault, however, maintains that the lotus was a date; Victor Bérard is doubtful, but contends that it was certainly a tree-fruit. If either of these be correct, then the lotus of *Od*. iv. 603-604 is quite a different plant, a kind of clover.**[6]

Before Harry procured the morphine for the woman on the second floor, the lotus was a date, but shortly afterward, it became a clover:

> **Now Strabo (xvii. 829*a*) calls the lotus ποαν τινα και ριζαν. Putting these two references together with Sulpicius Severus, *Dialogi* i. 4. 4, R. M. Henry suggests that the Homeric lotus was really the ποα of Strabo, i.e. a kind of clover .**[7]

Or it had been a clover all along. These are matters of interpretation. Philologists of this period cared deeply, going so far as to retrace Odysseus's steps, traveling the wine-dark seas to ascertain the truth, expressing dismay that the earlier generation of scholars, those of Harry's childhood, had not pursued the real lotus. To correct the course of the discipline, philologists at the turn of the twentieth century wrote and published tracts of proof.[8] But the wave and the stream of the sea, sea currents and the waves and the North Wind swept me from my course as I was doubling back around, fierce winds drove me away from there, across the fish-filled seas, thence for nine whole days was I borne by ruinous winds over the teeming deep, foul winds washed me up

> **probably near the Little Syrtis on the coast of Africa. The lotus mentioned here is a prickly shrub with a yellow fruit like a plum, if it is to be identified with the jujube tree that still grows in that neighbourhood.**[9]

Lotus, date, clover, jujube. Any of them who ate the honey-sweet fruit of the lotus by any name was unwilling to take any message back, or to go away, but wanted to stay there with the lotus-eating people, feeding on lotus, which made any man who tried it lose his desire ever to journey home, and whosoever of them did eat the honey-sweet fruit of the lotus had no more wish to bring tidings nor to come back, but there he chose to abide with the lotus-eating men, and ever feed on that weird plant, which was so delicious that those who ate of it left off caring about home, and did not even want to go back and say what had happened to them or bring back word to us, but wished to stay and chose to abide, and to remain, among the Lotus Eaters, and inclined toward staying and munching lotus with the Lotus Eaters, feeding on the plant without thinking further of

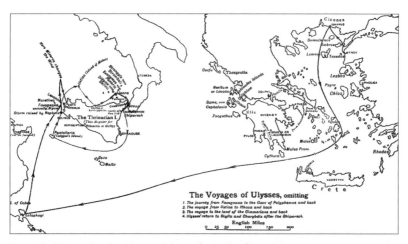

From *The Odyssey, Translated into English Prose for the Use of Those Who Cannot Read the Original by Samuel Butler*, 1900. Courtesy of The Fales Library and Special Collections, New York University.

their return, eager to forget about their homeward voyage and forget the way home.

Lotus—be it date or clover or jujube—is a metaphor for all the plants from which Homo sapiens sapiens have derived agents of drowsing and forgetfulness, not some innocent dreamy luxuriation, but a cultural undoing, or never having done, for divestment from the work of settlement, accumulation, empire. If lotus carries those meanings, Lotus Eaters threaten civilization itself. If the threat is contagious, Odysseus's men have caught it; they could become carriers. The only way out of this chapter is to be carried, weeping, by force. By force, we will embark once more, tied to the thwarts by others; those who understand the need to get word back will propel the narrative onward. Whosoever understands the locomotive force of narrative will have to remind us that the need for word is greater than the thirst for the unutterable sweetness of the lotus.

Whosoever Weeps

And who are the Lotus Eaters? Somewhere between 1904 and 1906, philologists located the Lotus Eaters of the Odyssey as members of a Libyan tribe in northern Africa.[10] Students of Odysseus placed him in North Africa for the purposes of Book IX the same year that Harry procured morphine for the Lotus Eater on the second floor, and fair planners and anthropologists collected fifteen to twenty thousand indigenous people from all over the world, including a number of North Africans, to make up part of the education and entertainment at the World's Fair in St. Louis. A particularly large Filipino contingent stood to educate fairgoers about the US protectorate that in turn stood for the imperial achievements of the United States. Domestic dominion was displayed by Native Americans from all over the country. The fair taught viewers that white Americans were the vanguard of human evolution; people who ate dogs, other humans, and lotus were bringing up the rear. Slowly. They came from many longitudes, fewer latitudes, to crowd together on the lower rungs of the ladder that led up to St. Louis.

Though we put our departure at risk, we will linger, tarry, hang back, rest and recline a while, hang out with the legendary Lotus Eaters—meet us in St. Louis or Libya. But what people are these, who live and laze in the land of lotus-eating? They lurk in jungles eating, chewing, smoking, drinking. They languish on the second floor. Listless they may be, but leaky too. The virus of idleness sneaks onto the boat when Odysseus's good men are carrying back the comrades who have been bitten by the lotus leaf. Trade is a two-way street. Lotus Eaters will throw good men off course, and subvert their productive energies, turning innocent boys and boats into purveyors, vehicles, and tools of their own endless spiraling down. Lesson learned, no matter what drave me on the fish-filled seas past the point to where I let go the rudder, and floated, buoyed, landing on the tenth day . . . here?

For Harry and for Odysseus, the call of the temperate zone, clarion clear, prevails. The whistle blows. For Harry and Odysseus, then, for the captains of temperance, for the men in the metropoles, for the march of progress, therefore I led them back to the ships weeping, and sore against their will, I forced them, eyes full of tears, into our hollow ships, dragged them underneath the rowing benches, and tied them up. I myself took these men back weeping, by force, to where the ships were, and put them aboard under the rowing benches and tied them fast, dragged them beneath the benches, and bound them in the hollow barques. Because my men, they did not want to go, just as they had not thought to give word, had wished to stay and remain, forgetful of their home. So out of the ordure, contra the torpor, against the waves, for the order of things, for order itself, I ordered, I issued orders, I commanded the rest of my well-loved company to make speed and go on board the swift ships, race on board, go to their places, in haste, vite vite, lest—but let us not speak further of the specter of forgetting, forgetting the word and forgetting the way home. My men, refastened to the word, my men live out their sentences, tied fast to benches, to the rowing benches, eyes full of tears, dragged by force beneath the thwarts. Right soon, astride these selfsame thwarts, the rest of the well-loved company sat in good order in their rows, and struck the gray sea with their oar blades, and, sitting orderly, smote the gray seawater with their oars and smote the gray seawater. For fear that another comrade or companion might taste of the lotus, for the sake of argument, sentenced to suffer like civilized men, retreat we from the land of Lotus Eaters, many other women of the period, to morphine, a drug whose dangers most medical authorities did not yet recognize. All I remember was that I heard a woman in pain, whose cries seemed to fill my whole twelve-year-old being. Then her husband came running down the stairs, telling me I had to get into the cart and drive to town. I was to pick up a package at the drug store and bring it back for the woman.

I recall driving those horses, lashing at them, convinced that the woman would die if I did not get back in time. When I returned with the package—it was morphine—the man hurried upstairs to give the woman the dosage. In a little while her screams stopped and a hush came over the house.

I never forgot those screams. Nor did I forget that the morphine she required was sold to a twelve-year-old boy, no questions asked.[6]

Young Harry must have had questions about the whole affair of the woman on the second floor. Why was she screaming? What was the source of her pain—was it in her muscles or bones? Was it in her blood—"the river of life"? Where did it hurt? In her heart, "the busy little pump"?[7] Her skin? Her teeth? Did she have too much, or not enough, heat? Was it her digestion, something she ate? The relevant text was over his head: "Many harmful substances, as ether, morphine, and other powerful drugs, are oxidized within the body and furnish a certain amount of energy, and yet nobody classifies these as foods." "What is a narcotic poison?"[8]

Blue, green. No, red, *red*. RED. **RED.**

Harry hears a woman in pain. Her cries seem to fill his whole being. She might die. It falls to Harry to save her life. He must get into the cart, he must drive the horses, lashing them, lashing them, lashing them, to town. Through rain or mud, in the darkening blue light of dusk? If the hammers are muffled in the snow, his driving heart makes up the difference. The horses, the lashings, these he remembers later, along with the woman and the screaming—the emergency—the emergency fills up his emergent being. With his literal arms, he lashes the horses. With his figurative arms, Harry waves a Lamp, Flag, Hat, violently.

Harry arrives at the drugstore, ties the horses hastily, runs inside and otherwise withdraw, whosoever weeps. The whistle blows. The long blast sounds. I think I hear that old Pennsy bell now. Correcting the course, I take to the lines, refind Harry his story.

Straight they embarked, and sat upon the thwarts, and with their oars they threshed the foaming sea. And onward thence we sailed with saddened hearts.

12 THE EDUCATION OF HARRY ANSLINGER

When Harry applied for a job in Washington in 1917, he was asked for his employment history. In response to Question 5 on the application, Harry listed his first official job in the subject-less syntax of the résumé: "At age of 14, on or about August 11, 1906, entered the employ of the Penna. Railroad Company, at Altoona, Pa." To get back on track then, to resume the narrative, is to find Harry at work on the railroad, having reduced his school lessons to morning sessions. Afternoons, Harry routed cars. In this capacity, he mastered the signals and codes, throwing switches, connecting cars to cars to cars in ever longer trains. He spent the following year working days, still at the Pennsylvania Railroad—"compiling statistics on mail detentions required by government"[1]—and going to school at night. Although he had not received a high school diploma, Harry enrolled in the Altoona Business College in 1908 or 1909, once again taking classes at night, and working now in the Motive Power Department of the PRR at storehouse management.

By the end of that year, his sixteenth, Harry was in Requisitions. He ordered parts; the ordering of parts was essential to the functioning of the Pennsylvania Railroad, and Harry an essential part of the company. After a year in Motive Power, Harry spent a year as secretary to the chief of the Relief Department, once again compiling statistics. Next, Harry worked on the literal lines—telegraph and telephone, a virtual canopy of which now hung over Altoona—even as he worked his way through Altoona Business College. During his two-year program in

Question 5.   At age of 14, on or about August 11,1906, entered the employ of the Penna. Railroad Company, at Altoona, Pa., resigned in September 1916.

1918 job application. Harry J. Anslinger Papers, Special Collections Library, The Pennsylvania State University Libraries.

engineering and business management, Harry worked at the Company on weekends and vacations, circulating through the organization, closer and closer to its ticking heart.

Around the same time, halfway around the world, back in the Bern that was Harry's father's birthplace, ever so close to the ticking tock of a train station in Switzerland, Albert Einstein reviewed patent applications. Just across the street from his office in the patent office in Bern stood the station, with its several clocks, one above each track inside and one on the facade. As he walked out from his apartment to head toward his office, Einstein was faced with the Kramgasse Clock Tower. Bern hosted no fewer than twenty-six publicly displayed clocks, all telling the same time. As he worked as an Engineer Class II at the Federal Office for Intellectual Property, Einstein pored over an increasing number of applications for patents related to the electromagnetic coordination of time.[2]

After hours, following the long clock-faced walk home, Einstein worked in his physics papers on the problem represented by the clock-coordination craze. He called that problem "simultaneity," and he called his answer to it "a theory of relativity" in a paper first published in 1905. In addition to lots of clocks, the train station housed the thought experiment with which Einstein illustrated a new way of thinking about simultaneity. Two bolts of lightning strike the front and back of a moving train at the same time. To an observer standing on the train, Einstein proposed, the two bolts of lightning appear to hit the train simultaneously; to an observer standing on the platform, it looks as though the bolts of lightning hit the train at two different times. Einstein wondered about the speed of a person running inside a train. Einstein wondered "what it meant for an observer here to say that a distant observer was watching a train arrive at 7 o'clock."[3] Trains ran round the inside of Einstein's head.

Though there could be no certainty that the same year for one observer was the same year for another observer, convention allows that in 1907, Henry Ford was hard at work in the locked fifteen-by-twenty-foot space he called the "experimental room"; there and then, Ford and a team of assistants developed the Model T. Ford's industry was to eclipse the railroad in the long run, though the assembly-line production of automobiles was merely incipient in that locked room.

For a sustained moment, trains dominated—as a mode of overland transportation, and as the industry around which an incalculable number of inventions, discoveries, patents, imaginative exercises, laws and judicial decisions, goods, services, profits, and losses materialized. So it is no mere coincidence that Harry Anslinger and Albert Einstein thought their formative thoughts in and around trains and train stations and train times.

Just as the technics of electro-coordination of time, as called forth by trains, extended across the globe, so did the wires and cables of the telegraph system. They ran around the world, connecting disparate geographical points and the people living and working there. It was an unprecedented technical achievement to enable simultaneous conversation between hemispheres: a series of wires and cables that tracked

> down and across the North Atlantic, up onto pebbled beaches of Newfoundland; it tracks from Europe into the Pacific and up into Haiphong Harbor; it slides along the ocean floor the length of West Africa. Follow the land-based wires and the iron and copper cables; they lead up into the Andes, through the backcountry of Senegal and clear across North America from Massachusetts to San Francisco.[4]

Like the geodesic polygons of the longitude explorers—whose maps derived from journeys across lands and seas as well as from theoretical calculations performed in Paris—the drawings of the new cable system looked like nets capturing continents, connecting the dots of Buenos Aires, Valparaiso, Rio de Janeiro, Lima, and Panama, Latin America being hauled up north to, or by, Washington, and northeast to or by Europe, Latin America as the captured culprit. Now Altoona was an unstable dot in a field gone relatively global, telecommunications and transportation systems wrapping themselves around Harry and his neighbors to the far south and far far east, relating Asia to Latin America to Altoona, personal and corporate home and headquarters. At the same time, the diplomatic conversation about drugs now could—and did—go global.[5]

13 HORSEPLAY TURNS TO TRAGEDY

Lotus Eaters lurk around lots of corners. In 1909, the same year that Harry detached the retina in his left eye, an opium convention took place in Shanghai, its members appointed by President Roosevelt at the urging of Archbishop Charles Henry Brent, Episcopal missionary bishop in the Philippines. A Canadian by birth, Brent had gone to work in the Philippines in 1901, "against my taste and with a revulsion for work in a Latin country."[1] The tropics did not agree with him—time wasting and luxury revolted him—but as an obedient servant of the church, Brent set his reforming sights on the "degenerate, criminal, and immoral" Americans who populated the US occupation of the Philippines. The American attracted to the job was, according to Brent, "the adventurer, the irresponsible weakling, the human bird of prey" given to "unwholesome pleasure-seeking" and utterly ruined by "the

APPENDIX IV—Continued.

Importations into the United States of various forms of opium, showing per cent of increase in imports compared with per cent increase in population, per decade—Continued.

From *Report of the International Opium Commission: Shanghai, China*, vol. 1, *Report of the Proceedings*, 1909, p. 82. Courtesy of the Division of Rare and Manuscript Collections, Carl A. Kroch Library, Cornell University.

hitherto untried and cruel temptations of the Orient."[2] Such a man would taste the lotus, stay among the Lotus Eaters, and forget the word Brent preached. As Orientals, the Filipinos' constitutional fault was "sensuality," and though it was a racial flaw, it was also contagious. White Americans on tour of duty could catch it, too easily. Atchoo. Brent's proposed solution was to halt the flow of Chinese opium into the Philippines, one of the earliest examples of a prohibitionist strategy against drug flow.

The US commission to the 1909 Shanghai convention envisioned by Brent was led by Hamilton Kemp Wright, an inside-the-Beltway-avant-la-Beltway expert in tropical diseases who made his reputation misidentifying a pathogen causing beriberi. Before going to Shanghai, Wright helped expedite the passage of the Opium Exclusion Act on the premise that such domestic legislation would give the United States greater authority on the international stage of the convention. This act extended the work Brent had been doing in the Philippines, making it illegal in the United States to smoke opium, smoking being the mode of consumption for nonmedicinal purposes. But there were other methods of consuming opiates. The act may have reinforced the authority of the US commission, but it was demonstrably less successful at suppressing opium use.

Wright then authored the commission's report upon his return from Shanghai. In this report, Wright recapitulates the by-then decades-old narrative about the debauchery of "young, robust, Chinese immigrant coolies who arrived on our Pacific slope before 1880," and their disease, which spread to "depraved Americans who frequented the resorts of the Chinese sections of our large cities."[3] Though the conference did produce a series of resolutions, they were in essence recommendations that would languish unsubmitted for ratification by participating nations. An emergent American style of suppression was represented in the resolutions—for example, recreational and habitual opium smoking should be regulated—but the international opium trade, in which the United States was not a principal party, freighted even these mild resolutions with unnavigable political complications in China and India, among other countries.

Wright's report also imparted grave concerns about the domestic use of cocaine:

> A new drug problem appeared about twenty years ago, and had
> grown with a rapidity that marked the avidity of our criminal class-
> es in acquiring a new vice; latterly it had exhibited a strong tendency
> to spread, corrupt, and ruin many who belonged to the higher ranks
> of society. This new vice, the cocaine vice, the most serious that has
> to be dealt with, has proved to be a creator of criminals and unusual
> forms of violence, and it has been a potent incentive in driving the
> humbler negroes all over the country to abnormal crimes.[4]

Wright appealed to an unspecified authority in accounting for
"abnormal" kinds of crime: "It has been authoritatively stated that
cocaine is, often the direct incentive to the crime of rape by the
negroes of the South and other sections of the country."[5] I can't
guess what a "normal" crime might be, if not precisely this, but in
any event, drugs follow from deviance (even the passive deviance of
being nonwhite), and deviance degenerates into criminality. Drugs
turn people into criminals and only criminals seek out drugs, and
this becomes a central tautology underlying the argument for the
criminalization of the possession of drugs. Though there were local
ordinances and state laws, Wright described their inadequacy as he
pressed for federal legislation:

> All that is required by such laws is that the dealer shall keep a
> record of sale, and the name of the person to whom, and the amount
> sold. Many state laws are defective in that they do not make illegal
> possession of habit-forming drugs evidence for conviction.[6]

This was when the public health approach to drugs hit the high road,
forced out of town by Wright in a roguish rant on cocaine smuggled
into a report on the opium convention in Shanghai. Of "the lower
order of working negroes," by which he meant southerners, whose
laziness somehow proved that New York was the source of the drug,
Wright wrote that "at many public works, levee and railroad construction . . . cocaine is handled among them by some method largely obscure."[7] Wright's logic too would be obscure were it not clear
that he meant to link cocaine, African American identity, moral inferiority, and criminality.

In the debates on alcohol prohibition that occupied the country in these years, "morality" became a key, though sometimes tacit, term: morality and health did a do-si-do. On an individual level, drug addiction had been understood as a subset of medical treatments gone wrong; in the mouths of Brent and Wright, drug addiction became a moral problem. Criminals were not sick; they were immoral. When drug addicts went from *habitués*, like Civil War veterans, to *criminals*, they ceased to be sick, becoming bad instead. You can tell because they are no longer white or they are the worst kind of whites. Degeneracy is generous, knows no bounds, is generative, can seep in through borders, nostrils, lungs, and veins. Good (unmarried) white girls could be raped, or drugged, which robbed them of their agency, and then, with what was left of it, they would go bad, their ruination Wright's call to action:

> Looking at the wider aspect of the use of cocaine throughout the United States, there is absolutely trustworthy information that the use of drugs has spread widely among the criminal classes of our large cities, that it is used by those concerned in the white-slave traffic to corrupt young girls, and that when the habit of using the drugs has been established it is but a short time before the latter fall to the ranks of prostitution.[8]

The shift from disease to criminality coincides with the shift from opium and, to a lesser extent, morphine (lesser because of its closer link to medical treatment) as the problem drugs to heroin as the problem drug around 1910. In a sign of the times, Wright compiled some statistics to spell out the effects of his proposed treatment:

> There are in the United States about 500 houses importing, manufacturing, or dealing in drugs at wholesale, from which, under the special tax of $10 per annum, a revenue of $5,000 would be derived, and about 40,000 retail druggists who, under the special tax of $1 as provided for in the act, would yield a revenue of from $30,000 to $40,000.[9]

Blue? Red? Exploding cap? Wright included a table of "imports of coca leaves and cocaine since the first years of their separate enumeration in the customs returns," which spanned 1898 to 1909. And he went on to claim that 15,000 or 20,000 ounces would be sufficient to satisfy medical needs, whereas "to-day there are manufactured at least 150,000 ounces of this drug, the larger part of which is put to improper uses."[10] Perhaps in part because pharmacists down on Eleventh Avenue would purvey morphine to a twelve-year-old boy, no questions asked.

Meanwhile, back in Altoona, the delicate machinery of Harry's body had produced six feet of stature and a square jaw. His relation to an opium convention in Asia is in the future, in which Harry will operate on the global stage crafting treaties. In 1909, the relation was one of mere coincidence; Harry at seventeen only had to be becoming himself in order to converge later with the opium convention that will by then be long past. To become himself all he had to do was act naturally, as Harry worked at the railroad, but also played the piano and engaged in adolescent shenanigans with peers:

> **"Inky" Anslinger was involved in horseplay with several friends one summer afternoon when he was accidentally struck in the left eye by a thrown pear. He suffered a detached retina and never regained sight in that eye.**[11]

Harry would play piano in the local movie theater, around which Altoona was becoming most modern. Downtown, on Twelfth and Twelfth in Altoona, druggist A. F. Shomberg boasted that "very careful attention is given to the compounding of prescriptions." E. J. W. Keagy was a "personally popular" pharmacist whose "patronage increases daily."[12] Harry steered clear of drugs, which required no very great effort in his social circles—alcohol otherwise. But Wright's report shows that in 1909, long before Harry could participate in, much less shape, the public discourse on drugs, the idea of the drug user as a criminal had already taken root. Thus Wright ranted and Harry engaged in some last youthful hijinks; on parallel planes, drugs were discursified in the nearsighted document from Shanghai, their greater regulation endorsed there—and Harry and his pals tossed a pear around.

14 A HIGH-PRICED MAN

So Stupid That the Word "Percentage" Has No Meaning to Him

The race to drug policy led right back to race. Harry emerged from Altoona Business College with an associate's degree in the year that Hamilton Kemp Wright lined up Representative Foster from Vermont to sponsor a bill to control opiates, cocaine, and, in one of its early appearances at the federal level, marijuana. The bill was killed—by druggists, pharmacists, and drug manufacturers. Then, in 1911, the crusade that had brought Wright from Shanghai home to Washington led him to The Hague for the next international drug convention. In preparation for The Hague, Wright's fellow delegate, Henry J. Finger of the California Board of Pharmacy, forged a new link between the flow of drugs and a group of immigrants:

> Within the last year we in California have been getting a large influx of Hindoos and they have in turn started quite a demand for cannabis indica; they are a very undesirable lot and the habit is growing in California very fast.[1]

Like others before and after him, Finger pointed to the threat of recently arrived workers "initiating our whites into this habit," in this case a fairly small number of Sikhs and Punjabs who had come to San Francisco in 1910.[2]

But it was Sir Williams Collins, British delegate to the convention, who sealed the connection between addiction and criminality, reporting that at the convention there was

> a disposition in some quarters to regard the morphinist and the cocainist merely as invalids and objects of pity, but . . . many of them are social pests of the most dangerous kind. Bankrupt of moral sense and will power they are lying and deceitful. Prodigal

of time, plausible to a degree, backbiting and contentious, prone to vice and apt for crime.[3]

Collins explicitly distinguished the criminal addict from a person with a health problem, countering any sympathy associated with the fact that addiction very often began as medical treatment.

To Collins, the degree of "plausibility" (credibility, viability) of the morphinist and the cocainist, not so very great by definition, decreases as the dosage increases; they waste time in addition to themselves. Time originates from Greenwich in the new temporal empire, and the degrees of longitude emanate from the same origin, the y axis that runs through the epicenter of the electro-coordination of time, one of 360 degrees of great circles, each running the entire circumference of the globe, and then the lines of longitude begin again, as opposed to those of latitude, of which only the equator is a similarly great girdle, where things grind to a languorous pace, ever approaching the asymptotic limit of morbid pleasure seeking, the likeness of another race, the birthplace of abnormal kinds of crime, and the threat of exceeding the axes, the specter of the flow, however slow, where time itself might run right out.

Meanwhile, the antidote was being synthesized in Bethlehem, about two hundred miles as the crow flies east of Altoona, where miners, manufacturers, and moneymen worked with the minerals and metals that would form the interlocking parts of trains and rails that led in and out of town, parts that Harry requisitioned. There, at the Bethlehem Steel Company, Frederick Winslow Taylor displayed his gifts for observation and for compiling statistics therefrom.

Taylor watched as a man stooped to pick up steel and stood up again. The man moved, carrying the steel some number of feet or yards; then he put it down on the ground or on a pile. He had used no tools but his hands. Taylor observed that the work was "so crude and elementary in its nature that . . . it would be possible to train an intelligent gorilla so as to become a more efficient pig-iron handler than any man can be." For Taylor, the workman best suited to the job was, also by nature, unable to understand the real science of doing this class of work: "he is so stupid that the word 'percentage' has no

THE PRINCIPLES OF SCIENTIFIC MANAGEMENT   59

From Frederick Winslow Taylor, *The Principles of Scientific Management*, 1911, p. 59. Edited from the original version to move up the final paragraph. Courtesy of the New York Public Library.

Now one of the very first requirements for a man who is fit to handle pig iron as a regular occupation is that he shall be so stupid and so phlegmatic that he more nearly resembles in his mental make-up the ox than any other type. The man who is mentally alert and intelligent is for this very reason entirely unsuited to what would, for him, be the grinding monotony of work of this character. Therefore the workman who is best suited to handling pig iron is unable to understand the real science of doing this class of work. He is so stupid that the word "percentage" has no meaning to him, and he must consequently be trained by a man more intelligent than himself into the habit of working in accordance with the laws of this science before he can be successful.

meaning to him."[4] Therefore, the right kind of worker would have to be trained by a more intelligent scientist of management.

A pig weighed 92 pounds. On average, a man at Bethlehem Steel Company moved 12 tons of pig iron a day, but Taylor found that if he talked to the man the right way, the man could move 47 or 48 tons a day. Here is how Taylor had to talk to the man, and how the man would talk to him:

> "Schmidt, are you a high-priced man?"
>
> "Vell, I don't know vat you mean."
>
> "Oh yes, you do. . . . What I want to find out is whether you are a high-priced man or one of these cheap fellows here. What I want to find out is whether you want to earn $1.85 a day or whether you are satisfied with $1.15, just the same as all those cheap fellows are getting."
>
> "Did I vant $1.85 a day? Vas dot a high-priced man? Vell, yes, I was a high-priced man."
>
> "Oh, you're aggravating me. Of course you want $1.85 a day— everyone wants it! You know perfectly well that that has very little to do with your being a high-priced man. For goodness' sake answer my questions, and don't waste any more of my time."[5]

Apparently, Schmidt could barely understand English; therefore, it was important to speak to him as though he were more gorilla than man. Or, Taylor could shovel the shit as fast as Schmidt could haul pig iron. Maybe Schmidt was no Einstein when it came to the science of his own labor, but his confusion of past and future tenses seems right on the money. Taylor had to repeat himself:

> **"Now do wake up and answer my question. Tell me whether you are a high-priced man or not."**
> **"Vell—did I got $1.85 for loading dot pig iron on dot car to-morrow?"**[6]

Did Schmidt got $1.85 to-morrow? Yes. Schmidt proved able to move 47.5 tons a day and averaged a little over $1.85 for the three years that Taylor continued to study the workers at Bethlehem.

Working with statistics (as Harry had done for the PRR) put Taylor on the standardization bandwagon, regarding task performance as well as time. Like Charles Henry Brent in the Philippines, Taylor deplored the inefficiency of work practices in the trades and counted its costs. Noting that "there are in daily use, say, fifty or a hundred different ways of doing each element of the work," Taylor advocated "having only one way which is generally accepted as a standard." Over and above standardization of procedures, Taylor called for a reconceptualization of management as "a true science, resting upon clearly defined laws, rules, and principles, as a foundation."[7]

Like the education of Henry Adams before him, the education of Harry Anslinger schooled him in *e* for energetic systems though the medium of the moment had shifted away from the electromechanical media of Adams's day to the E for Einsteinian relativity in which the force of E for Empire equals the Mass of Commodities circulating globally, winners take all, losers sit at the sideshow watching, at the World's Fairs from Chicago in 1893 to St. Louis in 1904, no very great distance, around the world and back, except for the work of capturing new natives in lotus-eating lands and putting them on display to stand for earlier points in the march of civilization toward the latest discoveries and inventions, which by 1913 included the assembly line made thinkable, if not necessary, by Frederick Winslow Taylor's work at Bethlehem Steel identifying the waste and inefficiency in then-prevalent production practices.

Taylor was a Pennsylvania Quaker whose principles of scientific management lay in establishing systematic management, "rather than in searching for some unusual or extraordinary man."[8] Harry J. Anslinger was born of tolerable European stock to a hardworking father and was therefore eligible for training. Indeed, Harry trained at the knees of captains of industry, those magnates who made the Pennsylvania Railroad Company the king of modern corporations. When he turned to government work, Harry would import all the insights of the Taylorized trades into bureaucratic practice. He was not an unusual or extraordinary man; he had the skill set to make the trains run on time rather than the genius-for-evil bone.

Harry did not have to be an unusual or extraordinary man to realize Taylor's vision of the application of the principles of scientific management to

> **all social activities: to the management of our homes; the management of our farms; the management of the business of our tradesmen, large and small; of our churches, our philanthropic institutions, our universities, and our governmental departments.**[9]

He just needed to grow up along with corporatism, to study at the feet of the Principles that put their pedal to the metal in the mass production of commodities, and to eat his Quaker Oats. He needed to gain the minimal experience, and minor credentials, necessary to ride that train out of Altoona and into loftier circles, beginning with the state capitol. Meanwhile, in the Altoona of 1911, when Harry walked on Eleventh Avenue, he passed by pool halls, tobacconists, cheese shops, clothing shops, and chemists. The town boasted no fewer than eleven pharmacies and drugstores, all legally dispensing the narcotics that would come under federal control within less than five years.

This is the Altoona in which Harry continued to live and work, even as he, aged nineteen, stopped growing. Altoona's expansion amounted to "over 25 miles of finely paved streets, and a sewer system capable of meeting the requirements of 100,000 inhabitants."[10] One of those Altoonans might step into a pharmacy on Eleventh Avenue as a young man, turn, walk out of Altoona, and head south and east for the national and international arenas of drug policy. As he leaves the pharmacy, he might pass a row of windows on the face of a new building on a straight street in Altoona, with many such buildings lining the sidewalk (a sidewalk now), come to the corner, look right, look left—twice to the left and with a little twist now to compensate for the detached retina—cross the two perpendiculars, where motorcars increasingly replaced horses as the motive power, to the next block, to catch the streetcar to Hollidaysburg on its electrical grooves, wires and cables overhead and always peripherally present.

15 KEYSTONE STATE OF MIND

Altoona was growing up. Circulating through the little city, in addition to thousands of railroad workers: currency both hard and electrical, the first automobiles, and sewage. According to boosters for the city, Altoona's progress could be measured by the development of a comprehensive sewer system, subsidized by the Pennsylvania Railroad Company. Though the system had been conceived back in 1888, four years before Harry was born, the city's four natural drainage areas were now supplied with large main sewers, and "no better sewered city can be found in the state, although the work of laying smaller branches and feeders has not yet been completed."[1] No, there was no better sewered city anywhere.

The tracks underfoot (with Altoona's modern sewer system flowing quietly below) and the lines overhead (with their heaven above) formed a grid, two grids, that sandwiched the city and its train shops and drugstores, while Harry, as he waited for the streetcar, stood parallel to the poles sprouting up from the tracks to hold lamps to shine down upon them, Harry and the other ambulatory Altoonans figuring as the third dimension, the z axes, the verticals that ran from the sewer to heaven, the mobile perpendiculars relative to the horizontal movement of the streetcars, as well as trains and electrical impulses, except the ones that zagged in jagged bolts of lightning. As an employee of the PRR, Harry now held various versions of that grid, the x-by-y one, Altoona's tracks and wires, in his hands, writ small. If Harry was surrounded and contained by grids, he contained them right back, in timetables framed with names of towns, crowded with times of day and night, columns running up and down crossing row after row, and in so many graphs and charts, plotted as labor costs and parts of cars and body parts lost and wages earned and hours and minutes x-ing and y-ing their way through so many pieces of paper,

Fatty Joins the Force,
Keystone Kops movie
poster, Jordison & Co
Ltd., Middlebrough &
London, 1913.

reports, requisition forms, actuarial tables, as Harry read across and down and filled in blanks, and all was correspondence.

Taylor's concepts and models for efficient production would quickly seep into the corporate bloodstream, as Henry Ford would evidence shortly. The year that Taylor published *The Principles of Scientific Management* is the year of The Hague International Opium Conference is the year that Clarence Weaver published *The Story of Altoona, the Mountain City: Railroad, Industrial and Commercial Center* is the year that Hamilton Kemp Wright of Shanghai International Opium Commission fame failed to push through the Foster Bill is the year that Harry completed his course at Altoona Business College and began working full-time for the Pennsylvania Railroad Company. Or is they?

The theory of relativity seemed to say so at or about this time. So maybe the first Keystone Kops movie struck movie theaters in Pennsylvania the same year. Or maybe it came out the following year. And maybe moviegoers were hit with *Fatty Joins the Force* and *The*

Bangville Police the next year, or the year after *that*. Other Keystone Kops features, like *The Gangsters*, came out at, or about, the time that Harry went on furlough, but there was no relation, except perhaps to some of the more recent immigrants, the Sicilians, skulking along the tracks and menacing fellow workers. For Harry, there was nothing funny about police; they exercised a sacred social function, kept things running smoothly.

It didn't take a high school diploma for Harry to make his way to Penn State or, by 1915, to the Intelligence Division of the Pennsylvania Railroad Company, where he did some policing of his own. Harry made a mark in Intelligence, displaying his gift for detection when he exposed the fraudulent claim of a widower, thus saving the Pennsylvania Railroad as much as $50,000.[2] The case: A local woman's shoe got caught in the track at a grade crossing as she was heading home with the groceries. Because she neither heard nor saw the approaching train, which was obscured beyond the curve of the track at that point, the woman made little effort to dislodge the shoe. Stuck there, she was struck and killed by the Broadway Limited. Or so her widower claimed in a negligence suit against the Company, whose lawyers, convinced that the woman's death was accidental, prepared to settle the case.

But Harry was not convinced. He thought twice and scoured the scene again, finding the dead woman's basket of groceries undisturbed in a wooded area near the tracks. It was intact, the groceries not strewn about as they would have been had the Broadway Limited struck a woman carrying them. The basket just sat there, unperturbed but speaking volumes to Harry's sensitive interpretive apparatus, seeming to indicate that the woman had put it down before going to the tracks, disclosing that this was no accident. On further investigation, Harry learned from their neighbors that the woman and her husband had "quarreled violently" on the morning of her death. On further interrogation, the husband admitted that his wife had threatened to commit suicide. Suicide is a crime, the only crime in the picture, to which the serene basket tacitly testified. The Company had no responsibility if a person threw herself under a train, and bore no obligation to compensate a survivor who might even have driven the person to do it, for all the Company knew. The suicide walked into town. She bought groceries. She carried them as far as the tracks. She put them down in a wooded area nearby. She walked to the tracks and stuck her foot there. And the mourning widower? Dogged in his pursuit of truth, Harry revealed him as a fraudulent claimant. The Company was blameless; it would not pay. No Keystone Kop, Harry. Nothing farcical for miles around. Not *A Misplaced Foot*, like that of the filmic pranksters Harry couldn't have found funny, because he couldn't have seen it yet. Or could he? A purposefully placed foot and a widower who wouldn't succeed in defrauding the Company was what Harry saw. When he looked down. When he looked up, he saw wires that connected Altoona to Valparaiso.

American railroad companies extended their reach beyond the borders of the United States, running into Mexico's railroads, such as the line that connected El Paso to Mexico City. But traffic in the opposite direction, that of Mexicans into Texas, seemed to carry the familiar threat of drugs and otherness. In 1914, El Paso passed an ordinance outlawing marijuana. It was the first time any approved legislation had named marijuana, but it was not the first time that a drug had been linked to foreigners, to a surge across a border—though here flowed the Rio Grande rather than the Pacific Ocean, and here flowed Mexicans rather than Chinese. El Paso's local ordinance was followed by state laws in California, Wyoming, Utah, Vermont, Massachusetts, and Maine. Local rippled into state, state into national, like concentric circles. At the epicenter, the presumptive American citizen—individual, sovereign, choice-bearing, vote-bearing (Go, suffragists). Liberal theory runs smack into relativity and *boom*, or should I say *big bang*:

> A human being is part of the whole called by us universe, a part limited in time and space. We experience ourselves, our thoughts and feelings as something separate from the rest. A kind of optical delusion of consciousness. This delusion is a kind of prison for us, restricting us to our personal desires and to affection for a few persons nearest to us. Our task must be to free ourselves from the prison by widening our circle of compassion to embrace all living creatures and the whole of nature in its beauty. The true value of a human being is determined by the measure and the sense in which they have obtained liberation from the self. We shall require a substantially new manner of thinking if humanity is to survive.[3]

So said Einstein. But much thinking remained Euclidean, persistently gridlike, and if anything expanded infinitely, it was the table, the graph, the x and y axes that governed statistical representation. Those axes writ large, longitude anyway, and even the less equatorial latitudes reached right round the globe, every Altoona, every Shanghai, every Hague, running imaginarily right through every El Paso, every Valparaiso, so many points on another imagined line, multiple lines, all straight, amounting to a pictographic prison girdling the globe, loops and coils tightening like a noose, perversions of a peacenik's metonyms of circle as a force of connection and compassion. Einstein's theory of relativity may have changed physical and metaphysical thought, but his free thinking, his bleeding-heart values of x, y, and z in which we are a "we" called "humanity" and are one with a "we" called "the universe," all in the same lot, has languished in the back pages.

In Altoona, in 1915 or so, Harry tried to exert some compassion while he was supervising railroad landscape construction gangs. Made up largely of recent Sicilian immigrants, the work gangs hammered the idea of a Mafia into Harry's head. He loved to hate the "Black Hand," or *La Mano Nera*, as "they called it in Italy," he liked to say knowingly. Adjudicating an incident among PRR workers, Harry threw his weight behind one innocent Sicilian, Giovanni, who came to America to be "the equal of all other men." His own Americanness one generation more established than Big Mouth Sam, Harry defended Giovanni's reluctance to pay for protection: "Why should he pay tribute out of his small earnings to some man the others called Big Mouth Sam?" When Giovanni resisted, "someone had put twenty-five bullets in his body, and dumped his blood-drenched form at the side of the road." Miraculously, Giovanni survived, but "while he battled for life," Harry personally confronted Big Mouth Sam.[4] Harry sets the scene:

> Squat, black-haired, ox-shouldered Big Mouth lived off fellow immigrants by his simple "terror tax" formula. Whoever balked was beaten, stabbed or shot. The little eyes glinted at me. He was startled, I gathered from his look, at my size. I stand six feet and weighed at that time about two hundred pounds.
>
> I said, "I'm Giovanni's boss and friend."
>
> "What about Giovanni?" he protested, excitedly waving

his hands. "What I got to do with Giovanni? I don't know no Giovanni."

I told him I knew he was the one who pumped all that lead into Giovanni's body and dumped him in the ditch. "If Giovanni dies," I warned him, "I'm going to see to it that you hang. Do you understand that?"[5]

Whatever else Harry may have been, he was, apparently, extremely persuasive; maybe he was as intimidating as his hard-boiled prose would attempt to demonstrate. His six feet may have contributed to an appearance (or self-understanding) as intimidating. Later, and in retrospect, the commissioner went back and retrieved this episode, for the very same reason I do, to show how it conditions later developments. Although he was not a profoundly introspective man, Harry's account shows the influence of psychoanalytic theory, which was developing while Harry was out-toughing Big Mouth Sam. In this one belief about individuals, if no other, Harry and I absolutely converge, a belief that would be all but universally accepted by the time he retired:

For most of us, the future has its roots in the past.[6]

As America went to see the Keystone Kops' *In the Clutches of the Gang*, and Altoona mastered all "the requirements of clearing waste," Harry took up the charge, figuring himself as an operator of a certain kind: a discerning tough, a detective, able to discover and interpret clues, sneaky, a Company loyalist, an effective enforcer, an executor of justice, delivering the good to good citizens, quashing evil, correct, acting on behalf of others, a protector, someone who keeps track. An agent. A supervisor in and of large and complex systems, marshaling force, going on, by literal and figurative train, from Altoona to Harrisburg to Washington, on a long tour of duty, and ultimately back to Washington, to apply fellow Keystonian Taylor's principles, as Taylor had recommended, to governmental forces.

Taylor himself had felt the wrath of the workers in Bethlehem. They may not have understood scientific principles, but they knew he was not their friend. Taylor's friends, by contrast, had warned him not to take his evening walk home from work by the relatively isolated railway track, that he put his very life at risk when he did.

> **In all such cases, however, a display of timidity is apt to increase rather than diminish the risk, so the writer told these men to say to the other men in the shop that he proposed to walk home every night right up that railway track; that he never carried a weapon of any kind, and that they could shoot and be d-----.**[7]

Like Harry, Taylor was a Christian and a cowboy, turning the other cheek in the mode of sheer courage, seeming to dare any of his enemies to go so low as to shoot an unarmed man. Righteousness was his shield, and if there was any intimidation to be done, "the writer" would do it himself. A contemporary of theirs philosophized about the cost of the kind of moral absolutism that was already Harry's signature, already in play with and against his fellow workers:

> **If an individual enjoys well-ordered thoughts, it is quite possible that this side of his nature may grow more pronounced at the cost of other sides and thus may determine his mentality in increasing degree. In this case it is well possible that such an individual sees in retrospect a uniformly systematic development, whereas the actual experience takes place in kaleidoscopic particular situations.**[8]

Harry enjoyed well-ordered thoughts. His was a Manichean belief system, untroubled by complexity. We might speculate that this side of his nature grew more pronounced as Harry matured. Soon, he will meet and marry Martha Denniston Leet. If Harry, looking back later, saw a linear development between his police work on the tracks of the PRR and his commissionership, we will have to throw in the kaleidoscope, favoring concurrency over causality and chartography in order to un-uniform the development of prohibitionist drug policy and law, which happened in circles, and understand Harry, whose actual experience, his whole life, like any, differs from biography by virtue of plotlessness, and orders of complexity. Lotus Eaters will lend us the kaleidoscope.

16 THE HARRISON ACT

Back in Altoona, as Harry began to act the dick, the dogged Hamilton Kemp Wright turned over the next iteration of a drug bill to Francis Burton Harrison, under whose sponsorship it finally passed in December 1914, going into effect March 1, 1915. To be administered by the Treasury Department, the Harrison Act would be the cornerstone of prohibitionist drug policy domestically and internationally for over six decades, and Harry J. Anslinger would be its delivery mechanism from 1931 to 1962. The Harrison Act was essentially a stamp act, meant to generate a lot of records and a little bit of revenue, but it very quickly became the legal means of establishing and maintaining a moral and social program that had no necessary relation to drugs. Just as the prohibition of alcohol would create a black market whose actors in every transaction would be, by definition, criminals, so would the Harrison Act generate a black market in drugs, a market that has grown ever since, along with a vast array of illegal practices associated with it, several classes (and races) of criminals, and the industrialization of the criminal justice system to process and administer them.

At its heart, the act requires registration by physicians and a tax payment on the transfer and sale of any opiate, except those between doctor or pharmacist and patient. Yet from the moment it went into practice, the Harrison Act was applied with special gusto against those very exceptions. Thousands and thousands of arrests, convictions, appeals, and judgments under it undermined the ability of doctors to prescribe narcotic drugs; in effect, medical decisions that had previously been made by doctors were made by judges and juries, curtailing medical authority in the act's first thirteen years.[1] Thus, whether or not Wright or Harrison intended it to do so, this piece of legislation buried the public health approach to drugs—as doctors had known it would:

Sixty-third Congress of the United States of America;

At the Third Session,

Begun and held at the City of Washington on Monday, the seventh day of December,
one thousand nine hundred and fourteen.

AN ACT

To provide for the registration of, with collectors of internal revenue, and to
impose a special tax upon all persons who produce, import, manufacture,
compound, deal in, dispense, sell, distribute, or give away opium or coca
leaves, their salts, derivatives, or preparations, and for other purposes.

---

*Be it enacted by the Senate and House of Representatives of the United
States of America in Congress assembled,* That on and after the first day of
March, nineteen hundred and fifteen, every person who produces, imports,
manufactures, compounds, deals in, dispenses, sells, distributes, or gives away
opium or coca leaves or any compound, manufacture, salt, derivative, or
preparation thereof, shall register with the collector of internal revenue of the
district his name or style, place of business, and place or places where such
business is to be carried on: *Provided,* That the office, or if none, then the
residence of any person shall be considered for the purposes of this Act to be
his place of business. At the time of such registry and on or before the first
day of July, annually thereafter, every person who produces, imports,
manufactures, compounds, deals in, dispenses, sells, distributes, or gives away
any of the aforesaid drugs shall pay to the said collector a special tax at the
rate of $1 per annum: *Provided,* That no employee of any person who produces,
imports, manufactures, compounds, deals in, dispenses, sells, distributes, or
gives away any of the aforesaid drugs, acting within the scope of his employment,
shall be required to register or to pay the special tax provided by this section:
Provided further, That the person who employs him shall have registered and
paid the special tax as required by this section: *Provided further,* That officers
of the United States Government who are lawfully engaged in making purchases
of the above-named drugs for the various departments of the Army and Navy,
the Public Health Service, and for Government hospitals and prisons, and officers
of any State government, or of any county or municipality therein, who are
lawfully engaged in making purchases of the above-named drugs for State,

---

The Harrison Narcotic Act of 1914, Pub. L. No. 63-223, 38 Stat. 785 (1914). Courtesy of the
National Archives and Records Administration.

> As was expected . . . the immediate effects of the Harrison anti-
> narcotic law were seen in the flocking of drug habitués to hospitals
> and sanitoriums. Sporadic crimes of violence were reported, too,
> due usually to desperate efforts by addicts to obtain drugs, but
> occasionally to a delirious state induced by sudden withdrawal.[2]

The public health perspective on drugs became an endangered point
of view, a minority opinion represented in editorials rather than leg-
islatures, as evidenced by this piece in the *New York Medical Journal*
two months after the effective date of the Harrison Act:

> The really serious results of this legislation, however, will only
> appear gradually and will not always be recognized as such. These
> will be the failures of promising careers, the disrupting of happy
> families, the commission of crimes which will never be traced to
> their real cause, and the influx into hospitals for the mentally disor-
> dered of many who would otherwise live socially competent lives.[3]

Influx into prisons also resulted from the application of the Harrison Act as everything from its constitutionality to its enforcement was
tested over the next fifteen years. Because it was a matter of federal
purview, enforcement of the act was bound to step on the toes of the
states and state police power. Jurisdiction was negotiated unendingly,
just as it was in the case of federal agencies responsible for enforcing
the Volstead Act of 1919. Oversight by the Treasury Department created particular problems, as alcohol prohibition would demonstrate,
and narcotic law enforcement would have a hard time finding a comfortable location in the federal government. Nevertheless, by 1925,
one-third of federal prisoners would be doing time for drug violations.

Also unresolved in the act was the question of "maintenance," that
is, whether physicians were allowed to prescribe cocaine or heroin to patients who had been prescribed the narcotics to which they
had then become habituated. The test of the legality of maintenance
treatment would take Harrison to court many times, along with any
number of doctors. Although the act did not explicitly criminalize possession of drugs, as the exemption for possession of small amounts
for medical purposes suggested, it did establish, in law, a rhetorical

link between drugs and criminality. The Harrison Act would come down hardest on habituated medical patients, and their physicians, rendering them criminals overnight on March 1, 1915.

Eight months after the act went into effect, another editorial appeared, this one in *American Medicine*:

> Honest medical men have found such handicaps and dangers to themselves and their reputations in these laws . . . that they have simply decided to have as little to do as possible with drug addicts or their needs. . . . The druggists are in the same position and for similar reasons many of them have discontinued entirely the sale of narcotic drugs. [The addict] is denied the medical care he urgently needs, open, above-board sources from which he formerly obtained his drug supply are closed to him, and he is driven to the underworld where he can get his drug, but of course, surreptitiously and in violation of the law.[4]

Although the author-doctor condemned the Harrison Act, in sympathy with the addict, a shadowy figure is waiting to be born here—one despised by both doctors and feds, though these two parties usually opposed each other in the courtroom. Feds and doctors aligned against a specter worse than all the delirious, desperate, and disordered addicts. That specter, almost inarticulable here, merely *underworld*ly, frequented a niche waiting to be born. In order to arrive at a narrative about the nascent dealer, *one has only to think* about his victim. She is a white woman. Think about her over and over. Though she is not his only victim, she is his most picturesque:

> Afflicted individuals are under the control of the worst elements of society. In respect to female habitués the conditions are worse, if possible. Houses of ill fame are usually their sources of supply, and one has only to think of what repeated visitations to such places mean to countless good women and girls unblemished in most instances except for an unfortunate addiction to some narcotic drug to appreciate the terrible menace.[5]

One is obliged to imagine repeated visitations to houses of ill fame, doubling back down back alleys with a contagious disease that like the other vices leads to other vices, or vice versa. As in prohibitionist tracts, good girls' goodness was at stake—whether ill fame begets addiction or it's the other way round. In this early bid for public health service, moral judgment lands more heavily on dealers than on *unfortunate* addicts. The real criminal was the dispenser of drugs, just emerging out of the spectral shadows, or rather into them, taking dark form in the cultural imagination. A drug-distributing devil who would promote the disease for his own profit. Like any Mephistophelean demon, this distributor and his effects would multiply, spread, like a cancer, a plague, a scourge. Like a network of tracks or a hypodermic needle carrying this to here and that to there, and thus contaminate the social body. And like any good villain, the drug dealer would call for an equal and opposing hero.

17 BECOMING A FED

By Harry's account, he left Altoona in 1916 for a job in state government at Harrisburg. Having distinguished himself at the PRR with his flair for intelligence, his commitment to protocol, his administrative purpose, and his willingness, Harry was hired to organize and reorganize units and divisions:

> **SEPTEMBER 1916 TO SEPTEMBER 1917**
>
> Upon the appointment by Governor Brumbaugh of the Commonwealth of Penna., of the Hon. G. Chal. Port, was in turn appointed by the latter to assist in the re-organization of a department at the Harrisburg Capitol, created by law, and after organizing an office and field force of 2500, the department was placed on a comprehensive basis, whereby the citizens of the Commonwealth derived benefit which hitherto had not been accomplished.[1]

The absence of the subject "I," conventional enough in résumés, does not account for the tortured syntax here. Nested appointments do: Pennsylvania Governor Brumbaugh installed Port who installed Harry. Thus Harry left the intelligence arm of the railroad and accepted the first of a long string of appointments *created by law*. The use of the passive voice might be noteworthy if there were a choice, but the only way to be appointed is passively. Harry was a career appointee. Even Franklin Roosevelt, the only president among the five under whom Harry served who believed that the position of commissioner should not be an appointment, would appoint and reappoint Harry to that post throughout his four terms.

By the time Harry left Harrisburg, he was a self-professed "Expert in Business Administration," married to one widowed Martha Denniston Leet. Harry's 1917 marriage, or rather Martha, came with a teenaged

1918 job application. Harry J. Anslinger Papers, Special Collections Library, The Pennsylvania State University Libraries.

son, Joseph. Harry had provided bona fide benefit to the common-wealth. It was a more experienced Harry who occupied his first position in Washington. It was the moment of his arrival as a G-man.

> **I began my government career as a member of the efficiency board of the Ordnance Division, War Department, in Washington in 1917.**[2]

With these words, Harry opens *The Protectors*, the memoir of his career. With this post in Washington, he launches that career. At the same moment, April 6 of Harry's year in Harrisburg, the United States launched itself into war. Harry was moved, but his compromised eyesight kept him from being admitted or even enlisted:

> **In September 1917, having been refused admission to the Officer's Training Camp and enlistment, the applicant, actuated by patriotic impulses accepted a position in the Ordnance Department at a salary of $1200, as a clerk, and upon reporting was assigned to assist in organizing the Equipment Division.**[3]

In this first job in Washington, DC, Harry put his clerical skills to materiel, but within a month, he was reassigned to work with personnel. His gift for detection was manifest in his duties as an inspector, and his deficient vision ended up revealing his flair for supervision. *Actuated by patriotic impulses*, this organization man had found his métier.

If Harry had had a phrenological chart, *organization* and *reorganization*, *office*, *department*, and *division* would have taken up frontal lobal locations. In Harry's files, there is an organizational chart indicating that in his next job in DC, Harry was responsible for furnishing personnel records to the Finance Division, he worked in the building at Sixth and

B in room A-3-211, and his phone extension was 2180. Whether Harry's patriotic impulses were gratified by working in a beehive with so many similarly actuated coworkers (their office locations crafted of a code by and for initiates, probably indicating the floor and the wing, like microlatitudes and microlongitudes and altitudes), whether he liked his comrades in the division (whose office locations A-dash and B-dash down the first column in the chart), and whether they liked him more or less than the black-handed workers at the PRR had, the chart does not reveal. But in Ordnance, as at the Pennsylvania Railroad, Harry moved up, or rather was passively moved up, the ranks:

> Upon re-organization, was placed in charge of entire Equipment personnel, later assigned to act as Assistant to the Chief of Inspection of Equipment, inspection of Textiles, Leather, Hardware, Metal Stamping, Aluminum and Mess Equipment. Jurisdiction of 130 commissioned men, 100 enlisted men and 1200 civilians receiving salaries up to $400.00, on the inspection of equipment at 490 points of production throughout the United States.[4]

The only thing better than organization was reorganization. In Washington, as in Harrisburg, reorganization opened doors for Harry.

In 1918, Harry was designated as a member of a divisional efficiency board representing the Inspection Division of the Ordnance Department, as per Office Order No. 147, dated February 21, 1918. The divisional efficiency boards fed into the general efficiency board, whose duties included developing *uniform methods and standards* for personnel matters, second nature to Harry, trained as he was at the Pennsylvania Railroad.[5] Such language was commonplace in private industries and in government offices; Harry trafficked in it. *Uniformity* and *standards* were the dye in which the wool of Harry's persona was dipped in Ordnance. Standardized uniforms had come in with the Civil War; now Taylor's vision of scientific management governed the administration of World War I. Harry had arrived in Washington at the right time with the right skill set to apply those business ideals to government work. Though he remained in federal government service forever, he didn't stay in town long. By June, he found himself "attached to the American Legation at The Hague," and by the end of that month, he had set sail.[6]

18 ONLY WORDS FROM WHICH THERE IS NO ESCAPE

Jin Fuey Moy

One of the earliest landmark challenges to Harrison came from a doctor in Pennsylvania. Born Moy Jin Fuey in 1861 in Sien Ning, China, Moy emigrated to San Francisco in 1875, the year of that city's first ordinance against opium smoking. With his name reordered to reflect American convention, Moy left California quickly, made his way to New York, and, with some philanthropic assistance, completed seminary in New Jersey a few years later.[1] After a stint as superintendent of the Chinese-American Union in Philadelphia, Moy entered Jefferson

From Louis Joseph Beck, *New York's Chinatown: An Historical Perspective of Its People and Places*, 1898, p. 267. Digitized by Yale University. Courtesy of the HaithiTrust.

Medical College, from which he graduated in 1890. In the year of Harry's birth, Dr. Moy began practicing medicine. Constrained by a history of laws barring Chinese physicians from treating white patients, or by custom built up around that prohibition, Moy depended on a Chinese clientele, but he found, as did other Chinese physicians, that most of his community favored traditional Chinese medicine.

Perhaps to supplement an unstable medical career, Moy got himself appointed official interpreter in the criminal courts by two successive district attorneys. Apparently a model citizen, Dr. Moy happened to be in a China-

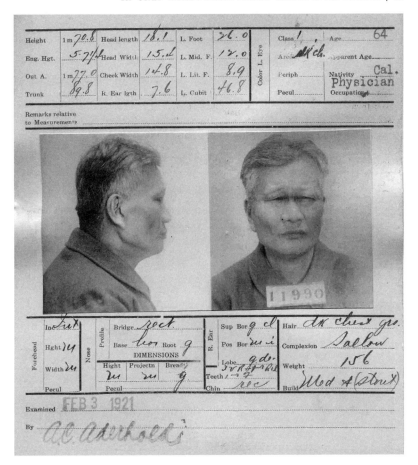

Height	1 m 70.8	Head length	18.1	L. Foot	26.0		Class 1	Age 64
Eng. Hgt.	5-7¼	Head Width	15.2	L. Mid. F.	12.0	Color L. Eye	Arc Mch.	pparent Age
Out A.	1 m 77.0	Cheek Width	14.8	L. Lit. F.	8.9		Periph	Nativity Cal.
Trunk	89.8	R. Ear lgth	7.6	L. Cubit	46.8		Pecul	Physician Occupation

Remarks relative to Measurements

United States Penitentiary, Atlanta, GA, record of the physical examination of Dr. Jin Fuey Moy, February 3, 1921. Courtesy of the National Archives and Records Administration, Atlanta, GA.

town laundry on February 1, 1901, when a twelve-year-old girl came in and offered the proprietor a roll of pennies. Moy noticed that all the pennies were "of precisely the same tinge," deduced that they were fakes, and turned her over to the police. It was soon revealed that the girl worked for a gang that, according to the headline, made "a profit of sixty cents on every hundred," and that Moy's intervention had con- tributed to the arrest of the youngest counterfeiter the court had ever seen.[2] It should be clear on what side of the law Dr. Jin Fuey Moy lived.

Indeed Dr. Moy was seen, by at least one observer, as "perhaps the most happy exemplification of the highest attainment of polish and education, made possible for all his race in Free America." A book of profiles of Chinese citizens in 1898 noted that Moy married "an American lady" and had a daughter; he had arrived at as high a station as a person of his race could hope to attain.[3] But by the same account, he remained troubled about his medical practice in the Chinese community. Moy is reported to have described his patients as

> **superstitious and . . . prejudiced against the scientific method of administering medicines, putting faith in various root and herb formulas handed down by bygone generations and to which they still cling with the simple faith of childhood.[4]**

Perhaps the modern medical methods to which Moy refers here included the hypodermic needle or administration of narcotic preparations. He may have felt they would be more effective. Is it the author of the vignette (such biographical sketches were a popular genre) or is it Moy who paints the Chinese patients as irrational children digging in their heels against the forward march of a science that would render roots and herbs obsolete? Moy's own feet marched to several drums, his training in "the genuine American school" rejected by the patient body to which he was socially bound.[5] In 1915, then practicing medicine in Pittsburgh, Dr. Moy was charged with violation of the Harrison Act.

All the several arguments put forward in the case took as a matter of fact that the doctor had prescribed a dram of morphine sulfate to an addict named Willie Martin.[6] The Harrison Act compelled Dr. Moy to register with the Treasury and pay one dollar, which he had done. Physicians were exempt from the prohibition on dispensing the drugs named in the act, so long as they were registered and produced the relevant revenue. Willie Martin on the other hand was no physician, and had not attempted to register, probably because he was a patient. Or could an addict be construed as a patient? If not, Dr. Moy was in violation:

> **The indictment charges a conspiracy with Willie Martin to have in Martin's possession opium and salts thereof, to-wit, one dram of**

> morphine sulphate. It alleges that Martin was not registered with
> the collector of internal revenue of the district, and had not paid
> the special tax required; that the defendant, for the purpose of
> executing the conspiracy, issued to Martin a written prescription
> for the morphine sulphate, and that he did not issue it in good
> faith, but knew that the drug was not given for medicinal purposes,
> but for the purpose of supplying one addicted to the use of opium.
> The question is whether the possession conspired for is within the
> prohibitions of the act.[7]

The act allowed doctors to issue "prescriptions" as long as they were written "in good faith" and "in the course of legitimate professional practice." Most addicts had been given morphine, for example, in the course of treatment of a primary ailment, and once they were habituated, their physical well-being depended on continuous use. Could a doctor, in good faith, prescribe narcotics for the sole purpose of staving off the physiological rigors of withdrawal, rather than effecting a cure, in a protocol known as "maintenance"? Also at stake in *U.S. v. Jin Fuey Moy* was whether Congress should have the authority to make that decision, namely, the power to determine what constituted legitimate professional medical practice, and how to understand "maintenance," in particular. Should Congress, as the authorized dealer of the Harrison Act, be further authorized to construe the act in relation to medical ethics and treatment? The court thought not.

In this early test, decided in June 1916, the court limited the federal government's ability to make a blanket determination about medical practice under the sign of a revenue act, which restored the authority to the doctor, though only very temporarily. In *Jin Fuey Moy*, the majority opinion explained that a law that made so many citizens into criminals in a single stroke was *unbelievably* unlikely to be within that limit. In other words, the court tried to stave off interpretations of the Harrison Act that would support its use as an instrument of criminalization:

> Only words from which there is no escape could warrant the conclusion that Congress meant to strain its powers almost if not quite

**to the breaking point in order to make the probably very large
proportion of citizens who have some preparation of opium in
their possession criminal.**[8]

Only words from which there is no escape could force us to believe
that Congress would have made criminals out of *us*, as we, the justices
implied, already were, with our preexisting condition: being in possession. And yet such words had already been composed, and were well
on their way to ratification. The oncoming steamroller of Prohibition
laid down the words of Volstead, from which there would be no escape
for thirteen years. The Eighteenth Amendment was the war cry that
curdled through the three years in which Harry was wading into the
waters of government service, setting sail for Europe, and getting wet
behind the ears with import and export. Though the prohibition that
would turn the vast majority of US citizens into violators overnight
related only to alcohol, the entire "experiment" would have—should
have had—profound lessons for the development of drug policy.

Jin Fuey Moy begged for further court cases to test the development
of popular and judicial thought about narcotics and addiction, disease and criminality. This one was at the front of many such cases
that addressed this medical and ethical ambiguity, along with the
legal ambiguity in the language of the Harrison Act. Captured here
in his mug shot, Dr. Jin Fuey Moy was one of the first doctors to be
prosecuted under the Harrison Act; many others would follow in his
footsteps. Tens of thousands of doctors were charged between 1915
and 1928. Dr. Moy himself went to the Supreme Court again in 1920,
convicted that time of dealing on a large scale from 1915 to 1917. The
one dram he had prescribed to Willie Martin became, in the subsequent case, hundreds of drams prescribed to many patients, some
total strangers, in systematic cahoots with at least one manager at
a Pittsburgh drugstore. In this case, Dr. Moy charged his "patients"
a dollar per dram. He also prescribed narcotics to a fictitious wife.
Let's call her Martha. Always elsewhere, seeing what the unreal see,
Marthas weave by day, and unweave at night. Even if they don't fill a
prescription, they fill a need.

As Dr. Moy wove his way through judicial circuits, the newspapers
fanned the fear of Bolshevism—whatever that meant, something for-

eign that was brewing abroad—which would soon breathe hot on the collars of laborers, and on labor reformers at home. Sacco and Vanzetti met in 1917 and might have been conspiring the whole time, and might even have been Bolshevik to the untrained eye. After he had taken a train from his childhood home in Milwaukee to Kansas, and from there to worldwide fame, the foreign little Houdini could be seen in several states contorting himself into and out of a "Chinese water torture cell." Houdini met his end in the performance of just such a water-torture trick in Detroit.[9] Places that had no water, Houdini could sink himself under it anyway, and stay trapped below, while so many citizens waited breathless above the surface for him to perform the impossible escape.

19 NOT ONE MINUTE DARKNESS

> 9.   Convoy appears from every zone on horizon. In course of one
>   hour twelve destroyers take formation. Dart in and out and
>   entire convoy zigzags. Several dropping depth charges.
>   Dangerous waters. Large dirigble joins convoy. Up north
>   so far not one minute darkness. Passengers sleep with clothes on.
>   With Sir Janes and blinker signals direct search lights on
>   two submarines. Bang biff crack.

July 1918 travel diary. Harry J. Anslinger Papers, Special Collections Library, The Pennsylvania State University Libraries.

Maybe Harry was asked or advised to keep a diary of his dip-lomatic sojourn to and through Europe. Maybe he thought his journey was of sufficient moment to warrant a record. Maybe he wanted to remember. In any case, from the moment he launched, Harry kept a regular, though not quite daily, diary.[1] In it he utilizes the syntactic abbreviations that mark telegraphic texts, short bulletins, or perhaps other diaries he had read. The diary reflects Harry's careful observation, a skill he had already honed; future tête-à-têtes with congressmen and undercover assignments will benefit from his close attention to the customs and expectations of those around him. In this journal, Harry begins to develop a small range of written voices, to try on some vocabulary, some stances, stylistic and political, and to elaborate a written self.

JUNE 1918

25th.	**Left Washington midnight.**
26th.	**Arrived New York Visas and passport.**

When he himself is the subject of a sentence, his "I" is absent, as above, which is conventional in a diary (as in a résumé) but can pro-duce ambiguities. For example, on June 30, can we be certain who "swore at the captain of a phantom submarine"?

> **Army Chaplain in next stateroom had a nightmare. **x#"**
> **Swore at captain of a phantom submarine.**

The entry continues:

> **Lieut. Walker, Phila. aboard, constantly**
>   **occupied with sick troops.**
> **Deck strewn with troops flat on backs.**
> **Not a light on deck. Difficult to see other ships in convoy.**
> **Stateroom door left open, adjust life belt and give yourself up.**

Note that articles have gone the way of the "I." Note also what Harry notes: the presence of a fellow Pennsylvanian, the signs of tension, and the difficulties of life on a ship during wartime, particularly the difficulty that troubles seagoers, even in peacetime, motion sickness. Later, in the new year, postwar, Harry will wax eloquently about the carnage in European capitals, but here, he is spare with words. There is a flavor to the prose, a leaning. The troops and the convoy are some of Harry's favorite things. As is the "phantom submarine," like the imagined enemies who will both haunt and animate Harry for the rest of his life in government service. The winking cryptography of the expletive. The cryptic, hyperbolic final phrase: "give yourself up." Does this phrase merely resonate with the ideal conclusion to every enforcer's plot, in which the apprehension of the bad guy follows the Law's command to surrender? Or does the open door of the stateroom reflect Harry's fear? Does it imply that the captain might abandon ship—or be taken by the enemy—in which case you, or rather Harry, would be up shit creek without a paddle. No matter how I interpret Harry's passage, that's where retrospeculation leads. (And a generative space it is. Ask a Lotus Eater.)

In other entries, Harry focuses on numbers of troops, kinds of ships—transports, cruisers, destroyers, even dirigibles and hydroplanes—and their formations. Harry observes about the troops from Texas, "Many Mexicans among them." He names noteworthy fellow passengers—"Lady Muriel Paget aboard"—and records ship routines: "Wear life belt always" and "Revellie disturbes at six and troops clatter about. Sleep impossible." On July 4, patriotic impulses are again expressed:

> British cruiser fired salute of twenty-one guns. Boxing
> matches, singing, Signal corps dames performing and speeches.
> Colonel Creach toasts America.

On the eighth, internal enemies, some of the rottener troops, engaging in nefarious recreations, double for the enemy outside:

> Troops and lookout want to see submarine. Lookout doubled.
> Light visible my port, examined at 2 am. Zigzagging course
> Ken. Witherow sold bathing for swimming
>   pool seven decks below.
> Poker parties. Officer going to shoot up game.

The hunt is on. And on July 9—*Eureka!*—signs and signals from all zones point to real and present danger. Adrenalin!!

> Convoy appears from every zone on horizon. In course of one
> hour twelve destroyers take formation. Dart in and out and
> entire convoy zigzags. Several dropping depth charges.
> Dangerous waters. Large dirigible joins convoy. Up north
> so far not one minute darkness. Passengers sleep with clothes on.
> With Sir James and blinker signals direct search
>   lights on two submarines. Bang biff crack.

Oof. There it is: the most comical, most literally cartoonish commentary, the battle cry of the modern white man—"bang biff crack." *Bang biff crack* means *It's very hard to distinguish between the testosterone days of summer we spent tossing a pear around and matters of state with hundreds of thousands of lives on the line.* *Bang biff crack* means *I hardly have words for this moment of fear, exhilaration, commitment.* Anslinger must have been turbocharged, converting fear to imagined force, burning and yearning after some kind of knuckle-in-the-face tough. Scouring a horizon broken into zones, searchlights discover that sneaky submarine. *Hit it!* And all for good, goddammit, that the world may be made safe for democracy, civilization itself seeming to be in the balance. As it was and as it ever will be for the future commissioner of the Federal Bureau of Narcotics. Here was Harry's authorizing moment, where he self-substantiated. Grown up now, far from Altoona, and swelled to bursting with the expansiveness of his country. And this was the closest he would brush with war (not counting the metaphorical one with drugs).

Sure enough, Harry is one with the troops, for when the ship arrives in England:

JULY 11.

Dock Liverpool. One submarine reported credit to us.
Town decorated in American flags each time convoy appears.
British band plays our national anthem.
Interviewed by Intelligence and leave ship.
Reception accorded Americans in England different than before
      the war. Are you in Mufty Yank. Minature trains to London.
Go along with party on ship, Mrs Campbell. Lady Paget, etc.

National means *We make Me bigger* means *We means Me* means *Where we followed now we lead.* Our *national anthem* sets these meanings to music. *American flags* and the *reception accorded Americans* mean more of same, on successively larger stages. Now Harry has been an Odysseus of his own, putting finishing touches on a big war, enduring the bobbing sea, ever vigilant, a man's man rubbing elbows with *dames* along the way, arriving finally at the heart of the empire at its peak, point of origin, point of pride, stealing the very thunder. It was a great time to be alive. A miserable time to die.

Even with one bad eye, Harry could see the effects of war as he toured

Through Hyde Park. Wounded quite a sight.

Harry was led through London as a member of a diplomatic corps, as close to royalty as an American of modest means could get. London Bridge, Tower of London, Trafalgar Square. Though "London not penetrated," the effects were audible as well as visible. On July 16, he wrote:

11 P.M. sounding air raid alarm.

> Children make for subways in groups of four. Women hysterical.

From London, the SS *Notts* carried Harry, among others, to Hook van Holland:

> . . . Mine sweepers clear way, pick up
> 50 mines in lane, and returning pick up 300 in same lane.
> So close to mines, and just missing, worse than shell fire.

And finally, as "big guns" were heard pounding on the front, the last leg of Harry's journey took him from Hook to The Hague, and there he stayed until the middle of February 1919. Six years too late for the drug conference, Harry did nevertheless make it there in time for some proximity to war action. In his diary, Harry noted a range of sights and activities: the queen's birthday party, food riots, and miscellaneous events, all recorded without comment:

SEPTEMBER 10

> Wilson and Dyar knock out two German Jews.
> Old Dutch sea captain spins a few yarns.

NOVEMBER 23

> . . . Soldiers
> corraling women who had to do with Boche, shaving hair off
> and branding cheeks. Women go insane.

Harry's straight-faced prose, his unadorned reportage, set major historic events and diversions of the day on the same plane, through both consistency of tone and juxtaposition: one day, "bathed in North Sea," another, "threatened revolution." Presumably, Harry was the implied subject of the former and the Bolsheviks the latter, yet they shared a stage, like the private and the public, the personal, such as it was, and the political, the small and individual that was Harry and one or two of his mates and the large collectives that were nations, armies, and revolutionary movements:

> Bolshevik crowds threaten to interrupt dinner with vanHee
> and Dyar account us eating meat.

Same Dyar who knocked out two German Jews with his pal Wilson, not Woodrow. German Jews would be distinguished from Germans for Harry's German and Swiss-German parents, and evidently for this Dyar as well. In leaving the United States for the first time, Harry became completely American; he was one with national identification, shot through with patriotism, and it gave him both pleasure and purpose.

In this diary, Harry issues the founding document of himself as a function of nation: he becomes the government; it becomes him. *Dulce et decorum est pro patria memento mori.* Written as he spanned the Atlantic, grounded in his firsthand view of the tail end of the great war, describing the unspoken subject as a patriotic American man, Harry's diary is literately his self-constitution, Harry the founding father of himself hanging in the balance. Hysteria is always elsewhere. Women go insane.

Less a personal story than the story of an aspiring public personality, this study focuses on Harry's emergent persona, because it houses, or fronts, the mind that will, at full maturity, guide the development of prohibitionist drug policy. Just as the language of the Harrison Act, as well as its construction and deconstruction and reconstruction in federal district courts and in the Supreme Court, would produce a career for Harry, so too did his own prose produce his public persona as G-man.

20 WITHIN THE WORDS

Back in 1919, as Harry composed himself in the present tense of his travel diary, the Supreme Court wrote two key decisions affecting drug policy, judicial reviews that would furnish Harry's conceptual chamber when he became the chief enforcer of tried-and-tested law ten years thence. In *Webb* and *Doremus*, the court interpreted the Harrison Act (and its 1919 addendum) as a weapon against an imagined scourge of narcotics, offering language that would equip Harry for the good fight.

Language was under active construction and reconstruction in 1919, like so much else. Like Europe. Like all kinds of national borders and entities in a two-hemisphere world of crumbling empires. Global communications and transportation systems gave millions of people the flu. Theoretical physics predicted time dilation. It was one hell of a year, by all accounts; by some, it was one hell of a month. By dint of a solar eclipse, Arthur Eddington was finally able to prove Einstein's theory of relativity on the West African island of Principe. Worlds did not collide when Harry circulated through The Hague the same year Bertrand Russell met Wittgenstein there. Russell was working on language, and mind and matter, and coming to believe that language was insufficiently abstract to correspond with the world. Language might be symbolic. All kinds of dynamics tilted at the idea of correspondence between signifier and signified. Meaning might or might not matter more or less than grammar. The ruling class might try to limit the meanings of certain social signs. Or status. Consciousness—or even unconsciousness!—might play a role. Language was a manifestation of culture understood as something all peoples had, near and far, however strange, us too, autonomous or not autonomous, purely structural, not unlike grammar, without respect to time or place or, alternately, a material artifact, entirely

WEBB ET AL. *v.* UNITED STATES.

CERTIFICATE FROM THE CIRCUIT COURT OF APPEALS FOR
THE SIXTH CIRCUIT.

No. 370.   Argued January 16, 1919.—Decided March 3, 1919.

The first sentence of § 2 of the Narcotic Drug Act of December 17, 1914, c. 1, 38 Stat. 785, prohibits retail sales of morphine by druggists to persons who have no physician's prescription, who have no order blank therefor and who cannot obtain an order blank because not of the class to which such blanks are allowed to be issued under the act. P. 99.

This construction does not make unconstitutional the prohibition of such sale. *Id.   United States* v. *Doremus, ante,* 86.

If a practicing and registered physician issues an order for morphine to an habitual user thereof, the order not being issued by him in the course of professional treatment in the attempted cure of the habit, but for the purpose of providing the user with morphine sufficient to keep him comfortable by maintaining his customary use, such order is not a physician's prescription under exception (b) of § 2 of the act. *Id.*

THE case is stated in the opinion.

Webb v. U.S., 249 US 96, 1919. Reproduced by permission from the Washington State Law Library.

dependent for operation on historically situated users. Theories proliferated. Theorists agreed without agreeing that language is open to interpretation. In St. Petersburg, *the formal and the sociological method* was—or were—offered by Bakhtin and Voloshinov, unless *and* is the wrong conjunction there, locating meaning in the usage of language, which might vary according to various dynamics. For example, "Red" and "scare" signified differently in Washington, DC, in 1919 from the way they had for a switchman in Altoona in 1902.

For another example, if a prescription form was used to facilitate narcotic addiction or dealing, the text written on it ceased to be a "prescription." For the Supreme Court. Indeed the prescription form— meaning a particular kind of blank paper authorized for that purpose, and also the genre written on it—came under consideration by the court in *Webb v. United States* in 1919. Webb was a practicing physician who appeared to be in cahoots with Goldbaum, a retail druggist in Memphis. Dr. Webb was charged with writing prescriptions that were not inside the language of the new law, four thousand of which had been filed by Goldbaum as he dispensed more than thirty times the average amount (per druggist) of morphine to bearers of "Webb's so-called prescriptions":

> **It was the intent of Webb and Goldbaum that morphine should thus be furnished to habitual users thereof by Goldbaum and without any physician's prescription issued in the course of a good faith attempt to cure the morphine habit.**[1]

Dr. Webb also wrote several questionable prescriptions to "one Rabens," an addict from out of state, "at one time ten so-called prescriptions for one drachm each, which prescriptions were filled at one time by Goldbaum upon Rabens' presentation, although each was made out in a separate and fictitious name." So Goldbaum had to have been in on it, if he sold drugs to one Rabens presenting as ten inventions, Rabens's fraudulence, in turn, authored by Dr. Webb in his violation of the conventions of the blank form, and the letter of the law. When Dr. Webb took poetic license in the filling of the forms, he changed their genre from prescription to crime. The court appears to have taken some poetic license of its own.[2]

And yet, as to the questions of the meaning of a "physician's prescription," and whether the act permitted a doctor to dispense drugs to maintain an addict's addiction, the court was stark and clear; the very prospect strained their sociolinguistic structures of credulity:

> **As to question three—to call such an order for the use of morphine a physician's prescription would be so plain a perversion of meaning that no discussion of the subject is required. That question should be answered in the negative.**[3]

Dealing drugs with fraudulent prescriptions not only nullifies the meaning of "prescription" but also of "physician." If no discussion of this particular subject was required, maybe that was because the word "prescription" had been so extensively discussed. In effect, the doctor dealing drugs in this way was not a doctor; he was a perverter of meaning; he was a criminal.

Energetic prosecution called the question to the floor again and again. In Dr. Jin Fuey Moy's first Supreme Court case, maintenance and the authority to decide what constitutes bona fide medical practice had been at stake. *Webb* picked up on the problem of maintenance, but the court's perspective seems to have shifted, from ethico-medical to cynical; the physician himself was a legal, rather than a medical, actor, thus the decision seems to be trying to cover its linguistic bases as much as anything else. The Supreme Court would then refer back to *Webb* in 1920, in a second round for Dr. Jin Fuey Moy. This time, Dr. Moy was not vindicated. And this time, the justices took yet another occasion to redefine "prescription":

> **the act of selling or giving away a drug and the act of issuing a prescription are so essentially different that to allege that defendant sold the drug by issuing a prescription for it amounts to a contradiction of terms, and the repugnance renders the indictment fatally defective.**[4]

This passage reflects and elaborates on the court's use of "perversion" in *Webb*—there was a definitional opposition between writing a prescription and selling or giving away drugs. If he sold drugs, the doctor was, by legal definition, no longer a doctor; a dealer was born. No mere snake-oil salesman, the dealer was more than perverse; he was, by virtue of rhetorical contamination, repugnant, defective. Harry would have plenty of uses for the dealer when he became commissioner. Meanwhile, in *Webb*, the court pronounced definitively on the question of maintenance and awarded the federal government greater power of regulation.

Unbeknownst to Harry, *Webb* was argued the day that he attended the "Drexels New Year Party." Three months later, the same day that the Supreme Court handed down the *Webb* decision, it delivered another landmark ruling for the development of drug policy. In *Doremus*, the court upheld the constitutionality of the Harrison Act, which effectively supported federal power to regulate, as against state and local policing power, and further polarized inevitable jurisdictional struggles. In the same week that *Doremus* was submitted, Harry enjoyed both "Dancing at Ministers" and "Tea at Ministers." Harry partied, aspirationally and with postwar pep. Late the night of the day that *Webb* and *Doremus* were decided, Harry left Paris for Brussels. The next day, Harry "heard wonderful tribute to fighting qualities of Americans."[5] The Supreme Court reconsidered the conviction of socialist Eugene Debs for espionage, and Justice Oliver Wendell Holmes wrote the decision reflecting the court's unanimous confirmation of Debs's ten-year sentence a week after the same court rendered the anti-maintenance decisions of *Webb* and *Doremus* that brought into existence the middleman, a figure crucial to a functioning black drug market, the dealer.

The most stigmatized of dealers were perhaps those doctors who abused the privilege of their professional office to sell substances that thereby ceased to be medications. Perhaps the repugnant dealer figure is an effect of the Supreme Court's attempt to negotiate between the initial revenue basis of the Harrison Act and its subsequent moral repurposing. Indeed, it was the revenue lost through fraudulent transactions that made the Treasury Department the relevant federal agency as well as the bulldog. If the Harrison Act, as a revenue act, regulated the market for drugs, then the systematic prosecution of physicians under that act—by restricting the legal flow of commoditized narcotics—was bound to produce a black market.

In *Doremus*, in particular, the court parsed the morality encoded in the Harrison Act, giving voice to a popular strain, perhaps introducing a new object, matter, or substance of intemperance—the moral umbrella under which alcohol and drugs can walk together is abstinence, a value, or term, so staunch that it will easily expand to include sexuality later in the century:

> It is true that it also had the moral purpose of discouraging the use of drugs except as a medicine, but its main purpose as a tax revenue measure was to see that dealers in the drugs do not escape the tax.[6]

And is it "true" that the Harrison Act had the moral purpose described? Or did it become true by virtue of being a pronouncement of the court? Unsurprisingly, the court ruled that the federal government was within its powers to tax drug transactions and did not step on states' toes in so doing. Yet this was a close call, a court split 5–4 in an era in which the court rarely split.

Charles T. Doremus was a San Antonio physician charged with sell-ing narcotics not "in pursuance of a written order on a form issued on the blank furnished for that purpose by the Commissioner of Internal Revenue." Dr. Doremus ceased to be a doctor when he violated profes-sional codes of conduct. These tropes were familiar from *Webb*. But in *Doremus*, the Supreme Court also brought into existence a "dope fiend" to go with the dealer—or rather, brought into legal subjecthood a figure already "popularly known"—an addict who seeks gratification, not a patient seeking treatment or even the permanent deferral of withdrawal, and not merely a criminal, but another kind of pervert, as communicated by "appetite." Justice William R. Day described the case:

> **The second count charges that: Doremus did unlawfully and knowingly sell, dispense and distribute to one Ameris five hundred one-sixth grain tablets of heroin not in the course of the regular professional practice of Doremus and not for the treatment of any disease from which Ameris was suffering, but as well known by Doremus, Ameris was addicted to the use of the drug as a hab-it, being a person popularly known as a "dope fiend," and that Doremus did sell, dispense, and distribute the drug, heroin, to Ameris for the purpose of gratifying his appetite for the drug as an habitual user thereof.[7]**

Whenever the court saw large amounts of narcotics being dispensed (like five hundred grains), it noted that the recipient could take them at any time and in any manner or—given a lack of supervision by a physician—not take them at all but turn around and sell them to others. There was no way of tracking the number of sales that might take place as a given quantity of narcotics circulated through the black market until it had been fully consumed—and none of those sales were documented or, at least as importantly, taxed.

The black market in drugs experienced the usual, and predictable, concomitants of other black markets: increased risk to producers and distributors, correspondingly inflated prices, compounded disparity between the incomes of the lowest- and highest-paid workers, no legal recourse for any of the workers with respect to the conditions of work, inducements to corruption on the part of law enforcement, and total lack of regulation of the quality of products; and if all the parties to a market are either criminal or law enforcement, it makes it very difficult for journalism to perform any kind of "independent" watchdog function. The effect has been a criminal justice system that displaces responsibility for a black market, one that is radically ineffective in remediating drug-related, social and medical problems.

To circle back to *Webb* and *Doremus*: to issue law is to call for judicial interpretation, and to construe a crime is to produce criminals. Put another way, disabling a legal market for the distribution of drugs produced a black market—in the classic chicken-and-egg problem of capitalism, consumption of drugs calls for production. But also, consumption itself must be produced, with commodities in general, drugs no less than others. Discourse is productive—like capital, like addiction, discourse produces consumption; drug consumption, in turn, reproduces itself like nothing else. Perhaps the doctor's prescription on the authorized blank is the literary form that called drug consumption into being, in tandem with the linguistic dynamos that put drug prohibition on the social map. The Supreme Court's authorization of the use of the language of the Harrison Act to prosecute people distributing narcotics produced all kinds of convictions, at about the time that the dynamo theory was waning in popularity, giving way to all kinds of quanta. It is no small irony that *Webb* was submitted to the court on the same day that the Eighteenth Amendment's ratification in Nebraska sealed its inclusion in the Constitution. It is, by contrast, a coincidence. Theories about why notwithstanding, the world kept turning; for almost as long, the court's language in *Webb* and *Doremus* would exert a strong hold on the field of drug policy.

21 I WOULD NOT ENDEAVOR TO DESCRIVE

At the end of September 1918, Harry received his "first letter from America."[1] Was it from his father or mother? A brother or sister? His wife, Martha? Or was it a business letter? Harry's diary was all business, and a little pleasure. Certain parties. Food riots. Two months later, the diary is characteristically closemouthed about a defining event: on November 9, "Kaiser abdicates, comes to Holland." It was the day that Wilhelm II went into exile.

It was also an opportunity to be seized, a perfect confluence of Harry's abilities and the exigencies of the moment, of being in the right place at the right time, what luck. And also, with what dogged persistence did Harry produce his opportunities, write his ticket. Harry, November 10: "Kaiser arrives. Baggage came to Hague first." Possibly because of his Dutch- and German-speaking skills, probably also because he was trustworthy, Harry was assigned to make direct contact with the kaiser. *Biff.* Possibly because he was sneaky and ambitious, he spoke his fluent German as he

> **bluffed his way past Dutch security guards and gained clearance to travel with the Kaiser's entourage without interference. Passing himself off as a member of the Dutch intelligence corps, he relayed information to one of the Kaiser's court counselors that abdication was entirely useless and unnecessary.**[2]

The kaiser abdicated—it's the opposite of being appointed. That much is history. Yet his colleagues and higher-ups agreed that Harry had dispatched himself ideally and had established himself as useful. His self-understanding comported with his growing reputation as an agent. Now his diary was all decoy. The entire episode, upon which he would expand in one of his memoirs, boiled down to a couple of words in his war diary. Yet those words stand as ciphers, with a

```
10.   Kaiser arrives.  Baggage came to Hague first.
11.   Armistice.  Celebrations.
12.   Prisoners leaving.
14.   Threatened revolution.  Liquor sales prohibited. Bolshevik
      sentiments throughout country.
```

November 1918 travel diary. Harry J. Anslinger Papers, Special Collections Library, The Pennsylvania State University Libraries.

meaning that he would keep secret until his retirement. The secrecy only heightened the value, for Harry, of the episode itself—his brush with such a powerful figure had already elevated him. Later writing would reveal the crucible nature of this moment, the forging of Harry's persona as the undercover operative operating in the confidence of men of state, all of which was concentrated in the word "Kaiser." Now he owned that word.

"Armistice." "Celebrations."

Harry did not mention that French, British, and German leaders signed the armistice in a train car, though it may have been a hit of the home front for our Altoonan abroad. Lowlier types all around him were laid low by *le cafard*, the mind disease that outlasted the war, everywhere rubble and gas, or fear of gas, or memory of gas and worse, or shrapnel where memory once was housed was now trapped forever in a foxhole, lidless, but yes indeed, celebrations there were. Victory. It had been an occasion on which Harry had almost had an impact on historical events.

As the fronts ebbed, Harry toured Europe, by train. February took him through Belgium and France in excruciatingly slow measure. He continued to record the state of things, attending especially to damage to infrastructure and industry.

FEB 15 1919

Train was slow as walk
. . .
Train proceeded slow as walk. Everywhere all wires down.
Rails blown up every other joint. Telegraph and telephone lines
destroyed. Stations blown up. All bridges down. Factories either
blown up entirely, or all machinery removed, or machinery
dumped along the way in broken twisted and damaged condition,
utterly useless.

Harry's own frame of reference was useless too, along with everything he knew from home, from Altoona in its heyday, about huge and heavy metals, wires and lines and stations. Back home, these were sign and signal of prosperity and social health. Here, all those engines of good were out of order; Harry's prose takes on the properties of the landscape he saw out the train window; he is not up to the task of articulating. Mere words are utterly worthless. Compromised communications systems. *Bang, crack.*

> The destruction and devastation can never be pictured described nor imagined. The perfect destruction of factories, complete railroad destruction and absolute destruction of bridges has wiped out great industrial centers. I would not endeavor to descrive [*sic*] what is to be seen as the most that could be said would be so very trifling in comparison that it would not be worthwhile mentioning. Magnify the imagination twenty times.

Here Harry signs on with Bertrand Russell, confronting the inadequacy of language to correspond with the brokenness of the world around him, and the limits of the imagination of an implied reader who had not seen it, the *perfect destruction*. He can't even put *describe* into writing, much less describe. Even seeing was not believing. Comprehension was . . . elusive, subjective, conditional.

> Barbed wire by the acres. Flanders
> Mud can only be comprehended by sight. Trench life
> must have been unendurable. Village clocks appear to
> have been the favorite target for shooting mark.

Comprehending mud, trying to imagine the life of the soldier in the foxhole—no roof and the danger showering down from above, but unpredictably. Clocks had taken a hit. Einstein no longer ambled to work along the Kramgasse contemplating clocks. There was . . . something about the speed of the trains.

> Great amount of war material and railroad equipments turned

over by terms of armistice to be seen everywhere.

. . .

Train as slow as walk and possible to get out and step into diner while train is in motion at most any point.

Now if two observers (one on the platform and one on the train) saw two bolts of lightning hit two ends of the train, it would seem to both of them that two bolts of lightning had hit the train at the same time, one at the back and one at the front. Even if one was a poet. Yet, even in the chaos, signs of civility persisted; during "tulip time" in Holland, Harry especially appreciated the color schemes he saw and found the "symmetry of planting very beautiful." Harry plumbed European manners for civility as well:

> Even after a struggle worse than any football scrimmage round the door of a carriage in the underground, good manners survive, I have been driven backwards by a vehement Frenchwoman and my ribs have been sore where her elbows dug into them, but when we have both at last got in I forgive her. For she turns to me with the brightest of smiles, making me, once her victim, a friend and comrade. "Mon Dieu," she says, "quel voyage."

The fresh air of Switzerland afforded Harry a good night of sleep, but in Geneva on the eighteenth of February, Harry struggled with European manners again: "Hotel a tipping organization, at least twenty coming in for their change, in all directions." Because Harry was not familiar with tipping mores, and perhaps because he didn't like them, he sensed an organization at work among the hotel workers, meaning, in his view, a system, if not a conspiracy, a racket. Organization, per se, was a good thing, except when put to use for bad ends, as it was with the Black Hand, *La Mano Nera*, the Mafia, and hotel workers.

Brussels, at which he arrived in the spring of 1919, Harry described as "sad." The price of a meal was too high. There in Brussels, Harry observed, "Society at standstill." His own prose almost ground to a halt. He wrote: "Pronunciation of name." In his diary, Harry recorded things that troubled him. But for all these ills, he proposed a cure:

> **A good cleaning up, police organization, food commissioner and good coat of paint would serve to bring the town to its feet.**

A good cleaning up, check. Police organization, check. But a *food* commissioner? Maybe. Maybe Harry was concerned with the distribution of victuals—surely some of the broken characters Harry paraded by were hungry. But maybe, as above, Harry hit the neighboring key by mistake. On his typewriter, *g* is to *f* as *b* is to *v*. If so, the typo tips the hand Harry's been dealt. His solution for a war-torn nation is a *good*, not a *food*, commissioner. For who could repair that kind of ravage but a man wearing the kind of suit that makes a man, and makes of him a good commissioner. The kind that Harry will wear when he conducts his own war, on drugs. As Harry reported,

MARCH 7TH.
_____

> **Throughout the whole trip to be well heeled was to be well armed.**

And to be well armed was everything, even after the fighting stopped. Harry now stood for something.

Returning home from Hell, doughboys poured back into the United States to flow through parades, officers with Sam Browne belts across their torsos, too many of them with heads bowed low by *le cafard*, which struck harder than tear gas, mustard gas, phosgene, and bullets, and went on disturbing afflicted veterans long after the war and the parades were over. Confetti. Kissing. War and Prohibition—along with other reaffirmations of law and order on the domestic front, notably immigration restrictions—would marry and give birth to a new and better peace, a stable world civilization whose imperial powers were invested in the benign expansion of markets, and laborers who begged to differ didn't beg for long (see Sacco and Vanzetti). A globe where rule ruled rather than rulers. The people had died and decided on it, in no particular order; they had spoken through the Women's Christian Temperance Union and the Anti-Saloon League—grassroots movements by any standards—and on the scorched grass of European fields, the people had voted with their guts.

The doughboys came home, but Harry stayed over there, over there.

22 ON THE BASIS OF SCIENCE

Harry settled into The Hague, where he remained in the legation until 1921, at which point he took the position in Hamburg of vice consul for the American commissioner in Berlin. There, by his own account, Harry's trajectory began to converge on the story of drug policy. He would later claim to have had his first exposure to an "international narcotics problem" in that first postwar post: two years in a Hamburg Harry characterized as "a worldwide distribution center for illicit drugs."[1] The little city just up the Elbe from the North Sea had been well situated as home to legal cocaine manufacture earlier in the century, but now opiate imports moved by legal pharmaceutical companies seemed to spill over into an illicit market; and the synthesis of heroin made it hard to track the origin of the opiate from which it had been derived. In Hamburg, Harry began to track.

While Harry was tracking imports and exports in northern Germany, the temperance movement had been gathering steam stateside, the Reds were storming the gates, and the Harrison Act was being acted upon. Women should vote but not drink. Men should go to war but might or might not come home. The latter should earn so the former could buy. Buying things was good for the U.S. of A. Back in Washington, D. of C., a special committee of investigation reported back to the secretary of the Treasury on "traffic in narcotic drugs." From the point of view of the national interest and federal organization, the traffic in narcotics was a subset of illegal markets, which is itself a subset of import and export. Customs is always financially interested in what commodities come and go, but the Treasury was perennially hamstrung by the challenges of enforcement. This is the intractable administrative conflict at the core of any federal prohibition designed to suppress international and interstate black market activity.

The Treasury's *Traffic in Narcotic Drugs* proposed to focus on drug

Number of narcotic prescriptions dispensed, as reported by druggists.

States.	Narcotic prescriptions reported.	Per cent of druggists replying.	Estimated number of prescriptions for 100 per cent replies.	States.	Narcotic prescriptions reported.	Per cent of druggists replying.	Estimated number of prescriptions for 100 per cent replies.
Alabama	264,443	47 5/12	540,124	Montana	4,612	2 3/4	169,000
Alaska	1,427	72 3/5	1,965	Nebraska	88,420	75	117,893
Arizona	28,187	(1)	28,187	Nevada	2,997	100	2,997
Arkansas	141,903	78 1/2	180,768	New Hampshire	23,267	23 2/3	98,311
California	270,334	100	270,334	New Jersey	380,073	67 1/5	565,584
Colorado	87,234	60 2/3	143,792	New Mexico	23,007	(1)	23,007
Connecticut	151,857	73 1/5	207,455	New York	1,381,646	50	2,763,292
Delaware	23,650	44 1/4	53,446	North Carolina	313,048	67 2/3	462,632
District of Columbia	88,676	44 1/4	200,963	North Dakota	38,612	32	120,662
Florida	132,619	62 1/2	181,059	Ohio	361,886	75 1/3	480,379
Georgia	311,226	64 1/2	490,273	Oklahoma	148,075	56	264,419
Hawaii	551	(1)	551	Oregon	82,351	73 3/5	109,470
Idaho	2,794	2 4/5	99,786	Pennsylvania	1,012,223	42 4/5	2,365,007
Illinois	454,761	27 2/5	1,659,711	Rhode Island	85,019	73 1/2	118,877
Indiana	188,005	73 1/5	256,837	South Carolina	138,533	(1)	138,533
Iowa	111,909	72 4/5	153,721	South Dakota	39,285	32	122,765
Kansas	150,297	78 3/5	191,217	Tennessee	322,583	67 3/4	476,137
Kentucky	213,434	66 2/3	320,151	Texas	65,429	8	817,862
Louisiana	227,681	87 1/5	261,102	Utah	433	2 4/5	15,464
Maine	50,612	23 2/3	213,853	Vermont	26,855	23 2/3	113,472
Maryland	284,809	44 1/4	643,636	Virginia	229,881	37	621,300
Massachusetts	401,180	81 1/2	492,246	Washington	106,237	72 3/5	146,332
Michigan	201,418	53 9/10	373,688	West Virginia	130,881	76 1/5	171,813
Minnesota	157,126	92	170,789	Wisconsin	169,549	76 1/2	221,632
Mississippi	130,447	47 5/12	271,593	Wyoming	6,674	60 2/3	11,001
Missouri	253,782	67 4/5	374,309	Total	9,511,938	52	18,299,397

[1] Per cent replying can not be given, as collectors summarized the data and did not furnish the number of reports.

"Number of Narcotic Prescriptions Dispensed, as Reported by Druggists," in Treasury Department, *Traffic in Narcotic Drugs: Report of Special Committee of Investigation*, 1919, p. 11. Courtesy of the University of Michigan and Google.

consumption and drug addiction from a "humanitarian" as well as "administrative" point of view:

> **In order to make a thorough and complete survey of narcotic drug addiction in all its phases, the committee formulated seven questionnaires, embodying questions covering the important points on which it appeared desirable to secure information. Each of these questionnaires was so arranged that it would bring forth the information which the persons addressed might possess, and at the same time be best adapted for the compilation of the statistics given.**[2]

In other words, the Treasury's exercise in humanitarianism depended, rather logically, on the collection of information from all relevant parties. The need for information spurred the development of new methods of gathering it, such as questionnaires.[3] Questionnaires were sent to individual professionals and to institutions: physicians, druggists, police, penal institutions, almshouses, health officers, public and private hospitals, and sanatoria. Functionaries, clerks, secretaries, and well-meaners filled out these forms, along with doctors and pharmacists. Social scientific methods clearly governed this procedure, the questions designed to elicit expert accounts, and engineered to yield results optimally quantified for statisticization. So what is knowable by such methods?

Social scientists could know numbers of gallons of paregoric (2,814), as against Bateman's Drops (12), as against Godfrey's Cordial (62), consumed in Maryland. Or the committee could estimate what the number would be had 100 percent, rather than 44 percent, of druggists in Maryland responded to the questionnaire. In Missouri, 3,882 addicts were reported by 14.5 percent of physicians questioned; had 100 percent replied, they would have reported 26,958 addicts in the state. This was where the social scientific technology broke down; the methodology seemed sound but the data did not flow. Moreover, "most of these officials replied to the effect that they kept no records of the number of drug addicts, nor had they any means of securing such information."[4] The responses of the health officers to the committee's questionnaire were not atypical:

> **Questionnaire No. 4 was addressed to 3,023 State, district, county, and municipal health officers. To this questionnaire, 983 replies were received, or 33 per cent of the total number sent out. Only 777 of these, or 26 per cent of the total, contained any information of value to the committee.[5]**

Much numeration but little data and even less information. Extrapolation could help the social scientists fill out the report. Thus estimates were ventured: anywhere between two hundred thousand and four million drug addicts in the United States;[6] larger cities tended to have greater concentrations of drug addicts than smaller towns and rural areas; there was no evidence of correlations between drug addiction and intelligence, gender, age, national origin ("except the Chinese and certain other nationalities of the Orient"[7]), and occupation, although drug addicts were disproportionately unemployed; and the report noted this important but thoroughly unsurprising observation:

> **In recent years, especially since the enactment of the Harrison law, the traffic by "underground" channels has increased enormously, and at the present time it is believed to be equally extensive as that carried on in a legitimate manner.**[8]

As early as 1906, Bishop Brent had called, from the Philippines, for sound methods for assessing conditions and behavior, for forms of knowledge that would serve as foundations for policy: "why could we not hope to have an investigation on the basis of science as well as of practical observation."[9] Now, in the 1920s, such methods came into widespread use, statistics proliferated, and the field of surveying expanded exponentially in the federal government. The Treasury, with its odd bailiwick, continually enhanced the sophistication of its statistical representations of narcotics traffic, use, and enforcement. Research and reports proliferated inside and outside of government.

The year the Johnson-Reed Act of 1924 was passed, curtailing immigration from non-European nations, the Lynds—Robert and Helen— went to work surveying Muncie according to nascent social scientific methodology. They published the survey results as *Middletown* in 1929, went back to Muncie to study cultural change in 1935, and published that survey as *Middletown in Transition* in 1937. The professional statisticians found the Lynds' work more valuable than "the sociological novel," but insufficiently scientific.[10]

In 1927, Elton Mayo began his experiments with workers at the Hawthorne Works of the Western Electric Company. The experiment ran for years—it was a way of life for the workers of Western Electric— and revealed the degree of influence that a group has on an individual in a group setting. The experiment ended in 1932, at which point there were no more workers. Similar data and methods for investigating social behavior were just beginning to inform industry practice and academic study, market research, campaign strategy, and the allocation of state resources. Budgets of governmental agencies, for example. Mayo and the Lynds were just part of a trend toward the methods and language of statistical thought and practice.

12

For detailed statistics of the sales of these various preparations, see the following tables.

Bateman's Drops, Godfrey's Cordial, and paregoric dispensed, as reported by druggists.

BATEMAN'S DROPS.

States.	Per cent replying.	Reported to collectors.		Number for 100 per cent. estimate.	
		Gallons.	Bottles.	Gallons.	Bottles.

GODFREY'S CORDIAL.

13

Bateman's Drops, Godfrey's Cordial, and paregoric, etc.—Continued.

GODFREY'S CORDIAL—Continued.

States.	Per cent replying.	Reported to collectors.		Number for 100 per cent. estimate.	
		Gallons.	Bottles.	Gallons.	Bottles.

PAREGORIC.

"Bateman's Drops, Godfrey's Cordial, and Paregoric Dispensed, as Reported by Druggists," Treasury Department, *Traffic in Narcotic Drugs: Report of Special Committee of Investigation*, 1919, pp. 12–13. Courtesy of the University of Michigan and Google.

In retrospect, earlier methods looked truly primitive. Even at the time, the Treasury's 1919 report betrayed a frustration with the methodological lag in the area of narcotics and articulated a hope for exactly the kind of social scientific knowledge and authority that did indeed materialize in the following decades. The special report offered some recommendations: Provide clinic and ambulatory treatment for the increased numbers of addicts generated by the Harrison Act. Strengthen the Harrison Act. Lay an absolute prohibition on anything to do with heroin. Support The Hague convention. Methodological recommendations were at least as important: Appropriate authorities should keep records. Record-keeping methods should be compatible with compiling statistics—on import and export, on the traffic in the illicit narcotics market, on the compliance of physicians and druggists, and increasingly, on the behavior of individual addicts.

It was not clear how these improved methods of gathering and storing information would serve the "humanitarian" perspective the committee wished to take on drug consumption, in addition to the "administrative" one, but this much they could say: authorities should "undertake studies to determine the nature of drug addiction with the view of improving the present forms of treatment or evolving some new and more efficient method of handling these patients."[11] Harry would inherit the value on statistical modes of representation, the opportunities and pitfalls of social scientific accounts, the bearing of both of these on both policy and enforcement. He was already at school in them, tracking imports and exports in Hamburg, on a course headed for authority, but only in retrospect.

23 HUMAN WRECKAGE
Wally Reid

On March 3, 1919, the Supreme Court affirmed the constitutionality of the Harrison Act in *Doremus* and opposed maintenance in *Webb*, the case of the infamous "scrip doctor" who sold drug prescriptions to all and sundry. Just the day before, on the opposite coast, an accident had befallen one of the greatest stars of the silver screen. Wallace Reid was arguably the most popular male actor of motion pictures at the time, having acted in well over one hundred movies, from shorts in which he starred with his wife, Dorothy Davenport, to the epics of D. W. Griffith and Cecil B. DeMille. Reid played opposite all the leading ladies of the day; he changed the wearing of neck collars; he brought the audience to the box office for film after film after film; his was the face of the birth of an industry. Across the country, Reid was the picture of fresh, benign, white masculinity—athletic, open-featured, young, kind to the workers. In the valley of San Fernando, over which Wally towered as a Hollywood phenomenon, he opened his home to all comers while he played music, having turned in the violin of his youth for a more contemporary sax. Often described as "manly," he had his pets and habits—the music, the fast cars, his wife, and the chemicals he liked to mix in the basement. Good clean fun.

But in *Valley of the Giants*, Wally ran into trouble. On March 2, 1919, director James Cruze put his troupe on a train headed out to shoot on location in the Cascade Mountains; Wally was playing guitar and crooning to castmates and crew in the caboose. In the movie, Wally saves the valley from the hostile corporate takeover of an unwelcome easterner by teaming up with a railroad agent and falsifying plans to build a line connecting the valley to the transcontinental railroad. Wally gets the backing and the girl, who is the daughter of the easterner. A scene with a runaway train—Wally saves the girl and her ungrateful father—provides extra thrills. But in real life, the train

Wallace Reid, 1922. From the personal collection of E. J. Fleming. Published in his book *Wallace Reid: The Life and Death of a Hollywood Idol.*

that the cast and crew took to the shoot that day jackknifed off the tracks at Noisy Creek Bridge, all the cars falling fifteen feet and landing on their sides on the embankment below.[1] At Noisy Creek Bridge, or rather under it, the red blood of Wally Reid ran down the back of his neck, from a cut deep enough to require at least six stitches. This dramatic incident within a dramatic incident would leave Reid permanently debilitated—and addicted to morphine. The next day, the Supreme Court would deal, with its double decision, a legal blow to doctors who prescribed narcotics for maintenance and a moral blow to doctors who dealt drugs to nonpatients. Given the taint associated with an emerging class of dealers, a guy who began as an innocent victim could fall into degeneracy. Wally Reid had far to fall. What began with medical treatment ended in the wages of sin less than four years later.

The studio doctor was equipped with morphine and authorized to dispense it to studio employees, and not infrequently did, in order to keep production on schedule. Wally's neck and arm were visibly injured but studio-supplied medication enabled him to work. Shooting the runaway train scene—uncanny in retrospect—must have been a special challenge with its replay of the accident. Because or in spite of being medicated, Reid continued to work at quite a rate—appearing in over twenty-five movies between the time of the crash and the time of his death. Yet pain, or its treatment, or both, became chronic. Wally had injuries, never quite specified, internal somehow, perhaps from the train but perhaps from an earlier accident he never talked about, injuries that never healed, or never stopped hurting. Always on the lookout for hijinks, Wally had experimented with substances even before Prohibition turned all the social gatherings in his house into crimes. Perhaps descriptions of unending pain from unhealed injuries made Wally into a bona fide patient, and offered the studio doctor some sense of immunity from the law; perhaps studio money and power inhibited Treasury interference; it is doubtful that doctors in Hollywood could have been unaware of legal developments.

Wally's account was hazy sometimes—or he lied about his level of consumption and his sources, or both. In the beginning, doctors prescribed morphine as a painkiller, but with Wally being Wally and Hollywood being Hollywood, already in 1920, there was no shortage of sources. Even when Dorothy could persuade doctors not to prescribe to Wally, Hollywood "had dope for sale":

> *Los Angeles*: **Thomas H. Tyner, alias Claude Walton, alias Bennie Walton, was taken into custody here on a local lot with seven bundles of heroin on his person, according to the arresting officer. He was arraigned before U.S. Commissioner Long and held for $1,000 bail for delivering the dope to one of the best-known male picture stars on the coast and that it had been the second time he was engaged to deliver to the same star, whose wife, in the hope of having him break the habit, informed the authorities.[2]**

It was said about town that the guilty party was Hughie Faye, a minor character actor from the Keystone Studios, and the "best-known dealer" in Hollywood, onto whom the criminality was projected for the moral protection of the star.[3] Thus rumors had begun right away, well before the strain began to show, but on with it anyway, at any cost.

In 1920, in *The Love Special*, Wally played a civil engineer who finds love on the tracks. Reid's character mistakenly assumes that a pretty young woman is his new stenographer; she is, in fact, the daughter of the president of a railroad line. Wally and the girl take a train ride, going loco through a high mountain pass in Yosemite, falling in love. Before Wally nods off offscreen. From Sleepy Cat to Medicine Bend, their little train trip takes them. It could be said that Medicine Bend is where the plot of Wallace Reid's life took a critical turn.

In Wally's real-life love special, his wife tried, for all she was worth, to control Wally's story and enter it into the record just so. While he was alive, Dorothy took charge of representing Wally to the press, crafting careful messages for his public as his private life went off the rails. She fed reporters a story of Wally's doings that featured his innocence earlier on, and his courage later. Dorothy went to great lengths to arbitrate between truth and falsehood, pleading in the kangaroo court of the media, and placing, too evidently, too much faith in the testimony of her darling addict. In a letter to the *Los Angeles Herald*, she wrote that

> **a young man was arrested with narcotics in his possession and explained he was "going to see Wally Reid." The explanation is true but the innuendo was false. Gossips immediately said the young man was taking the drugs to Wally to "make a delivery," as the saying goes. That was not true.**[4]

But if Dorothy herself was fooled, she was not fooling anyone else.

In 1921, Wally starred in *Across the Continent*, but his reputation extended even farther than that—he was the most popular American movie star in Europe. Now his reputation began to suffer, as did Reid himself, with the effects of long-term use of morphine, and its complications when mixed with alcohol. Dorothy too became the object of speculation:

> **It is known the wife of one of the most popular of the younger male stars has time and again had the peddlers of dope supplying her husband arrested, but she has been unable to get her husband to break his habit.**[5]

Peddlers could be arrested but the all-consuming habit could not; dope and her husband joined ranks with the peddlers and lined up against a railing Dorothy, who bore the standard for free will and good health. She blamed pushers and doctors, but mainly the film industry. Will Hays resented the inference and the interference, preferring to hold the standards himself, preferring the picture of a good industry with a few bad apples.[6]

Variety bore the standard for the film industry and its fans; a review of *The Hell-Diggers* was laced with unsubtle insinuations that Wally's drug and alcohol use were interfering with his art and its appreciation. Reviews were not all bad, but when they were, they often implied that Reid's drug-assisted decline was lit up on the big screen, visible in the hang of his trousers on his thinning body, and the hang of his skin on his frame, in the cash cow of a grin that he still sported despite his less robust health. Referring to drugs and alcohol, respectively, one critic opined that "a continuance of this attitude at this particular time and he will discover the vogue he has enjoyed in the last few years has slipped away from him. He'll be high and dry on the lot."[7] With the one word, "snow," another critic referred simultaneously to drugs and to the condition of overexposure to stage lights known as "Klieg eye," from which Wally was reported to be suffering:

> **An exclusive photo of Wally Reid, made just before he collapsed and went in out of the "snow"—into a sanitarium where the bootlegger can not break in and corrupt.**[8]

Notice that the "bootlegger" is holding the place for the "dealer," as the purveyor of black market goods antithetical to the mission of the sanitarium. Yet another critic summed up the paradox by which Wally's condition was both visible and invisible: even in character, Wally seemed to be "keeping his discomfort to himself, doing his bit with a high and gay courage."[9] Following a critique of Reid's lackluster performance in 1922's *The Ghost-Breaker*, one critic predicted that "things of this sort are about as sure a road to oblivion as far as the screen is concerned, as being involved in some unsavory scandal."[10] By then, Wally Reid had clearly peaked. Though he had enjoyed stratospheric heights of popularity, Wally was visibly compromised after three years of dependence on opiates since the train crash. He lost some teeth to the so-called side effects of drug use.[11] Addiction was the unsavory condition that would take him to oblivion.

The fact that *Webb* and *Doremus* came down at exactly the same time Wally's real-life train fell, and that his figurative star started to tumble after it, are matters of pure coincidence. But Wally was a very public figure, and his addiction was a matter of public discourse. Discourse of which the Supreme Court might well have been aware as it continued to interpret Harrison for years after Reid's death. The period was one of alarmist moralizing amid fear of all kinds of foreign forces. Wally's decline was indeed a matter of public alarm, and must have provided an occasion for the huge public that attended movies—already millions of people a week in the 1920s—to develop and articulate a feeling about narcotics, an opinion. Cures proliferated, or rather, scores of courses of treatments were advertised as "cures." And cures were called for:

> What happened to Wally happened to many a soldier released from hospitals after World War One, and happened to patients, men and women, released from hospitalisation, cured perhaps of their ailments but made into hopeless addicts through the then abysmal ignorance of the medical profession.[12]

In 1922, with Wally on his way down fast, the court delivered a decision that put new force into the legal campaign against doctors who prescribed narcotics. A doctor whose case went to the Supreme Court in 1922, Behrman had prescribed—to one Willie King and at one time—enough heroin, cocaine, and morphine to constitute over three thousand doses, but his indictment was a kind of legal trick. Behrman was tried as though he had been prescribing a "treatment . . . for the purpose of curing the addict."[13] His conviction made it effectively illegal for all doctors to prescribe narcotics (in any kind and amount) to addicts, and this questionable legal strategy, which became known as the "Behrman indictment," was invoked repeatedly in the legal harassment of many thousands of doctors, a good number of whom were never convicted. As Rufus King points out about this crusade against physicians:

> In cases that went all the way to trial, the ratio between arrests and convictions remained notably low, indicating abusive use of the indictment processes: in 1920, 3,477 arrests produced 908 convictions; in 1921, 4,014 arrests produced 1,583; at the peak, in 1925, 10,297 federal arrests produced 5,600 convictions.[14]

In a cultural shell game, the moral values attached to alcohol were grafted onto drugs—the 1920s is the decade of this grafting—so that chronic use of drugs began to reveal a flawed character, as alcoholism had previously done. Now chronic alcohol use constituted a socially acceptable rejection of a repressive (and silly!) state apparatus. When libertinism and libertarian privacy defeated puritanical moralism with respect to alcohol, drugs stepped in as whipping boy. When alcohol and drugs divorced, at the end of Prohibition, the former would be largely redeemed, but the latter would keep the moral—and legal— taint. Maybe drugs took the rap so that alcohol could be rehabilitated.

Wally Reid's reputation could not be. Wally was the boy every-one had loved, a victim, close to home, a hero whose death must be avenged or made good, if only after a necessary moment of disavowal and repudiation. Other stars, after all, had not fallen; neither Douglas Fairbanks nor Mary Pickford had turned to drugs, for example, nor had Chaplin, though all three had their share of physical discomforts in the course of also-unrelenting film production.

Dorothy Davenport, who took up the call against narcotics after Wally's death publicly, that is, oratorically and cinematically, came to represent a now-conventional view of Prohibition:

> **Before we had wine in the home, which Wally drank temperately with friends for relaxation after strenuous hours in the studio, and then it became a crime, and the bootleggers came with their poi-sonous Scotch and Bourbon, and their insinuating drugs.**[15]

As a star, Wally Reid failed spectacularly, and in so doing, he succeed-ed in giving life to an addict figure driven by bad values, Hollywood values, hedonism, lack of will, overindulgence, sin. Hollywood had only just become bad; it had only just become anything but a desert. But there were parties—and there was Fatty Arbuckle, whose trials forced fans to face the fact that movie stars who shone on screen might be sinners in real life. The popular media were already making regular charges of lax morality in Hollywood.

Wally walked the walk from star to sinner in the public eye while Dorothy talked the talk of the brave fight against a monstrous foe— *two* foes: opiates and the unceasingly greedy studio heads. Out of greed, the studio pushed morphine on Wally from the day after his train accident up until the end. In his last days, the too-late days of the foregone conclusion in the sanitaria and the wooded cabin retreat, the days of no longer going to the studio, Wally did go off the narcotic, ultimately dying a natural death. Dorothy lionized his clean and sober departure from this world accordingly. He was a perfect prodigal son, forswearing the sin, though it cost him his life. But what, exactly, killed Wally Reid? He wasn't on morphine—and medically supervised withdrawal, no matter how painful, doesn't usually kill young men. He had lost a tremendous amount of weight, which could certainly result directly from morphine use, and he had dysentery, which can also cause dramatic weight loss. And dysentery could kill, indirectly, through kidney failure, for example—and "renal suppression" was indeed listed as a cause of death. The legal certificate identified the cause of death as lung congestion and organ failure, but headlines named "drugs," "dope," and "narcotics."[16] But the moral of the story is, and has always been, that morphine killed Wallace Reid. As he returned to innocence, the drug absorbed the guilt.

Also guilty was the newly minted dealer, himself a step down the ladder of evolution from the prescribing doctor, the Hollywood flunky who animated the black market. Whatever unscrupulous corporate personnel and medical practices may have precipitated Wally's death, the dealer was the fittest, the cockroach who survived the era, the one whose evil would be reified in this role and brought down through generations as the lowest of the low, intrinsically irredeemable and unrehabilitatable over time, scurrying on the outskirts of society, a parasite called forth by a nascent prohibitionist regime. Law enforcement was Dorothy writ large, an ineffectual agency of intervention reduced to pronouncement on morals.

The Hearst papers, including the *San Francisco Examiner*, gave Dorothy Davenport a platform for spinning her husband's story, with stories like "Wife Pens Dramatic Story of Wallace Reid's Drug Ruin."[17] Dorothy was determined to use Wally's death for good, to educate an ignorant public about the dangers of narcotics. In 1923, Davenport produced, starred in, promoted, traveled with, and spoke about *Human Wreckage*, a film addressing the subject explicitly and boldly. Although her movie was fictional, Dorothy wanted the audience to connect the story with Wally's addiction and death. To make the moral point, however fictionally, the film has the taxi-driving protagonist crash his car into a train, killing himself and his passenger—the dealer who got him hooked on drugs to begin with. Although the movie is lost, "at speeds near 90 miles per hour the taxi careened in and out of traffic before a final shot of a head-on crash with a moving train."[18] This is the crash of time.

Wally loved cars, and he had a raging thing for driving fast, on and off camera. A number of his biggest hits were roadster films in which he performed the driving himself. And one of the close calls of his leisure time involved a determination to drive in the Indy 500 in 1922 when he was already quite weakened from drug use. As though with a will, as though some original sin kept reasserting itself, Wally's roles would take him through one re-creation after another of an early car accident, a head-on collision on the Pacific Coast Highway in 1915 in which Wally had driven into an oncoming car. Wally was twenty-three, his star just rising. The father of a family of five was killed. Wally escaped uninjured and somehow untarnished, perhaps as an effect of the czar-like power of his studio head.[19] Or had he? Maybe those were the injuries that never healed, the whiplash and the guilt—the replays on the big screen, the cars, trains, accidents, speed, and the narrow gauge track referring back to the earlier scene, re-raising the specter of the repressed returning, head-on.

Of *The Love Special*, one critic wrote, "steam engines and racing cars, bursting dams, and snowstorms are, to be sure, the chief actors, but Mr. Reid smilingly takes what bows there are. Whether he is bowing for himself or the steam engines—well, anyhow."[20] Not the first person to stand in for a steam engine, Wally reported confusion about who was really driving the train in a particular scene, one that hearkened back to the 1915 car accident or maybe the 1919 train crash. According to Wally,

> It was great sport to feel the big engine pick up as I pulled the throttle but I felt lost without a steering wheel. At times when we went around a sharp curve, I would instinctively grab for the wheel, only to remember that I was in a locomotive and didn't have to do any steering.[21]

Wally had already lost control of his personal narrative by the time he shot that scene in 1921. But still he instinctively grabbed for the wheel. Was Wally trying to turn back time, to go back before the bend, and this time turn the wheel before hitting that other car on the Pacific Coast Highway in 1915? Dorothy's *Human Wreckage* ends with a head-on collision between a car and a train killing the car's driver as well as the antagonist in the passenger seat, like a doubling back around the curve to the repressed accident, lapping back to the pre-condition of Wally's addiction, bringing the locomotive force of the film's narration to an end.

> **A shadowy figure runs through Dorothy Davenport Reid's narcotic crusade film "Human Wreckage," although [sic] his name is not in the cast. You get an impression that the film is haunted by the phantom of Wally Reid, to whom it is dedicated.**[22]

Then the film itself came to a permanent end; no known copies have survived.

Webb and *Doremus* came down at the very moment that Wally's star peaked and began to fall. But *Behrman* was decided while Wally was thrashing around in the throes of addiction, putting a cherubic face on habituation and thus lending the extraordinary cash—and cultural—value of his innocence to the power of the narcotic to corrupt it. Wallace Reid was perhaps the first to make national news as an addict, an early celebrity doper. *Behrman* was decided—in favor of arming the feds against minor as well as large-scale offenders—in the early days of Prohibition when alcohol was still a moral struggle, until death, disease, financial ruin, a black market amok, and pervasive corruption had forced morality offstage entirely, or turned it to full-on farce. At the same time, a drug market opened up, creating an opportunity for reinvestment of the cultural values that attend temperance, abstinence, sobriety, and the like.

Wally Reid was fading in the rearview mirror. *Human Wreckage* was on its way to being as lost as Wally. The millions of motor vehicles on the growing number of roads had begun to have a serious impact on train travel and distribution. The court put a last twist on its indictment of the Behrman indictment; it cautioned in the most severe terms against this interpretation of the Harrison Act:

> **Enforcement of the tax demands no such drastic rule, and if the Act had such scope it would certainly encounter grave constitutional difficulties.**[23]

Too late! The Harrison Act would no longer be used to interfere with medical practice, but too many doctors had already lost to it their livelihoods. And too many addicts, Wallace Reid among them—as well as the victim of his 1915 car accident—lost their lives.

24 LOTUS EATERS

In Dolce Far Niente

He walked soberly, past Windmill lane, Leask's the linseed crusher's, the postal telegraph office. Poles and cables radiating up and out. He continued past the sailors' home. He turned from the morning noises of the quayside and walked through Lime street. Deviating from a straight path along the quays, always captaining himself, Bloom made a choice, chose, crossed Townsend. Now he drave past the end of town, over the edge of town, into a nontown. Nine days later, in Westland row, he halted before the window of the Belfast and Oriental Tea Company and read the legends of lead-papered packets: choice blend, finest quality, family tea. Another big plant with leaves to hang dry and magical mind-changing proper-

Photo by H. J. Anslinger

THE STATION AT ZIG-ZAG

"La Guaïra–Caracas Railroad" clipping. Originally published in the *American Consular Bulletin*, vol. 6, no. 9, September 1924. Harry J. Anslinger Papers, Special Collections Library, The Pennsylvania State University Libraries.

ties. Poetries. Poet teas. Launching him, linguistically, into uncharted waters. The far east. Ceylon was Oriental in the last measure of completeness—utterly Oriental, also utterly tropical, and indeed to one's unreasoning spiritual sense, the two things belong together. The costumes were right; the black and brown exposures, unconscious of immodesty, were right. And there was that swoon in the air which one associates with the tropics, and that smother of heat, heavy with odors of unknown flowers.[1] Lovely spot it must be: the garden of the world, big lazy leaves to float about on, lily pads sans logic, snaky lianas they call them, so many leasky vessels. Wonder is it like that. In those tropics, where good men get lost, imbibing flowery meads, forgetting all about. What. But what people are these floating like so? Those Cinghalese lolling around in the sun, *in dolce far niente*, sneaky lines snaking about them. Teas circling, circling teas, circulating eastly. Those Cinghalese lolling around in the sun at the tip of the widow's peak of India, surrounded everywhere by her rolling ocean, a large tear-shaped island, a last drop of the continent poised to plash through Buddha's own basin toward the equatorial latitudes. In southern tongues, sotosay, *in dolce far niente*. Not doing a hand's turn all day. Not acting one's part in the machine, and soaking instead in sweet succulent nothingness, little hope of a war to sink one's teeth into, to keep one alert. Hard to scare up a hunt once in a while. Sleep six months out of twelve. Too hot to quarrel. Influence of the climate. Lethargy. Flowers of idleness.

The narrative, such as it was, ground to a halt in Westland row. Off the western edge of town they sailed, Bloom and crew, off the pages of an American journal in July 1918. The machete had been hung, and was still hanging, wavy in the heat, having swung but once or twice before quitting time, which brought the crew to chewing loosely on rubber, sitting and chewing. Though James Joyce's *Ulysses* was far from complete in 1918, the *Little Review* began serializing the first several sections that year. The January and July issues were seized by US Customs officials, who, in some accounts, burned it, in others, confiscated it, perhaps in Canada, perhaps New York. It is written elsewhere that postal workers burned copies of the book. Be that as it may, dirty bits of *Ulysses* were not legally available in the United States in 1920. Common knowledge, this. Same story

England. Editors Margaret Anderson and Jane Heap could not have been surprised, or disappointed, since they prospered by the controversy about *Ulysses* in their journal: while they stood by the originality, ambition, and effects of Joyce's work, they ran angry and uncomprehending letters from readers, fomenting, fermenting, foruming, fostering a public debate.

Also legally unavailable, following virtual decades of debate: alcohol. January 16, 1920, was the first day of Prohibition in the United States. Later that year, a section of *Ulysses* that involved Bloom masturbating invited obscenity charges by the New York Society for the Suppression of Vice. He waited by the counter, inhaling the keen reek of drugs. He rustled the pleated pages. Better leave him the paper and get shut of him. For most critics, scholars, and readers of critical editions, the thorny heart of the publication history of *Ulysses* is the problem of error correction in a manuscript of extreme length, one that was prepared for printing by several different cooks. But it was the obscenity charges that succeeded in scaring off certain American publishers at the time. Alcohol and *Ulysses* were both banned in the United States in 1920; black markets and bootlegs ensued.

> **About a fortnight ago, sir?**
> **Yes, Mr. Bloom said.**[2]

From that time on, rum ran up the east coasts of the Americas because

> on or about the same Day that the Volstead Act went into effect, an executive order was signed excepting the citizens of the Bahamas, Bermuda, Cuba, St. Pierre et Miquelon, in fact every place used by the smugglers as a base of operations, from the necessity of having a passport or visa to enter the United States on a visit. While it is understood that this executive order was promulgated to relieve war time restrictions, no consideration was given to the fact that a new war had started and that for the Treasury Department it was just as necessary to control the movements of the smugglers through passports and visas as to control the movements of those suspected during the war.[3]

Here, the Eighteenth Amendment produces a "war" on alcohol. (You heard that particular phrase here first.) Empires at stake. And warriors on both sides of that law had it rough. A two-master is much harder to handle in the heavy weather of the North Atlantic winters, and terribly dangerous in tropical squally weather, where things can happen with very short notice. Water water everywhere, slopping over the sides of vessels, language like liquor trickling down the sides of the hemisphere like so much molasses through the bunghole of history, and always as a function of intemperateness: "too much heat could make the molasses expand, causing a combustion which could blow or fracture a bung, and the molasses would overflow." So says Hugh H. Corkum, whose *On Both Sides of the Law* makes his life an open book, "the exciting personal story of a former rumrunner and flamboyant police chief."[4]

Rumrunners were in constant danger, with the US Coast Guard on watch, either one an army rotten with venereal disease: overseas or halfseasover. Half-baked they look: hypnotised like. Eyes front. Mark time. Table: able. Bed: ed. The King's own. Like the scurvy Dog. What an officer he would have made, but for the affliction of demon rum. He would go ashore a fine-looking man—tall, dark, husky, solid—and come back drunk and disgusting. A skyride on a keg of rum is not the best way to enter heaven. Maybe it was not good thinking, but our basic strategy was to keep trying the escape route as long as there was any possible chance of getting away. And away the ship sailed, around the headlands of Lunenberg Harbour, never to be seen again.[5]

The King's England then extended from Cecil's "Cape to Cairo," from Calcutta to Canada. The sun, sotheysay, never set on the empire, the vast vista of spud, spore, sprout, those fruits which once squoze yield up the sauce. Kookaburra to cocker spanning the globe, some 570 million heads under the Crown. Clean not a one, sober my eye-are-land. In this light, some small sea it was from Dublin to Ecum Secum. Twixt here and there, just some small boats, and on them, some rum. It's a pretty tough run up the coast on those little fellows because they roll like hell, and things smash around so much that it's hard to keep your set together, and if you succeed in doing that, the vibration is so hellish that your tubes go to pieces fast, and are so noisy while they do work that you can't hear much in a heavy sea. Then too, as you know, having been around Halifax for some time, that coast is no place for a nervous man. The ledges are very bad, practically all the way from the Lurcher Light vessel until after you pass Canso and Scatteree going into Sydney, and the fog is terrible, excepting for about two months in the fall. Of course you can't put in anywhere with a load so you just either head her straight east in a storm or take a chance on smashing to hell on one of the million reefs that lie in wait for you just beneath the innocent-looking shoal waters. Then if you are lucky, in passing the Lurcher on the way home, you still have the Bay of Fundy to reckon with, and if you've ever been out there in a blow on a night thick as SH--, you know that the nastiest weather in the world comes from northern Quebec and tears down four hundred miles thru that bay and comes out like a blast from hell to whirl you into the yawning black abyss of Davy Jones's Locker.[6]

I had been told to get the lifeboat prepared for evacuation in a hurry, which I did, but I was not told to cast everything overboard.[7] Not in so many words, more in the way of thinking. Thinking therefore I am an incoming train clanked heavily above his head, coach after coach. Therefore I am emergence, unurgencee. More thought experiments in a train. Barrels bumped in his head: dull porter slopped and churned inside. The bungholes sprang open and a huge dull flood leaked out, flowing together, winding through mudflats all over the level land, becoming the sea that surrounds. Thoughts released, foamed up, and fell flat, sporadically or staccatoly. Rectal flatitude. Antiphony of lassitude, this analysis and reuse of *Ulysses*, of literary and alcoholic prohibitions, of a couple of rum-running writers.

Harry J. Anslinger heard the call—and was launched across the puddle and into these latitudes. From 1921 to 1923, Harry had kept his eye on shipping, immigration, and trade, among other matters of US interest in northern Germany. There, he was a little fish in the little North Sea, but in his next post, Harry was a slightly bigger fish in a much, much bigger sea.

> However, it is not of the new appointments, even though they be to fascinating places, that we intend to speak, but of the weird shifts

of consular locations, recorded in Secretary Hughes' order. Thus, Mr. Anslinger is to be moved from Hamburg to La Guayra—from the bustling city of North Germany struggling . . . [word missing] after-war difficulties, to the ultra-Latin port of Venezuela.[8]

Although Harry pleaded for assignment to another location, something less weird perhaps, he agreed to take the post in the small coastal town. He could only imagine the tropical zone. Was this a demotion, a rung down the ladder of evolution, a backward step in the march of civilization?

In a poem entitled "The Lure of La Guaïra," an anonymous colleague of Harry's describes a place "of donkeys, heat and sordid smells." "This," the colleague laments, "after Broadway, theatres and dinners only a few nights before."[9] Yet it was understood that undesirable assignments were the fate of the appointee. As Harry himself toured La Guaïra, old-timers pointed out notable landmarks: the leper asylum, the hospital, and the graveyard. Years later, in his own poem, Harry recalled his anticipatory fears of La Guaïra, fanned in the first place by reading an entry in an anonymous "encyclopedie." He remembered worrying that

fevers of a malignant and putrid nature prevail and life here is very dangerous to strangers.[10]

All food and water must be boiled. What might one catch. Or be caught. Watch out or be boiled and eaten, probably sans sauce.

In fact, though he feared the difference, Harry's work in Venezuela followed logically from his work in Germany. Harry crossed back over the Atlantic, vehicle after vehicle, finding his way west and south some, station to station, and stopped for a while in this teeny-tiny coastal town in Venezuela to ply his trade—which was to track same. As he had in Hamburg, Anslinger tracked shipping—imports and exports—though he certainly found his job in La Guaïra less glamorous. "Down here," he grumbled, "my activities are smothered as there is absolutely nothing of interest. I cannot even find a little Communist about." Although the "ultra-Latin" locale compared "favorably with any tropical country where negro blood predominates,"[11] Anslinger continued to press the State Department for reassignment. He's not going out in bluey specs with the sweat rolling off him to baptise blacks, is he? The glasses would take their fancy, flashing. Oblivion then? Sure but why. Cured of all apparition and apparent bleeding, maintaining. Gastritis not too Good and not too Bad, though they have their days of battle in the gut now and again. Not unlike East West. North South. South East of a sudden. Unspeakably hot. The equator is arriving again. We are within eight degrees of it. Ceylon present. Dear me, it is beautiful! Whole libraries of sentiment and Oriental charm and mystery, and tropical deliciousness.[12] Look at them. Metropole and its unequal opposite, empire to outpost. Only coming to a stop at the post office.

While Harry waited to be reassigned, he amused himself with local color, and of it all, he reported only on a local train that ran through a high and picturesque, or perhaps truly sublime, pass:

> **Climbing from sea level to a pass about 4,000 feet high, the train descends 1,000 feet into Caracas, having traversed 22 miles to reach a point six miles distant. A straight line is not always the shortest distance between two points.**[13]

His byline attached to this puff piece, which described "The La Guaïra–Caracas Railroad" for the *American Consular Bulletin* in September 1924. Altitude obtains at all latitudes. And Harry J. Anslinger knew of what he spoke. Altoona, Horseshoe Bend, the old work whistle, the inexorable, however effortful, forward movement of the train all came crashing back:

> **The bell clangs, the conductor whistles, the engine breathes, the train starts. It runs along the sea for several miles and then does a succession of curves and reverse curves over colossal excavations and astonishing precipices which make one shudder and think that youth's dream of falling through endless space will at last come true but with a crash at the end of the dream.**[14]

Unlike Wallace Reid, whose train crashes had caught up with him in January 1923, Harry survived his thirty-first year; his crash dreams had not in fact come true. Yet at the time of Reid's death, Harry's youth was coming to an end; he was approaching thirty-two in a godfor-saken outpost in the Southern Hemisphere. Would that he had been able to leave the tracking of trains behind him already, but no. Would that a train or plane or ship would come and hie him from here to another there. A there where we would not have to mine so hard for metaphor in the mountains.

> The sea disappears from view. The train passes over 15 steel bridg-es and through no less than fifteen tunnels, four of which are driven through solid stone. The track debouches from one of these upon a rocky shelf at a sheer vertical drop of 1,600 feet above the gorge of Boqueron.[15]

Above all, the piece suggests that Harry had enough time on his hands to twiddle his thumbs as his vision of a cosmopolitan career faded in the rearview mirror. Romance, let alone debauchery, elud-ed him. But all around him, or at least in the waters just northeast, bootleggers and rumrunners partook:

> I stowed away in the lazaret, which was aft of the cabin by the rudder post, where the paints, oils, ropes, spare sails, and many other items are stored for a long voyage. It was my favourite spot on a ship because of the wonderful aroma of oakum and hemp rope stored there.[16]

While Harry waited to be carried out of this chapter, word for word, other words were beginning to make their way around Europe, worlds away. The whole time Harry languished in La Guaïra, the metropole that was Paris was still there. There in Paris, in February 1921, Sylvia Beach lent the preeminent French writer Valery Larbaud the issues of the *Little Review* that contained early chapters of James Joyce's mag-num opus. A week later, Beach received a letter from Larbaud with his famous appraisal: "I am raving mad over Ulysses."

From 1914 to 1921, Joyce had been writing *Ulysses*. During that time, a war raged and then ceased raging. *The Little Review* that could, did. Then in 1921, the writer tried to pull his manuscript together for printing, quibbling with the editors about its particular manifestations, worrying the printers at all turns. Coming back at them again with changes. And again. Three visits are written, three visits the Buddha made to the island, to the island and back, to see those snakes who can appear human, the Nagas, the Naga Kings, who never really existed. Yet Buddha made those three trips. For a symbol and some symbolism. Balangoda man migrated from here to the mainland, passing Buddha like a ship, doubling back, Hey was that Buddha? at approximately the time that humans rode, walked, and otherwise slunk their way to the Indian subcontinent from Africa. The printer managed to set the outsize novel in astonishing time. Celebrated, desirable, strange, but in production restricted to the hot belt of the equator; and out a little way in the country were the proper deadly snakes, and fierce birds of prey, and the wild elephant and the monkey.[17]

Although he would not have been able to purchase that book in the United States in 1923, Harry J. Anslinger could, theoretically, have read *Ulysses* in La Guaïra, because it had indeed been published in Europe, though not England, the sweat of the assignment falling onto the page where Bloom sets sail for Ceylon. Harry and Bloom could have hovered within three degrees of each other, just above the equator, Ceylon a little farther east from Greenwich than La Guaïra is west; both are as hot as hell and lazier. But Bloom takes his stroll at an earlier date: June 16, 1904. Could have been the day Harry had to get morphine for the woman on the second floor. Overdose of laudanum. Sleeping draughts. Lovephiltres. Paragoric poppysyrup bad for cough. Clogs the pores or the phlegm. Poisons the only cures. Remedy where you least expect it. Monkey in the medicine. Clever of nature.

Contemplates not only his navel but that other friendly nubbin buoying up in the bathtub, a man's own ocean, under a moon's own shine, the limp father of thousands, a languid floating flower, of a lotus variety, amid the dark tangled curl of his bush floating, floating hair of the stream, around which. Could have been that night too. Bloom dried off is an everyman walking around town, all the protagonists are doing it. Bloom is a petit bourgeois everyman. The odyssey is the universal journey, each man's early life a plot, or a trajectory anyway. The rest of life the blossoming consequences of following the impenetrable clues. Bloom's pen name, his code name, is Flower. A Lotus Flower.

As intemperate, practically hot-headed, Henry Flower, Bloom posts an ad: "Wanted, smart lady typist to aid gentleman in literary work." From among the respondents, Bloom opts to correspond with one Martha. Harry had a Martha too. A rose. A Martha whose son encountered "substandard educational facilities" in La Guaïra.[18] A Martha who consequently repaired to, and took up residence in, Caracas, a Martha who may or may not have been the writer of the "letter from America" Harry received back in Brussels in September 1918. How can Flower's Martha aid in literary work? She has done enough already, a character we do not meet whose absence animates the groundbreaking protagonist. There was another Martha, real but more important for the purposes of this book, *another*. A Mrs. George Washington Reed who may, in philanthropist garb, have sponsored Dr. Jin Fuey Moy in seminary. She was married to an editor at the *Brooklyn Eagle*—and isn't anyone married to a George Washington a Martha? The Reeds lived on Berkeley Place.

Could have given that address too. Could have given a fictitious port. Could have done like Roy Olmstead, one of the touchables, a young police lieutenant in Seattle who moonlit as a bootlegger, giving fake orders on the phone that was tapped and giving real orders on the untapped line, trying to beat Volstead. Olmstead's wife transmitted coded instructions to his reception committees and wholesalers in the specially written children's bedtime stories she read on the radio. Dirty that. Dirty this, Roger that. In other codes, *Anchored in Harbor. Where and when are you sending fuel?* became *MJFAK ZYWKH QATYT JSL QATS QSYGX OGTB*.[19] All instructions were in code and transmitted in CW. Sometimes at a drop, orders would be passed by word of mouth, but only to those who we knew for sure could be trusted. The code of ethics was strict, and trust was very important. Our code book was our bible; it was complex and closely guarded. It held secrets to the whole operation, so in the wrong hands its contents could be ruinous. Unmasking the devil, devilishly difficult.

The devil take the threat of discovery, snakes unasped. Secret letter writers unmasked. Hot as Hades holding on to the letters from Martha and the other applicants at the post office. Heating up the whole potted place, and the officially original garden of the world. Storm without *drang*. Trying his best to break codes and bust up illegal operations, but way off his axis, Harry rode out the first wave of Prohibition in a historical humdoozer of hurricane force, just as bad as one of the previous year. His Martha hung out in Caracas so her son Joseph could take tutoring with a Harvard man.[20] But there was only so much tutoring he could take.

> **The material available is voluminous and pages could be written, but an effort has been made to confine it to a brief readable analysis of what was actually accomplished and any theorizing indulged in was only included because it was regarded as pertinent.**[21]

The chemist turned back page after page. Sandy shrivelled smell he seems to have. Shrunken skull. And old. Quest for the philosopher's stone. The alchemists. Drugs age you after mental excitement. Lethargy then. Why? Reaction. A lifetime in a night. Lots of time lines up against the page, lots of timelines, telling you somely about the ways of Harry J. Nagaslinger, a dead man, an exciting tale. If you desire that any changes be made in the story, and you will so advise me, I shall be glad to make them.

Meanwhile, Martha and Joseph in Caracas, Harry in La Guaïra, hot in their hellholes like it would never end. Off the coast of Venezuela, boats hove to and rode it out without any trouble, but with some concern, because we were a little too close to Sable Island for comfort, with Dad as our captain.[22] I was learning the ropes.

The *Quadra* was busted "on or about October 13, 1924, while hovering at a point about five or six miles from the Farallone Islands," and then the rumrunner *Coal Harbor* was "seized in the vicinity of Farallone Island, on February 17, 1925, with a cargo consisting of approximately 10,000 cases of assorted liquors, all of which were consigned to the usual fictitious destination, John D. Douglas and Company, Libortad, San Salvador."[23] Same night, years later, all in the same swim: from the *Chief Skugaid*, on Thursday, October 13, 1932, 8:15 a.m.: "Moderate SE gale. Vessel drifting in distress," and by 12:30 a.m., morning of the fourteenth: "Fishing vessel unable to tow us across Straits of Juan de Fuca in rough, confused sea & swell." Time topsy-turvied. Nine days became thirteen years. Spiraling down the drain at the uncorked core of the earth, emptied out and refilling with all that alcohol, sailors too, tanking in the deep text. Fictitious port. Rough, confused sea & swell. Such pouring forth: The commander of base six at Fort Lauderdale received a note which read, "SAMUEL ROLLICKING DRA BROADSIDES 6786-10-NEPB-K3 or GOING WITH VERONA ON 6786 TO HI-JACK BRILL'S ---------- BOAT 10 MILES northeast of Palm Beach K-3." I had the helm, and we were passing one of the little islands on our port side, with what we thought was plenty of distance, when suddenly all hell broke loose. Crash! Bang! Boom! Bing! She shook, trembled, and stopped.[24] Juan de Fuca?

> **Such historic happenings have been passed down verbally from generation to generation and have been instilled so vividly in the minds of the natives of Lunenberg County that, when looking out on Mahone Bay, one almost expects to see a ghost ship on fire.**[25]

This happened to him, Hugh Corkum, whom we left bobbing and weaving on the high seas back in the 1920s, still sailing around the law, yet to go straight, which he will when repeal runs rum-running aground:

> **We moved to the east coast of Cape Breton. The Flora Anne towed us the whole way around to the south of Louisburg, where we took on 300 kegs of rum and awaited orders for our next drop. It began to blow very hard; in fact, it turned into a northeaster, which can last for several days. With a northeast gale and a strong southwest tide you can drift four or five miles an hour. . . . I suggested it would be a good idea to go into Main a Dieu and run in the lee of Scatari Island until the storm blew over.**[26]

A tide, a gale, a good idea blows us over. Several days. You can drift. Christened the *Santa Cecilia* and built for the fourth Henry Paget, son of another Henry Paget on up the line of Marquesses of Angelsey, just two degrees up and two to the right from Dublin. This in 1881. Same boat became *Selma* in 1917, sold same year by the All Red Line, in Canada. In Canada in those days, they renamed all the boats, according to custom, all Indian words all beginning with *C*, see? *Camosun, Capilano, Cassiar, Cheakamus, Chehalis, Cheslakee, Comox, Coquitlam,*

Cowichan, Coutli, Chelohsin, and *Selma* she joined them as the *Chasina*, just another C word in a crazy world of code, not an anachronistic reference to the author hereof, Chasin, A.

How did she get over there? Must've swum. Then they had her running the Vancouver Powell River route for a time. Sold again, older now, to sail under the umbrella of the Consolidated Exporters Corporation, "a band of the most highly organized smugglers with which the Treasury Department has to cope."[27] From Victoria to Shanghai, she sailed, the *Chasina*, arriving June 16, 1931, then on to Hong Kong, from which she hied on September 6, then to Macao, and thence on September 25 but never made it to Ensenada, going down somewhere between there and there, a leaky lady fifty years old, out of her lane, lost, but at least not running anymore. Maybe we were in the process of lowering our sails and anchoring when several fairly heavy squalls hit us quite unexpectedly. They became quite strong with heavy puffs of wind and rain.[28]

One almost expects to see a ghostly customs agent sit down and bard this story. I understand so don't know what wave she is using now. There are so many ways of circling back, of writing [h-i-s-t-o-r-y]. History writes up the crops of import-export for which Ceylon is positioned to perfection on the map: rubber, coconuts, coffee, tea. The home of cinnamon. Found in Egypt as early as 1500 BCE, suggesting commerce which suggests contact, did we stopover perhaps on the northern coast of Africa? Sleep six months out of twelve and the other six, sleep.

Back home in Dublin, Bloom more than is, is more than, a flower, though indubitably he is one, and a snaker through town, a traveler to the edge of it. Over and back. Hothouse in botanic gardens, the glass bottle in which we display the southern plants transplanted in the northern cities. Keep they their noses in nosebags. . . . Men are beasts. Poor jugginses! Damn all they know or care about anything with their long noses stuck in nosebags. Too full for words. Too full for words. Too dear to send them home. The spice emanates through the nosebag, the newspaper, the prescription, the decision, the riddle book, speaks soakingly of the fruit, the leaf, the seed the way nature intended them, spiralizing into the steamy upfunnelling of fragrance—what matters simple distance when Ceylon's seeds are essentially mine? Sleeping sickness sucks us down the airzone of time backwards. How will we get out of this chapter, how rise froth-like forth? Weeping? Back to the ship, to the memory of words, to the need to send one back? Even though we experienced some long smooth spells going down, we also had several heavy gales, and our deck load was in grave danger of spewing its lashings.[29] Will he purge, or will we, or will the book ingest and then disgorge itself? The danger is imaginary. Cigar has a cooling effect. Narcotic. Thinking is one thing. Go further next time. Quotating Martha now. It's not meant to be like Joyce or not like Joyce but in this context, it has no choice.

> **Complying with your request for a story of our activities in the Southeastern District during the past year, permit me to attach hereto, in triplicate, a resume of the salient features of the work carried on in that territory.**[30]

A place where excess can exceed itself, foam over and become so many snaky lianas, winding through mudflats all over the level land, a lazy pooling swirl of liquor bearing along wide-leaved flowers of its froth. Doctor whack. He ought to physic himself a bit. Electuary or emulsion. The first fellow that picked an herb to cure himself had a bit of pluck. Simples. Want to be careful. Enough stuff here to chloroform you. Test: turns blue litmus paper red. Chloroform. From here to there. Safe in the arms of kingdom come. Lulls all pain. Wake this time next year. Blowing it all to kingdom come also lulls all pain.

Speaking, or speaking of, the King's English, all that slang slung together and the rumrunner and the future police chief in Corkum could improve his facility with code, which behooved both sides of the law. Thus he spent part of 1930 taking the course at Dodge's Telegraph Railway Accounting and Radio Wireless Institute in Valparaiso, Indiana. Codes went with the territory, and given his familiarity with wireless communications, Corkum sailed through the class. "There is very little difference between the land line and international codes, so that part of the course was a piece of cake." Corkum could have taught Mr. Johnson's nine-month training in telegraphy and railway accounting, which should have equipped him for a good clean job, but there weren't any, so he reverted to dirty ones, and he dusted off his code of pirate conduct. What happened could hardly have surprised

Corkum: "as they were coming on board on the starboard side, our wireless operator was throwing the code book and some other things overboard on the port side."[31]

And where the book lies open, the Lourdes cure, waters of oblivion, and the Knock apparition, statues bleeding, if you uncork 'em—and swirling in the "t" until you get United Statutes at Large. There's a big idea behind it. Thing is if you really believe in it. Religion. Christianity, as the opium of the people, the body and the blood as the narcotic cause and effect of the funeral mass, Paddy Dignam's, for example. If you really believe in the self-advertisement of the saints and their descendants saving the Dark Continent. Going on from there to Save China's millions. Wonder how they explain it to the heathen Chinee. Prefer an ounce of opium. Celestials. Rank heresy for them. Prayers for the conversion of Gladstone they had too when he was almost unconscious. What does he know of the Chinese? Or the Cinghalese, Buddha their god lying on his side in the museum. Taking it easy with hand under his cheek. Joss-sticks burning. Fragrance swirling up *far niente*, all *dolce* like, like, no not like, unlike, Ecce Homo. Crown of thorns and cross. But not. Chopsticks. Who needs saving. Not those Chinee who send the medicinal wines across the water from Canton to California. Sir:

> These wines are in the nature of the less reputable patent medicines on sale in the United States, being regarded as a panacea for human ills, particularly those affecting the sexual functions. Various kinds of drugs and animals are steeped in the spirits to add special virtue to the medicine, such as the monkeys in Saw Weung, night storks in Goo Hawks wine, sparrow in Woo Deck wine, a kind of lizard in Kop Kai, the urine found in the bladder of a wild fox of the North River District of Kwantung Province—it is supposed to have both male and female sexual organs; the reproductive organs of the tiger, deer and panther in Sam Bin, and so forth. In some cases the names of spirits are merely trade names used by the dealer to specify their particular brands. However, in other wines, the animal ingredients are actually steeped in the liquid.[32]

I have honor to be, Sir. Your obedient servant. Wo Kurk was produced in South China by steeping Paddy birds in twenty-five percent Spirit;

Wu Kot, wild cat; Pank Hook, stork; Sam Weung, monkey; Sem Sem, urine found in the bladder of a slain tiger. Fu Kwat, tiger bones. Kop Kai is said to prevent "dripping" after syphilis. Kwat the fu? Liquorice root is a stomachic; szechuan worm grass, a tonic for kidneys; Heun Pak Tsze, a carminative. Other spirits treat debility, leucorrhea, and emissions. And

> on account of the fact that these wines are locally regarded as aphrodisiacs, it is also recommended that an investigation be made to ascertain whether these medicines may not be excluded from the United States under the provisions of Section 245 of the Criminal Code, Page 493, Paragraph 396 of the Code of Laws of the United States, Volume 44, Part I, The United States Statutes at Large.[33]

Their codes are very crude, as you may glean from a little dope we got at the Boston CG Hqtrs. They told us about a code that was being used on one of the little runners that simply consisted of writing off the message in plain English and then dividing it up into five letter groups. My code was a little better than that. However. I had a sliding double alphabet with which to encipher my stuff; altho it is simple enough, still it takes a while to find the code word and minutes count plenty. The points of the compass were also encoded so as to make it impossible for the CG to figure your course,[34] like telling fact from fiction, Bloom from Flower. Better follow your own stars.

> On the way home we had several bad storms, one in the vicinity of Bermuda and the worst one close to Sable Island. Salt was a dangerous cargo; many ships have had trouble with salt clogging their pumps. A leaky vessel with a load of salt could cause real problems. When we encountered the August gale close to Sable Island, two sailors were lashed to the pumps because our ship was leaking quite a bit and Dad was worried.[35]

Tied to the thwarts, we were. Whether she goes down unknown or the US Coast Guard shoots her up, like an American boat, the *I'm Alone*, we all float solo, or fail to do so, in the end. Code only slows both boats down a little bit. And who among us lives not on both sides of the law? Not a Royal Navy expert: Consolidated Exporters Corporation hired a retired Royal Navy expert to devise and modify its codes every few weeks, paying him a $10,000 retainer. The two-timing law would meet its unmaker, the repeal of Prohibition, in 1933. Meanwhile, Marthas waited while Henry Flower and Harry J. Anslinger charted their courses and captained their destinies, however circuitously.

25 *LINDER V. UNITED STATES (1925), OR VICE VERSA*

Once the damage has been done, the reputation of a ruined physician can hardly be restored. Dr. Charles O. Linder foreverafter remembered the Saturday afternoon on which his medical career, along with his good standing, came to a premature end. I. had brought it with her when she came to him that morning of the first day of April in 1922. Having practiced as a physician in Spokane for well-nigh thirty years, Dr. Linder was generally able to discern the nature of a patient's distress before the patient described it (and could detect a tubercular before he even opened the door), but I.'s trouble did not make itself known to him in this way. She presented as a healthy native Caucasian woman of maybe twenty-five years of age, with the appearance of one who lived in town, evidently unbowed by labor in the field, though marked, he thought, by mill or childbirth, or both. Her hair was unribboned, her frock a bothersome blue, not unlike the sky when the sun has sunk behind Rimrock but night has not yet fallen, and on account of the light wind and damp of the day, she had covered it with a well-worn shawl of gray. She smiled as she stepped, with laced boot, over the threshold, her demeanor so casual that had a certain apprehension not flit through him just then, Dr. Linder might have guessed that I. was calling on behalf of a family member too infirm to make the voyage into his cabinet.

Presently, I. revealed a story so unheard of as to be preposterous on the face of it, involving ulcers, invisible pox and caries, and physicians licentious, brutal, missing, and dead. But her manner of revelation discovered another, a moral or mental condition, Dr. Linder could not say, manifest in the flute of her voice and the tic of demurral in her wrists, an inability to distinguish between her own Truths and Falsehoods, though Dr. Linder himself could tell the difference. He was convinced of the reality of the ulcer. Yet, as he knew, "there is no reason to suppose that only one coherent body of beliefs is possible,"[1] and so Dr. Linder intended to record the case in elaborate detail. I.'s condition, thought he, could be the stuff of philosophical, if not medical, history. *I. presented as a healthy native. . . .*

Spokane was a growing municipality with a hundred-some thousand residents, and was, around that time, deemed in the papers "the healthiest city in the world."[2] Dr. Linder did not credit himself for that designation, which was not only patently unscientific, reminding one of the dubious claims of a local faith healer, but he had enjoyed a thriving practice among the good families of his neighborhood. Neither the richest nor the poorest that could be found in Spokane, his patients were those who worked in both new and familiar professions: a few schoolteachers, journalists, social workers, shop clerks, insurance men, but also a growing number of proprietors and landlords, and those who oversaw the work of others in the mills and power stations, those of the middle and higher ranks. Some Snodgrasses and some Posts. They knew the doctor by his true and only name, the same Dr. Charles O. Linder advertised on the shingle and the door.

Saturdays Dr. Linder reserved for patients of dubious means, hoping in this way to contribute to the upkeep of a population that dwelt on the margins of respectability. Most often, the people who came on that day were ones he had not seen before and would not see again. It had been raining throughout the better part of that Saturday afternoon, but the sun shone clear into the pantry in the last half hour Dr. Linder would ever practice medicine. He thought fleetingly of the twilight in her dress. He had treated eleven patients already, and he saw five more sitting in the waiting room, having just concluded business with an elderly man whose dyspepsia was more easily addressed than the lifetime of work in a local mine that was now laboring his breath. With a formula for his digestion, the physician dismissed him, knowing full well the man's industry would catch up with him soon, perhaps before he could develop his next minor ailment. But it was with cheer that Dr. Linder issued the script for the dyspepsia, for what is the good in—

Knowing what happened, whose account would be awarded veracity, is a matter for the court. Records indicate a sudden intrusion, a disruption of business, a rough and disorderly charge by four Narcotics Division agents, a search and an arrest on the afternoon of Saturday, April 1, 1922. At four o'clock, while Dr. Linder was examining a female patient, with other patients still waiting, the law burst in upon him and, "boisterously and in an ungentlemanly and forcible manner," took charge of his office. While Dr. Linder protested, the agents showed their Treasury Department badges, telling him, "This is sufficient."[3] After a rowdy search, they took him off to jail, where he was indicted under the Harrison Act in a word-for-word repetition of the recent Behrman indictment, though Dr. Behrman had issued script for over three thousand doses of heroin, cocaine, and morphine to a single "patient," Willie King, and charged a small fee for each dose. Dr. Linder had done nothing of the sort.

So what warrant went before said intrusion? What had Dr. Linder done wrong? It was for the courts to decide how events had trans-pired between him and I. earlier that same day—memory belonged to them alone. But whatever I. may have remembered, her testimony convicted Dr. Linder in the district court, and if the court saw right through her, it nonetheless favored her version over his. Known by the name of Ida Casey, I. was an instrument of the law, her cravings turned against him.

Written into the transcript of record, her account went like this: "Sure I was working for the bulls." And: "Ain't that unreal." What Ida Casey didn't say was, that's the way it always was with stoolies: if you got pinched, you spoiled or you went to jail. If you went in the hold, not only were you in the hold, but you couldn't get any dope. The pen was two pens then, so thinking it over was unnecessary "when the buttons fingered me to peach. Aw, you wouldn't understand." On the instructions of said buttons, and with the promise of freedom this one time, Ida Casey put on her best ritz and paid a visit to Dr. Linder's office, where she plainly told him that she was a fiend, according to herself. She didn't say whether she had got a little hopped before going in to see him, or if her memory of that visit was at all addled. She testified that she was a known addict. She was called upon to emphasize this point. The police, for example, knew her well, too well. Thus, when Dr. Linder dispensed to her three small tablets of cocaine and one of morphine, he knew, she claimed, that he was giving the drugs "to a person of habit, in the maintenance of that habit, neither in the treatment of any illness nor in the exercise of withdrawing her from the drugs to which she was addicted."[4]

In his version, she complained of a painful abdominal ailment consistent with an ulcer or a cancer. What Charles O. Linder didn't say was that I. fascinated him, with something unspoken, somehow charismatic, emanating from the complainant, her skirted insouciance notwithstanding. She told him, Linder said, that the doctor who regularly treated her was away from Spokane. He testified that he did not know she was an addict. How could he have missed it; I. could not have been using such preparations for much above a year; and anyway, there was something else about her more corkscrewed than that. The court was reminded of Dr. Linder's degree and license, his membership in a medical association, his contributions to ozone injection. Following a personal interview, he prescribed the medicine in question according to his best judgment as an experienced practitioner, Dr. Linder told the court—in modest quantity, in treatment of a bona fide ailment, and, above all, in good faith.

What the court says goes. In convicting him, the lower court decided that Dr. Linder erred when he put narcotics

> in the possession or control of Ida Casey with the intention on the part of the defendant that Ida Casey would use the same by self-administration in divided doses over a period of time, the amount of said drugs dispensed being more than sufficient or necessary to satisfy the cravings of Ida Casey therefor if consumed by her all at one time; that Ida Casey was not in any way restrained or prevented from disposing of the drugs in any manner she saw fit and that the drugs so dispensed by the defendant were in the form in which said drugs are usually consumed by persons addicted to the habitual use thereof to satisfy their cravings therefor and were adapted for consumption—contrary to the form of the statute in such case made and provided and against the peace and dignity of the United States.[5]

The particulars of Dr. Linder and I.—a shade of blue, the missing hook on Ida's left boot, the stains of tincture on Linder's thumb and index finger, the canon of coughs coming from the waiting room, the mud puddle outside the front door—give way to the thousands of prosecutions of physicians under the Harrison Act between 1915 and 1928, all some version of Behrman or Linder, those rightly convicted for the wrong reasons, and those vindicated in vain, and the indictments that never went to trial. The one and only Ida Casey goes down as less than a footnote; the receipt of that one Get Out of Jail Free card shows her as the recidivist she probably was—a probability to which scores of anonymous Idas attest—and predicts her eventual Return to Jail.

In reconsidering Dr. Linder's conviction, the Supreme Court also reconsidered the lower court's version of Ida Casey, noting that "the unfortunate condition of the recipient certainly created no reasonable probability that she would sell or otherwise dispose of the few tablets intrusted to her."[6] The court hereby refrained from diagnosing the scores of other Idas that composed an addict class, and restored medical authority to the doctors:

> The Narcotics Act says nothing of "addicts" and does not undertake to prescribe methods for their medical treatment. They are diseased and proper subjects for such treatment, and we cannot possibly conclude that a physician acted improperly or unwisely or for other than medical purposes solely because he has dispensed to one of them in the ordinary course and in good faith, four small tablets of morphine or cocaine for relief of conditions incident to addiction, and we cannot say that by so dispensing them the doctor necessarily transcended the limits of that professional conduct with which Congress never intended to interfere.[7]

Found, in his turn, not to have interfered with the collection of revenue—the practice with which the Congress did, by contrast, intend to interfere—Linder found his 1922 district court conviction overturned in a unanimous decision by the higher court in 1925. What the Supreme Court says is, was. Dr. Linder was no longer guilty, and maintenance was no longer in the congressional or judicial bailiwick. Although the right to determine their own professional conduct was restored, the reputations of thousands of doctors had been irreparably damaged in the course of repeated trials of the Harrison

"Health Talks by Dr. Charles O. Linder," *Spokane Daily Chronicle*, March 22, 1930. Reproduced by permission from the Spokesman-Review Newspaper Library.

Act, and these cases had the cumulative effect of deterring many doctors from prescribing narcotic drugs to patients for years to come.

If I., in an odd free moment, ever returned to the physician's neighborhood, ever revisited Dr. Linder's cabinet to find it locked, windows unwashed, once overturned chairs now uprighted but facing helter-skelter, of this there is no written record. For the doctor's addresses on hygiene, exercise, God and health, and the benefits of Ultra Violet, there is an advertisement in the *Spokane Daily Chronicle* years later. Of rainfall in Spokane in 1922, '23, '24, '25, the years Charles Linder spent in court and out of work, dry and bootless graphs. I. offered periwinkles of Falsehood to liven the account. She never wore the shoe and lace invented here, though the one and only Ida Casey must have worn something on her feet, a something unknowable, perhaps even then. "It may be that, with sufficient imagination, a novelist might invent a past for the world that would perfectly fit onto what we know, and yet be quite different from the real past."[8] Like the near future. Now never mind the boots. Invent the peace and dignity of the prosecuted.

26 A SET OF FALSE TEETH IN ITS STOMACH

We last left Harry dying on the vine in Venezuela longing for a more cosmopolitan assignment, one closer to the corridors that line the halls of power, or at least something in a more reasonable climate. We can believe that Harry wanted nothing more than to leave La Guaïra where it was hotter than hell. The juggler was there, with his basket, his snakes, his mongoose, and his arrangements for growing a tree from seed to foliage to ripe fruitage before one's eyes; in sight were plants and flowers. Finally, in 1926, Harry was reassigned. And that sudden invasion of purple gloom fissured with lightnings—then the tumult of crashing thunder and the downpour and presently all sunny and smiling again.[1]

Suddenly, the machine in the garden: a heavy tramcar honking its gong slewed between.[2] Remember the lot of Altoona. Better yet, the verdant Hollidaysburg. Though it is still hot in Nassau, there is plenty of traffic. Harry's new post will bustle with commerce, the coming and going of carriers, the import and export of goods. For all his hatred of La Guaïra, Harry's reassignment occasions a short personal essay in which he strikes an ambivalent pose. In "The Assignment, or Infinite Echoes" (possibly to be retitled "Infinite Echoes, or the Assignment," according to his own marginal notation), Harry points out the inevitable irony: you have come to love the post you had at first protested and now reject the prospect of the post you would have loved last time around.[3] Now Harry reflects on his initial approach to La Guaïra:[4]

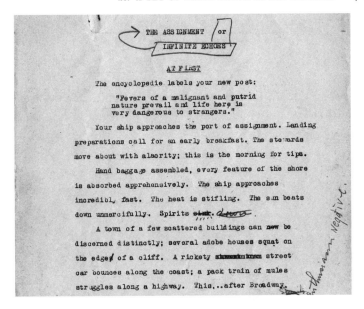

As he recalls his arrival at the tropical destination, his new post, "Spirits"—Harry has crossed out "sink"; he has crossed out "down." It is hard to descrive. Over time, the appointee, the assignee, becomes accustomed if not acclimated to that which he had previously only feared. He has even been able to identify some local charms. Like the railroad. By the time headquarters in its wisdom relocated him, "at last," Harry notes his "qualms about leaving the glorious sunshine, superb bathing, the swaying palms, the fresh fruit, the overhanging cliffs, the stupendous mountains."

The new post is in the north—"climate cold clammy"— Spirits sink. down . There is the irony—catch it if you can. Harry has never had more trouble editing his own typewritten prose: "repeat" and "ad infinitum" are x'ed out, retyped, re-x'ed out. He writes by hand:

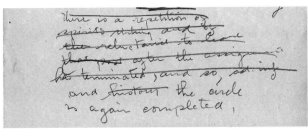

History never had a chance. Anslinger's prose is unalarming, weaker than moonlight; his crossings-out reflect his doubt that his prose is working at all. He tries again. His transfer. His ironical emotions as he is reassigned.

Finally, Harry's *Spirits sink—ad infinitum*, infinite like the coastline, sinking like the spirits aboard the leaky rum-running vessels he will attempt to interdict in the Caribbean pit stop en route to the United States. This piece of prose is as close as Harry will ever get to getting lost in the tropics, or to succumbing to its "spells," as his anonymous colleague had it, dripping with sweat as well as minor irony:

> **La Guaïra, I love you,—fleas and banana,**
> **I'm here to stay,—HASTA MAÑANA.**[5]

Gaining sixteen degrees on the ladder of latitude and losing seven longitude, Harry went to Nassau to work as consul under Brigadier General Lincoln C. Andrews in 1926. Andrews was a career army man who had just been appointed by Secretary of the Treasury Andrew Mellon to head a reorganization of the Prohibition Unit. Nassau was a favorite hotbed for rumrunners, who ran raw materials up to the United States, and ran liquor from the Bahamas to Nova Scotia and Cuba, landing and unloading liquor that would leak across the borders into the States, and lying about where they had come from, what they were carrying, and where they were going. In conferences in London and Paris, Harry put his administrative zeal for prohibition to work. That is, he put his administrative zeal to work for Prohibition, persuading Great Britain to require each ship to record a destination when it left port, and then to prove that it had in fact been there, with a landing certificate to be filed when the ship came back through Nassau. General Andrews personally witnessed Harry's testimony, his powers of persuasion, his cool head, his attention to certification. For negotiating this new mandatory form, Harry would be noticed, and rewarded. Mellon himself would borrow Anslinger to achieve similar agreements with Canada, France, and Cuba.

While in Nassau, Harry investigated the question of attacks attributed to sharks. Anecdotal evidence convinced him that barracudas were solely responsible for attacks on swimming human beings, and sharks only came in to swallow what had already been killed, and to take the rap. He published an article in defense of sharks in the *Saturday Evening Post*.[6] Dismissing the "overdrawn" reports that poured in from readers and eyewitnesses in Australia and Hawaii, among other places—who objected that it was irresponsible to print material that might lead people to imprudent bathing—Harry held his watery ground. Just because a shark had "a human skull and a set of false teeth" in its stomach, or "a hand, a knee, two whole arms, one leg bone and the first and second cervical vertebra [sic]," along with "a pair of swimming trunks," or a little native boy, that didn't prove anything.[7]

> The shark could have severed the head of a dead body as well as that of a live body. . . .
> Whether the shark had killed the man or swallowed the corpse of someone drowned at sea remains a matter of conjecture. The shark's stomach gave mute evidence.[8]

Thus, in Nassau, holding fast to his false belief, Harry coughed up the metaphor for which we have been casting: "It is difficult for our plastic minds to discard the shark bugaboo and to fear the real enemy."[9] Here is the killing irony, and I don't mean the barracuda. Harry's argument may be a little hard to swallow (though surely no harder than a knee or vertebra), but his interest in shark attacks is noteworthy, if only because it is the most idiosyncratic thing in his entire archive, and does seem to indicate that identifying enemies was an ongoing preoccupation. It is not difficult for our plastic minds to imagine that subsequent eyewitness accounts—from Hawaii, Australia, and New Jersey—of shark attacks on humans failed to change Harry's mind.[10] A similar commitment to a folder full of drug bugaboos, tales of the barracuda, and the metaphorical piranhas, or pariahs, that are dealers and addicts, would soon prevent Harry from registering evidence about actual drug use.

Back in the Keystone State in 1926, Philadelphia made the news with the First World Conference on Narcotic Education, which was convened as a meeting of the American Pharmaceutical Association and held on the roof of the Bellevue-Stratford Hotel. The meeting ran high with emotion as Captain Hobson, the president of the International Narcotic Education Association, charged the Treasury Department and Bureau of Public Health with suppressing a report commissioned in 1918. The missing report, initially issued in 1924, estimated that there were one million addicts in the United States, though it had since been lost, according to the feds. Hobson persisted:

> But I found a copy in the Library of Congress. Then we asked for a copy from the Public Printer. He answered that the type had been ordered destroyed by the Treasury Department. Then Congressman Rainey asked the Secretary of the Treasury for two copies for himself and fifty copies for distribution. He got them.[11]

The government's unsuppressed estimate was of a different order of magnitude; Uncle Sam reckoned there were 110,000 or 120,000 addicts. Statistics were debatable, institutionally located, politically motivated.

An agency could and would use information to its advantage, presenting statistics in ways that would mitigate toward certain political conclusions, and ultimately decisions about its warrant, its budget, its tactics, its effectiveness, and so on. For example, in its 1926 annual report *Traffic in Opium and Other Dangerous Drugs*, the Treasury Department summarized the year in the quantities of time sentenced, that is, 10,342 violations and 5,120 convictions amounted to 6,797 years, 11 months, 10 days in prison. In 1928, 8,653 violations and 4,738 convictions was recorded as 8,786 years, 4 months, 28 days of prison time.[12] This framing of the information valued prison time as a measure of justice served with respect to drug violations. Prison time was the end of the equation.

One set of statistics persistently challenged the Treasury's law enforcement efforts:

> Between January 1920 and February 1929, 187 agents were fired or forced to resign for "intoxication and misconduct," 121 for "extortion, bribery, or soliciting money," and 118 for "unsatisfactory service and insubordination." A total of 752 agents, or 28 percent of the agents employed, were dismissed for collusion, dereliction

of duty, submitting false reports, perjury, illegal disposition of liquor, and embezzlement, and other charges.[13]

Alcohol agents were considered more vulnerable to corruption than narcotics officers, partly because the former were a poorly paid lot, and were not required to take civil service exams, while the latter were. Oversight and accountability eluded the alcohol agents, who were, statistically speaking, more "touchable" than their buddies in narcotics; bribes, booze, and the barrel end of a gat touched many an agent.

Gunshots rang out in hotel lobbies and outside their front doors, like the thousand rounds of rat-a-tat-tats that ripped through the Hawthorne Inn as Hymie Weiss pockmarked Al Capone's own hotel in Cicero in 1926. Capone and his ilk had transformed Cicero from a "typical American community" just west of Chicago, replete with Rotarians, Kiwanis Clubbers, and Lions, into a hotbed of racketry: "Overnight, Cicero seceded from the Volstead United States and went wilder West, and wilder wet, than Chicago."[14] A local saloonkeeper described a situation that was perhaps not atypical, even beyond the environs of Chicago:

> **When the cops and the prohibition agents come here after hours all the time to get drunk, why, of course, they go along with us. They always tip us off to the raids. An injunction means nothing.**[15]

Many of Al Capone's closest associates had never heard of him when the police came around the next day, temporarily sober and asking questions. Capone was invisible too, or so said eyewitnesses, which is how he stayed alive so long. And Cicero and Chicago played the Sherwood Forest of the Midwest where lone gangsters were either credited with redistributive justice or blamed for the crimes of invisible syndicates, and either way earned outsized legends.

Ever since he'd seen Giovanni roughed up on the tracks in Altoona, Harry'd been seeing the syndicates that others couldn't see, and Prohibition proved him right. Prohibition seemed to be the main event, bootleggers the bogeymen of law enforcement in the 1920s. Alcohol was the only real contraband in question, and newspapers and movies abounded with stories of busts. Not that there weren't drugs—just that the black market in narcotics wasn't as large or developed as that in alcohol, and culturally speaking, recreational drugs were no more than short fringe on the flapping skirt of booze.

And booze it was that busied Harry in the Bahamas, when he wasn't observing barracuda behavior in shark's clothing. Harry's formal innovation in the procedures of Prohibition, the form for tracking traffic, with which he prevailed in London and Paris, drew the attention of the Treasury, which would bring him into its fold and out of the State Department. When Brigadier General Lincoln Andrews, who had worked with Harry in London, handpicked him and installed him in Washington as chief of the Division of Foreign Control in the Prohibition Unit late in 1927, all those intervening latitudes collapsed. Harry now had a position which would allow him to engage in the combination of diplomacy and covert operations that was already his signature. He never left headquarters again.

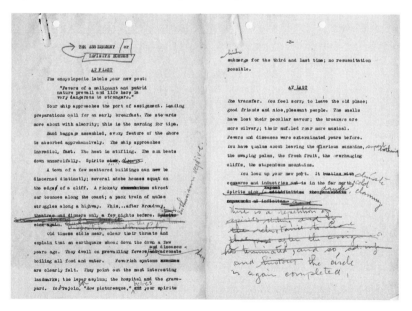

27 PROHIBITION AS SUBSTANCE:

Putting the Bureau in Bureaucracy

Over there, over there, in The Hague, Harry had put on ideological weight: His patriotic sentiments had been actuated in the moment of great war, world war, then calcified in the tropics with nothing to do but watch over third-rate trade, and finally fully realized, optimized, buffed, and polished in the mold of Prohibition, which the United States clownishly modeled in the global fishbowl of the Caribbean. He had brushed shoulders with greatness that one day. As he moved up through consular oversight of import-export, from station to station, as he came closer and closer to sitting in the seat his ass was carved for, in a certain office chair in the Treasury, Harry crafted a persona and completed a small collection of beliefs that would fill the compartments of his mind and remain there unchanged for the rest of his career. He adopted this very finite set of ideas in the mode of law enforcement, no jurisdiction too tricky, no bootleg operation

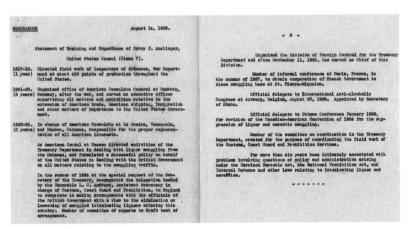

"Statement of Training and Experience," 1929. Harry J. Anslinger Papers, Special Collections Library, The Pennsylvania State University Libraries.

so covert that he could not uncover it with the equal and opposite operations of agents.

As chief of the Division of Foreign Control in Washington, Harry proposed ever more measures.[1]

> **At the offices of this company should be kept (1) an alphabetically arranged central register containing data regarding all persons with whom the company has in anyway [*sic*] come into contact; (2) a sales register, containing the names of approved customers in the order of their registered numbers, and (3) a register of all purchases made.[2]**

Because more than anything else, Treasury agents needed operational expertise—they needed, that is, to outflank, outpace, outspend, outshoot, outnumber, outwit, and otherwise outman bootleggers, but not to study the sciences of alcohol or its effects on individuals and collectives, or to familiarize themselves with current research. In this sense, Harry's intelligence was formal, police-procedural. He neither had nor needed substantive knowledge relative to the sciences of alcohol and its effects, nor had he studied law or history. He had read neither political philosophy nor literature. His on-the-job training in Europe extended to a self-taught tutorial in narcotics smuggling when the matter picked up postwar. For this reason, among others, Harry's work in alcohol prohibition was all the training he needed, or got, for his post as drug commissioner; Harry's complete lack of scientific or medical education would not disqualify him for leadership in the field. A rising through the ranks took the form of a series of appointments in tracking, then policing, international traffic.

Traffickers ran circles around agents of all stripes. There was drama on- and off-screen, the hotfooting it in and out of hotel rooms, shooting 'em up, like the Marx Brothers those gangsters, the Mafia lurking in every immigrant, Which staying one step ahead of Whom, tires screaming as the car pulls out, the whistle ditto the train, the ship to shore, the story of the young man who hailed from Altoona, equipped with a set of answers he'd never have to question. Like a bat out of hell out of the building, the alley, round the corner of the street, the ave. Out of town. Out of the city, county, state. Out of the jurisdiction. Out of the country. Crossing national boundaries was the gauntlet thrown down by the trafficker, the dare mission. Harry double-dared; Harry double-crossed. Harry did traffickers one better, believing about alcohol what he would say explicitly about drugs: "There are no national boundaries in our work. You can't afford national sovereignty when you're trying to break up the narcotics racket."[3]

Alcohol prohibition in the United States amounted to pure farce, deadly for sure, but comedic in essence given the bald ubiquity of alcohol. Nothing unknown about it. Sin won, hands down. In 1929, Harry rose to the rank of assistant commissioner of the Bureau of Prohibition. He believed or professed to believe that Volstead would work, if only enforcement could be improved.[4] The same policies that Harry would endorse and implement relative to drug prohibition got a trial run with alcohol, such as coordination among government agencies, mandatory sentencing, and harsh penalties. Harry believed that these strategies would deter trafficking. He was not alone, as the Wickersham Report would soon reveal, though he was in a diminishing minority.[5]

Though Prohibition had been moved in the mid-1920s to the Department of Justice, the Narcotics Division had remained in the Treasury through the decade. Drug prohibition gestated in the liminal zone between departments, notably Justice and the Treasury. In another interdepartmental zone, in January of 1929, Harry traveled to Ottawa to attend a conference on commercial smuggling between Canada and the United States. He did so in his capacity as "liaison officer between State and Treasury Departments," an occasional title that acknowledged the inadequacy of any one department to oversee the work of prohibition.

Then, on June 9, 1930, President Hoover signed a bill designed by Representative Stephen G. Porter of Pennsylvania to create the Federal Bureau of Narcotics. The functions of the Bureau of Narcotics would be "closely parallel" to those of the Bureau of Prohibition, which was also housed in the Department of Justice.[6] Secretary of the Treasury Andrew Mellon immediately appointed Harry J. Anslinger as acting commissioner of the new bureau. Harry's by-then background in Prohibition stood him in good stead as he strode toward the office that would define his career as well as US drug policy in the twentieth century.

Having made a ripple in the pond of Prohibition, Harry was now poised to make a splash in Narcotics, even if he had to make waves to do it. Harry was just one more appointment away from heading the new agency, but arguably more qualified men sought the post as well. Although he lacked a medical background, Harry had the short-lived support of the American Medical Association, as well as the National Association of Retail Druggists. In another of Harry's corners were those pharmaceutical companies to which he would award the few coveted legal licenses to produce narcotics for medical purposes: Merck, Mallinckrodt, and New York Quinine & Chemical Works in Brooklyn. Harry further benefited from the advocacy of a senator and representative from Pennsylvania, and California state senator Sanborn Young (who twice wrote to Hoover on Anslinger's behalf, and mobilized the support of Paul Shoup, president of the Southern Pacific Railway, among other magnates). But perhaps the most important man on Harry's team was the one who most nearly cornered the market on news, who made and broke careers for breakfast, William Randolph Hearst, who would publish the message and assist the messenger for years to come.[7] Hearst might publish anything he pleased, but he could honestly, truthfully say about Harry that the latter was one heck of a bureaucrat.

On September 23, 1930, President Hoover appointed Harry J. Anslinger as the first commissioner of the newly established Federal Bureau of Narcotics. He was confirmed by Congress in December, a day after his bureau made a spectacular one-million-dollar drug bust. Thus Anslinger the commissioner was constituted. Martha Anslinger looked like opera might come out of her lungs or Groucho Marx might come out from under her skirt, and cheerful for all that. Harry was heavier now, but he still had the bearing of the aspiring concert pianist he had once been. The rest is history. The rest is, he could hardly have done differently. The rest is, if it hadn't been Harry, it would have been someone else like him. There were others like Harry, guys who didn't even know the meaning of *le cafard*, guys with their own version of "Kaiser," patriots galore. Guys who *biff bang crack*—there have always been guys who *biff bang crack*. But it was Harry.

28 THE FEDERAL BUREAU OF POLITICS

With Camel Hair Glued Over Them

Though it seemed to many that the world was coming to an end at the end of 1929, for Harry, it was just the beginning. In 1930, the Federal Bureau of Narcotics was established, inaugurating Harry's long reign as drug czar. With his appointment, Harry launched a thirty-year speaking tour, a veritable odyssey through oceans of faces, all kinds of audiences, including law enforcement authorities, pharmaceutical industry and pharmacist association events, and civic and social clubs. Harry spoke to organizations like the Women's Christian Temperance

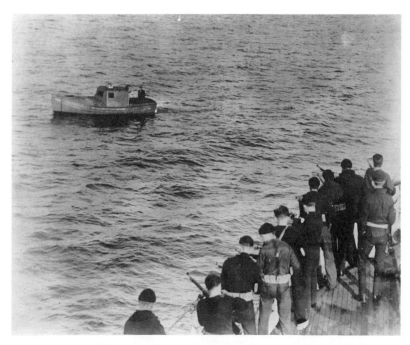

Coast Guard cutter USS *Seneca* chasing and capturing a "rumrunner," 1924. The Library of Congress Prints and Photographs Division, Coast Guard Collection, LC-USZ62-50077.

Union and the Benevolent and Protective Order of Elks. In most of his addresses, Harry traced the history of antidrug legislation in the United States. He led listeners through the international treaties to which the United States was, or should be, bound: The Hague Opium Convention of 1912; The Geneva Drug Convention of 1925; The Narcotics Limitation Convention of 1931. Anslinger frequently argued that the need to comply with these conventions obligated the United States to adopt federal legislation. Then he would wax increasingly poetic about the terrible ravages of narcotics and the evils of those who traffic in them. He won the women. Go figure.

Altoona's population peaked at eighty-two thousand in 1930. If there had ever been dirt in downtown Altoona, no sign remained, though a rain might remind citizens of the old mud, the return of the compressed under the tarred roads. Governor Pinchot had campaigned on a pledge to pave the rural roads of Pennsylvania, and pave he had. But after a rain on a hot summer day, steam might sizzle up from bituminous surfaces all over the state, and under that the very earth that used to count as dirt. Dust having long since become grime, now dirt stood for a primeval Altoona, for the floor of a farm back before the memory of any Altoonans who could make it out to the Logan Theater, which would open on Eleventh Avenue in 1938. Any Altoonans who passed through in the thousand years before that left the dirt floor much as it had been before.

Originally Altoonan Commissioner Harry J. Anslinger made the rounds of towns not unlike his own, and towns very much unlike his own, reaching out to the standard-bearers of value from coast to coast. The message depended on the audience with Harry. To social clubs, he bemoaned the threat from narcotics to youth, families, and neighborhoods in narratives that echo his propagandistic writing in magazines. He adjusted his diction again as he told reporters about his crusade against horse dopers, detailing his tactical prowess.[1] To law enforcement officials, Harry appealed for cooperation, carefully stating the limitation of the federal government in dealing with drug traffic, diplomatically deferring in cases "over which the Federal government has no jurisdiction."[2]

In his 1931 address to the International Association of Chiefs of Police in St. Petersburg, Florida, for example, Harry began with his habitual timeline: the use of opium by Egyptians and Persians, and references to opium in writings by Homer. From there, Harry expanded to the East, tacitly justifying contemporary prosecution of Chinese drug lords in the United States and paving the way for some strong accusations against post-revolutionary China. He identified drug use as early as the Tang Dynasty, seventh century CE, and brought the police up to date with the litany—Shanghai convention, 1909, and Hague convention, 1912, the latter of which, Harry pointed out, the United States was the first to ratify. Opium was still being grown "in faraway India" with impunity in 1933, the government of British India promising to "end its distasteful but profitable export business in the sinister drug by 1935."[3]

The cost of noncompliance with conventions was civilization, as a State Department press release of February 25, 1936, indicated. Released by Mr. Stuart Fuller, assistant chief, for publication in the newspapers the next morning, this top-secret report referred to narcotics as "the menace to civilization and to the human race" and went on to descrive that menace: devastating deterioration, delusion, and death. Confidential intelligence was disclosed confidentially to the readers, methods of smuggling you would not believe:

> **Hollow heels of shoes, brass bedsteads, grindstones, journal boxes of railway cars, camel saddles, automobile cushions, bibles, coffins, and even tombstones have been found to have drugs concealed within. Bricks of hash had been glued to camels' humps, with camel hair glued over them.[4]**

Imagination was stirred. "An apparently innocent shipment of ozokerite" turned out to be heroin. Egypt was exotic. "Not long ago a caravan of camels arrived at the Egyptian Land frontier." Ladies were a padded lot. Men were for martinis. "He went up to one camel and stroked it." Harry recounted the mischief of the international trafficker, and he tied up his business in neat statistics by the end of the speech. Not unusual were such luncheons. Camels' humps were smoothed over in the office of the Permanent Central Opium Board; well-fanned shirt collars prepared each year a statement showing, in respect of each country or territory for the preceding year:

(a) The estimates in respect of each drug;

(b) The amount of each drug consumed;

(c) The amount of each drug manufactured;

(d) The amount of each drug converted;

(e) The amount of each drug imported;

(f) The amount of each drug exported;

(g) The amount of each drug used for the compounding of preparations, exports of which do not require export authorizations.[5]

With a metaphor that recalled his textbook of yore, Harry ended his speech to the police with a plea for increased cooperation:

> There should be team-work to transform the squeaking, creaking, unwieldy, awkward enforcement machinery into a well-oiled, efficient mechanism, to work with such precision and telling effect that the people of this country will again place confidence in those who are their protectors against evil forces seeking to destroy the foundations of society.[6]

Harry also spoke on the foundations of society, or on the floor of Congress, anyway, testifying for and against various legislation, for the maintenance or expansion of his budget, before key committees.

And Harry did a lot of things sitting at a desk rather than standing at a podium. He oversaw the legal market in narcotics, controlling the licenses of pharmaceutical companies to distribute synthetics as that market exploded midcentury. By the end of the 1930s, Harry's small list of favored companies expanded to include Hoffman-LaRoche, Parke-Davis, Eli Lilly, and E. R. Squibb & Sons. He attempted to collect data that was statistically meaningful on a national level. He assigned personnel to cases of interstate trafficking and other federal violations—that's where things began to get clandestine. He didn't piss off too many people above him. An appointee has to play it just right; Harry played it just right. His media campaigns were well placed, well supported, and reached a large audience in newspapers and magazines. Which helped, in turn, with the lobbying.

When Harry took office as commissioner of the newly formed Federal Bureau of Narcotics in 1931, he assumed new responsibility for a process that had already been underway for four years—the drafting of a Uniform State Narcotic Drug Act. In compliance with the Harrison Act, the vast majority of states already had legislation on the books prohibiting the sale and/or possession of cocaine and opiates, and a handful had prohibited the possession of syringes. But the laws were inconsistent, as were the penalties for violations, and all too often, given the states' limited budgets and the constraints of jurisdiction, the feds made a disproportionate number of busts. A Uniform State Narcotic Drug Act would standardize legal practices surrounding enforcement of Harrison, like, and yet unlike, a pharmacopoeia.

Initially, marijuana was not covered by the Harrison Act, and neither was it in Harry's sights as he sought to get the Uniform State Act adopted by more states, but he heard complaints from jurisdictions in the Southwest and the Pacific Northwest. New Orleans, too. Self-fashioned experts offered early commentary in that hotbed of narcotic mischief. In 1931, Dr. Fossier addressed the Louisiana State Medical Society with a paper called "The Marijuana Menace," while Dr. Stanley ventured into politics with his "Marijuana as a Developer of Criminals."[7] As a busy port city, New Orleans had its share of publicity showing that drugs came in from out of the country on boats, and narcs were there on the scene to bust up the rings. Deportation recurred as a solution, something to get narcotics offenders farther out of town than prison, part of the cyclical looping of immigration restriction—the 1930 Fish Bill had reauthorized the deportation of foreign violators.

Following the campaign of prosecuting doctors, and a few high-profile cases like Wally Reid's, it was widely agreed that cocaine and opiates were socially detrimental, but marijuana was a little-known substance as the drafting process began for the Uniform State Narcotic Drug Act in 1925. Intended for states to sign on to individually, the act represented Volstead-like prohibition legislation applied to narcotics and, like any state-by-state legislative strategy, was proceeding slowly. For the first five years of his term, Harry's principal objective was to pass the act. During this period, he tended the garden of international cooperation, he seeded political alliances in Washington and beyond, he licensed (and withheld licenses from) pharmaceutical companies, he primed the pumps of undercover work, and he set about to popularize marijuana as a major social problem.

For this purpose, it helped Harry to have friends like William Randolph Hearst in the media.[8] Not that there's anyone else in media like William Randolph Hearst.[9] Newspapers liked Harry because he and the Federal Bureau of Narcotics fed them stories that in turn fed the public appetite for juicy stories—crime stories were all the rage—which in turn boosted sales, even while serving the "public good." And if the media created the appetite for such stories, well, the people were biting and buying. And Harry and his agents were feeding. It was a righteous life cycle.

But publicity, like or unlike a camel, could bite back. As observers waited to see if newly elected president Roosevelt would reappoint or replace Harry, the latter wrote a problematic memo to agents describing an informer, Edward Jones, as unreliable and unsatisfactory. With reference to his personal features, Harry wrote further that Jones "might be termed a ginger-colored nigger."[10] Anslinger was criticized throughout the administration for this affront, which reached the president, who would never speak this way, as the assistant secretary of the Treasury was quick to state. Pennsylvania senator Guffey called for Anslinger's resignation, protesting on behalf of Pennsylvania's Black citizens. Yet Harry rode out the scandal, buoyed by the pharmaceutical lobby, the Hearst enterprises, claims for bureau heroics and declining drug use, and political allies. In 1934, Harry faced qualified competition, as well as dissension from within his own ranks, as his deputy commissioner, Louis Ruppel, agitated against him. Yet Anslinger was reappointed, and Ruppel hit the high road. Anslinger managed his friends and enemies carefully.

Sometimes, with friends like Harry's, who needed enemies? Harry reported knowing William G. Walker "very favorably," when he personally endorsed Walker for a position as chief of narcotics in California. Harry sent that endorsement to the California state senator who had, three years earlier, written to President Hoover twice to support Harry's own initial appointment as commissioner. Senator Young did go on to appoint Walker, but Walker went on to feed Bay Area newspapers embellished accounts ("lurid stories") of white women abducted into addiction and prostitution in Sacramento. As Harry's earlier endorsement of Walker hardened on his face, his erstwhile friend was charged with allowing reckless distortion of his records "in the interest of a hysterical campaign," and ultimately "bringing the law and the state into contempt."[11]

Closer to home, there was yet more contempt for the law and the state, colleagues who had to be handled: the office in New York frequently dealt with corruption (which didn't look so good on Harry) and sometimes was out to get him. In New York in 1931, a couple of bad agents offered a fellow agent one thousand dollars not to testify against a certain drug dealer, and Harry had to send some good agents to catch the bad ones conspiring in a speakeasy on Fifty-Second Street. Subornation, attempted bribery, and obstruction of justice were added to their names. Representatives Fiorello LaGuardia and Hamilton Fish from New York, along with Representative Loring Black, accused New York narcotics agents of interfering with the local police's handling of mobster "Legs" Diamond, as part of an intermittent effort to bring the Federal Bureau of Narcotics under investigation. New York was a perennial thorn in Harry's side, between the corruption and the liberalism—there were political and ideological differences that found different expression over the years.

Harry demonstrated his political savvy by not showing how he evaded or suppressed any investigation, not leaving any evidence of the private conversations through which he secured support that made him unfireable. With Franklin Roosevelt in office, Harry mobilized the considerable, if conservative, support he had garnered. Not only was FDR distracted with the economic woes of the country; Anslinger's odd-bedfellowed coalition of pharmaceutical execs, racetrack owners, and reforming women joined his pre-Beltway friends in pressuring Roosevelt into keeping Anslinger on. The Women's Narcotic Defense Association, for example, issued three resolutions at their Special Meeting in the Offices of the Chief Justice of the Court of Special Sessions in New York City, January 25, 1933, all supporting Anslinger and lauding his performance as commissioner.[12]

Anslinger successfully navigated both the little craft of his career and the little bureau that could through the corridors of Washington.

> **In appearance the railroad is dangerous, but there has never been an accident involving loss of life. The engine runs backwards in front of the train so that the man at the throttle has a clear view of the track in case rocks, boulders, goats or other obstructions express an intention of interfering with the normal movement of the train.**[13]

A straight line is not always the shortest distance between two points, as Harry had learned on that mountain train back in La Guaïra. And as Wally Reid learned in Yosemite at the throttle of a vehicle with no wheel, it's hard to tell who's driving the boat. Anyway, the risk is only to the progression of the narrative of progress.

Before heading home to Martha and Washington after a speaking engagement with a briefcase full of To Do, Harry fit right in. Wherever he went, Harry was at home away from home with the cops when he went to speak among them and stroke relations, "heartily commending the members of your Association on their splendid spirit of cooperation in the enforcement of the narcotic and marihuana laws."[14] Hardy har har with the good old boys of the Elks, Masons, and Lions, and decent Dashiell with the ladies, perfectly capable of blustering over a small gap in knowledge. "On the camel's hump he felt something which did not seem to be camel."[15]

29 A PLASTIC PALIMPSEST

Before Prohibition itself finally fully foundered, excluded beverages kept the Coast Guard busy with a task of Sisyphean proportions, though it pushed those proverbial pebbles from the Sandwich Islands twenty-six miles west of San Francisco and Puget Sound off the west coast, to Nantucket, Martha's Vineyard, Montauk Point, the Hamptons, and Sheepshead Bay off the east. It is commonly acknowledged that the feds never intercepted more than 5 percent of smuggled contraband at the border, though this is perhaps less a function of their infamous corruption and ineptitude and more a function of the infinitude of the border itself. Mere hundreds of agents patrolling two long coasts, one long dry border, and one long oozing sore hadn't

SS *Selma*, 1913, renamed *Chasina* in 1917. Courtesy of the City of Vancouver Archives, Major Matthews Collection.

got a prayer. According to the Department of Commerce, the National Oceanic and Atmospheric Administration, and the National Ocean Service, in figures taken in 1939–1940, the general coastline is 12,383 miles long and the tidal coastline 88,633 miles long.[1] But according to the principles of fractal geometry, the calculation depends on the length of the measuring rod; using units of measure so small they count on the scale of subatomic particles, or smaller, the US coastline is infinite. From the shore, Harry scanned for barracuda.

Under these conditions, it was easy to ship liquor to fictitious ports, and to tip off the Coast Guard to decoys while real boats unloaded nearby. These are just two of the tricks of the trade of Bill "The Real" McCoy, the most famous rumrunner ever. It turned out he was not nicknamed for not watering down his booze, but rather from a phrase in James Bond's *The Rise and Fall of the Union Club, or Boy Life in Canada* of 1881. Not *that* James Bond, not even his namesake, just another doppelganger. And not the M'Coy Leopold Bloom struggles to get away from so he can read the letter from Martha burning a hole in his pocket. The real one.

In naming boats, Canadians appropriated native North American nomenclature no less colorful than the imports of Chinese medicinal wines. Likewise, internal locutions of liquor, local patriotics, backyard poetics of preparation of potato, cactus, iodine, and burnt sugar, amounted to no less a Ma-and-Pa menagerie: Panther Whiskey, Red Eye, Cherry Dynamite, Old Stingo, Old Horsey, Scat Whiskey, Squirrel Whiskey, Happy Sally, Jump Steady, Soda Pop Moon, Sugar Moon, Jackass Brandy. The suchlike populated tubs, barrels, crates, canteens, casks, flasks, and likewise leaked from nonliteral bungholes. Labels on bootleg liquor maintaining the appearance of compliance with law were written in a code called irony:

> **Caution: do not place the liquid in a jug and put it aside for twenty-one days because it would turn into wine. . . . And do not stop the bottle with a cork because this is necessary only if fermentation occurs.**

> **Caution: will ferment and turn into wine.**[2]

With the ship of Prohibition on its way down after a decade at sea, President Hoover commissioned the National Commission on Law Observance and Enforcement in 1929, which would, among other things, assess the work of relevant federal agencies. Popularly known as the Wickersham Commission, it published in 1931 a series of thirteen reports, known as the Wickersham Report, constituting a thorough attempt to understand criminal justice on a national scale. The second of these, a "report on the enforcement of the prohibition laws of the United States," released in early January of that year, detailed what most Americans already knew: Prohibition tended to produce corruption in enforcement agencies, and failed to control alcohol production, distribution, and consumption. Given incontrovertible evidence that alcohol violations had not been effectively prevented, the votes for continuing with Prohibition came from members of the commission who—like Harry J. Anslinger—thought that enforcement had not been given a robust enough effort. Yet proposals for greater personnel and funding were no longer credible. Among those in favor of revision, Commissioner Roscoe Pound opined that "it is futile to seek a nationally enforced general total abstinence."[3] Though it concluded that the amendment was ineffective as well as unenforceable, the commission proposed revision rather than repeal of the Eighteenth Amendment: of eleven commissioners, two voted for straight repeal, five for revision, three for a further trial, and one, Commissioner Wickersham, to preserve. Harry sided with those who felt that there could be more robust enforcement, though he would later recant.

But given the mood of the country, the Wickersham Report did little to support the Eighteenth Amendment. On one side, giddiness, on the other, hysteria; Prohibition was a national, even an international, joke. The commission's ambivalence was expressed in comedic, if not farcical, terms in a much-quoted ditty by famed columnist Franklin P. Adams:

> **Prohibition is an awful flop.**
> **We like it.**
> **It can't stop what it's meant to stop.**
> **We like it.**
> **It's left a trail of graft and slime,**

It don't prohibit worth a dime,
It's filled our land with vice and crime.
Nevertheless, we're for it.[4]

The failure to suppress alcohol consumption went hand in hand with the failure to frame and address alcoholism as a public health problem. In favor of revision, Commissioner Kenneth Mackintosh suggested that Congress "take the private profit away from the criminals and make the business help support Federal and state social service, public health, child welfare and development, and the many kindred public humanitarian agencies, including teaching of the necessity of temperance."[5] This acknowledgment of the social cost of Prohibition concedes that it had definitely produced a black market run by gangsters, in increasingly centralized organizations, who purveyed alcohol with unregulated ingredients at inflated prices, ran numbers rackets among other gambling opportunities, sold women and sex, and offered the greatest inducements to corruption that organized law enforcement had ever seen, concomitantly forfeiting taxes on alcohol.

The Wickersham Commission's work represented the federal government's first attempt to tabulate the literal cost of crime to the taxpayers. Black market transactions, like most sales and purchases of alcohol and those of illegal narcotics (by definition), were criminal offenses, but they were financial offenses as well. When those sales went untaxed, the loss of revenue was considerable, and in fact, the restoration of alcohol revenue was one of the strongest arguments made for repeal. Furthermore, the enforcement of the amendment cost the federal government two-thirds of its total law enforcement budget, over and above what enforcement cost individual states. The commission estimated that $52 million had been spent on law enforcement in the fiscal year that ran from July 1929 through June 1930, and $34 million of it had been spent on enforcement of Prohibition, on top of which were unpaid taxes it was impossible to ascertain and calculate. Yet they agreed that "it should not require the dramatic effect of some lump-sum total figure to emphasize the importance and necessity, from a purely economic standpoint, of dealing adequately with the problem of preventing crime and controlling the criminal."[6]

The Wickersham Report's articulation of a particular social goal—"controlling the criminal"—suggests that "criminal" had become a nearly generic term. Categories of criminality had proliferated; and the criminal character transcended the actual commission of crime. It was a whole social element that needed controlling. Progressivism and the growing (or rather immigrating) discipline of sociology helped locate the roots of crime, the hotbed of criminals, in poor, immigrant, and racially marked urban communities, places where traditional American mores and institutions were weakest.

At the same time, other American mores were challenged by an immigrating literary text, and textual imports were subject to legal control themselves. In 1932, in the hope of publishing James Joyce's *Ulysses* domestically at long last, Random House had a French edition travel to the United States on the SS *Bremen*, while its lawyers alerted customs to its arrival. Publisher Bennett Cerf was angling for the fight, and agents did seize the book upon arrival, but then the district attorney's office took its time bringing the case. What finally lit the fire under the district attorney was news that a book pirate, one Joseph Meyers, was planning to print unauthorized copies, which would have undermined a copyright claim for Joyce. What ensued was *United States v. One Book Called "Ulysses,"* put before a single judge in November 1933. In "the monumental decision of the United States District Court rendered December 6, 1933, by Hon. John M. Woolsey, lifting the ban on 'Ulysses,'" Judge Woolsey explained that

> **Ulysses is not an easy book to read or understand. . . . It is brilliant and dull, intelligible and obscure by turns. In many places it seems to me to be disgusting, but although it contains . . . many words usually considered dirty, I had not found anything that I consider to be dirt for dirt's sake.**[7]

Woolsey had to measure *Ulysses* against this standard of obscenity: "tending to stir the sex impulses or lead to sexually impure and lustful thoughts," according to the reasonable man. The precedent had been set, in part, by *United States v. One Book Entitled "Contraception,"* and you can guess how stirring that text might have been. Satisfied that the author's intent was not pornographic, the judge found that reading Ulysses "did not tend to excite sexual impulses or lustful thoughts but that its net effect on them was only that of a somewhat tragic and very powerful commentary on the inner lives of men and women."[8]

In his defense of Ulysses in court, Morris L. Ernst articulated a cultural connection between temperance and antiobscenity sentiment (and even law), when he hypothesized that "squeamishness in literature" went hand in hand with Prohibition, and that "sex repression found vent in intemperance." In the end, the booze and the book entitled Ulysses had faced exactly the same tenure under the table: thirteen years; they were unbanned, as they had been banned—at the very same time. "The first week of December 1933 will go down in history for two repeals," Ernst claimed as he celebrated the convergence. "We may now imbibe freely of the contents of bottles and forthright books."[9]

Ernst also hailed the court's decision as a work of art in itself. Subsequent legal US editions printed Judge Woolsey's work along with the text of Ulysses and a foreword by Ernst, in which the latter estimated that Judge Woolsey "has written an opinion which raises him to the level of former Supreme Court Justice Oliver Wendell Holmes as a master of juridical prose."[10] Here is Woolsey's prose at its wildest wooliness:

> Joyce has attempted—it seems to me, with astonishing success—to show how the screen of consciousness with its ever-shifting kaleidoscopic impressions carries, as it were on a plastic palimpsest, not only what is in the focus of each man's observation of the actual things about him, but also in a penumbral zone residua of past impressions, some recent and some drawn up by association from the domain of the unconscious.[11]

Plastic palimpsest? O he can look it up in the prescriptions book. Looking through Einstein's kaleidoscope from another angle, Woolsey faces full frontally into aesthetics; he must in order to rescue Ulysses from the bunghole of indecency, the veritable dung heap of so much porn. He has no choice. Ulysses must be literature, but how to say why:

> **It is because Joyce has been loyal to his technique and has not funked its necessary implications.**[12]

Rock on, Woolsey. Joyce's prose must evidence technical skill. But here too the Honorable Judge is playing around with the boundaries of decent language; it's so tempting. God keep us from funking the necessary implications of our techniques. The judge and the two other reasonable men Judge Woolsey consulted, his trusted literary assessors, all agreed that *Ulysses* represented a sincere and serious attempt to devise a "new literary method for the observations and description of mankind," mankind whose arts are gross.[13] Woolsey concluded that,

> **whilst in many places the effect of "Ulysses" on the reader undoubtedly is somewhat emetic, nowhere does it tend to be an aphrodisiac. . . . "Ulysses" may, therefore, be admitted into the United States.**[14]

Real aphrodisiacs may not. Something for leucorrhea and emissions. Tiger wine. Two men half-blind. Must drink from the eye of the storm. Must sleep through the cure. Remedy where you least expect it. Please pass the calumet.

Boats like the *Chasina* went down, as did Prohibition, but *Ulysses* stayed afloat. Stephen Dedalus said, "History is a nightmare from which I am trying to awake."[15] And then a rocket sprang and bang shot blind and O! then the Roman candle burst and it was like a sigh of O! and everyone cried O!O! in raptures and it gushed out of it a stream of rain gold hair threads and they shed and ah! they were all greeny dewy stars falling with golden, O so lively! O so soft, sweet, soft! when all hell broke loose. O Crash! O Bang! O Bing! O Boom! O History! O Leopold! O Bloom! Flowers circulate, swiveling down rivers, vining up tall mountains, spiraling down the other sides, or lifting off and flying over, so species can cross-pollinate and C words transmigrate seawise. Then come out a big spreeish. Let off steam. A carminative. Corkscrewing down into, yet battling upward like hell out of Dodge but for what? O Cargo! O Cuba! O Contraband and Convention!! O Captain, who here can steer?

30 THE COLLECTED STORIES OF HARRY J. ANSLINGER

For all of his thirty-eight years, Harry had been the repository, the receptacle, the resting place of all kinds of stories—from scripture to health texts, railroad rules and regulations, rumors about Sicilians, references to Odysseus and the Lotus Eaters, diplomatic dope on the kaiser, stories in the newspapers, fears of Communism, laws and documents relating to Prohibition and its violation. He had been briefed on drugs and their evils, on the Harrison Act and the enforcement of it. Though he had already begun to compose his own persona in a travel diary when he joined the US legation, now, as commissioner, Harry became an authority, a status he took literally. For the next thirty years, he would author—and often coauthor—a very small number of stories, with only slight variations on the stories he had been collecting all along. But he also continued to collect them. In the service of pushing the Uniform State Narcotic Drug Act in his first years in office, Harry collected stories about a little-known drug called marijuana. Court cases and tabloids had popularized the dangers of narcotics, but there had been little said and written about marijuana; the field was his to cultivate.

Harry's bureau—picture the etymologically related piece of furniture—housed all kinds of files, memos, reports, and correspondence, most of it coming from his agents, local police, and newspapers around the country. Soon he could say, "In 1931, the marijuana file of the United States Narcotics Bureau was less than two inches thick, while today the reports crowd many large cabinets."[1] This bureau had compartments for each story he liked to trot out when it was time to give a speech, write an article or annual report, or testify before Congress.

When speaking or writing on marijuana, Harry typically began by

MARIJUANA

Assassin of Youth

Marijuana, a stalk of which is
shown above, is contributing to
our alarming wave of sex crime,
according to many police officials. The weed can be easily
recognized by its seven-bladed,
saw-tooth leaves. It grows in
stalks from 3 to 8 feet high

July 1937.

THE sprawled body of a young girl lay crushed on the sidewalk the other day after a plunge from the fifth story of a Chicago apartment house. Everyone called it suicide, but actually it was murder. The killer was a narcotic known to America as marijuana, and to history as hashish. It is a narcotic used in the form of cigarettes, comparatively new to the United States and as dangerous as a coiled rattlesnake.

That youth has been selected by the peddlers of this poison as an especially fertile field makes it a problem of serious concern to every man and woman in

friend produced a few cigarettes of the loosely rolled "homemade" type. They were passed from one to another of the young people, each taking a few puffs.

The results were weird. Some of the party went into paroxysms of laughter; every remark, no matter how silly, seemed excruciatingly funny. Others of mediocre musical ability became almost expert; the piano dinned constantly.

"Assassin of Youth," *American Magazine*, July 1937, p. 48. Harry J. Anslinger Papers, Special Collections Library, The Pennsylvania State University Libraries.

offering a little history. He located the origins of a modern drug problem in a mythical Orient:

> In the year 1090, there was founded in Persia the religious and military order of the Assassins, whose history is one of cruelty, barbarity, and murder, and for good reason. The members were confirmed users of hashish, or marijuana, and it is from the Arabic "hashashin" that we have the English word "assassin."[2]

Here, barbaric Others incriminate marijuana from the get-go; they lend the name of their own criminality to the drug, assigning assassination to its use. At the same time that the Persian assassins were smoking the hash in the Near East, medieval balladeers in Europe were tuning up their Romance languages to tell tales of heroes on adventures, sometimes singing of the setting of antiquity, such as the Trojan War, sometimes locating their heroes closer to home in time and place, as in *The Song of Roland*. The latter, identified by scholars as the original chanson de geste, the proto-romance, was composed in 1098—within eight years of the founding of Anslinger's Assassins in Persia in 1090. Those late eleventh- and twelfth-century romances are marked by simple sentence structure and spare language. Incorporating fantastic elements, episode after episode of the exploits of heroes endow their idealized characters with signature, even superhuman, strengths.

Similarly, Anslinger's public poetics tended toward the hard-boiled, making use of spare language and simple sentence structure (though in his correspondence the language is often tortured by efforts at diplomacy). And like the romances of yore, Anslinger's own tales were filled with heroes and antiheroes, endowed with almost equal and diametrically opposing superstrengths. For example, according to Anslinger's files, one murderer who had put his victim's body in a trunk had thirty marijuana cigarettes, which he had been selling in a Miami restaurant; this man explained that he was "fearless after smoking marihuana cigarettes but would not have done this without marihuana." After a gang of young men was apprehended in 1937 following a string of over thirty-five robberies, "one of the youths admitted that he had smoked 'reefers' on and off for at least 2 years, and said that when he went with the others on stick-ups, he was 'ready to tear anybody apart' who opposed him."[3] Law enforcement demonstrated matching heroics. In Columbus, police

> were called upon to investigate a disturbance on a public street, where a young man, Howard Horn, was menacing citizens with a pistol. The officer, while attempting to subdue Horn, was attacked by him and wounded three times. He was obliged to return the fire to save his own life and Horn was killed instantly. Investigation by the vice squad showed that Horn, who was 19 years of age, was a

marihuana addict and at the time of his attack on the officer was under the influence of this narcotic.[4]

Here, marijuana boosts the addict's strength, drives an attack on a police officer, and calls forth "return" fire; a force that matches his own kills Horn. The superstrength of both parties to a violent attack hearkens back to the romances of the late Middle Ages.

As much as narcotics do, the genre of *romance* ties Odysseus to Anslinger and his antiheroes, from Hereward the Wake forward: "at lower levels the Narcissus or twin image darkens into a sinister doppelganger figure, the hero's shadow and the portent of his own death or isolation." These verse and prose narratives tie the classical epics to the modern novel, according to the commonplaces of Western literary history. According to Anslinger's article, even before the Persians sealed these links, "the weed" had made an appearance in the *Odyssey*: "Homer wrote that it made men forget their homes and turned them into swine."[5] Here, Harry conflates a few episodes—mashing up the Lotus Eaters and Circe—just as he continued to do with the cases he liked to collect and re-present to sensational effect. Bearing these traces, Harry Anslinger's personal mythology is self-making, yes, but far from self-made.

In addition to drawing on literary tradition, Harry drew on expert knowledge. In a 1942 letter to the editor of the *Journal of the American Medical Association*, Harry asserted

> **the great danger of marijuana due to its definite impairment of the mentality and the fact that its continuous use leads direct to the insane asylum. . . . Marijuana precipitates in certain persons psychoses and unstable and disorganized personality.**[6]

The same letter quotes sources going back to 1838 and 1877. For years, Harry peppered his memos with the following citations: Dr. Moreau's "Du hachich et déalienation mentale" (1845), whose title speaks for itself; the French colonial Dr. Henri Bouquet's "The Insane of Tunis" (1900), which identifies "Indian hemp as an etiological factor in the greater part of mental disorders"; and Dr. Gueche's "Chronic Intoxication Led, in the End, to Hallucinatory Insanity" (1933). Harry frequently invoked a Dr. Dhunjibhoy, "the Director of one of the Hospitals for the Insane in India," who observed that the prolonged use of Indian hemp leads to insanity.[7] Indeed, in Columbus, Ohio, in 1937, "the killer of a hotel clerk blamed his deed on insanity resulting from use of the weed."[8]

Insanity and superheroic strength also pervade the "Gore Files" that Harry Anslinger and the Federal Bureau of Narcotics collected, a series of abbreviated reports of crimes involving marijuana. But these files also articulate a linchpin in the growing case against marijuana, the case for race. As portrayed in the Gore Files, the vast majority of offenses committed under the influence of marijuana were violent, notably armed robbery, murder, and rape, and southern and border states seemed most heavily afflicted with these crimes. Already in the 1930s, Black and Latino men were disproportionately arrested, and likewise identified in Anslinger's files, with phrases like "Negro, crazed by smoking marihuana." Harry's files also named those arrested for cultivating marijuana or possessing large quantities; in Ohio in 1935 alone that number includes large quantities of Latin names: Teofilo Chavez, Fred Chavez, Frank Chavez, Marjorie Chavez, Emmez Guzman, Joe Garza, Sylvestro Gonzalez, Pedro Mandez, Pedro Nieto, Salvador Capetilla, Harry Horlendez, Louis Gonzalez, Antonio Navarro, Florentino Garcia, Jesus Fierro, and Rafael Tolento.[9]

African American men posed a threat, particularly, and familiarly, to white women and girls in the Gore Files. One incident among many took place in West Virginia "before Jan 1937":

> **Negro raped a girl eight years of age. Two Negros took a girl of fourteen years old and kept her for two days in a hut under the influence of marihuana. Upon recovery she was found to be suffering from syphilis.**[10]

In 1937, in the same state, "M 26 Negro charge raping 9-year old girl."[11] These cases were used again and again—not only by Anslinger, but by other experts citing Anslinger—without any reference to whether they resulted in convictions.

Also familiarly, if and when white women appeared willing, the crime had to be slightly relocated in order to order any scene of interracial sex. In other words, it's hard to know which specter was more threatening: rape or consensual sex. Harry's files contained some observations on the matter, but what could he say about race in public, officially, especially in Roosevelt's administration, and especially since he had already made one costly gaffe? Some of Harry's files never left the bureau, never made it into print or onto the radio airwaves, and never were heard at the podium. These observations were confined to a private pigeonhole:

> **MARIHUANA**
> Colored student at Univ. of Minn.
> partying with female students (white)
> seeking and getting their sympathy
> with stories of racial persecution. Result
> pregnancy.[12]

This account lacks credibility, but it says something about Harry's fears of the social disorder that results from the combination of marijuana and non-whiteness.

These were recurring motifs in the talks that Harry gave to law enforcement associations and to the "opinion makers," members of women's clubs and men's clubs. But Harry did not just opine from the podium. He also lobbied lawmakers. And he sought to control the content of the stories about marijuana that circulated in the media:

> On radio and at major forums, such as that presented annually by the *New York Herald Tribune*, I told the story of this evil weed of the fields and river beds and roadsides. I wrote articles for magazines; our agents gave hundreds of lectures to parents, educators, social and civic leaders. In network broadcasts I reported on the growing list of crimes, including murder and rape.[13]

Harry's bully pulpit was handed to him, in significant part, by William Randolph Hearst. More than anything, this is why Harry J. Anslinger is known as a propagandist. In addition to his speaking engagements, radio gigs, and cowritten magazine articles, Harry and his stories showed up in newspaper after newspaper all over the country, decrying drugs and dealers, and singing the praises of narcotics agents. When he addressed the topic of marijuana, Harry worked from a limited repertoire, tailoring his talk for particular audiences, but his signal message never changed: marijuana is evil; it is brought into the United States by foreigners, especially men from Italy, Mexico, the Caribbean, South America, and Asia; marijuana drives people insane and turns the people weak enough to consume it into crazy evildoers—especially murderers and rapists. Marijuana threatens social order.

Even as he and his agents filled the bureau with stories, Harry redeployed them in popular magazines. When he published in the popular press, he tended to take a sensational angle. Sourceless examples of marijuana causing insanity blossom all over Harry's articles and speeches; his texts are littered with the bodies of nameless youths driven to nonsensical violence that ends in handcuffs and total incoherence. Stories that begin like this:

> Not long ago, a fifteen-year-old girl ran away from her home in Muskegon, Mich., to be arrested later in company with five young men from Detroit marijuana den.[14]

and this:

> A newspaper in St. Louis reported after an investigation this year that it had discovered marijuana "dens," all frequented by children of high-school age. The same sort of story came from Missouri, Ohio, Louisiana, Colorado—in fact, from coast to coast.[15]

and end like this:

> Staggering about in a human slaughterhouse . . . he seemed to be in a daze.[16]

This last is a quote from an article Harry cowrote with Courtney Ryley Cooper. "Marijuana: Assassin of Youth" is the paradigmatic example of Harry's penchant for sensationalism and propaganda. Published in 1937 in the *American Magazine*—a popular and well-

established periodical with broad national circulation—this article
represented the public relations arm of Harry's campaign to sell anti-
marijuana legislation. To do so, he first had to introduce the largely
unknown drug and, with it, the specters of personal and social dev-
astation. The piece opens sensationally:

> The sprawled body of a young girl lay crushed on the sidewalk the
> other day after a plunge from the fifth story of a Chicago apart-
> ment house. Everyone called it suicide, but actually it was murder.
> The killer was a narcotic known to America as marijuana, and to
> history as hashish.[17]

Locating this apocryphal scene in Chicago makes the link between
an unknown drug, crowded urban conditions (the apartment house
with at least five stories stands for urban density, if not poverty), and
illegal vice and murder (Chicago being the province of bootleggers
and gangsters).[18] Further, the article's assertion that marijuana is a
known narcotic is performative; that sentence, printed in a widely circulated magazine, makes marijuana known. Readers knew of
marijuana after reading the article, but they knew only what Harry J.
Anslinger and Courtney Ryley Cooper had to say about it. The Federal
Bureau of Narcotics files include fifty letters from readers reporting
that they first heard of marijuana in this article.

Making its appearance in "Assassin of Youth" was one of Harry's
favorite stories from the Gore Files, one that he trotted out uncountable
times over the next couple of decades. It portrays the case of a young
Mexican man rendered violently insane by marijuana:

THE MOST HEINOUS CRIME OF 1933

Victor Licata, Tampa, Florida, on October 17, 1933, while under
the influence of Marihuana, murdered his Mother, Father, Sister
and Two Brothers, WITH AN AXE while they were asleep.[19]

Anslinger used Victor Licata, again and again, as the wake-up call to
the dangers of marijuana (and Mexicans). According to Harry, Licata's case—in which the youthful addict killed his family—had woken

America to the danger of the weed. Here is Licata's cameo appearance in "Assassin of Youth":

> **"I've had a terrible dream," he said. "People tried to hack my arms off."**
> **"Who were they?" an officer asked.**
> **"I don't know. Maybe one was my uncle. They slashed me with knives and I saw blood dripping from an ax."**

Some time after the crime, Licata killed another patient in the hospital and finally hanged himself. Psychiatrists said he had dementia praecox, a long-lasting psychosis that had preceded his killing spree, but Anslinger's retelling omits this part of the record. Licata seems to have gone spontaneously crazy after smoking marijuana:

> **He had no recollection of having committed the multiple crime. The officers knew him ordinarily as a sane, rather quiet young man; now he was pitifully crazed. They sought the reason. The boy said he had been in the habit of smoking something which youthful friends called "muggles," a childish name for marijuana.**[20]

Licata's youth is central to the narrative. It makes him more susceptible to corruption—to friends bearing muggles—and also more dangerous. Harry's account of Licata's story loosely imports additional young people into the crime, friends who have no actual role in it. But now there is a muggles-bearing gang where there had been a lone crazed axe-wielder. The specter of shadowy gangs animates a great deal of Harry's writings. Marijuana performs this transformation rhetorically—one becomes many—just as it transforms sane young people into wild and crazy ones:

> **Much of other irrational juvenile violence and killing that has written a new chapter of shame and tragedy is traceable directly to this hemp intoxication.**[21]

In these tales, Harry reveals his own addiction, his habitual dependence on this one line of thought. There's a compulsive aspect to

Harry's reiterations of Licata's story and the claim that marijuana causes insanity. His conviction, his belief in the easy equations
between inner-city squalor, racial otherness, organized crime, and
drug traffic and consumption, remained virtually unchanged for the
next thirty years. Harry is unable to change course even when confronted with contradictory scientific and social scientific information, or with changing mores. Yet it would be unfair to consider Harry
closed-minded. His files contain the occasional bit of evidence that
Harry was receptive to new research, especially if it forged a link
between drugs and vice:

> **Mazhar Osman Uzman states that homosexualism was common
> among hashish addicts.**[22]

Harry was covering all his bases on every possible angle; if there was
an aspersion to cast on hash, Harry wanted to know it. (He never
sought to publicize the intelligence in this clipping.)

As reported by a number of Hearst papers, Harry tried to keep the
clippings in perspective, admonishing an agent who boasted of the
agency's voluminous files:

> **Gently Anslinger said, I don't see how those clippings are going
> to help you or the bureau. I think you'd be smarter if you concen-
> trated on getting convictions, instead of headlines.**[23]

Harry contradicted himself on the subject of sensationalism, though
he kept pushing the same stories. Later, in an attempt to double
down on the suppression strategy that is a function of prohibitionism, Harry professed to believe that any mention of drugs at all in
the media ran the risk of glamorizing the stuff. He claimed to reject
drug education programs for this reason—though it is likelier that
he rejected them more because of the liberal skew of such curricula as began to emerge in the 1950s. Just as Harry controlled the
licensing of the distribution of legal narcotics, he wanted to control
the distribution of stories about drugs. The meta-suppression media
strategy worked about as well as Prohibition did to suppress the use
of alcohol. Alcohol, drugs, and stories—and their carriers—circulated
throughout.

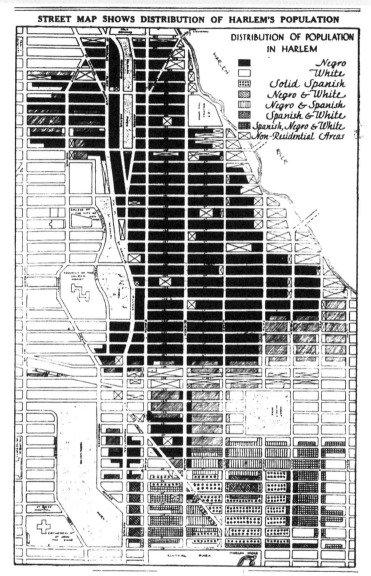

STREET MAP SHOWS DISTRIBUTION OF HARLEM'S POPULATION

DISTRIBUTION OF POPULATION
IN HARLEM

Negro
White
Solid Spanish
Negro & White
Negro & Spanish
Spanish & White
Spanish, Negro & White
Non-Residential Areas

Idleness, Harlem's Chief Threat

Negroes Lured Here When Labor Was Needed Now Find Themselves Hungry.

Harlem. This thing can be fairly singled out as the great reason for the migrations that filled Harlem to overflowing, crowded its tenements. There came, in the years after the war, a need for cheap, strong labor in New York and in other industrial areas.

Free Trains Lured Them.

From "Idleness, Harlem's Chief Threat," *The Sun*, March 23, 1935. Courtesy of the New York Public Library.

31 FUNKING THE NECESSARY IMMIGRATIONS

For drugs to circulate promiscuously in the body politic, they first had to enter that body. In Harry's reliable narrative, drugs entered the United States on the backs of foreign bodies—or hidden inside their false-bottomed commodities, or taped onto their camels—that is, with human foreigners. The introduction of opium to the United States, for example, and its spread into white communities, had long been associated with Chinese immigrants by the turn of the century. Harry had spent his time in the Bahamas in the 1920s trying to stanch the flow of alcohol from the Caribbean into the United States. Now, as commissioner, he set about to establish that "marijuana was introduced into the United States from Mexico."[1] He maintained this claim, even though he knew, and often said, that in the modern United States, cannabis plants grew wildly in many parts of the country; WPA workers, Harry noted often, were put to work uprooting them.

Even so, so stealthy were marijuana's Mexican purveyors that it, or was it "they," "swept across America with incredible speed."[2] A member of the American Coalition living in Sacramento opined:

> Marijuana, perhaps now the most insidious of our narcotics, is a direct by-product of unrestricted Mexican immigration. . . . Mexican peddlers have been caught distributing sample marijuana cigarets to school children. Bills for our quota against Mexico have been blocked mysteriously in every Congress since the 1924 Quota Act. Our nation has more than enough laborers.[3]

Abuse after abuse was heaped upon Mexicans in connection with a new social problem in a now-familiar linking of narcotics with immigrant populations, in the same breath with which they were linked with the already-chronic problem of foreigners underselling

From Frederic M. Thrasher, *Chicago's Gangland* (Chicago: University of Chicago Press, 1926). Original held in Map Collection, University of Chicago Library.

white people's labor. With variations for region of the United States, country of origin, and substance, the federal government had entertained several previous proposals for deporting violators of narcotics as well as Prohibition laws. In 1922, the Senate Committee on Immigration and Naturalization had heard estimates that as much as 98 percent, or at least 80 percent, or, anyway, the "majority" of narcotics and Prohibition violations were by foreigners, based on identification by surname. Acting Bureau of Prohibition Commissioner James E. Jones had cited the sheriff of Clackamas County, Oregon, as stating that "in looking for moonshiners he goes by the name—meaning foreign names," and the tax collector in Wichita wrote in to say that "fifty per cent of the violators in Kansas are foreigners or foreign birth or blood." Admittedly, the expert witnesses were not able to offer statistics, substituting "general information" and anecdote, or "having daily contact with arrests and convictions."[4]

Thus, at a rhetorical level—that level at which rhetoric informs policy—Mexicans threatened to bring criminality and nonproductivity with them under the sign of marijuana. Anslinger's files list twenty-one cases of seizures on the Mexican border for the year 1939 (again, without reference to convictions) for amounts as little as one joint, and in one case "the defendants admitted that the marihuana had been obtained in Mexico and smuggled into the United States."[5] For this, immigration restrictions are the prophylactic, and deportation the cure.

Not much had changed rhetorically when, ten years later, the Committee on Immigration and Naturalization held hearings on a new bill for the deportation of aliens convicted of violating narcotic laws and a new authority testified. In support of this bill, H.R. 3394, in January 1931, Commissioner Anslinger put it on record that there were "approximately 500 such deportations a year and that aliens were, indeed, at the root of the narcotics problem."[6] Prohibition was on the wane, narcotics on the wax, as Commissioner Anslinger's very presence indicated. Mexicans infiltrating the country brought the new marijuana with them across the border and, along with the Spanish language, spread it everywhere they went. The 1932 annual report of the bureau drew the map of the marijuana problem:

> **This abuse of the drug is noted among the Latin-American or Spanish-speaking population. The sale of cannabis cigarettes occurs to a considerable degree in States along the Mexican border and in cities of the Southwest and West, as well as in New York City, and, in fact, wherever there are settlements of Latin Americans.**[7]

This formulation highlights what the Mexican border has in common with New York City—they are points of entry, testaments to the porousness of national boundaries, those impossibly thin lines of thought where security and vulnerability converge. The southern border collapses into New York City, which is set to become a very efficient setting for a certain urban morality play. The character of the characters (of the dealer, addict, etc.) slips into the character of the setting (of the city).

Importing the study of modern industrial culture from Europe, American sociologists in the 1920s and 1930s turned to characterizing the big city in a new movement called "ecological community studies." This school originated with Progressivists in Chicago and spread to New York City, brought by Frederic Thrasher, among others. Born in Indiana in 1892, the same year that Harry was born in Altoona, Thrasher attended college at DePauw and went on to study sociology with Robert Park, the University of Chicago scholar who spearheaded the new approach to urban studies. Assisted by the native informants he called "superior boys," Thrasher wrote his dissertation on 1,313 gangs in Chicago. In this work, he contrasted Old World societies and mores with those of the immigrant in American cities. Focusing on the "child's social world in the modern industrial community of the metropolitan type," Thrasher explained the delinquency that arises from the confusion and inconsistency that itself arises from

> **the fact that divergent social worlds which were formerly distinct have been thrown together through modern means of communication and migration and now interact and interpenetrate, for the child at least, at many points.**[8]

In addition to the difficulty of assimilating Old World practices to a New World milieu, including the shift from a backward background to modern living conditions and communications technologies, the immigrant child goes from a monocultural setting to a multicultural one:

> **The child of the immigrant in the American city is conditioned not only by a social world represented in the cultural background of his parents but by many other sorts of backgrounds presented by his contact with other nationalities in his local community.**[9]

Thrasher's thesis became an influential text in the field of criminology, and Thrasher took a job at New York University. There, he supervised any number of graduate students who did for East Harlem what Thrasher had done for Chicago.

Those aspiring sociologists in New York matriculated downtown and did their fieldwork uptown, studying the boys' clubs of East Harlem. In this literature, the neighborhood itself was routinely described in pathological terms:

> **The street was very dirty, refuse of various kinds such as watermelon rinds, banana peelings, broken glass, old boxes and papers was everywhere in evidence . . . an empty store [had a broken window]. The sidewalks, the doorsteps, the windows, all showed people in great numbers."**[10]

It was the storied people of Ellis Island, the wretched refuse, the homeless, the tempest-tossed, who were responsible for the mess:

> **Always, where so many tongues are found, Old-World mores of mothers and fathers temper the New World habits of their boys and . . . retard their progress.**[11]

Instead of progress, this was what the retarding immigrants produced:

> **Old brick buildings row on row, dingy, dreary, drab, wash flying like strings of pennants from the fire escapes, garments of a none too selected choice; streets littered with rubbish from push carts,**

> **busy curb markets of the district; "mash" in dark heaps in the gutter, silent evidence of a flourishing illegal industry; garbage in piles, thrown from kitchens where heavy oily fare is prepared for gluttonous gourmands; penciled or chalk lines on walls and sidewalks, indecent expressions of lewd minds; ground floor shops; unattractive warehouses of dusty stock; cellar pool rooms, "drink parlors," many curtained or shuttered, suggestive of their real business; human traffic busy about nothing in this squalid congestion."[12]**

In East Harlem, immigrant populations provided fodder for all kinds of dissertations based on the proposition that pathological social conditions obtained.[13] The immigrants were "busy about nothing," producing nothing but squalor, prostitution, and drug use, not to mention looking different, talking different, wearing the wrong clothes, and eating the wrong foods. Researchers collapsed these conditions with both biological inferiority and crime, locating this collapse in East Harlem:

> **There is much delinquency and there are feeble-minded and morons in the neighborhood.[14]**

People in East Harlem came from a number of places. White ethnic populations (from Ireland and northern and eastern Europe—Poland, Germany and Scandinavia—Jews among them) formed the first large groups of immigrant settlers, many of them in the five or so decades preceding World War I. There was more than one wave of immigration from Italy, particularly southern Italy and Sicily. Yet others came from the Caribbean, including a fair number of Puerto Ricans, even before the Great Migration in the years immediately following World War II.

These groups, living in closer and closer quarters as their populations grew, accounted for the "divergent" (to use Thrasher's term) linguistic landscape. But there was also significant migration from the American South; African Americans relocated to a number of neighborhoods in Harlem, including East Harlem. In the mid-1930s, it was not uncommon to hear references to "Spanish Harlem," "Italian Harlem," and "Negro Harlem"; these collapsed into "East Harlem," or "The Barrio," over time. An editorial in *Time* magazine summed up the soup:

> **[It] is a venomous, crime-ridden slum called East Harlem [popu-lated] by hordes of Italians, Puerto Ricans, Jews, and Negroes."**[15]

In the representations offered by sociologists, among other observ-ers, immigrants brought social deviance with them, but at the same time, the pathology of the crowded city as the hotbed of social evils communicated its disease to its denizens, who were, not incidentally, poor people and people of color. East Harlem, in particular, is suscep-tible to this slippage, with its multiplicity of ethnic communities; East Harlem covers the map, providing a setting for the non-whiteness of immigrants to slip into the non-whiteness of African Americans. While Irish, Polish, German, and Jewish people managed to become white in direct relation to the proportions in which they moved out of East Harlem and into other New York City neighborhoods (or out of New York City altogether, and into Westchester, New Jersey, Long Island, and Los Angeles), those who stayed in East Harlem retained racial difference as well as responsibility for urban pathologies.[16] By dint of inner-city contiguity and shared non-whiteness, African Amer-icans, who raised the special specter of miscegenation—the contam-ination of the genome—easily came to share the marijuana burden with immigrants in the neighborhood. Deportation was not an option. That's what incarceration was for.

Ultimately more mobile than their African American peers, first-generation children had the ostensible privilege of self-invention, but generational privilege accrued to, or from, the date of arrival in the United States. Harry Anslinger himself was a first-generation Amer-ican, his most virulent distrust reserved for immigrants who had arrived only a bit later than his own parents, the Sicilians he had supervised in his hometown. Some immigrants are different from others. Harry ascended from his parents' immigration like a crab from a bucket, his Americanness shored up by the attribution of degeneracy to more recent arrivals from south, east, or west, to those who spoke less English. The discourse of immigrant pathology in East Harlem in the early 1930s was not unprecedented, not a brand-new fabrication of the sociologists—it was an acquired trait they had caught from their own parents. When Harry was just one year old, learning English as only a "native" can, the *New York Times* printed a piece on "the lawlessness and vindictive impulses of the many immigrants from southern Italy living in East Harlem."[17] Those very Italians were the ones Harry identified as the Black Hand, *La Mano Nera*, the Mafia, the kind he ran across in Altoona, and would see as the single greatest bogeymen of organized crime, more dangerous even than Communists, until his dying day.

32 THE MARIJUANA TAX ACT

Having inherited the legislative campaign to pass the Uniform State Narcotic Drug Act in individual states, Harry spent the early 1930s propagandizing against marijuana, trying to establish it as a national rather than a regional problem. Once the larger public was aware, and afraid, of marijuana—and the crimes committed under its influence—popular sentiment would tend more toward federal legislation. Harry's proficiency as a bureaucrat helped win the subscription of thirty-five out of forty-eight states by 1937, but he could see that the Uniform State Narcotic Drug Act would perpetuate some of the very problems it was intended to solve, especially with respect to enforcement. Jurisdictional issues and inconsistencies between states would undermine the efficacy of state laws. Though he didn't want

crime

The State's Attorney in a New Mexican town estimated that approximately fifty per cent of crimes of violence committed in that city are attributable to marihuana addicts. A District Attorney in New Orleans stated that it has been the experience of the Police and Prosecuting Officials in the South that immediately before the commission of many crimes the use of marihuana cigarettes has been indulged in by criminals, so as to relieve themselves from a sense of natural restraint which might deter them from the commission of these criminal acts, and to give them the false courage necessary to commit the contemplated crime. *There is*

From files on Marijuana Related Arrests [Gore Files], 1937. Harry J. Anslinger Papers, Special Collections Library, The Pennsylvania State University Libraries.

the bureau to be responsible for enforcement that was clearly beyond its capacities, he could see that federal legislation would avoid these issues; moreover, it could be used to criminalize marijuana. Many Prohibition agents had been reassigned to narcotics. For a country that had been divided on the question of alcohol, unanimity of public opinion on the evils of narcotics provided a common goal. Thus Harry had turned, as of 1935, to supporting a proposed piece of legislation known as the Marijuana Tax Act. By March 1937, when the bill was heard in Congress, it was the only real proposal on the table.

Harry had moved his machine into high gear—through access to Hearst print organs, speechifying for social clubs and law enforcement organizations, personal calls to members of Congress, and the photogenic staging of narc heroics—and as alcohol was rehabilitated, momentum gathered for federal legislation outlawing marijuana. Drafters took their cue from the National Firearms Act of 1934, which set such high taxes on machine guns that the latter were effectively outlawed. The proposed marijuana legislation would set a prohibitively high tax on marijuana—for legal tax stamp registrants, the transfer tax was one dollar per ounce; for nonregistrants, it was one hundred dollars.

This approach was developed by the Treasury's general counsel. Anslinger favored treaties as a mechanism for compelling domestic federal action, but he couldn't get his treaty working, and this bill had "the backing of Secretary of the Treasury Henry Morgenthau, who has under his supervision the various agencies of the United States Treasury Department."[1] We must forgive Harry the redundancy; he meant to stress the multiplicity of agencies at work. Referring back to the Harrison Act, Harry went on: "It is a revenue bill, modeled after other narcotic laws which make use of the taxing power to bring about regulation and control."[2]

In his famous "Assassin of Youth" article, Harry had restored rhetorical order, and he hoped to do so in life as well with his bill before Congress. Drawing on the original meaning of tax—*tassein*, "to put in order"—Harry proposed to attack organization with organization, to mobilize the power of ordering against the forces of social disorder. He reached into the right desk compartment to find a crime to fit the crime. Rape! Murder! Insanity! The sprawled body of the young girl! She appeared, again and again, like a victim of ataxia, a condition that attacks the cerebellum, causing a failure to regulate posture and muscles, and manifesting as lack of coordination, which might manifest on the larger polity as social spasticity should the many necessary and relevant agencies fail to coordinate their attack on narcotics.

The roots of taxation policy aside, scientific and medical establishments differed with each other and internally, providing contradictory evidence of the prevalence of drug addiction, the effects of different drugs, and the prospects for both medical and legal responses to drug use. Pharmaceutical companies differed too. When Anslinger brought the marijuana act before the Ways and Means Committee in 1937, there was little resistance, though there was even less familiarity with the narcotic he proposed to outlaw. Representing the American Medical Association, legislative counsel Dr. William C. Woodward gave lonely testimony against the act.[3]

Woodward was a thorn in Harry's side and Harry had tried to pluck him out of credibility before. It would not be hard to do so again on the floor. Woodward began by noting that although he had cooperated with the preeminent Hamilton Kemp Wright in drafting previous legislation and had been to visit the Federal Bureau of Narcotics at least ten times in the two years preceding the hearing, no one had informed him of the proposed act. He went on to object to Anslinger's use of an editorial in the *Journal of the American Medical Association* as evidence of the AMA's support for the act. As Woodward pointed out, the supposed evidence in the editorial, which Harry had cited in his testimony, was composed of quotations from Anslinger and the Federal Bureau of Narcotics. What's more, Woodward added, an editorial does not necessarily represent the official opinion of the association. Woodward argued that Federal Bureau of Narcotics claims about addicted children were unsubstantiated—no information had been solicited from the Children's Bureau—and there was, in fact, no medical evidence that marijuana was addictive. On a political level, Woodward took the position that Harry had espoused until 1935, preferring that states, not the federal government, handle any marijuana problem. But he was two years too late. The Ways and Means Committee savaged Woodward, discrediting him professionally and pointing to the lack of footnotes in the editorial in *JAMA* as evidence of his unprofessionalism.

The circularity of the argumentation, twisty almost, rippled out, like Harry the pebble in the pond, like narcotics rings inside of rings, the circuits of capital, indifferent to the legality of its particular equivalents. I repeat, in case the Kafkaesquely recursive nature of the discourse is not clear: Woodward entered into the record the editorial in the *Washington Herald* that quoted the editorial in *JAMA* that quoted Anslinger directly and indirectly, and which Anslinger used as evidence that "this industry has spread its tentacles throughout the Far East and has direct connections with the narcotic rings in Europe and the Americas."[4] In effect, Anslinger quoted himself, to which Woodward objected:

> **I have here a copy of the editorial referred to and clearly the quotation from that editorial and from the editorial in the *Journal of the American Medical Association* do not correctly represent the views of the association.**[5]

But the committee would have none of it. Even though Harry's data stock had been called into question, his act carried. *The Herald* said:

> **The United States is the big-money market, and happy is the syndicate that can perfect its lines to that country.**[6]

These were the very crooked lines that Harry meant to straighten out, those syndicates run by crooks, undermining the legal market licensed by Harry's authority. He would weed them out. And who could argue? Who could even think straight? Who needed to? The rest of the testimony didn't require the same powers of concentration, or concentricity.

The rest of the testimony called for a sense of humor. At the eleventh hour, it became evident that hemp seed figured in the recipe for certain house paints, so Harry took it up with Sherwin Williams and the Department of Commerce. There remained one commercial interest he had to "satisfy": birdseed makers who used hemp seed in their product. The committee had little time for shenanigans, but it did have time to entertain this problem. Harry explained to the committee that musicians reported that marijuana heightened their musical capacities. So this must be why hemp seed was used in birdfeed:

> **Marijuana has a strangely exhilarating effect upon the musical sensibilities (Indian hemp has long been used as a component of "singing seed" for canary birds).**[7]

Not according to Raymond G. Scarlett of William G. Scarlett & Co. of Baltimore (a member of the National Institute of Oilseed Products). As a representative of the seed industry, Mr. Raymond G. Scarlett sought to cooperate with the committee to the fullest, asserting that "we are not interested in spreading marihuana, or anything like that. We do not want to be drug peddlers."[8] Scarlett claimed he had never observed birds getting high from hemp seed. Rigorous interrogation ensued:

> *The Chairman:* **Does that seed have the same effect on pigeons as the drug has on individuals?**
> *Mr. Scarlett:* **I have never noticed it. It has a tendency to bring back the feather and improve the birds.**[9]

Though both laws changed the tax code and the moral code, the Marijuana Tax Act differed from the Harrison Act in intention. The latter, designed to bring documentation and control to a legal distribution of narcotics, was then applied in a way not strictly intended by its drafters, as a means to effectuate moral, specifically antinarcotic, values. But the Marijuana Tax Act, with Harrison in its rearview mirror, was clearly meant to authorize enforcers to suppress narcotic trade. Despite the differences, both acts were designed to criminalize those self-selecting criminals who would take liberties with the code. Law enforcement made recourse to tax evasion time after time to bring down syndicated crime leaders who covered their tracks with enough degrees of separation from the bloodier crimes they supervised to evade being charged for them. While gangsters had underlings break proverbial knee caps, the government broke gangsters for breaking tax laws. The feds lent new meaning to epistaxis—paying through the nose.

The Marijuana Tax Act ultimately did less harm to gangsters and even large-scale traffickers and dealers, and more, much more, harm to untold numbers of individuals convicted of possession. The first in a series of laws that stipulated harsh punishment, increased penalties for repeat offenders, and mandatory sentencing, the act classified and penalized marijuana and its possession as a narcotic like heroin, cocaine, and opium. This law, and its successors, would provide the central mechanism for the incarceration of millions of poor people of color—but it would not prevent marijuana from being imported into the country and widely distributed here.

Days after the Ways and Means Committee heard and approved the Marijuana Tax Act, the *Hindenburg* exploded. Public response was mighty, acknowledging the tragic effects of the crash on innocent riders and their friends and families. When the act went live a few months later, on Friday, October 1, 1937, the feds lost no time putting it to work on individuals, though its passage made few headlines. On Saturday the second, Samuel Caldwell and Moses Baca were picked up by the FBI in Denver, the former on charges of dealing to the latter, and both on charges of possession. They were the first of millions. By Tuesday the fifth, Baca and Caldwell had been convicted and sentenced by Judge Foster Symes, who took the occasion to pledge to "enforce this new law to the letter."[10] The Mexican American Baca got eighteen months for possession. An unemployed worker with prior alcohol violations, Caldwell got a steep $1,000 fine for possession, and for dealing, four years in Leavenworth, sans parole.

Oh, the humanity.

33 THE UNBRIDLED POWERS OF A CZAR

As a staunch Republican appointed initially by a Republican, Harry sought to secure his place in the Roosevelt administration. It behooved him to give nonpartisan demonstrations of his authority, his effectiveness, and the advisability of keeping him in his office. One of Harry's strategies was to garner positive exposure by fostering public awareness of a relatively limited phenomenon: horse doping, the illegal practice of giving racehorses stimulants to enhance their performances on the track. President Roosevelt had a declared interest in cleaning up the racetracks, but it can't be said that there was popular outcry on, or even attention to, this issue.[1] Because the practice was even less well known to the general public than marijuana use, horse doping was, like the weed, open to representation by Harry.

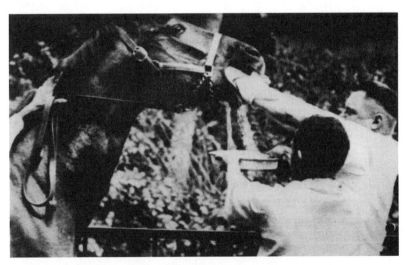

Chemist Virgil Ashley is shown above holding the tray while veterinarian J. S. Catlett obtains saliva for a drug test in Miami. From Bradford Wells, "A Landis for Racing?," *Post Time*, June 1935. Harry J. Anslinger Papers, Special Collections Library, The Pennsylvania State University Libraries.

In the piece "Hopping Horses," in 1936, *Esquire* let Harry tell the story his way. He began by explaining that in 1932 his agents had reported that doping was taking place on the Maryland tracks. When the 1933 season opened, Harry sent men "posing as track loungers or itinerant trainers" to investigate further. Fearing interference and damage to their reputations, racetrack executives asked him for permission to clean their own stables. Harry acceded to this request, but after two years of inaction, he decided that they had failed: "so the Narcotics Bureau shortly will start a new war on the use of narcotics on race horses and that will be a war to the finish."[2]

Meanwhile, in leading trade magazines, calls went out for greater organization and oversight in racing and against industry corruption. In *Polo*, columnist G. F. T. Ryall called for a "central governing body of the highest order with complete authority."[3] Anslinger seemed to agree with that vision:

> **Oddly enough, Mr. Anslinger suggested the best solution: a central governing body—men of the highest type, rich, disinterested, with no social or political aspiration—who would have an under-cover squad of operatives and chemists, and veterinarians with no professional contacts. Such a squad would not only do much to stamp out the narcotic evil, but also the spongers and other undesirables.[4]**

Or it agreed with him. Bradford Wells imagined horse racing cleaned up by "a man with the unbridled powers of a czar and integrity beyond all question" in an article for *Post Time*, "America's authority on racing."[5] Though Wells had an internal governing board in mind, Harry rode in from Washington for the job, or rather, sent his agents into the stables for the Herculean cleanup.

Harry's tactics with the horse dopers were familiar from his work with human dopers. Undercover operations at horse farms handily revealed workers who had so little fear of being caught that they often boasted openly about their doping practice. In a series on "combatting the dope evil" in horse racing, *Post Time* reported that the agents' job proceeded unobstructed; they just walked around barns pretending to be "country horsemen" and found the dopers at work.[6] Harry relied, as usual, on "reports of operatives who had either seen the act committed or offered sufficient circumstantial evidence to stand in a court of law; photostatic copies of so-called 'prescriptions'; letters seized by operatives."[7] According to the *Esquire* article,

> **The powers within racing never knew that Anslinger had all the aces in the game. He had a list of about 1500 horses which had been subjected to drugging within the year. He had names of owners and trainers, dates, speed charts, form charts, and a vast quantity of data. Anslinger also had copies of prescriptions his men had seized together with syringes, hypodermic needles, "speed balls," (pills), etc. In short, he had all the ammunition to start a war and wage it to successful conclusion against those who had prostituted the sport of horse racing.**[8]

Through the kind of covert intelligence work for which he had a penchant, Anslinger and his men identified those horses drugged by trainers whose real rivalry played out in the stables, less on the track, and more in the concocting and administering of "optimal prescriptions, and administering narcotics to horses just enough time in advance of a race to send them 'flying.'"[9] Optimal narcotic formulas were usually composed of a combination of heroin and cocaine squirted into the horse's mouth with a syringe. Less popular methods included injecting the horse with a hypodermic needle, dusting its mouth, or dosing it with pills.

When his agents caught a number of trainers "red-handed," Harry hoped for support from "newspaper turf writers." Somewhat disingenuously, he evinced surprise that his campaign to drive disreputable horsemen out of racing encountered "opposition from the very people whose interest would have been bettered."[10] Anslinger batted away the charge that his agents only went after poor horsemen, explaining that they simply couldn't get into the better-guarded stables of richer outfits. In one poorly guarded outfit, an agent who broke through was held by stable hands and poked with a pitchfork for his troubles.

Joseph Murphy, a track director in Detroit, published a broadside claiming that the "snooping" was a publicity stunt for the Federal Bureau of Narcotics. Now Harry ceased to narrate and the *Esquire* writer filled in the blanks:

In due course of time, a copy of Murphy's letter reached Anslinger. Just what followed is not publicly known. But it is a matter of record that Murphy quickly announced that he was in favor of ridding the turf of those owners, trainers, or stable hands who drugged their horses.

So far as is known, the writers who loosened billingsgate at the Narcotics Bureau never again uttered one word of criticism or condemnation.[11]

This was one of Harry's long suits, the private negotiations that turn enemies into friends, or, anyway, collaborators. This was bureaucratic savoir faire. Harry threw another trick of his trade into the ring to bust the horse dopers; he collected and then supplied agents with statistical information: "names of owners and trainers, dates, speed charts, form charts, and a vast quantity of data."[12]

In the climax, the feds conducted a spate of raids and arrested a number of trainers, attesting to the muscle of the Federal Bureau of Narcotics under Anslinger's leadership. Further, Harry made friends in the bargain by arresting trainers rather than track owners, for whom he did the extra favor of restoring the integrity of the sport. If Harry's racetrack triumph did not endear him to Roosevelt, he nonetheless won positive public exposure—and reappointment.

Dope was not the only issue dogging the races. Gambling had gone underground and south of the border as temperance geared up. Just after alcohol became legal again, between 1933 and 1939, twenty-one states restored legal betting on horses. At the same time, reinvigorated by the repeal of Prohibition, racketeers sought to substitute other illegal goods and services for the illegal alcohol market. The smallest of small fries, the numbers runner, ran around urban neighborhoods recording numbers in his book. In spite of repeated crackdowns, the numbers racket persisted, particularly in New York City. In 1934, Harry could well have seen the newsreel of Mayor Fiorello La Guardia smashing slot machines or throwing them into the Long Island Sound, as though La Guardia were his ally in the fight against crime.

But Anslinger and La Guardia were not political allies. La Guardia opposed legal slot machines because they lifted revenue from the people who needed it most. Anslinger took his stand against illegal gambling, not regressive taxation schemes. Also contra Anslinger, New York's mayor requested a report from the New York Academy of Medicine to evaluate the effects of marijuana on users in order to evaluate, in turn, what kind of social threat the drug posed. Commissioned in 1938, the study began in 1940 and concluded in 1941 that the dangers of marijuana had been greatly exaggerated.

The commission had taken a page from Harry's book, mobilizing "plain clothes" investigators who

> **circulated in the districts in which marihuana appeared to be most widely used, particularly Harlem, associated with marihuana users, and found out as much as possible about sources of supply, means of distribution, and effects of marihuana on users.**[13]

Not surprisingly, this circular methodology confirmed the starting assumption that users were concentrated in Harlem. But surprisingly—and problematically—at least to Harry Anslinger, the commission concluded that

> **the marihuana user does not come from the hardened criminal class and there was found no direct relationship between the commission of crimes of violence and marihuana.**[14]

For their research into the direct effects of the drug on individual users, the researchers used the men in the penitentiary on Rikers Island, a stone's throw from East Harlem. The research subjects exhibited no psychosis, no violence, and no tendency to dependency; the prisoners were as docile as horses grazing in the grass.

Least surprising of all, Anslinger suppressed the publication of this study that contradicted his conviction that marijuana was linked to violent crime. The La Guardia report, "The Marijuana Problem in the City of New York," was not released until 1944. If not altogether unbridled, Anslinger enjoyed significant authority to control the representations of drugs and their users and their effects.

34 ANSLINGER NATION, OR DOUBLE AGENCY

In the end, Harry was a collection of stories.

> He usually said he was born in Romania on October 16, 1893, and
> came through Ellis Island at age five. But . . . there were no records
> of an Itzhak Donenfield, his wife, or their sons Harry and Irving
> ever having entered America. Harry said he'd worked his way
> through New York University to learn business, but there was no
> record of him there either.[1]

Wait a minute. This is not our beautiful Harry. This is a Romanian
Jewish Harry, our Harry's doppelganger,[2] born around the same time
to parents who had just immigrated to the United States, bringing
older children from the old country (the old country a mid-western-
European state), and who would go on to bear American-born children.
This is Harry's *unheimlich*, a discomfiting yet familiar figure who also
went to business college, though records of certain claimed university
degrees are likewise unlocatable.[3] Of our Harry too it could be said,
"The passage of the Eighteenth Amendment in 1919 changed Harry's
life, although a few years passed before he knew it."[4]

By his teens, this Harry too had "learned to dress like a 'cadet'" and
had learned "the power of fashion," just like our Harry, who found,
during the war, and in military company in its aftermath, that to be
well dressed was to be well armed. "It was a low-cost way to look like
a big shot. . . . Harry wanted to be a bigger shot than that though."
Both Harrys worked hard on developing their personas; both wanted
to be seen as toughs; both manufactured narratives brimming with
"bravado." And "sometimes the stories soared to the ridiculous."[5] Yet
both Harrys truly did gain insider knowledge of the gangs that ruled
so many urban streets in the 1920s and 1930s, one by belonging and

Film stills from *The Public Enemy* (1931) (*left*) and *Bullets or Ballots* (1936) (*right*). From University of Washington Libraries, Special Collections, UW36371 and UW36372.

one by framing, closely observing, and occasionally infiltrating. Where Donenfield would work this knowledge into the frames of the first comic books, Anslinger would work it into faux journalism and equally faux evidence of the need for legislation. If it might be said that both men engaged in caricature, then it might be said of either one that

> **the unabashed self-promotion, the absurd claims to glory, the refusal to submit to the tyranny of the real or the possible, the understanding that the story is all that matters—all these would be Harry's gift to the industry he helped create.**[6]

So if Donenfield helped create the comic industry, what industry did Anslinger help create? By deploying stories strategically—as much as by policing and doubling, in as much as that's not redundant since policing is doubling, as hailing is bringing into being, and policing is tailing, too often trailing so much more than leading—Harry helped create, if not the gangster himself, the ever-expanding field of professional gangsters, whose organizations developed, as doubles do, in the image of their opposing organizations, first the Bureau of Prohibition and then the Federal Bureau of Narcotics. Though he did not fashion the lone drug addict who had been overprescribed morphine by a well-meaning local physician, Harry did help create the international drug cartels whose organizations became every bit as elaborate, operating exactly as covertly, as his own organization, and operating more profitably than their overt counterparts, the pharmaceutical companies.

Unlike Harry Anslinger, Donenfield got his gang smarts on the streets of New York City. New York was no stranger to street gangs, or to the political organizations that matched them. Al Capone, for example, was born in New York City, in 1899, growing up to straddle the line that distinguishes legal and illegal markets, like so many professional gangsters, covering his tracks and evading arrest with dummy companies. How anonymously cash can cross that line, leaving little trace. Like the railroad industry, Capone moved his center of operations, in the early twentieth century, from New York to Chicago; then, like trains, he crisscrossed the plains.

Like a ganglion on the Midwest, gangsters proliferated in the City on the Plains in the 1920s, and from there they radiated and circulated, in small and large overlapping and competing networks, kind of like trains, headquartering and roundhousing in cities, and changing magazines, before heading out again and blowing through small towns. But trains themselves were heading out of town, and gangsters increasingly used cars, finding in them the advantages that bootleggers had found: cars had hiding places and cars went door to door; cars were mobile steel shields out of which you could shoot while you fled. For the selfsame reasons, narcotics agents wanted cars to match those of their quarry. In 1934, in his testimony to the Appropriations Committee, in one of a string of annual and unsuccessful attempts to keep his budget from being further cut during the Depression, Harry Anslinger argued that the Federal Bureau of Narcotics needed new cars, one for each of its fifteen districts, in order to match, that is, catch, the gangsters: "They use fast cars—Lincolns or Cadillac cars."[7]

In the same plea for updated resources, Anslinger complained of the clumsy Army .45s that his agents had to use. Difficult to conceal, these guns impeded undercover work, so Harry requested "detective specials," those swank little numbers, blued finish or nickel-plated, with the wood grip, or textured, pearl-handled for ladies, black-and-white pattern of spats, deadly. Thus in materiel, Anslinger fashioned himself after gangsters, while the commodities' names identified them with enforcement. The detective special is a snub-nosed Colt .45, the kind used by undercover cop Johnny Blake, as played by Edward G. Robinson in 1936's *Bullets or Ballots*. Hot-headed Johnny infiltrates the gang, getting in with the big guys, making it up to No. 2 in the organization, only to blow the racket wide open. For *Bullets or Ballots*, read *crooked or straight*. The gangster Dillinger carries a detective special in *Dillinger* in 1945. In real life, John Dillinger met his maker outside the Biograph Hotel on July 22, 1934. Same year Harry made the above request to the Appropriations Committee.

In the movie *Scarface* (1935), a fictionalized account of Al Capone's career, Tony Camonte first appears as a shadow sliding against a wall; then the shadow morphs into a silhouette, the film playing with its own possibilities for rendering doubleness. Blackened profile of a man, gun pointing out of his midsection: *pop!* As he rises to the top of the Chicago organization, always willing to use a gun, Camonte explains that he wants his bootlegging "scheme" to run "like a real business." In real life, bootleggers professionalized partly by mirroring legitimate business, seeking profits according to similar, but by definition illegal, mechanisms of production, distribution, and consumption, yet seeking higher profits, and with reason to expect them, given the heightened risk and the relative value of illegal booty. So bootleggers needed, in effect, even tighter organizations; they needed to go business one better, in order to stay a step ahead of the cops. In film after film, the gangsters are literally one step, or one car length, ahead of the cops. Eat my dust, copper.

Until the end. In the movies, the coppers always got the last word. The Hays Code called for endings in which the law triumphs as an instrument of morality, as it does in *Public Enemy* and *Little Caesar*, both released in 1931. In the first, a petty criminal works his way up through a crime organization, while in the second, an entrepreneurial young man gets rich on the black market; in both, the criminals meet with the requisite reversal of fortune. Bootlegging narratives of the early 1930s reached back to the 1920s, when Prohibition called into being not only a black market for alcohol but professional bootleggers like Capone. Because black market activity must compensate a risk that is legal as well as financial, Prohibition encouraged bootleg-ging on a large scale, which in turn called for a hierarchical criminal organization—the higher-ups moving greater quantities of product, thereby taking on greater risk, and controlling knowledge that must be held secret if the risk were to pay off.

In this way, the Eighteenth Amendment produced crime *syndicates*, the word itself suggesting that illegal collaborative networks have something in common with agencies that sell stories for publication. Controlling print and transportation run and rerun round and round each other, doubling or perhaps reproducing organizational structure in triplicate: legitimate business, black market business, government. All of it running circles around the consumer citizen who pays for it all. *G-men*, which played across the country in 1935, has early agents hunting down career criminals who are wreaking mayhem from New York to the Midwest. Stories—like capital, the outlaws who chase it, and the law that chases them—circulate. Endlessly.

As Harry's own stories recirculated, he received a call for help from the wild west. Emerging from a landscape of gangster sprees, a letter from a small-town editor to the Federal Bureau of Narcotics appealed to Harry in terms he would have recognized. Floyd Baskette, of the *Daily Courier* in Alamos, Colorado, requested the bureau's assistance in "handling the drug" on behalf of the civic leaders and law officers of his community:

> **I wish I could show you what a small marihuana cigarette does to one of our degenerate Spanish speaking residents. That's why our problem is so great; the greatest percentage of our population is composed of Spanish speaking persons, most of whom are low mentally, because of social and racial conditions.**[8]

Baskette's own doppelganger had passed through Colorado a few years earlier, getting picked up in Pueblo for vagrancy. Pretty Boy Floyd was charged with violation of Prohibition in Sioux Falls, South Dakota. Putatively, he had also peddled drugs. Inarguably, Pretty Boy had traversed the Midwest, stinging folks, and maybe offing a couple of law enforcement officers, in Kansas, Missouri, Ohio, and/or Iowa. Did he rob banks? Pretty Boy was heroically evasive. En route to Ohio, he likely crossed Illinois and Indiana too. Yet, in the words of the folk song, "Oklahoma knew him well." He was born in Oklahoma, and in Oklahoma, Pretty Boy was legendary. "Every crime in Oklahoma was added to his name."[9]

> **Less than 24 hours after Federal agents announced that Floyd was wanted as one of the Union Station killers, he was flushed out of an Iowa farm by two peace officers. In his first brush with authority this year, he showed that he had lost none of his finesse. Jumping into a car with two companions, he led the police on a wild chase to an empty house at the dead end of a road. There he turned on them with a machine gun and automatic rifles, shot his way out and away.**[10]

Here, *Time* betrays a between-the-lines appreciation of Floyd's "finesse," and even his getaway. If America was ambivalent about gangsters, gangsters were ambivalent right back. They carried the double meaning of *romance*, over and above earning our love-hate. Though he bit the dust at the hand of the heat on the East Coast of Ohio, on the straight unrivered boundary with Pennsylvania, in 1934, Floyd had briefly reanimated the legend of Robin Hood. On, or should I say with, the one hand, Pretty Boy Floyd stole money; on or with the other, he gave some away.

> **But many a starving farmer**
> **The same old story told**
> **How the outlaw paid their mortgage**
> **And saved their little homes.**[11]

Time's homage replayed the old story of the crook with the heart of gold, like the one told about Pretty Boy Floyd, who brought bankers to their knees while, or thus, thrilling the families on relief.

> **Yes, as through this world I've wandered**
> **I've seen lots of funny men;**
> **Some will rob you with a six-gun,**
> **And some with a fountain pen.**[12]

Which brings us back to Floyd Baskette, the editor with the *b* in his bonnet, hard at work with his fountain pen, echoing Harry's fear of foreigners right back at him. Justifying the law's war on drugs. And the beat goes on.

The land is littered with the bodies of the murdered and the murderers; gangs doppeling each other to death coast to coast, in hotel rooms, bullet-pocked cars, coffins, hearses, cemeteries, bursting with the boys who romanced each other across state lines. Crazies and criminals lit up in taillights. Marthas shimmering by their sides, escaping unscathed, lost innocence implied. Hearsay. Blammo. Boss. Their nicknames on headlines, bylines, and marquees. Magazines, movies, radio shows boasting chills and thrills, spilling over with the stuff of our love of story, kept reminding citizen-consumers not to turn that dial. Sponsored by Chevrolet, one such entertainment premiered on the radio as *G-men* in July 1935, to be reborn as *Gang Busters* on January 15, 1936. After which it ran for another twenty-one years.

> [Alarm. The cranking up of the siren.] Woooo . . . Woooo . . . [machine-gun fire] . . . [In the voice of the dispatcher/announcer:] Tonight *Gang Busters* presents, "The Case of The Cincinnati Narcotics Ring," whose deadly dealings in drugs spread across two nations, until the Royal Canadian Mounties, the Federal Narcotics Bureau and the Cincinnati police cornered the ringleader in a final duel to death.[13]

In the end, Harry was a collection of stories, packed in archives, like the one lying in boxes at Penn State not far from where the literal Harry lies in a box in Hollidaysburg, still on one level, but on another level still reaching out from that grave and into courtrooms, alleyways, and squealing squad cars, everywhere and forever turning the screw:

> [Whistle.] Now, *Gang Busters*, presented in cooperation with police and federal law enforcement departments throughout the United States. The only national program that brings you authentic police case histories.[14]

35 FICTION ALONE HAS NO MONOPOLY IN THIS FIELD

Real Detective Stories

In 1845, the wily and incorrigible George Wilkes published his proposal for a "national railroad from the Atlantic to the Pacific Ocean for the purpose of obtaining a short route to Oregon and the Indies." A journalist and railroad promoter, Wilkes believed railroads, along with magnets and steam engines, had "annihilated space, and exploded

James W. Booth, "New Orleans' Dope Secret," *Startling Detective Adventures* 21, no. 122, September 1938, 34. Harry J. Anslinger Papers, Special Collections Library, The Pennsylvania State University Libraries.

all theories which rested on the accidents of time and distance."[1] Preceding Einstein's related theory by more than fifty years, Wilkes derived from this physical revolution a warrant for Manifest Destiny, a cosmic demand to master the continent by train.

Wilkes put great stock, literal and figurative, in the belief that developing the railroad was the most effective route to developing the nation, and that "the Railroad is the GREAT NEGOTIATOR, which alone can settle our title more conclusively than all the diplomats in the world."[2] The Pennsylvania Railroad Company's title in Altoona would soon prove Wilkes right. The railroad would raise Harry right and send him forth from Altoona, send him to the table with the diplomats of the world to become the human great negotiator. Wilkes, by contrast, never left New York, gaining there firsthand knowledge of the sordid social circles whose stories would stimulate readers to plunk down pennies for papers, by borrowing and owing money, ruining women and consorting with prostitutes, sleuthing and being found out, and going to jail, finally, where he did time for libel.

In the same year he issued his train vision, Wilkes founded the *National Police Gazette*, a forerunner in lowbrow journalism in the United States, a periodical that lasted well into the twentieth century, an early bird in the genres of vice, true crime, sporting magazines, and detective stories, ostensibly designed to present matters of interest to police officers in the service of reducing crime in New York City, but actually designed to titillate the general public with tales of sex, crime, drugs, and the perennial visuals of the scantily clad. One hundred years later, there were dozens of "exploitation" magazines in the same market, whose themes ranged from romance to the military, all tapping the same old trove. Wilkes had struck the central vein of a mass story mine when he realized that if he took the stock elements of a certain class of crimes—an illegal substance, a swarthy kingpin, a white woman, a locale, and a cop—and threw them against a broadsheet, they would magically arrange themselves into a story. Of persistent capitalizable interest to readers of this kind of periodicals were police and detective stories, all the way through to the middle of the twentieth century. In latter days, one more element—Harry J. Anslinger—would pull a Hitchcock, showing up once or twice per story, as the tough and tweedy boss, the great negotiator, the one who made the trains of morality run on time, to get the story rolling. Or to pose for the occasional glossy photo, with twined bundles of confiscated dope and other agents. Or to get the final word.

> Weird shadows like bony strangling fingers clutched at the desert town of Reno, Nevada, "biggest little city in the world," as we skidded down the skyways late one afternoon in March, 1937.[3]

It was a recent night in a small, stuffy room in a downtown building in Grand Forks—window shades closely drawn, doors carefully locked, key-holes and other openings tightly stuffed, lights softly dimmed.

> *Narcotic* is a bizarre story that accurately mirrors the true lives in the little known world where depraved and degenerate men and women give over to bestial passions.

Whooping Indians, clowns, cowboys, gaily-bedecked Oriental potentates and suave courtiers who looked as though they had stepped from out of the musty past and the Court of Louis XIV, thronged Canal street and thoroughfares leading to it.

> Pretty girls, their masks failing to hide their beauty, flirted, laughed and danced.

Beautiful girls . . .

> " 'Dope' Makes Strange Creatures of Beautiful Women"

Esther Gordon, whose stabbed and battered corpse was found in a barrel in New York's East River, was linked to gang warfare for control of a gigantic dope syndicate.

> *Narcotic* is True Biography.

Rex, Lord of Misrule and King of Carnival, was in command of Crescent City.

> The sinister Oriental figures, flitting shadows, furtive meetings in dark alleyways and doorways in the "biggest little city in the world."

Everywhere the spirit of revelry prevailed.

But there were two men in New Orleans that day in early March who did not participate in the merry-making.

"Federal Men Had Their Orders but They Were Powerless Until a Beautiful Co-Ed Stepped in as an Amateur Detective and—"

"This is Jean."

She was a picture.

"If her story is true the blow off will rock Nevada."

From small-fry vendors she heard of a mysterious higher-up, "the Old Man with the Whiskers," and she was told that Woo Sing, czar of Chinatown, wanted to see her in his "private joint" at 219 Peavine Street.

And more than a half-million subjects of his realm had thrown all serious thoughts aside to join in tempestuous mirth.

Jean Nash, the dancer, swore that she had known the Chinese as Frank Gin since the preceding August, when she became acquainted with him through another girl.

I feasted my eyes on the tips of her stylish pumps, her shapely legs, seductive breasts in a snug-fitting white-silk dress.

"If it's true you have your job cut out for you."

The squalid, nauseating opium den on the wretched little back-street and the luxurious apartment house in the fashionable part of town, where drugs can also be procured, are both going to be scourged.

She admitted that she was an addict at the time and purchased the drug from him regularly.

Will you have breakfast with me at the drug store on the corner in 30 minutes?

"I'm wearing my red jacket."

This was too fantastic—too much like a fiction tale.

"Sit down, Harry," she said.

Harry is not my name, but I sat down.

"I know just the man. . . ."

Although posing as a legitimate business man and acting as president of a fruit company which operated between New Orleans
and the banana countries of Central America, he was a killer of
the most vicious type.

As these thoughts formed in her mind, a heavy thickset man of
perhaps sixty—but smooth-faced!—left a roulette table where
he had been idly watching the play and disappeared through the
office door.

Bianco slipped furtively into a telephone booth and dialed a
number.

"How do we know the Feds aren't wise?"

Commissioner Harry J. Anslinger, of the United States Bureau
of Narcotics, sat at his desk in the Tower Building in Washington
D.C., with a frown on his face.

"Okay, then, let us see the whole set-up and we'll play ball."

"Let's go!" she said, and slipped into the tight-fitting red jacket
which had become her uniform.

"He'll lead us to the rats."

He put a hand on her arm and slowly led her through the opium-
soaked haze.

Shrewd and crafty as Carolla was reputed to be in both his legitimate and illegitimate dealings, he readily accepted the narcotics
agent as one of his kind and never suspected his identity.

Judah was like a magician putting on an act. He opened the container. Suspended within the can was another can, soldered in
position so that it would be entirely surrounded by milk. And
within that second can was—morphine!

"One false move and . . ."

Suddenly a blinding flash of fire sprang out of the semi-darkness; the explosion of a gun blasted through the house.

The shadow crumbled to the floor and then the bedroom door was slammed shut.

McCarty felt a sharp sting in his right thigh. It spun him half around but as he fell he fired back.

"If you want to slough somebody, why don't you get a big shot?"

He shrugged his broad shoulders, grinned, shook hands.

"Got to bait with small ones like you to get the big ones."

"If you can handle twenty-five pieces at one time, I might be able to put you right next to the big boss," he said.

How many are selling their souls to Hell for one more bindle.

The receiver clicked.

"I just got a fast call about some queer twenties."

One was H. J. Anslinger, United States commissioner of narcotics.

In front of him was the report which had just been teletyped by Supervising Narcotics Agent J. B. Greeson, of the New Orleans District, advising of a seizure of pure heroin from a local peddler, the sixth in as many days.

How many of these disillusioned persons have turned to the false, alluring dream of the opium pipe, the burning needle, the crude syringe and knife of the crazed narcotic addict?

The big plane's wheels slewed onto the hard rubber with the shriek of agonized rubber like the screams of a crazed "junkie" kicking the habit.

Nobody came to the Philadelphia rendezvous, and Louise's prints weren't in the Bureau files.

Louisiana—Clever narcotic peddlers ply their vicious trade until a shrewd agent leads them into a trap.

We landed.

They found no trace of the document, nor of any smuggled narcotic.

The only girl there wearing a red jacket sat alone at a small table.

This was Louise—pint-sized, older than he looked, small enough to have a woman's gait and a woman's fist, shrewd enough to choose a woman's name, but unable to hide the missing joint on one finger.

The customs clerk seized his hand. The first joint of the third finger was missing.

"Yes, it's a pinch," answered one of the approaching Federal Narcotics officers.

Through my mind flashed the words of my chief, Harry J. Anslinger, United States Narcotics Commissioner in Washington, D.C., as he bade us good-by. His last deep-voiced instructions still rang in my ear above the roar of the motors.

Anslinger did not always follow his own instructions. He had essentially fictionalized the story that provided the headline and warranted the claim that marijuana was the "assassin of youth." And yet he warned,

Fiction alone has no monopoly in this field. . . .
   . . . It is no field in which to experiment with unproved ideas, fanciful suggestions, or curbstone opinions.[4]

Having authored an essentially fictional story based on clippings in his Gore Files, Anslinger went on to opine in *The Traffic in Narcotics* that sensationalism was immoral. Having sold "The Assassin of Youth" to the *American Magazine*, Anslinger elsewhere deplored the fact that

> radio and television shows have featured the dope fiend, and publishers of cheap fiction have not hesitated to use indefensible and lurid stories involving addicts to enhance their sales.[5]

He had noticed that these lurid tales were morally and aesthetically bankrupt, with undesirable results, that in them

> generally, the facts are distorted, the plot abominable, and the youngsters' curiosity improperly and unduly aroused thereby.[6]

Harry feared that these lurid tales stimulated interest in sex and drugs. Which is why he tried to convince readers of the demonstrably counterfactual claim that

> certainly no one would want to drench the American public with illustrations concerning the techniques of sex perversion.[7]

Yet publishers and readers alike did want such drenching. Whether readers on the demand side, or publishers on the supply side, were responsible for the drenching in representations of the techniques of loathsome sex perversions caused by the degrading habit of drug addiction, it was clear, even to Harry, that

> for the past several years, the general public has been bombarded with stories, articles, pictures, programs, discussions, and speeches dealing with all phases of drug addiction.[8]

Harry himself gave such speeches. So the buck didn't stop with Harry, who deployed that which he deplored, though not in the same venues. It didn't stop with his friend William Randolph Hearst, whose editorials offered curbside opinions about the traffic in narcotic drugs and legislative solutions to associated social problems. There was no end of bucks with Hearst. But, however paradoxically, Harry did offer other publishers

> one final thought for both producers and sponsors—stop building detective stories around drug addicts.[9]

Would Harry have preferred a return to the mores of yesteryear? Here, railroad promoter and tabloid pioneer Wilkes gets the last word, however anachronistically:

> In conclusion, the Author has but to add that the project of a National Railroad across the Continent, though generally denounced as visionary and impracticable, will, upon the examination of the following pages, not be found more difficult than other plans now in the contemplation of the Government; and in presenting it again to the public, he claims for it that attention which every scheme deserves from its opposers.[10]

36 THIS FELLOW OUGHT TO BE THE FIGMENT OF SOMEBODY'S IMAGINATION

By midcentury, the drug war had become a stock play. Fictions circulated as promiscuously as drugs, running the exact same circuits from prescription form to camel, from the Far East to the Midwest, aliases abroad and at home, fooling foes everywhere. There was a growing role for the undercover agent, covert operations called forth by black market activity. A not-atypical story from the *Modesto Bee* demonstrates the fineness of the line between fiction and nonfiction in the black market and among its busters. The California paper reported on a "true 'thriller'" released by the Treasury Department on February 9, 1943:

> **The American undercover agents were taken on a trip into the mountains of Guadalajara, where "La Nacha" introduced them to "the chemist" and "the lawyer."**[1]

The Bee relates that the "principal character," the "brains" of the gang, La Nacha, was really Mrs. Ignacia Jasso Gonzalez, and offers the real names of her code-named coconspirators. Alberto Torres Ybarra and Luis Manuel Vazquez—a.k.a. "The Chemist" and "The Lawyer"— had hid up in the mountains with her, had stashed fifty-five ounces of morphine worth $8,000 in their gas tank, and were sentenced to five years in jail and fined $5,000 each. La Nacha had other runners, also arrested in Texas, who bore code names in the newspaper story: "The Interpreter," "The Old Man," and "The Old Woman." The Chemist, The Lawyer, The Interpreter, and others, all provide crucial functions for international traffickers; in the domestic drama, the cast of char-

FEDERAL BUREAU OF NARCOTICS (33-1)
TRAINING SCHOOL

Instructor_____ Class Period_____
Subject_____

UNDERCOVER WORK

I. "DEFINITION - Undercover work is an investigative process in which
disguises and pretexts are used to gain the confidence of criminal
suspects for the purpose of determining the nature and extent of any
criminal activities they may be contemplating or perpetrating.

II. PURPOSE.

    A. To determine if a crime is being planned or committed.

    B. To identify all persons involved.

    C. To obtain evidence for court.

    D. To locate contraband or stolen property.

    E. To determine a suitable time for raiding a hangout or arresting
       principals.

III. QUALIFICATIONS FOR UNDERCOVER OPERATIVE.

    A. Undercover work does not require any special type of individual
       so far as appearance or personality is concerned. Anyone can
       operate undercover if he is intelligent, resourceful and possesses
       the requisite qualities of individual initiative, energy and courage.

    B. Self-confidence.

    C. Good judgment.

    D. Mental alertness.

    E. Resourcefulness.

    F. Language.
       1. Accents.
       2. Foreign languages.
       3. Colloquialisms.
       4. Underworld slang.

FOR OFFICIAL USE ONLY

- 1 -

Federal Bureau of Narcotics Training School curriculum, 1950s. Harry J. Anslinger Papers, Special Collections Library, The Pennsylvania State University Libraries.

acters that collaborate with The Dealer(s) often include The Ingenue
and The Doctor. On the side of the law, no one plays a bigger role than
the American Undercover Agents.

Harry Anslinger knew well that "the spy or intelligence agents had
to have a 'cover' story, a fictional life, so intimately a part of him by
long practice and indoctrination that it became more true to him than

the reality of his existence."[2] He employed and supervised a number of undercover agents, some of whom moonlighted for the CIA. Charles Siragusa was just one of a number of agents so special they were not bound by law, not bound to one department or division, and not bound to one cover story or one reality.

> The embassy didn't know it, but it had just opened its doors to a character straight out of murder-mystery fiction, the kind of shrewd, steel-nerved and intuitive undercover agent that detective-story writers spend their lives dreaming up.[3]

With a nod to the blurring of genres that characterizes the work of the narcotics agent, the *Saturday Evening Post* sings the praises of this special agent, who worked for both the Federal Bureau of Narcotics and the CIA:

> This undercover agent's name is Charles Siragusa. In the five and a half years since he set his brief case down in that embassy cubicle he has run through enough hair-raising exploits in Europe and the Near East to give those same detective writers an acute sense of job insecurity.[4]

Equipped with preternatural self-control, all six senses, and a brief-case (in it, the tools of the literary trade), Siragusa wrote his own ticket from one bureau to another, one continent to the next,

> making up his plots as he goes along . . . using as many aliases as Alec Guinness—all of them with horn-rimmed spectacles and a Bronx accent. . . . The very file names of the cases he has broken read like a rack of newsstand paperbacks—The Green Trunk of Alcamo, The Case of the Lebanese Caramels, The Schiaparelli Affair, The Wehrmacht Leak, Operation Old Goat, The Queen Mother of Opium, The Just-Call-Me-Danny Case, to mention only a few. Obviously, this fellow ought to be the figment of somebody's imagination, if only his own.[5]

The prolific and poetic Siragusa was, like all successful undercover agents, a figment of his own imagination. It would have been in the job description, if there had been one.

In fact, among the texts Harry authored were curricula for training narcotics agents. In one such training outline, Harry offers this definition:

> Undercover work is an investigative process in which disguises and pretexts are used to gain the confidence of criminal suspects for the purpose of determining the nature and extent of any criminal activities they may be contemplating or perpetrating.[6]

Of course undercover work is also used in intelligence work with noncriminals, but in any case, the disguises, the pretexts are fundamental.

Harry was not a creative writer. Though his repertoire included some fairly purple rhetorical flourishes, as when he broached the social dimensions of the drug war—the evil of dealers and other dispensers, the violent insanity of the marijuana user, and so on— much of his writing was marked by the same habits of thought that he learned at the knee of the corporation; in these texts, he mere-ly expressed the bureaucratic mind. Throughout his oeuvre, Harry lists and enumerates, he has headings and subheadings, and he frequently uses outlines. The outline is a graphic equivalent of the bureau, an organizational aid that offers a format for hierarchical order or sequence, categorical distinction, comprehensiveness, and classification—and these are a few of Harry's favorite things. His love for them manifests in habitual recourse to statistics, and in the cur-ricula for training narcotics agents.

These curricula instructed trainees in their own writing, in the textual production that attended the institutionalized intelligence and enforcement operations (production that ended up calling forth amnesiac shredders, redactors, burners, buriers). For example,

VIII. EXECUTION OF ORDER FORMS

1. Execute them in triplicate.
2. Written, Ink, Indelible Pencil or Typewriter.
3. Signed by authorized person.
4. Power of Attorney.
5. Distribution.
6. Lost Order Forms. Notify Commissioner of narcotics.
7. Improperly executed, erasures or mutilated. Retain.

Writing itself was in question, as Harry laid out the parameters for various writers. Doctors, for example, faced certain rules for writing prescriptions, legal strictures involving the name of the doctor himself (Harry's assumption about the gender of doctors), as well as the names of patient and institution, how to write prescriptions for dogs, cats, and mules, and the purpose of the prescription. Even a prescription form could bear fiction. Which leads to all kinds of trouble—doctors had better leave fiction in the hands of the agents.

C. PRESCRIPTION WRITTEN IN FICTITIOUS NAME.
1. **For office use.**
2. **Unlawful supply.**
3. **Conceal the true name and address of the addict.**[7]

Agents also had recourse to those liminal characters known as informants. Like the narcs who tapped them, informers operated in between legality and illegality, fiction and reality, close enough to the latter to have access to information about drug trafficking, but paying enough of a service to the Federal Bureau of Narcotics to earn a certain immunity, a contact privilege, a prerogative transferred from cop to rat fink. One of the persistent ironies of undercover police work is that the greatest single resource is the corrupt criminal, the double agent in the streets; agents depend on the intelligence of the crookedest crooks, the most treacherous of the underworlders, from penny-ante neighborhoodlums to Lucky Luciano. One narcotics agent recalls the difficulty of tracking down a Willie Gilhooley, "the biggest dope peddler in the Middle West," whom he found thanks to an informer named Earl Benedict.

Benedict stepped up and pointed the way to Gilhooley:

> **The big South Side peddler was just the man we were looking for. We had stumbled onto the biggest game in Chicago. By pressing the buzzer over the mailbox marked "Bennett"—obviously a fictitious name—we could get Mr. Gilhooley in person.**[8]

The real Benedict (Arnold to his friends) exposed a fictitious Bennett as the real Gilhooley. Just as fake names were de rigueur for trafficker

Incognito Operations   (33-7)

     5. Do not duck out to make call. Always give logical
       reason for departing.

  D. Notes and reports.

     1. Notes may be made on match book covers, toilet paper,
       magazines or other available bits of paper.

     2. Take only necessary notes and write in such a way that
       information would be unintelligible to anyone else.

     3. Numbers may be written as mathematical problems or as
       part of a fake phone number.

     4. Written reports to headquarters may be addressed to a
       fictitious name or organization at a prearranged general
       delivery address. Do not put your return address on the
       letter.

     5. Less risk if reports are written in Post Office and
       immediately mailed.

X. AUXILIARY SURVEILLANCE.

  A. If appropriate, undercover activities should be augmented
    by a shadowing detail.

  B. Undercover man must always try to move slowly and cause such
    delays as may be necessary for shadow men to maintain contact.

  C. Direct meetings with fellow officers are dangerous and should
    be avoided if possible.

  D. Secret signals should be prearranged between undercover man
    and shadow detail.

     1. Method of wearing or carrying hat or coat.
     2. Handkerchief showing from coat pocket.
     3. Smoking, etc.
     4. If care is exercised, brief notes may be dropped for
       fellow officers.

       a. Written on empty match book covers.

       b. Written on empty cigarette package or cigar band.

       c. Written on scrap of paper rolled up and pushed in
         one end of cigarette. Cigarette is lighted, then
         crushed and abandoned before fire has reached note.

F O R   O F F I C I A L   U S E   O N L Y

- 7 -

"Incognito Operations," Federal Bureau of Narcotics Training School curriculum, 1950s. Harry J. Anslinger Papers, Special Collections Library, The Pennsylvania State University Libraries.

and agent alike, they were also sometimes connected with the cross-over figure, the one with one foot in each world, the stool pigeon.

Whalen isn't his real name, though that is what he is called by the few in the department who know him. He is sometimes called "the man of a hundred names." The department guards his real

> identity zealously, for if it ever becomes known to the underworld, his days of usefulness will be over.[9]

It's not just that narcs and stoolies perform, in busts, heroics of material and ideological value for the security and defense of the United States; they make great narrative too. In one account, another special operative for the Federal Bureau of Narcotics, George White, was a "gin drunk" his colleagues found sitting on the curb ranting one morning.[10] But he was also good for top-secret missions around the world, and better yet, he was into sadomasochism.

Braver, more thrill-seeking, perhaps characterologically duplicitous, agents were barely themselves as they broke international drug rings. Writer-turned-agent-turned-writer Harry Edward Neal broke it down in his unpublished fictional work:

> An undercover agent, a "roper," may work for weeks or even months to convince a gang that he is one of them, that he will do anything "to make an easy buck."[11]

Maybe personality disorder helps too:

> In one crucial moment the agent destroys the personality he has struggled to make convincing. He discards it like the disguise it is and reveals his true identity.[12]

Another Harry doppelganger along the way, Neal began his career as a stenographer for the Secret Service, transcribing other people's words. Snatching the negative of a counterfeit ten-dollar bill out of a furnace, and thus providing crucial evidence for court, Neal won himself a promotion to agent, going on to become assistant director of the Secret Service, a career he left to become a full-time writer. Among his publications are the law that made the Secret Service a permanent agency and thirty-one books, including *The Story of the Secret Service*, and a book about how to write nonfiction. The former president of the Association of Former Agents of the United States knew, as did any undercover agent past or present, that the production of fictions in the service of the gathering of nonfiction is the name of the game.

(33-2)   Undercover Work

    G. Cultural background.

    H. Special talents and hobbies.

    I. Trade, profession, occupation.

    J. Good memory for names, faces and information.

    K. Knowledge of underworld methods and the modus operandi of crimes.

IV. DISGUISE.

    A. Abandon official identity.

      1. Remove badge and all credentials.

      2. Remove cards, letters, note books and all other items that might cause suspicion of official status or that can be traced to its source, unless consistent with background story.

    B. Adopt a completely different identity.

      1. Assume a character compatible with the suspect and the neighborhood involved.

        a. Select a remote background city with which you are familiar, but if possible one not well known to suspect.

        b. The background story should include names, addresses and descriptions of assumed education, places employed, associates and neighborhoods.

        c. Try to select fictitious information that cannot be readily verified by the suspect. Arrange for principals in story to be persons who have been coached to corroborate the story in case the suspect investigates.

        d. Corroborating persons should be bartenders, waiters, hotel clerks, pool room operators and others in occupations that would not arouse suspicion in the mind of the suspect.

FOR OFFICIAL USE ONLY

- 2 -

"Undercover Work," Federal Bureau of Narcotics Training School curriculum, 1950s. Harry J. Anslinger Papers, Special Collections Library, The Pennsylvania State University Libraries.

37 IN DOCTOR NATION

In the words of the old truism, "Truth is stranger than fiction." But as Harry wrote at the proverbial curbside, "Fiction alone has no monopoly in this field." Indeed, in addition to dealing in fictions, the Federal Bureau of Narcotics and CIA also trafficked in truth. The OSS, the CIA's precursor organization, had begun searching for a truth serum in 1942. With interest, then, did a senior administrator in the TD, or "truth drug," program read the reports of scientists at Dachau concentration camp "for useful leads in extracting information,

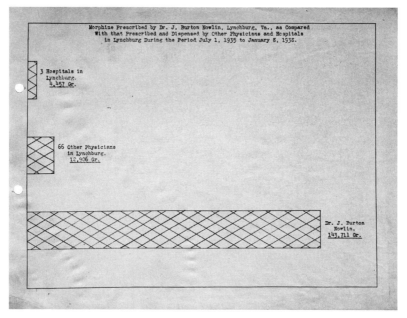

"Morphine Prescribed by Dr. J. Burton Nowlin, Lynchburg, Va., as Compared with That Prescribed and Dispensed by Other Physicians and Hospitals in Lynchburg during the Period July 1, 1935 to January 8, 1938." Harry J. Anslinger Papers, Special Collections Library, The Pennsylvania State University Libraries.

including speech-inducing drugs." At Dachau, a Dr. Kurt Plotner had administered high doses of mescaline to Jewish and Russian prisoners "and had watched them display schizophrenic behavior."[1] Nevertheless, Dr. Plotner's experiments with prisoners seemed to indicate that mescaline might have some role in inducing speech, or even in mind control; his results might have intelligence applications for good or for evil, depending on who recruited him. Thus, in the name of national security, the navy brought Dr. Plotner to the United States. (In Operation Paperclip, the United States adopted, and shielded from prosecution for war crimes, a great number of scientists and doctors who had run experimental programs for the Nazis.)

The CIA's Project Bluebird included the reproduction and furthering of that work. Replacing mescaline with LSD, it launched its experiments with a dose of 150 micrograms each for twelve Black men "of not too high mentality" followed by a hostile interrogation. The work was continued on a larger scale at the Edgewood Chemical Arsenal in Maryland, where more than seven thousand soldiers were unwitting subjects. Commanded to ride exercise cycles, the men in the experiment were given face masks sprayed with various hallucinogens: LSD, mescaline, BZ, and seryl. One of the objectives, to be attempted in future experiments as well, was to produce complete amnesia in the subjects. (Ironically, no single group was more afflicted by amnesia than special agents.) Over one thousand of the subjects suffered epilepsy or grave psychological complications, and there were dozens of suicide attempts.[2] In the end, it turned out that there was no such thing as a truth serum. Most subjects maintained their personalities, their values, and their dispositions toward truth and falsehood under the influence of a range of drugs.

There was a worldwide culture and history of experimentation no more authored by the Nazis than anti-Semitism was. As in other Western nations, Americans shared the Nazis' logic behind the ethico-administrative decision to use certain social groups as subjects.[3] Prisoners, racial and religious others, people with mental and physical disabilities and diseases, elderly and children—all these made up the natural constituency of subjects, partly because they inhabited an intermediate rung of being, somewhere between monkeys, dogs, and rats, on the one paw, and human experimenters, on the other, and partly because of the administrative ease of using preprocessed and on-site, incompetent, or disenfranchised groups.[4] As commissioner, Harry confronted such questions with respect to experiments that involved drugs.

For example, drug testing was conducted at the Narcotics Farm in Lexington, Kentucky, under the direction of Dr. Harris Isbell, with the hospital staff assisting. The Lexington team often tested human subjects; they had easy access to patients, and they did early research on Demerol, in which Harry became particularly invested. The addictive potential of the new synthetic and hazards attached to occasional use were the qualities that might bring a new drug under existing legal controls and therefore within his direct purview. The scientists and doctors at the United States Public Health Service Hospital in Kentucky published their results in the *Journal of Pharmacology and Experimental Therapeutics* in 1942.

Five prisoner-patients, serving sentences long enough to ensure clinical recovery after withdrawal, volunteered for the study. They were all former addicts who had been clean for at least six months; withdrawal was not unknown to them. Given varying but always increasing dosages of the substance, the five men were observed closely, and their "brain potential" was registered in a four-channel electroencephalograph and recorded on photographic paper. "An observer was always with the patient to record movements and to insure the absence of sleep." While the general trend in patients was bad enough, with results like "constipation, exaggerated tremors, graduating into muscle twitches and finally gross jerking of the extremities, hallucinations, increased sensitivity to sudden noise, and weakness in the extremities," case histories read like pure torture: On day 15, having received twelve doses for a total of of 1,700 milligrams, one subject "staggered against the wall and raised his hands to protect his head" as he walked about the ward. He felt claustrophobic and believed something had hit him in the head. Four days later, he was hallucinating that people were touching him. Three weeks after that, he had trouble talking. Ten days later, he was disoriented and walked aimlessly around the ward. After seven and a half weeks, he attempted to cool off his urine specimen with a fan; he was being given 2,660 milligrams over the course of fourteen daily injections. Eight weeks in, his head felt numb.[5]

Another patient was constipated, jerking in his sleep, and perspiring profusely by two weeks into the trial. On day 47, he found that he had bitten his tongue in his sleep, in which state he also laughed. On the sixty-ninth day, given fifteen injections amounting to 3,180 milligrams, he fainted and hit his head on the cement floor while the hot coffee he had been holding burned him.[6] Subjects were intermittently withdrawn from the Demerol as part of the trials. This subject was not atypical in reporting an "absence of aching" nor in saying that " if he was on the street he would seek Demerol for relief."[7]

In less concentrated and prolonged usage than was employed in these experiments, users tended to fall asleep. Or worse, feel good:

> **Demerol kicks me right up. It produces feelings I have never had and really desire. It relaxes my insides and I feel good. I forget my worries and feel exhilarated. All aches, pains and nervousness leave me. . . . Sexual pleasure is short-lived and easily satisfied; the pleasure obtained from Demerol is intense, sustained, and you want to keep that feeling all the time.**[8]

The Lexington study of 1942 had concluded, somewhat lukewarmly, that serious harm might come to addicts who could obtain very large quantities, a conclusion too mild for Harry. Harry was less concerned with the chemical than the legal properties of Demerol among other barbiturates. For Harry, the acid test of a chemical substance was whether it was controllable, and for a drug to be controllable, it had to be either addictive or dangerous on an occasional basis.

By 1946, Harry was engaged in a print war in the correspondence column in the *Journal of the American Medical Association*. A recent article in *Reader's Digest* had described Demerol as "God's own medicine" and seemed to deny its addictive capacity. Harry took to the pages of *JAMA* to issue an exhortation against the "blurb for a drug controlled by one manufacturer," a statement followed up, luckily, if not mysteriously, with the report of another Lexington researcher, Dr. Herbert Wieder, who asserted that Demerol was indeed addictive. In a final sentence that was more congenial to Harry, Wieder decided that "the same precautions should be observed in its use as in the use of the opiate drugs."[9] Indeed, in the interval between the

publication of these two articles, Harry had succeeded in scheduling
Demerol with the opiates, so the precautions governing the latter
also governed the former.

Like his colleagues in the OSS, Harry felt the pressure to duplicate,
if he could not preempt, strategic scientific initiatives abroad. Discoveries about drugs could be used for or against the strategic interests
of the United States. Two world wars had made of the earth a world
after all. There was no place on the globe, and therefore no nation,
in which the United States might not have an interest. There were
no more third terms, no more unturned stones, neutral countries, or
cultures deep enough in the Amazon that they weren't divvied up
and rostered Us or Them on the big binary whiteboard of the coming Cold War. Other nations were either friends or enemies; their
scientists likewise. Like his colleagues in the nascent CIA, Harry had
heard of research in China that called for copycat experiments in the
United States. Soon "two dogs without brains survived more than a
year at the United States Public Health Services experimental hospital
for drug addiction at Lexington."[10] Harry appreciated Dr. Abraham
Wikler's reports on the "cortical dogs," representing the stakes and
standards as he understood them:

> **Our only way of testing it is to try it on dogs. If the dog's legs get
> tangled up the drug is potent.**[11]

It was a tough and elegant test! "If you go on giving the dog marihuana, his brain is destroyed."[12] Airtight logic! Suggestive results!
Vivisection! The cure for addiction was right around the corner.

Also at Lexington, and again using animal subjects, Isbell and
Wikler tested the "tolerance and addiction liability of 6-dimethylamin
0-4-4-diphenyl-heptanone-3," which is methadone (then called "methadon").[13] There would soon be significant implications for humans.
Meanwhile, the Lexington team caused addiction and withdrawal in
rhesus monkeys and dogs with various spinal configurations:

> **All the dogs that had been receiving methadon showed restlessness,
> severe muscle tremors, fever, tachycardia, vomiting, hypernea,
> hydrophilia and loss of weight.**

Spontaneous rhythmic running movement developed in the hindlimbs, the flexor reflexes were hyperactive and the extensor thrust reflexes were abolished.

After this the preparation exhibited almost continuous grubbing, gnawing and sniffling at the floor of the cage for four days and was prostrated for several days thereafter.[14]

The researchers at the Narcotics Farm upped the ante on methadone experiments as they turned once again to their captive population, selecting as subjects patients who had cancer. As one example, a forty-seven-year-old white man with lung cancer was injected three times daily with methadone, and on the forty-first day, the drug was "abruptly withdrawn."[15]

Beginning twenty hours after his last dose he was nauseated and vomited twice, complained of cramps in his abdomen, sneezing, yawning and sweating and had three or four bowel movements. He slept poorly and said that he was nervous, uneasy, jittery, but did not ask for medication. A 5 mg. dose at the end of twenty-four hours did not relieve his symptoms.[16]

From the experiment in which this subject participated, Isbell et al. concluded that methadone had the potential for addiction and would become a serious public health problem unless its manufacture and use were "controlled."[17] This report, too, Harry read with interest. These researches in Kentucky proved useful to Anslinger in Washington; Harry knew just where to file them.

While well-funded chemists and doctors reported on drug trials in medical and scientific periodicals, and Harry read their reports with an eye to policy and law, journalists reported on arguably less licit drug trials and tribulations for the mass media. These reports bore all marks of the sensationalism fostered by George Wilkes and officially deplored but nonetheless practiced by Harry. Cleveland police found a hysterical woman "sobbing over her husband who lay on the floor amid a litter of wrecked furniture. The rug was covered with blood." He had smashed a mirror and cut off two of his fingers in "a violent spell brought on by long and excessive use of barbiturates. When he came to in a hospital, he had no recollection of his mad spree."[18] A man slipped sleeping pills to his kindergarten-aged twins, which caused a divorce between himself and his wife. Barbiturates left another man sleeping completely naked in a heavy rain in a manure pile. Yet another fell asleep with his cigarette burning a hole in his chest and was found with one hundred boxes of pills in his bedclothes.[19]

True or false, barbiturates were the big news, growing in popularity all over the population. Thrill Pills! Goofballs!! There were already two hundred varieties, and three billion doses were distributed annually. There were stories in the papers. "Sleeping Pills Aren't Candy!"[20]

> **In a squalid apartment in Kansas City, police found the body of a woman. The evidence in that one-room hell showed that before she died, alone and haunted in the dim half-world of the sleeping-pill addict, she had become an animal, crawling about on all fours, eating food off the floor, tearing at the furnishings of the room.**[21]

A lot like the dog on methadone.

Along with Demerol, barbiturates were synthetic drugs, and they were developed by the score in the 1940s, changing the drug landscape in the United States. Here were drugs taken by noncriminals, drugs that didn't automatically transform people into criminals the way narcotics did. Unlike narcotics, synthetic drugs could come to the United States from other countries legally (though they could also do so illegally), and represented a nearly limitless legal market for pharmaceutical companies (though they could also be distributed illegally). As they crossed over, they became Red Devils! Yellow Jackets! Blue Heaven! Purple Powder! And like narcotics, legal synthetics crossed over to the domestic black market on the backs, or prescription pads, of physicians. Synthetics reestablished doctors as crucial points of diversion from one market to the other, figures that could turn medicine into dope. Because they had the keys to the medicine cabinet, doctors would come back under the scrutiny of the Federal Bureau of Narcotics in the 1940s.

Harry had the keys to the rolltop desk where he kept file after file on doctors. One of Harry's compartments was overstuffed with reports of doctors addicting women to narcotics, getting them pregnant, driving them around town, beating them with a belt, giving them abortions, in between giving them shots or grains of morphine, taking their money, and involving them in cons. The doctors Harry had in this compartment were predators; reports came in from all over: Kansas, Oklahoma, South Carolina.

Other compartments tracked addicted doctors. Among drug addicts, the proportion of doctors was eight times what it should be.[22] "The percentage of physicians who become drug addicts is extremely high" became "The percentage of drug addicts who are doctors is extremely high." This point was stressed in an article in *Collier's* magazine, which actually implied that the doctor figures as a "typical addict":

> **Call him Dr. Brown. His name is not actually Brown and his case history has been sufficiently disguised to prevent identification. But he *is* a doctor.**[23]

Popular representations hearkened back to the 1933 Dwain Esper movie *Narcotic* in which the doctor-protagonist's drug addiction destroys his career, his social standing, and his health. Now, in one magazine piece in the 1940s, "physicians become victims of own treatment, administering drugs become most dangerous prescriptions . . . to the risky point of experimenting on themselves."[24] Here the experimentation on human subjects comes full circle, with a loopy logic that will be at work with Special Agent George White in the next chapter.

Yet another cache of files in Harry's bureau tracked bogus doctors. A radio repairman posing as a physician managed to talk himself onto the staff of one hospital after another: "Dr." Groves became addicted to morphine and still assisted in "appendectomies, hysterectomies, leg amputations, gall-bladder removals and skin grafting," until he took over the practice of a retiring Flint physician and pasted his name over the old doctor's name on his diploma. Other bogus doctors included, for a brief moment, *Dr.* Harry J. Anslinger, author of "Marijuana Research"—or so he had been represented in a 1938 convention book.[25] Clerical error. Hardly the stuff of a "Dr." Groves.

Ironically, Harry was the biggest dealer of them all. In 1935, Harry had launched a program to stockpile opium for use in treating injured soldiers during wartime. Though the war had not even begun, Harry predicted that the national opium reserves would not last two years and that the instability in the international arena meant the United States should be prepared. So he raised money "to purchase a strategic stockpile of opium . . . in sufficient supply to outlast the war period."[26] Beginning with a 169,000-pound buy in 1936, Harry acquired opium from Turkey, Yugoslavia, Bulgaria, and Afghanistan, and by 1940 had amassed 300 tons, which sat in the Treasury vaults vacated by the movement of the gold to Fort Knox. Anslinger virtually cornered the already-contracted market on opium during the war years.[27] To his dying day, Anslinger took pride in the way he anticipated the call for the "critical and strategic material" that would reduce the suffering of soldiers, and how this maneuver had the side effect of indebting other nations to us:

> **The supply was adequate enough to furnish vast quantities of drugs to our Allies.**[28]

Anslinger's stockpiling contributed to the reduced flow of opium in the black market during the war.

For all of Dr. Anslinger's concerns with doctors and their sensationally bad behavior back at home, he became less concerned with physicians' ability to prescribe the old opiates and more concerned with their ability to prescribe the new synthetics. For all the media attention to the skyrocketing use of the new barbiturates and their addictive qualities—and in spite of stiffening narcotics laws and increasing stigmatization of addicts—efforts by antidrug reformers to have them controlled were thwarted. Neither Dr. Isbell nor the AMA nor Harry J. Anslinger wanted "to create another Volstead situation with the barbiturates, nor would we wish to put the barbiturates into the same category as those under the Harrison Narcotic Act." Harry didn't necessarily want to have prescription drugs "in the same compartment as morphine" because of the social and practical impossibilities of enforcement.[29] Doctors would have to police themselves, but Harry and his agents would keep an eye on them. The next question was, Who would police the special agents who took drug experimentation into their own hands?

38 SPINDOCTRINATION

Among the most fun Harry ever had was testifying before the Kefauver Committee, the Special Committee on Organized Crime in Interstate Commerce, in 1950. This was Harry's time to shine. He had been deeply involved with exposing the organized crime syndicate of whose existence he had been convinced since working on the railroad. His peer and counterpart most conspicuously unconvinced was J. Edgar Hoover, head of the CIA, who resisted Anslinger's intelligence. Hoover was not convinced until the feds busted up a confabulation of crime lords, kingpins, big bosses, in the backwoods of upstate New York in 1957, the so-called Apalachin Meeting even Hoover couldn't deny. But back before the Kefauver Committee in 1950, a compensatory moment of vindication was at hand for Anslinger, whose testimony was more than adequate enough to persuade.[1]

One of the few legislative outcomes of the Kefauver Committee was the 1952 Boggs Act for which Harry had testified. Boggs was a "mandatory-sentence law" that provided for penalties adequately harsh, Anslinger believed, to deter second and third offenses.[2] When

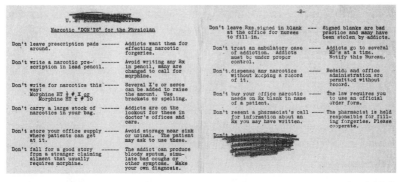

"Narcotic 'DON'TS' for the Physician," date unknown. Harry J. Anslinger Papers, Special Collections Library, The Pennsylvania State University Libraries.

he testified again in favor of a yet stricter revision of Boggs in 1955, Harry gave his take on marijuana, again, adding this time that "our great concern about the use of marijuana, that eventually is used over a long period, it does lead to heroin addiction."[3] It was the heyday of the gateway theory.

Harry had long advocated adequate penalties. In 1939, a *Washington Post* article, "U.S. Narcotics Chief for Stern Penalties," had summed up his view on the problem of narcotics: "Adequate punishment is Commissioner's answer."[4] What punishment for violators was adequate by Harry's standards? In 1945, *Newsweek* had printed his glib proposal to "jail offenders then throw away the key."[5] Harry spoke in favor of capital punishment for people who sold drugs to children: "If we have the death penalty for kidnappers, who only steal children, why not the same punishment for dope peddlers who destroy them?"[6] He came to reverse this position when he became convinced that such sentences would cause juries to acquit defendants out of fear of sending innocent people to the chair.[7]

In the language of the Boggs Act, revised nomenclature names an "addict violator" as the subject of its clauses, cementing the construction of addiction itself as criminal. Social scientists tried to account for addiction by different means. Certain psychological types had certain susceptibility to drug addiction: those who suffered from an inferiority complex, weak fathers or overbearing mothers, alienation. Certain social facts mitigated toward the use of certain prescription drugs: the overgrowth of cities, the cultural and historical vacuum at the heart of the new suburb, the fast pace of technologized living, the competition-on-fire that made the postwar era so prosperous domestically but also mass-manufactured fear and tension.[8] And projected them onto Soviet everything. Aldous Huxley kicked in again with *The Doors of Perception*, recommending mescaline for the exercise of the undisciplined Mind at Large with its capacity for creative and intellectual reach, and personal and spiritual insight. And regular suburbanites echoed experimental subjects whose worlds were turned inside out by synthetics: "Demerol relieved my nervousness and made me feel normal."[9]

By 1952, the CIA had constituted a working group known as MKULTRA, which took advantage of relative peace to fiddle around with some less predictable tactics, less conventional warfare, weapons even less visible than gas, mental maneuvers. With the help of certain specialists, it might be possible to compel people, say prisoners of war or criminals or staff people, to tell the truth, or to carry out posthypnotic assassination orders, or otherwise to comport relative to national interests. With the help of certain chemicals, it might be possible to manipulate minds, to force the truth out of unwilling interrogees, or to blank out the memories of those with state secrets. With the help of certain agents, it would be possible to test such chemicals on a range of human subjects, from involuntary to unwitting.

The legal synthesis of drugs for these experiments would theoretically have been in Harry's jurisdiction. The rerouting of seized opiates and cocaine for other experiments was also in Harry's bailiwick. Which is not to say that the CIA comported with Federal Bureau of Narcotics rules and regulations; that agency would run its course with or without Harry's say-so. Chemist Dr. Sydney Gottlieb, a.k.a. "Dirty Trickster," oversaw the bulk of CIA-funded drug tests in the 1950s and 1960s as head of the so-called Technical Services Division. Under Gottlieb's auspices, the famous skin doctor, Dr. Kligman, directed the experimental program at Holmesburg Prison in which dozens of corporations and a few branches of the military were invested, and together with colleagues, he ran tests with radioactive and carcinogenic materials—and with hallucinogens.[10] While the governmental agencies supported extensive testing with LSD at the University of Pennsylvania, other universities and private companies pursued morphine, Demerol, seconal, atropine, benzedrine, and psilocybin.[11]

Having noted mind control work being done in China and the Soviet Union, Gottlieb argued that the work of MKULTRA, begun in 1953, was "mandatory." This drug-testing program was part of a larger one of mind control, itself part of a broad study in chemical use in offensive as well as defensive intelligence arenas, in turn part of a larger project of world domination. It was Gottlieb whose direction of MKULTRA included the funding of Dr. Ewen Cameron, who contributed to the drafting of the Nuremberg Code governing medical research before going on to investigate the possibilities of psychosurgery. Dr. Cameron researched the possibility of "wiping the mind clean." One technique of which involved, over the course of two or three months, putting patients to sleep every day with a cocktail of "Thorazine, Nembu-tal and Seconal" and waking them with amphetamine injections to subject them to electroshock and reprogramming treatments; 150 patients underwent this regimen.[12] And it was Gottlieb, at Fort Detrick, who dosed Frank Olson, the CIA chemist who officially suicided out a tenth-story hotel-room window in New York City days later.

Gottlieb and his associates also tried drugging themselves and finally turned to pulling people off the street for unscheduled testing. For this work, he had the use of the supremely gifted narcotics special agent George White. White, operating under various aliases, set up an MKULTRA "safe house" in Greenwich Village, to which he invited random people—it is not known how many—to parties in order to test LSD on them. For this, White needed to hang around on the George Wilkes side of town, its underbelly, where his friend Gil Fox, the sleaze writer, and his various pseudonyms, drank and drugged and swung with other swingers and prostitutes—and then wrote "novels" about it all. Prostitutes could be used to slip drugs into subjects' drinks. Then again, White was pretty good at it himself—he is alleged to have dosed many people in an off-the-cuff extra-experimental way. White liberally dosed his friends and acquaintances (Clarice Stein, and Kai and Jo Jurgenson, among others), his colleagues from Fort Detrick to Los Alamos, and himself. He was accused of having dosed an actress named Linda King on September 12, 1953, whose reaction sent her to the hospital but not to a lawyer or the press. Later the same month, narcotics agent Crofton Hayes may also have tasted White's touch, according to the agent who alleged that White dosed an office clerk for the CIA (who went "berserk").[13] George White left a trail of LSD wherever he went; the gin he drank up.

Relocated from New York to San Francisco, White set up two more safe houses in the Bay Area. There he carried out Operation Midnight Climax, working with a team of prostitutes known as "George's Girls" to the SFPD—"many of them black heroin addicts whom he paid in drugs"—who would bring their tricks to the "CIA-sponsored drug and sex sessions."[14] What finally brought these extravagances and abus-es to light was a newly installed and careful inspector general, who objected to the $1,000 charge for liquor and $44 for a telescope. Earlier charges for red curtains and large mirrors had gone under the rug.

Surely White was uniquely arrogant, even among agents. I don't like to give him this airtime, but I am still paying his bill.

What has this to do with Harry or with drugs? Harry J. Anslinger is the wind beneath the wings of every one of these MKULTRA escapades whether the Federal Bureau of Narcotics funneled the funding or the CIA did—and not just because he knew a good deal of what the CIA was up to. The CIA unilaterally offered its agents Federal Bureau of Narcotics papers as covers, hiring Corsican drug smugglers as assassins, bringing narcotics in from Cuba, and "blackmailing spies, diplomats, and politicians at three Bureau safehouses."[15] Harry may not have been central enough to give or withhold explicit approval to or from all CIA projects, but Harry and the Federal Bureau of Narcotics supported what they did know, as well as what they didn't. Over and above loaning the CIA Harry's most special special agents, like Garland Williams, Charles Siragusa, and George White, the bureau supplied materiel for many government-run experiments involving drugs. If nothing else, Harry knew enough.

Harry sat just outside the clique of elites who took experimental intelligence enterprises into their own hands. And Harry did not himself perform brain surgery on people who were alive and awake. He did not force-feed anybody salt water or infect anybody with syphilis. But Harry kept the boat floating. If Dr. Gottlieb made the madness of Agent George White and Dr. Kligman possible, Harry in turn made Gottlieb possible every day of his working life, filing certain papers in certain compartments of the bureau and sweeping others under the rug. Unspecial people like Harry hold down the world with order forms and budgets. People like him made people like Hoover—never mind people like Williams, White, and Siragusa—possible. They balance the act of government bureaucracy, while mad geniuses with expense accounts for multiple martinis per diem tear around tipping international relations into the ocean of absurdity. With moral sleight of hand, Harry distracted the members of the social clubs, while very special operatives for the CIA and Federal Bureau of Narcotics did whatever the fuck they wanted (or thought was a good idea), and what they wanted (or thought was a good idea) was large-scale violent overthrow of foreign governments, unless a goofy little targeted assassination could do the trick. What they wanted was aliases. What they wanted was enemies' asses to kick. What they wanted was pussy. What they wanted was booze. What they wanted was clearance. They fucking loved clearance. They made their way past the point of corruption, these guys with those drugs and their overweening senses of prerogative.

Congressional approval was for straights. The Kefauver Committee hearings made good TV. Harry could have his little Boggs Act.

39 THE WORLD'S LEADING AUTHORITY

Harry arrived, approximately when he achieved high office in 1931. Anslinger, not fantastically wealthy, not highly born, not much educated, not a player or a sexy man, not magnetic, nevertheless went on to become quite powerful, with dense political muscle. The latter he flexed fiercely but without flamboyance, in national and international arenas, and his high rococo rhetoric he broadcast widely in the media and from podia everywhere. A Herbert Hoover appointee reappointed by Franklin Roosevelt by 1933, Anslinger had pushed through major legislation by 1937. He hit his stride in the 1930s, and strode through the next two or three decades, remaining in the one office through both Democratic and Republican administrations, wearing that strange political vestment, official nonpartisanship.

The name Harry J. Anslinger was synonymous with narcotics policy and law enforcement, and with the Federal Bureau of Narcotics. But was Anslinger made for the Federal Bureau of Narcotics, or was it made for him? The identity was close enough for confusion and allowed for a certain slippage:

> **Mr. Anslinger started the Bureau. He has made it the model for every government anywhere which seriously desires to fight one of the worst menaces of civilization.**[1]

And what was the gift by dint of which Anslinger accomplished this? The same commentator offers this tautology about Anslinger's model agency:

> **It is inevitably a monument to the enduring success of sheer merit.**[2]

It was sometimes asserted that Harry's merit lay in his job performance, which included a performance of modesty:

WASHINGTON, JAN. 4--ANNOUNCES CRACKDOWN ON DOPE TRAFFIC-- HARRY J.
A...NGER, U.S. TREASURY NARCOTICS COMMISSIONER, TODAY ANNOUNCES
A S...IES OF RAIDS IN THE NATION'S BIG CITIES AIMED AT CRIPPLING THE
NA...TICS TRAFFIC. MORE THAN 500 SUSPECTED PEDDLERS WERE BAGGED.
AN...NGER SAID A LARGE NUMBER WHO HAVE BEEN SELLING DOPE TO YOUTHS
WE...CAUGHT. (AP-WIREPHOTO)(EE61840STF-HWG)1952 (SEE WIRE STORY)

Narcotics Commissioner Harry J. Anslinger, in New York on January 4, 1958, "announces a series
of raids in the nation's big cities aimed at crippling the narcotics traffic. More than 500 suspected
peddlers were bagged" (AP photo).

> I do not know M. Anslinger personally, but year after year I keep
> hearing comments about the fine, devoted, and tireless job he is
> performing quietly, with a small staff, in a continually uphill battle
> against smugglers and dope peddlers.[3]

But it was much more often asserted that Anslinger's success was a
function of his administrative expertise—and his "authority":

> We have great faith in Commissioner Harry J. Anslinger, a world-
> renowned authority. The United States is fortunate indeed to have
> him heading its narcotic bureau. He is not only one of America's
> great administrators but one of the finest administrators in the
> world.[4]

Not only was he *an* authority, but he was *the* authority; specifically, "he is the greatest living authority on narcotic traffic," according
to Sir Lyle Leonard of the International Permanent Central Opium
Board.[5] This phrase was much bandied about, appearing, for example, in *Bangor Daily News* in 1946: "He is the greatest living authority
on the world narcotic drug traffic."[6] His authority now derived from
his authority and redounded to it in a self-legitimizing loop, a rep-
utational maintenance program in the Department of Redundancy
Department.[7]

For example, in January 1943, the *Journal of the American Medical
Association* printed a letter Harry had written to its editor in which he
contradicted a previously published paper asserting that marijuana
doesn't lead to physical, mental, or moral degeneration.[8] Harry's letter
offered a long list of passages from articles up to one hundred years
old as proof that marijuana causes criminal insanity. His commissionership rendered incredible claims quite credible, literally authorizing
his authority.

It was difficult to argue with Harry's claims, his rigid objectivity, his
hard lines. *Bangor Daily News* praised the Trojan job Harry had always
done, reporting that the

> big balding bureaucrat who began his government service as a
> typist 33 years ago . . . now has the unique distinction of being

> probably the only person able to get the Russians to cooperate in
> the dis-United Nations.[9]

A grandiose claim for a cold warrior, to be sure. Clearly Harry had
friends from Maine to California to the New York islands, from the
backwoods to the main stage, in Hollywood. But for all his important accomplishments, he was modest too and let others have the
limelight:

> Although the nation's top authority on the smuggling, distribution
> and consumption of narcotics did not appear openly in the sensa-
> tional seizure of Robert Mitchum and his marijuana companions
> a few weeks ago, his agents have had their eye on this problem for
> months. Anslinger, however, prefers to remain behind the scenes,
> letting the local police handle the cases on the spot.[10]

If there was anyone in the limelight for heading up a federal
enforcement agency, it was J. Edgar Hoover, the effective bureaucrat
from whom Harry differed most pointedly. Three years younger than
Harry, ascending to the directorship of the FBI four years after Harry
became commissioner of the Federal Bureau of Narcotics, Hoover was
a Washington native and a household word. Hoover was more powerful than Anslinger, in terms of reach and sway, access and control,
and Hoover's office was on the central corridor. Moreover, Hoover had
a personality over and above a public persona. But if he lived in the
shadow of the flashier Hoover, Harry was evidently comfortable there.
The two shared a zeal for intelligence work and they shared personnel. If Hoover knew more than Harry about certain covert operations,
Harry knew enough to cooperate with the CIA when asked. And if
chains of command sometimes ran around him in his odd perch in
the Treasury, Harry nevertheless had a very secure niche.

Anslinger did indeed figure as the world's leading authority on
narcotics—without contest—for about thirty years, a figuration
secured by having a job as the world's leading authority figure in the
field of narcotics. And who knew otherwise? There were researchers,
lawmakers, pharmaceutical company executives, journalists, law
enforcement officials, and agents galore, among other colleagues in

the Treasury and in the Department of Justice, so many spokes on the hub that was Harry in his bureau office. Not one of those hands could know what all the rest were doing about drugs, but Harry could, like or with the brain of the corporate octopus. And with that special vantage point, he could see that people would believe his claims about narcotics. Authority, like price, was a function of agreed-upon value. Until the late 1950s, when Harry's authoritarianism would begin to wear on his colleagues, most people who knew of Harry J. Anslinger seemed to feel that he was a qualified expert performing a valuable public service, and performing it well. As the clipping in Harry's own files said about Harry,

Men like him should get a pat on the back once in a while.[11]

And so he did.

SUNDAY MIRROR MAGAZINE, AUGUST 12, 1945

How OPIUM, *a Jap Weapon,* PERILS THE WORL[D]

By GERALD R. SCOTT

JAPAN was boasting. The louder the roar in the ears of her doomed citizens as whole cities collapsed under the cataclysmic broadsides of the American Grand Fleet moving inshore for the kill, the louder rang the Japanese boast.

Here is the form it took, as recorded by the Army's San Francisco listening post tuned in July 17 to a Domei broadcast out of Tokio:

"We have a secret counter-strategy in reserve against these indecisive enemy blows. We must bide our time, not move until the nour is ripe. We must not play into the enemy's hands.

"In the end the enemy will play into ours!"

Old stuff, some will say, remembering how Nazidom expired with the cry on its frothing lips that it, too, was luring the Allied armies to the gates of Berlin in order to exterminate them en masse with one sweeping blow from "a secret weapon in reserve."

But Japan HAS a secret weapon. It CAN reverse the military verdict now being won by our fighters at a mounting cost in American lives. It CAN double or triple that cost, and do so long after the purely military phase of the current death-struggle between East and West has ended. It HAS been timed to kill like a fabulous delayed-action bomb by the super-strategians of the Orient who lurk behind Japan's puny military tacticians.

The name of this secret weapon is known.

It is opium.

Against this deadly weapon, warns an Associated Press dispatch from Washington, the authors of the United Nations Charter, as recently "perfected" in San Francisco, have seemingly closed their global eyes.

Says the AP:

"What worries some authorities is that no specific provision has been made for international opium controls under the new Charter of the United Nations."

Ominous figures are quoted:

"The legitimate medical and scientific needs of the world for the drug derived from the opium poppy are less than 400 tons a year.

"The U. S. Government estimates that the world currently produces 5,200,000 tons!"

That Japan began planning long ago to exploit that fatal 5,000,000-ton discrepancy between civilized mankind's self-improving needs and self-destroying desires for the ruinous drug is attested by the known facts.

Those facts were hammered into the international conscience—if any—eight years ago, to the rhythmic thud of the Chinese headsman's axe, when an alarmed China decreed death for all opium addicts as a desperate counter-measure to Japan's open policy of "conquest by narcotization" of the Northern Chinese provinces which she now holds so securely.

How the poppy was pressed into service in Japan's fifth column by the late Mitsura Toyama, sinister head of the Nipponese Black Dragon Society, was an open secret at the time and has remained so ever since.

Toyama had dedicated the eighty years of an evil life to weaving all the elements of organized vice into a network of intrigue—from the stinking waterfront brothels of the port cities to the paradisical opium-smoker palaces operated for the enslavement of China's top leaders in the shadow of the last emperor's walled domain in Peiping. Toyama's main objective was conquest by drugs.

How far Toyama's Black Dragon cohorts had progressed in this planned offensive is attested by the desperate nature of the counter-offensive launched, in extremity, by Chinese authorities when, at long last, they struggled out of dope-induced sleep and promulgated the 1937 decree of mass extermination of the victims of the "Opium Offensive."

Mitsura Toyama, late Black Dragon head, began vicious drug warfare.

A two-day reprieve for the doomed was included in the edict which, on Dec. 28, 1937, ordered the police to deliver all opium addicts to the local headsman, without trial for instant decapitation starting Jan. 1 of the New Year. Wholesale executions ensued. A pathetic sidelight on the historic cleanup is thrown by yellowing copies of the Pieping, Nanking, Tientsin and Shanghai newspapers of the period, which were crammed with ads by quacks, making impossible promises of overnight cures.

Lest the average American remain lulled by the notion that Japan's all-out narcotic offensive of eight years ago against Northern China will remain an isolated incident of the past, worth only a foot-note in postwar history books, the latest release of the Foreign Policy Association on the subject of "drugs in the war" is quoted in the AP Washington dispatch.

The release reveals that "the Germans stole enough morphine and codeine in Belgium alone to supply the legitimate German medical needs for a year. At present prices in the illicit market in the United States, the stolen narcotics would bring approximately $17,000,000."

Here then is evidence of the trend of the thinking of at least one partner in the late unlamented Axis as to the postwar possibility of the addiction-drugs as a comeback weapon for the defeated foe.

But the possibilities of a deliberate release into the illicit international dope traffic of hoarded drugs of European origin are negligible when compared with the similar possibilities, or probabilities, of an organized attempt by a sullen, defeated Japan to seek her revenge on her occidental conquerers by pulling the plug on the East's enormous sources of opium supply.

Those sources were augmented before the war, and maintained during the war, because of the open "dope 'em and rule 'em" policies of at least one member of the Big Three who are now the self-appointed masters of the globe for at least a century to come.

Until a little over a year ago, when her political and military fortunes in the Far East were at low ebb, England pursued a policy of excepting her Asiatic colonies from accords reached by the old League of Nations on regulation of the world output of the opiates.

The gross hypocrisy of such a policy is obvious. It amounts to a pious statement that England is against peddling dope—except to a paying clientele that wants it. Until late 1943, as the AP dispatch points out, England held to the position, taken in the Permanent Central Opium Board of the old League of Nations, that she could not curtail her operations in India and Burma as official dope peddler to the native masses because the annual take from this lovely racket was the revenue which paid the salaries and operating expenses of her colonial ruling setup, from the Viceroy on down to the lowliest clerk in the government dope dispensaries. Encouraged or perhaps constrained by this example, The Netherlands operated a similar dope-peddling monopoly in her Far Eastern empire.

It took the lessons taught the British and the Dutch by the disasters of Hong Kong, Singapore, Java, New Guinea and Ceylon to bring about a belated change in this suicidal policy. The "poppy belt" provided the Japs with the avenue of none-resistance down which they marched and sailed to the shores of Australia in the first year after Pearl Harbor.

It is now known that that sweep down the Pacific was more a feat of calculated corruption than feat of arms. Its moves were planned in the Tokyo GHQ of the Asiatic Underworld years before they were ratified in any Japanese War College. Mitsura Toyama's "other army" of panders, pimps and peddlers had infiltrated the route of Japanese conquest long before Tojo gave the word which undammed the flow of Japanese armed forces into the ready-made breech.

A month after Pearl Harbor these facts were placed in the historical record in a remarkable statement, unheeded at the time, prepared by Harry J. Anslinger, U. S. Commissioner of Narcotics, for release by former Sec. of the Treasury Morgenthau. Said Morgenthau:

"Japan started war against western civilization 10 years ago, with narcotics as weapons. An illicit opium traffic was engaged in by Japan as an instrument of national policy for a decade before Pearl Harbor.

"This policy has had and WILL CONTINUE TO HAVE three official Japanese objectives: to gain revenue; to corrupt western nations; to weaken and enslave the peoples of lands already invaded or marked for inva[si]on by Japan.

"Wherever the Japanese army goes, the drug traffic follows. In every territory conquered by the Japanese a large part of the people become enslaved by drugs.

"But—Japanese troops are forbidden to use drugs!"

As a matter of fact Anslinger, whose "N-Men" fight dope fully as remorselessly and competently as J. Edgar Hoover's G-Men fight the kind of crime which dope engenders, did not wait for Pearl Harbor as a cue for his warnings against the Japs.

As far back as 1934, this able field officer in the Treasury's army of law enforcers was trumpeting his conviction that Japan's secret drive to capture control of the world's illicit traffic in habit-forming drugs represented a long-range plan to soften up the white man's world for an eventual war of conquest. He thus aligned himself with the select few who not only foresaw Pearl Harbor but spoke their pieces in useful time instead of waiting to join the chorus of second-guessers.

In 1934, Anslinger reported:

"The sources of the world's illicit drug supply has shifted from Western Europe to the Far East, and simultaneously the U. S. Government's fight to suppress this nefarious and vicious traffic at the nation's gates has shifted from the Atlantic to the Pacific Coast.

"Only a short time ago, illicit drugs were pouring into the United States from Western Europe in large quantities, but this flood has now been reduced to a thin stream by the operation of the Geneva drug-c[ontr]ol convention of 1931, the forceful representations o[f th]e American State Department to foreign countries which heretofore had been lax or indifferent to any program of stamping out the evil, and the vigilance of our Federal Customs and Narcotic Services.

"Scourged from one country to another as the international agencies seeking their extinction have been relentlessly closing in on them, the drug traffickers have now set up their clandestine factories in the Far East, principally in Japan and Manchukuo.

"Three years ago a dope trader could go to nearly any capital in Europe, call in a 'broker,' give an order for a ton of morphine to be delivered in New York, and the order would be filled. Now illicit morphine can scarcely be obtained at any price in Europe. The source of this supply was chiefly Turkey, where illegitimate manufacturers set up factories after being driven from France, Switzerland and Germany. But this haven did not last long, because the President of Turkey stepped in and shut all these factories.

"There have been some indications, disclosed by the seizure of several large shipments of illicit drugs at Marseilles in the past year, that some of the traffickers were creeping back into France. This was met promptly by the French Government by establishing a Central Narcotics Bureau, not only for the purpose of eradicating the traffic in France, but to co-operate with the United States in trapping the smugglers.

"The drug that is coming from the clandestine [fac]tories of the Far East is the deadliest of all—he[roin]. Morphine and heroin are derivatives of opium. Heroin is a reprocessed derivative of morphine and about three times as powerful as its parent. It make addicts almost instantly on first use."

The average clean-living citizen, being spared close contact with the painful human problem of drug-addiction, understands little about the difficulties involved in combating the spread of this special form of race suicide.

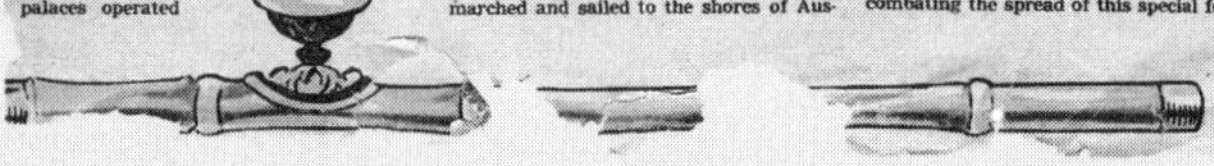

Gerald R. Scott, "How Opium, a Jap Weapon, Perils the World," *Sunday Mirror Magazine*, August 12, 1945. Harry J. Anslinger Papers, Special Collections Library, The Pennsylvania State University Libraries.

40 THE ORIENTAL COMMUNISTS HAD A TWOFOLD PURPOSE

At the top of the chain of command that reached all the way down into the drug-littered gutter of midwestern American cities, Harry J. Anslinger. With the authority he had accumulated, Harry pursued the agenda that would ossify into his legacy. On the domestic front, Harry continued to support harsh penalties, mandatory sentencing, and compounded penalties for repeat offenders. As he had throughout his adult life, Harry maintained his longstanding convictions that Black jazz musicians and Latinos purveyed marijuana, and he directed enforcement accordingly. His active relationships with pharmaceutical companies continued through the 1950s, as he continued to license distribution of synthetics (or tried to suppress them, as in the case of Demerol). And he continued to amass evidence that there was an organized crime syndicate controlled by Italians in cooperation with Jews, Greeks, and Asians, and whose members slunk across national boundaries, which in turn required *his* cooperation with other nations. The United States was the vulnerable white woman in a sea of narcotics purveyed by Others everywhere else. Anywhere from Sicily to Manila, people hopped boats, stashed drugs on camels, came to US cities, and destroyed them. Anslinger's jurisdiction, like his authority, necessarily attained global proportions. So did his paranoia.

Harry held a pan-Asian prejudice that was not uncommon among his fellow Americans. At least as far back as the 1909 conference in the Philippines convened by Hamilton Kemp Wright, there had been explicit invocations of the threat of criminal contamination through drugs in a geopolitically indeterminate Asia, a collapse of national and ethnic distinction called "The Orient." Harry was not the only one to use this designation: before and during the war, prejudices against both Chinese and Japanese immigrants and their imagined countries of origin easily slipped into a kind of pan-anti-Asian sentiment. As an occupying power in China and active Axis power in the Second World War, Japan focused a good deal of generic anti-Asian fear in the 1930s and early 1940s. Domestically, these fears manifested in internment camps for Japanese Americans, but Harry's scope featured the Japan in Asia, less so the one in the United States.

> Meanwhile, the Bureau has become an essential part of our national war-effort: Japan, as the Commissioner has elsewhere amazingly proved, systematically employs drugs not only to "reconcile" conquered peoples: she officially uses narcotics to "soften" populations marked for her enmity and during her open hostilities.[1]

I am unaware of such proofs, though similar claims pepper his pages and those of newspapers around the country. "How Opium, a Jap Weapon, Perils the World" appeared in the *Sunday Mirror Magazine* in August of 1945, lauding Harry for all of his work, including his perspicacity for having foreseen the Japanese drug war "plans" as early as 1934. He was frequently cited for his analysis of the Japanese strategy.

> Harry J. Anslinger, unrelenting head of the United States Bureau of Narcotics, more than once has accused the Japanese of using narcotics as an instrument of national policy, not only to poison the American people with their clandestinely imported drugs but also weaken their subjugated peoples.[2]

In fact, as Harry knew, global drug trafficking had decreased during the war for a number of reasons. Transportation was more difficult and more dangerous in all theaters. Commercial transportation was restricted and monitored more closely, and interdiction was likelier when everyone in the world imagined that everyone else was an agent of the enemy, and enemies were internal as well as external. Dealers and users enlisted or were inducted, and those men who didn't fight were busy with other entertainments and other avenues of profit; weapons tended to edge out narcotics as a popular black market commodity. Anslinger happily noted the decrease in global traffic, which naturally corresponded with a domestic decrease, though he accurately predicted that the traffic would pick back up again after the war. For the moment, Anslinger himself was the kingpin, having stockpiled sufficient opium to kill a great deal of Allied pain.

After the Allies bombed Japan in August 1945, the Soviets renounced their nonaggression pact with Japan and within two weeks had essentially defeated the Kwantung Army. Within a month, the Japanese troops in China formally surrendered. Thus, the Sino-Japanese War ended at the same time as World War II. Now the burden of suspicion and presumptive enemyhood began to shift from the Japanese to the Chinese. By the end of the decade, China would be more of an enemy than Japan.

Triggered by the Chinese Revolution of 1949, Harry's animus against Communism converged on his anti-Asian sentiment. During his first diplomatic dispatch to Europe, Harry's

> **devotion to his Government and its ideals is further evidenced by the astonishing revelation he made in 1921 while collaborating with the British Intelligence Service in relation to the Third International, and their plans to sow the seeds of revolution throughout the world.**[3]

In Harry's next post, in Venezuela in the 1920s, the absence of Communists lurking in the bushes had left him disappointed and bored.

By 1952, Harry's long-simmering conspiracy theories came to a boil:

> **America's top narcotics sleuth accused Red China today of drug warfare against the United Nations in the Far East. He said the Oriental Communists had a two-fold purpose: Selling habit-forming drugs to finance party activities and buy war materials, and spreading drug addiction to undermine morale of U.S. and other troops in the Far East.**[4]

Tarring Japanese and Chinese with the same brush, Anslinger identified a Communist official named Po, in what was then called Peking, who was "training 4,000 Chinese Communists to smuggle drugs, direct to Japanese workers, collect the funds, distribute a share to the Communist Party in Japan and purchase war materials."[5] By the time the domino theory was explicitly articulated by President Eisenhower in 1954, Harry described the mission of the Federal Bureau of Narcotics as "smashing Red China's Fifth Column."[6]

Theatermate North Korea was also implicated:

> Harry J. Anslinger, U.S. Narcotics Commissioner, drew what he said was a clear pattern of red Chinese and North Korean links with Japanese Communists to produce and smuggle opium products, "push" them through streetwalkers and brothels and smash the resistance of U.S. soldiers by making them narcotics addicts.[7]

Eisenhower's domino theory was in the air. As the threat of Japanese Communism floated away, other Asian countries seemed to become vulnerable to the infiltration of "Communist" logic. India, the last imagined domino in Eisenhower's schema, now made it onto Harry's map.

> If the soil of sprawling, misruled, India were to become the seedbed of a devious postwar assault against the hated whites, through rot-degeneration of the occidental nerve-system, we could easily and quickly sink to sub-standard rank in the family of mankind.[8]

India all by itself was contagious, sprawling rather than simply large, and if the West were not careful to suppress their flow, drugs would knock down the vulnerable pillars of our race defense, those young white US soldiers. And indeed, drug use increased dramatically following the war, especially among younger people.[9] Drugs were the weapon with which Communists would attack the men who would succumb to them, which would, in domino fashion, lead to the addiction of Christian white women and thence to prostitution, edging out procreation.

> The average clean-living citizen, being spared close contact with the painful human problem of drug addiction, understands little about the difficulties involved in combating the spread of this special form of race suicide.[10]

With such high stakes, enforcement was a pure force for global good, a mandate to protect the future of humanity, and it warranted the tactics of covert warfare, in addition to a public communications strategy. Therefore, no drug bust in the United States, no matter how small, was simply a local matter.

> **A world of meaning—or, one might better say, an underworld of meaning—is suggested by that obscure Baltimore seizure of what may seem like a drop-in-the-bucket consignment of the drug which destroys civilizations. The significance lies not in the amount of the haul, but its origin.**[11]

Here is a dose of uncut racism, where whiteness is simultaneously a condition of moral and organic supremacy, where the two are one, and where its opposite is the crooked and contagious enemy. Each little drop of drug waters the seed of decline and defeat—of whiteness, of civilization, of temperance; the flood of drugs causes rot in which whites will sink below the Others, whom they should, properly, rule. No wonder whites were nervous. Here is the cautionary tale of colonial misrule, not the trouble with the rule itself. Harry compounded the formula, conflating drugs and Communism—both weapons of enemies of free enterprise—and addicts and slaves.

Harry was willing and able to attribute almost any contemporary political problem, from the inner cities to the global arena, to drugs. So if Japan ceased to be an enemy of the United States and Japanese Communism failed to materialize in any really threatening form, China's Communism, by contrast, grew only more threatening. Harry never had any trouble identifying the threat, from Communists to sharks to nonwhite, un-Christian, and un-American people. For Anslinger, salvation lay in the passage, in the 1950s, of the further passage of harsh and durable prohibitionist law, the real legislative pillars of Nixon's later War on Drugs and the Rockefeller Drug Laws. Thus Harry threw all his weight behind the Boggs Acts of 1952 and its reincarnation in 1956 as the Narcotics Control Act—and their aggressive enforcement.

41 LOTUS EATERS:

1953, or The Imponderabilia of Actual Life

In 1953, William Burroughs set out for South America to seek the kicks of the Yage as brewed and administered by the natives, like a participant-observer in the rituals of drug taking as yet uncorrupted by actual anthropologists, unbusted by the Federal Bureau of Narcotics or its affiliates abroad, and inexhausted by the research for, and perhaps funded in part by a stream of royalties deriving from, *Junky*, published the same year (in which, coincidentally, Narcotics Anonymous was formed as a kind of friendly amendment to Alcoholics Anonymous by the famous Bill), by the pseudonymous William Lee.

> **When I went to score for Yage I was walking into strange territory.**[1]

On his way south as a stranger to paradise, to a place still beyond the pale of social scientists, deep in the vine-tangle of tropical climes, high high in the Colombian mountains, Billy Burroughs and William Lee

> **anchored their ship on an unknown coast, and were met by friendly natives who offered them lotus plant which had the peculiar property of causing all who ate of it to forget their business, their homes and their destination, and to settle down in dreamy apathy.**[2]

If Burroughs, singular, had sung that song, he'd have sung it along with one R. H. Boll. In 1953, Boll published an article called "Lotus Eaters" in *The Word and Work*, of which he was the editor. As a premillennialist, editor Boll believed that Jesus Christ would come back to Earth, no mere wafer and wine, but a flesh-and-blood man, before the thousand-year reign of global peace. In his article, Boll performed

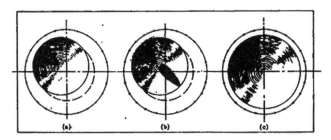

From Henry Ford Trade School, "Drills and Drilling Operations," *Shop Theory*, rev. ed. (New York: McGraw-Hill Book Company, 1942), p. 76.

a little parabolic application of the Odyssean myth to the approaching millennium. Like the Christian on his journey to Christ,

> after ten years of arduous warfare in the siege of Troy, Ulysses (so the ancient tale runs) with his companions, turned their hearts eagerly homeward.[3]

> At Home, the buying of the Christmas tree was a ritual. . . . And there were other customs.[4]

In 1953, Gwendolyn Brooks published *Maud Martha*, who likes to complicate the matter, as Marthas do. William Burroughs published *The Yage Letters* in 1963 in the form of his correspondence with Allen Ginsberg during the former's trip to Mocoa ten arduous years earlier. Stalking the wild hallucinogen to the Amazonian side of the Andes, Burroughs sent field notes home to the poet who would edit his letters:

> Yoka grows on high ground and it took us four hours to get there. The Indian cut a Yoka vine and shaved off a handful of the inner bark with a machete. He soaked the bark in a little cold water, squeezed the water out of the bark and handed me the infusion in a palm leaf cup. It was faintly bitter but not unpleasant. In 10 minutes I felt a tingling in my hands and a nice lift somewhat like benzedrine but not so tight. I walked the four hours back over jungletrail without stopping and could have walked twice that far.[5]

> How she loved a "hike." Especially in the evening, for then everything was moody, odd, deliciously threatening, always

hunched and ready to close in on you but never doing so. East of Cottage Grove you saw fewer people, and those you did see had, all of them (how strange, thought Maud Martha), white faces.[6]

Here in this country so dark and dreary,
I long have wandered, forlorn and weary—[7]

In *The Yage Letters*, written in 1953 and published ten arduous year later, Burroughs advises Ginsberg on the techniques of "Brion Gysin: an English painter, collaborator and friend of Burroughs from Tanger [sic], who suggested to him the application of XX Century painter's techniques—the collage—to written composition."[8] Ginsberg remembers Burroughs recommending collage as a

graphic exposition of an immediate way out of temporal literary and phenomenological hang-ups.[9]

As soon as these methods are applied, primitive society loses the appearance of absolute stability which is conveyed to the student who sees a certain people only at a certain given time. All cultural forms rather appear in a constant state of flux and subject to fundamental modifications.[10]

Whereas sociologists of the 1920s and 1930s had taken up the mantle of earlier Progressivism to extend the paradigm toward explaining the conditions of those inner cities where immigrants from plural places commingled far from their monocultural origins to produce bad odors and crime, psychologists emerged later in the century to explain why even North American white people were taking more drugs now, and participant-observers kicked in with participant-observations:

The urge to escape from selfhood and the environment is in almost everyone almost all the time.[11]

Could be nature, which had a seed or root, or an element (what do you want to call it) of constancy, under all that system of change. Of course, to say "system" at all implied arrangement, and therefore some order of constancy.[12]

> While in natural sciences we are accustomed to consider a given
> number of causes and to study their effects, in historical happen-
> ings we are compelled to consider every phenomenon not only as
> effect but also as cause.[13]

Cause and effect swam together in the cauldron of culture. Against
the backdrop of a universal and transhistorical account of the drive
to narcosis, and a foreground of constant change, Martha Gellhorn,
the pioneering war correspondent, expressed the uncertainty curi-
ously lacking by the men hot on the same trails. They knew themselves and others so surely.

> But all these years I have been writing against myself, as it were,
> and envying the writers who could give themselves importance
> and believe in the value and necessity of their work.[14]

Like Burroughs, Gellhorn hit the high road, but unlike her, he got the
hell out of Dodge to get himself into drugs. While city life drove many
urban North American whites to the suburbs, the suburbs drove Burroughs mad, drove him out of St. Louis and off the edges of the continent altogether, toward exotic locales in Africa and South America,
and all the way to Margaritaville. For Huxley, as for Burroughs, the
reasons to imbibe, ingest, inebriate, intoxicate, sprang eternal:

> The problems raised by alcohol and tobacco cannot, it goes with-
> out saying, be solved by prohibition. The universal and ever-
> present urge to self-transcendence is not to be abolished.[15]

Pace Harry J. Anslinger, who could not have differed more belliger-
ently from the former claim, though he shared some barely historical antecedents with Huxley and the social scientists:

> On the clay tablets of the Sumerians it was recorded that the
> juice of the poppy was "collected in the early morning," perhaps
> before the Eastern sun should have tempered its anodyne.[16]

In 1953, Anslinger published these words in *The Traffic in Narcotics*,
cowritten with William F. Tompkins (United States attorney for the
District of New Jersey and former chairman of the Legislative Com-

mission to Study Narcotics in the General Assembly of New Jersey). Having reviewed the anthropological literature, Harry J. Anslinger reported that

> this people of the land of Sumer in lower Mesopotamia—now the Arab kingdom of Iraq—cultivated the poppy plant five thousand years B.C. in order to extract its juice; *gil* was the name they gave it which translated means joy or rejoicing.[17]

In 1953, a cool seven thousand years later, the CIA backed the ouster of nearby Iran's Mohammad Mosaddegh, the democratically elected prime minister, and reinstalled the deposed shah.

> Do you want to get into the war? Maud Martha "thought at" Paul, as, over their wine, she watched his eye-light take leave of her. To get into the war, perhaps. To be mixed up in peculiar, hooped adventure, adventure dominant, entire, ablaze with bunched and fidgeting color, pageantry, thrilling with the threat of danger.[18]

On other fronts too, the United States advanced: "Nineteen-fifty-three was a banner year for the CIA's ARTICHOKE activities." Operation ARTICHOKE descended from Operation Bluebird and covered research into mind control and interrogation, and included experimentation with human subjects and a range of mind-altering drugs. Superagent George White was up to his neck in it. "On May 21, 1953, the CIA formally designated White's safe house as MKULTRA Subproject 3."[19]

> West of the Midway, they leaned against buildings and their mouths were opening and closing very fast but nothing important was coming out.[20]

> This lack of available details, moreover, was probably not wholly attributable to the destruction of MKULTRA files in 1973; the 1963 report on MKULTRA by the Inspector General notes on page 14: "Present practice is to maintain no records of the planning and approval of test programs."[21]

In 1953, Martha Graham wrote that "we learn by practice," just as Burroughs was studying the practice of drug taking in indigenous

352

NAME   : Joseph Mario BARBARA, Jr.

ALIASES   : None

DESCRIPTION   : Born 5-24-1936, Endicott, NY,
                  5'10", 280 lbs, black hair,
                  brown eyes, heavy build.

LOCALITIES   : Resides Castle Gardens,
FREQUENTED   Vestal, NY, frequents Red
                  Barn Restaurant and Vestal
                  Steak House, Vestal, NY.

FAMILY   : Father: Joseph, Sr. (de-
BACKGROUND   ceased); mother: Josephine
                  Vivona; brother: Peter; sister: Angela.

CRIMINAL   : Salvatore Monachino, Pasquale Turrigiano, Ignatius
ASSOCIATES   Cannone, Bartolo Guccia, Joseph & Salvatore Falcone,
                  Anthony Guarnieri, Santo Volpe,▬▬▬▬▬▬▬▬.

CRIMINAL   : No FBI # assigned   NYCPD #B-431573
HISTORY   Pleaded guilty to contempt of court 1959, received
                  a suspended sentence 1960 and placed on probation
                  until December 17, 1962. No other arrests.

BUSINESS   : Planning to enter the construction business with
                  a large amount of money left to him by his father.

MODUS   : Personally made all of the preparations for the
OPERANDI   1957 Apalachin Mafia meeting, at which his late
                  father was the host. In assisting his father he
                  became acquainted with many of the top ranking
                  Mafia racketeers in the nation. He has become a
                  trusted confidant in Mafia circles as a result of
                  his steadfast refusal to divulge any particulars
                  of the Apalachin meeting to law officials.

Property of U. S. Govt — For Official Use Only
May not be disseminated or contents disclosed
Without permission of Commissioner of Narcotics

From *MAFIA*, 1960, a facsimile edition of a United States Treasury Department / Bureau of Narcotics publication. Courtesy of HarperCollins Publishers.

Colombian culture and presently practiced lay anthropology, while the actual practitioners of the discipline studied "culture and the causes of culture."[22]

> Within this frame, the *imponderabilia of actual life*, and the *type of behavior* have to be filled in. They have to be collected through minute, detailed observations, in the form of some sort of ethnographic diary, made possible by close contact with native life.[23]

> I decided to try some Yage prepared Vaupes method. The Indian and I started scraping off bark with machetes (the inner bark is the most active). This is white and sappy at first but almost

immediately turns red on exposure to air. The landlady's daughters watched us pointing and giggling. This is strictly against Putumayo protocol for the preparation of Yage. The Brujo of Macoa told me if a woman witnesses the preparation the Yage spoils on the spot and will poison anyone who drinks it or at least drive him insane. The old women-are-dirty-and-under-certain-circumstances-poisonous routine. I figured this was a chance to test the woman pollution myth once and for all with seven female creatures breathing down my neck.[24]

This woman would come over, singing or humming her popular song, to see Maud Martha, wanting to know what special technique was to be used in dealing with a Negro man; a Negro man was a special type man; she knew that there should be, indeed, that there had to be, a special technique to be used with this type man, but what? And after all, there should be more than—than singing across the sock washing, the cornbread baking, the fish frying. No, she had not expected wealth, no—but he had seemed so exciting! So primitive!—life with a Negro man had looked, from the far side, like adventure.[25]

Like Burroughs, though not with him, North American human females were way into sex. In 1953, Kinsey proved as much in his social scientific study, *Sexual Behavior in the Human Female*, forgetting to specify *North American*.

They ate, drank, and read together. She read *Of Human Bondage.* He read *Sex in the Married Life.*[26]

At the same time, Hugh Hefner published the first issue of *Playboy*, with Marilyn Monroe spread across the centerfold.

The booths of Vanity Fair are filled with such wares. He stops and eats and grows forgetful of his high and holy destiny. A drowsy feeling enwraps his soul, a deadening of his spiritual sensibilities, a dreary indifference to the things of God. He has eaten the lotus.[27]

In two minutes a wave of dizziness swept over me and the hut began swimming. It was like going under ether, or when you are very drunk and lie down and the bed spins. Blue flashes passed in front of my eyes. The hut took on an archaic far-Pacific look with Easter Island heads carved in the support posts. The assistant was outside lurking there with the obvious intent to kill me. I was hit by violent, sudden nausea and rushed for the door hitting my shoulder against the door post. I felt the shock but no pain. I could hardly walk. No coordination. My feet were like blocks of wood. I vomited violently leaning against a tree and fell down on the ground in helpless misery. I felt numb as if I was covered with layers of cotton. I kept trying to break out of this numb dizziness. I was saying over and over, "All I want is out of here."[28]

By the time he can talk, he is the little creature of his culture, and by the time he is grown and able to take part in its activities, its habits are his habits, its beliefs his beliefs, its impossibilities his impossibilities.[29]

Is there, after all, a way out of phenomenological hang-ups? Per Boll, it was not too late:

Do not detain me, for I am going
To where the fountains are ever flowing.[30]

Like Boll and Burroughs, Aldous Huxley just wanted "out of here," and continued his quest for "frequent chemical vacations from intolerable selfhood and repulsive surroundings":[31]

By a series of, for me, extremely fortunate circumstances I found myself, in the spring of 1953, squarely athwart that trail. One of the sleuths had come on business to California. In spite of seventy years of mescalin research, the psychological material at his disposal was still absurdly inadequate, and he was anxious to add to it. I was on the spot and willing, indeed eager, to be a guinea pig. Thus it came about that, one bright May morning, I swallowed four-tenths of a gram of mescalin dissolved in half a glass of water and sat down to wait for the results. Half an hour after swallowing the drug I became aware of a slow dance of golden lights.[32]

Maud Martha saw people, after having all but knocked themselves out below, climbing up the golden, golden stairs, to a

> throne where sat Jesus, or the Almighty God; who promptly
> opened a Book.[33]

Huxley's trail led through a pit stop at the World's Biggest Drugstore in Los Angeles where the transcendent seeker, guided by his wife and a psychiatrist, pored over art books. Then he went home and looked at the legs of his chair for a while.

> How wonderful! Was it true? Were people to get the Answers in
> the sky? Were people really going to understand It better by and
> by? When it was too late?[34]

In 1953, the world began waiting for Godot. The millennium went and came and we're still waiting—it's a hard habit to break. For Huxley, as for Vladimir and Estragon,

> my actual experience had been, was still, of an indefinite dura-
> tion.[35]

For Boll, 1953 went on that long too. Nineteen fifty-three was before Christ all over again, which indicates that Boll, like Christ, had taken his time, had

> cut along the lines.[36]

Like Lotus Eaters like Huxley, Boll had deranged time, manifesting an affinity he would have disavowed with Burroughs who was also a writer:

> Cut-ups are seen as a way of duplicating drug states: non-linear,
> producing irrational or illogical material, they are a way of "de-
> ranging the senses." . . . They free the writer from the tyranny of
> grammar and syntax.[37]

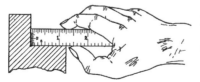

From Henry Ford Trade School, "Rules," *Shop Theory*, rev. ed. (New York: McGraw-Hill Book Company, 1942), p. 34.

Fig. 257. Using a Rule

Like Boll, Burroughs and Ginsberg had found a way out of literary hang-ups and doubled back to some literary history of interest here, according to Harry J. Anslinger:

> The poppy was old in Greek legend before Homer in the *Iliad*, recounting a concoction of it used by Helen of Troy, said that it had the power of "inducing forgetfulness of pain and the sense of evil."[38]

Like Homer, Burroughs was

> down as writer on tourist card.[39]
>
> When Burroughs uses this alias he assumes the cover of an "artist" and a "seaman." "William Lee," of course, is interested in narcotics and reputed to have contacts in the underworld and among seamen who are in or on the fringes of the narcotics business. . . . For one reason or another, he is able to get these people to his apartment at 81 Bedford Street where he tries to elicit information.[40]
>
> The method of reducing information, if possible, into charts or synoptic tables ought to be extended to the study of practically all aspects of native life. All types of economic transactions may be studied by following up connected, actual cases, and putting them into a synoptic chart.[41]

Like the sociologists before, alongside, and after them, anthropologists were tourists down on the writer card, at pains to defend their discipline as scientific. They were at pains to distinguish themselves from the patriotically motivated undercover agents to whom they bore an uncanny and tweed-jacketed resemblance, the participant-observers without the PhDs, the tourist-writers who

> refused to go back to the hardship and danger of the journey, and were content to dwell and live and die in the land of the lotus-eaters[42]

who

> know about Aristotle, Plato, who weave words like anachronism, transcendentalist, cosmos, metaphysical, corollary, integer,

monarchical, into our breakfast speech as a matter of course[43]

who

toiled wholeheartedly in the vineyards because it was fun, fun, fun. Where else could a red-blooded American boy lie, kill, cheat, steal, rape and pillage with the sanction and bidding of the All-Highest[44]

who

makes it clear that this account of an Andalusian pueblo is an anthropological account. It is not based primarily on documents, though these have been used, but on direct observation. The people he writes about are real people and not figures taken from the printed page or units in statistical tables[45]

who

was around 70 with a baby smooth face. There was a sly gentleness about him like an old time junkie. It was getting dark when I arrived at this dirt floor thatch shack for my Yage appointment. First thing he asked did I have a bottle. I brought a quart of aguardiente out of my knapsack and handed it to him. He took a long drink and passed the bottle to his assistant. I didn't take any as I wanted straight Yage kicks. The Brujo put the bottle beside him and squatted down by a bowl set on a tripod. Behind the bowl was a wood shrine with a picture of the Virgin, a crucifix, a wood idol, feathers and little packages tied with ribbons. The Brujo sat there a long time without moving. He took another long swig on the bottle. The women retired behind a bamboo partition and were not seen again. The Brujo began crooning over the bowl. I caught "Yage Pintar" repeated over and over. He shook a little broom over a bowl and made a swishing noise. This is to whisk away evil spirits who might slip in the Yage. He took a drink and wiped his mouth and went on crooning. You can't hurry a Brujo. Finally he uncovered the bowl and dipped about an ounce more or less of black liquid which he handed me in a dirty red plastic cup. The liquid was oily and phosphorescent. I drank it straight down. Bitter foretaste of nausea. I handed the cup back and the medicine man and the assistant[46]

who

have attempted to group the activities covered by the 149 subprojects into categories under descriptive headings. In broad outline, at least, this presents the contents of these files. The activities are placed in the following 15 categories:

1. Research into the effects of behavioral drugs and/or
    alcohol:
        17 subprojects probably not involving tests on human
            volunteers;
        14 subprojects definitely involving tests on human
            volunteers;
        19 subprojects probably including tests on human volun-
            teers. While not known, some of these subprojects may
            have included tests on unwitting subjects as well;
        6 subprojects involving tests on unwitting subjects.
2. Research on hypnosis: 8 subprojects, including 2 involving
    hypnosis and drugs in combination.
3. Acquisition of chemicals or drugs: 7 subprojects.
4. Aspects of magicians' art useful in covert operations:
    e.g. surreptitious delivery of drug-related materials: 4
    subprojects.
    . . .
10. Research on drugs, toxins, and biologicals in hu-
    man tissue: provision of exotic pathogens and the
    capability to incorporate them in effective delivery
    systems: 6 subprojects.
    . . .
15. Three subprojects cancelled before any work was
    done on them having to do with laboratory drug
    screening, research on brain concussion, and re-
    search on biologically active materials to be tested
    through the skin on human volunteers.[47]

Sure enough, when Burroughs drank the Yage, he met that human
with the yellow-periled skin, that specter of Oriental importation of
opium reanimated in the Cold War that carved the many peoples of
the earth into friend and foe all over again in the 1950s:

When I closed my eyes I saw an Oriental face, the lips and nose eaten away by disease. The disease spread, melting the face into an amoeboid mass in which the eyes floated, dull crustacean eyes. Slowly, a new face formed around the eyes. A series of faces, hieroglyphs, distorted and leading to the final place where the human road ends, where the human form can no longer contain the crustacean horror that has grown within it.[48]

They "marched," they battled behind her brain—the men who had drunk beer with the best of them, the men with two arms off and two legs off, the men with the parts of faces. Then her guts divided, then her eyes swam under frank mist.[49]

Maybe if I'd kept my eyes open then and noticed it and eaten it I would have formed the habit of self importance and self confidence and then the whole business of work would be easier.[50]

Or alternatively, of a perpetual present made up of one continually changing apocalypse.[51]

In 1953, the French were losing it in Southeast Asia, but far from bowing out gracefully, and closer to home, they deposed the sultan of Morocco and replaced him with his uncle.

"Beloved, I beseech you as sojourners and pilgrims that ye abstain from fleshly lusts which war against the soul," says the apostle Peter. That is the fatal lotus which makes the Christian forget his purpose and his calling and his inheritance. The love of money, the quest for honor among men, and popularity—"the lust of the flesh, the lust of the eyes, the pride of life"—these are the tempting lotus-leaves which are offered to God's pilgrims.[52]

In 1953, Anslinger recounted the pilgrimage through the lands of the heathen taken by an immigrating flower that would function as an intoxicant in places where religion forbade the consumption of alcohol.

Eastward from its ancient home through Persia to India was another road the poppy traveled to become naturalized.[53]

Anslinger went on to quote the observer Magellan or his friend Barbosa (the syntax makes it hard to tell),

who in 1511 could write of the "opium which the most of the
Moors and Indians eat."[54]

The effective object of worship is the bottle and the sole religious
experience is that state of uninhibited and belligerent euphoria
which follows the ingestion of the third cocktail.[55]

To India Chinese junks sailed the long, arduous voyage around
the Malaysian peninsula to secure the opium that became the be-
ginnings of the "traffic" as we use that word today.[56]

Today, in 1953, long arduous voyages were in. Mohammad Mosaddegh
was out. Nixon was unwelcome in Tehran on account of that afore-
mentioned ouster. Days of rioting over there, and what of it. Anomie,
alienation, ennui here at home, we were so fucking bored. We were
bored with the antics of coeds jamming themselves in phone booths,
all twisting torsos and wilting chinos, working up an appetite for retirement. We were bored with cigarettes. A smattering of philosophy was
too little, but any more would have been too much. After ten minutes,
in which our very boredom was explained, sociology, the hippest invention to come from the Germans since Rheingold Beer, fast became boring, like everything bound in books. We were bored with films. We were
bored with the tiddlywinking troops and Bob Hope's Buick Skylark. We
were bored with the tsk-tsking of ladies in Cincinnati, Newport Beach,
and Oxford, Mississippi, locating the breakdown of the moral fabric
of the country in our boring everyday entertainments. Dungarees, for
God's sake. Estes Kefauver was very boring. We were bored of congressional committees and did not yet believe in computers. If HUAC had
met the big adding machine ENIAC in a monster movie and duked it
out, we couldn't have cared less. Even DNA didn't rouse us out of our
stupefaction. I was blasé like my life depended on it. I was white. As
were most of my friends, actually. Holden Caulfield was white, and he
rang a lot of bells, but saying "damn" a lot didn't unknot our ties. We
were a population waiting for a drug to happen. Then heroin happened.
It livened up the cigarettes again.

For Boll, lotus-eating, lotus-drinking, or lotus-smoking, would deter
a Christian from the righteous path toward the City of God, kick the
second coming of Christ further on down the road. Boll kept his eyes

on the prize of an earth ruled by peace. But Burroughs, a.k.a. William Lee, differed:

> **This is a game planet. All games are hostile and basically there is only one game, and that game is war. Research into altered states of consciousness—which might result in a viewpoint from which the game itself could be called into question—is inexorably drawn into the game. One of the rules of this game is that there cannot be final victory since that would mean the end of the war game.**[57]

From the fall of 1953 to the late spring of the following year, Christ hosted a string of parties, inviting a stream of unsuspecting CIA subjects to Bedford Street, spiking their food and drink with chemicals such as sodium pentothal, Nembutal, THC and, of course, what the apostle Peter referred to as "the LSD surprise."

> **Among the perils of their journey there was one that proved well nigh fatal.**[58]

There was, for example, Frank Olson's final trip out the tenth-story window of a hotel in midtown Manhattan, on November 28, 1953. Olson had been working on biological weapons for the CIA. As the colleague and agent who had been in the room with him told it, Olson's death was a suicide. As Anslinger had it,

> **We could tell when we were on the right trail because someone invariably committed suicide.**[59]

But the subsequent exhumation of Olson's body by his sons revealed that he had suffered a blow to the head before he went out the window. "It is terrible to float like this, in one's work; terrible."[60] The CIA aside, swimming in Burroughs's spunk, and spiking the punch of the cold light of social science—Sputnik nothing:

> **She is singing or humming her popular song.**[61]

> **Somewhere in space, I hang suspended**
> **From all that I hunger for**[62]

> **But one day the song is hushed.**[63]

> **One evening the capsules are slashed with knives, either horizontally or diagonally. The cold war infusion is a light red color. Sun-**

light would cause the milky juice to turn brown and the product to be inferior. This is why the capsules are slit in the evening and the products collected in the morning.[64]

Take the enclosed copy of this letter. Cut along the lines.[65]

What has happened? A strange lethargy has befallen the pilgrim. Vividness of mental imagery, aphrodisiac results, silliness and giggling. New little patent leather shoes and white socks, the little b.v.d.'s and light petticoats, and for Harry, the new brown oxfords, and the white shorts and sleeveless undershirts.[66]

The anthropologist has forgotten his calling and the goal of his pilgrimage. His zeal, his aspiration, his hope, has well-nigh faded away. The world is full of lotus and lotus-eaters. Has he fallen in with them and eaten of the fatal weed? Likely so.[67]

I got a book by one William Burroughs, and that night I drank a quart of infusion over a period of one hour, read about forty pages and except for blue flashes and light nausea, thought I would be literally sick—though not to the point of vomiting. The juice comes out, it dries overnight, and is gathered in the morning. What a scurvy thing.[68]

Cut and rearrange in any combination. Read aloud. I can not choose but hear. Don't think about it. Don't theorize.[69]

And tell us that we need be
Strangers no more[70]

Athwart the trail, among the sweet songs we sing, this is one of the sweetest.[71]

I saw her face and I ascended
Out of the commonplace into the rare[72]

The war correspondent waved from the shore. The weather was bidding her bon voyage.[73]

From William Goodyear, *The Grammar of the Lotus*, 1891, p. 267. Courtesy of the Internet Archive (at archive.org) with funding from the Microsoft Corporation.

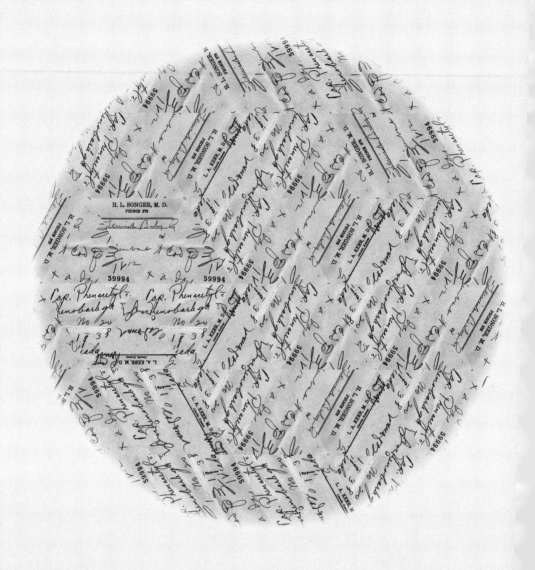

Kaleidoscopic prescription forms, 1940s. Courtesy of Jack D. Crispin Jr., RPh., proprietor of Crispin's Drug Store Museum, Lincoln, KS. Collage by Kayla Reopelle.

42 DR. JOHN BLANK

The pitchfork of Harry's philosophy of narcotics law enforcement had three prongs. He believed in the harshest possible penalties, mandatory minimum sentencing, and superadded punishment for repeat offenses, and he believed these would deter drug-related crime. In the early and mid-1950s, antinarcotic bills proliferated, like the Boggs Act of 1952, which encoded these values and beliefs with Harry's full endorsement, requiring across-the-board increases in penalties for narcotics law violations. A bill proposed (but not passed) in 1955 would have allowed the death penalty for second offenders. When the Narcotic Control Act was proposed in 1956 as a kind of reinforcement of the five-year-old Boggs Act, Harry hit the spotlight once more. He had spent a good deal of time preparing testimony based on a study conducted by the Bureau of Narcotics in the 1950s, and now produced some fairly far-fetched statistics about how few addicts there were nationwide; critics found his figures on addiction too low, and his data too precise, to be credible.[1]

Nevertheless, the Boggs Act and the Narcotics Control Act not only passed easily; they represented mainstream opinion on narcotics trade and use. The legislation did not go completely unopposed—it was the second version that won passage—and neither did Anslinger. In "Masterly Service, Cynical Reward," the *Christian Science Monitor* asserted, in 1953, that Anslinger had made the Federal Bureau of Narcotics "the wonderfully efficient engine it is today" and was still at the peak of his abilities. The article also allowed that Harry was the target of "an influential group of a certain sort of Republicans" who proposed to remove him from his job in order to make room for an Eisenhower appointee who could only be, the *Monitor* opined, "inferior in vitally requisite knowledge and experience!"[2] Harry's authority was certainly solid, but he had his detractors.

Challenges to Harry's hegemony in the field would pick up in the 1950s, especially with the joint committee convened by the American Bar Association and the American Medical Association in 1956. The committee, which included the lefty lawyer Rufus King and was supported by liberal funding from the Sage Foundation, concluded, among other things, that the criminalization of the addict was immoral and misguided. Sharing certain premises with Anslinger, the report would veer off in a different direction:

> At the present time the addict is treated by our statutes like a criminal. If he is found in possession of even the minutest portion of narcotics for his own use, or a hypodermic needle, he may be jailed. He may be jailed under some statutes because of the mere fact that he is an addict.[3]

While Anslinger favored these conditions, the so-called "Interim Report" called them into question:

> If the addict is, as the author believes him to be, a sick, maladjusted individual driven by a compulsion, then these statutes are wrong. They must be replaced with statutes which in the first instance require the treatment of addicts and not their incarceration in jails or prisons.[4]

This was a minority opinion, anathema to Harry, that began to gain traction in proportion to the slowly increasing activism of progressive doctors and lawyers, and as drug use by white people became accepted fact. For the time of its utterance—the late 1950s—the recommendation that untreatable addicts be allowed to obtain "a legal supply of narcotics," remained far-fetched. The "Interim Report" ended by calling for a great deal more research, and ultimately for law "based on the enlightened premises of a new social policy towards addiction."[5] That shift would come with the accession of the Kennedy family to the federal government and coincide with Anslinger's retirement a few years down the road.

Though invited several times, Harry declined to participate in the committee's investigation into narcotics—but he did not decline to decry the report's "glaring inaccuracies, manifest inconsistencies, apparent ambiguities, important omissions and even false statements."[6] And Harry did not refrain from attempting to suppress the glaringly inaccurate, and so forth, report, sending an agent to Indiana University where it was being prepared for publication. The agent nosed around the press, asked into the report's funding, and came too close for comfort to Alfred Lindesmith, the Indiana sociologist there who had criticized prohibitionist policy. It was not the first time Harry had suppressed a report that painted an insufficiently alarmist portrait. The New York Academy of Medicine remembered Anslinger's response to the La Guardia report over a decade earlier. The doctors from New York had never wiped Harry's slate clean.

One day, on his endless speaking tour, Harry addressed a gathering of pharmacists, detailing the relevant functions of the Federal Bureau of Narcotics. Pharmacists could be part of the solution—or they could be part of the very alarming problem. They must safeguard the narcotic drug stock—and safeguard prescription blanks. For Harry, blank order forms were the crime vehicle of doctors, the prescription a genre Harry must control, and pharmacists the gatekeepers of inventory, who could be manipulated by doctors and addicts, or who could be cooperating with their illicit schemes. From the podium, Harry instructed pharmacists in the proper writing of the prescription so that they could detect fraudulent use of the blank. To shore up the bona fides of a given prescription as he processed it, the pharmacist could do some writing of his own. Anslinger looked down and consulted his notes:

> **3. Suggest Pharmacist prepare notation on back of prescription**
> **"Delivered to Dr. John Blank, 2:30 p.m., January 20, 1956."**[7]

Inventing a fictional Dr. Blank who presented a narcotics prescription to an innocent pharmacist, Harry suggested that the pharmacist should record the time of the transaction and the name of the person to whom narcotics were delivered. Keeping written records was always important. Sometimes.

But what was Harry's Dr. John Blank doing on January 20, 1956, after he had presented a scrip to the pharmacist that afternoon, and walked away with a pocket full of drugs? All around him, Dr. Blank's country was doing what Eisenhower had called "waging peace" in the State of the Union Address two weeks earlier. So why was drug use on the rise again? Science—medicine, but also social sciences—would elaborate on the question of why twentieth-century Americans were ripe for barbiturate use, for addiction to opiates, for experimentation with everything in the kitchen. And garage. From government reports to *Reader's Digest* to scandal sheets, accounts would pour forth. New scientific and pseudoscientific accounts of more people taking new and old drugs. The popular media weighed in. If accurate facts were in short supply, theories abounded:

> **under the pressure of modern living, thousands are turning to barbiturates in search of escape.**[8]

In the hamlet of Apalachin, New York, a number of mobsters went running out the back of a large house in search of escape. In November 1957, New York state troopers busted a meeting of upper echelon operatives from organized crime—the very kind that Anslinger had identified, the very kind whose existence Hoover had denied. The meeting of one hundred Mafiosi took place at the home of Joseph Barbara, in a tiny town just west of Binghamton, New York, and just north of the Pennsylvania border. Had the meeting been able to go forward, the question of hierarchy would have been on the table. The dons would also have considered a proposal to foreswear, collectively, trafficking in drugs. Within twelve days, Hoover had established his Top Hoodlum Program. Robert F. Kennedy would ramp up on the McClellan Committee on Improper Activities in Labor and Management (covering union dynamics and racketeering), and would stay on the case against organized crime as attorney general, winning Harry's respect and loyalty. The Federal Bureau of Narcotics had all kinds of documentation to show at numerous hearings. Harry could say he told them so—his vindication came at about the time of his swan song.

Harry was nearing the end of his influence. The legal damage done, Harry started to come down from the heights of authority. He still believed that the best way to suppress was to suppress, all evidence to the contrary. *The Squared Circle* played at the Logan Theater in Altoona.

Harry turned a blind eye while Joe McCarthy lived out his last days in a morphine-assisted attempt to control his drinking, making sure the prescriptions ran through Harry's own pharmacist. According to Anslinger's biographer, Harry felt the moral burden of countenancing, indeed administering, McCarthy's morphine drip down to the last drop.[9]

Like Anslinger's at the close of the 1950s, my job is essentially done. There is no point explaining Harry as he prepares to clear his files out of his offices. Anslinger has gone from effect to cause. The legislation of the 1950s was the cruel capstone on a cold career. The Boggs Act and the Narcotics Control Act—in place for almost twenty years by the time Nixon declared his War on Drugs and passage of the Rockefeller Drug Laws—are the literal linchpins of the expansion of the prison-industrial complex. Mandatory minimum sentencing stripped the judge of discretion, the ultimate machination in the process of criminalizing the drug-tainted individual. The judge had to be dehumanized too, completely instrumentalized by the ideological commitment masquerading as law. Mandatory minimums also encouraged prosecutors to push for stiff penalties in order to compel plea bargains and, with them, much more efficient resolution of cases.

As Anslinger's star began to fade, other politicians came into a new kind of limelight. The 1950s was a decade of investigations and hearings, of the emergence of these proceedings as television fare. The emergence of anything, and everything, as television fare. The Herlands investigation into corruption in 1954 picked up on the work done by the Kefauver Committee three years earlier. As a condition for testimony by naval officers, the navy requested that the report remain unpublished. Though the investigation found conclusively that Lucky Luciano had been given his freedom and a ticket to Italy in exchange for assistance to the US government during World War II, Herlands kept his word and didn't publish the report. This gave greater weight to testimony about organized crime that had been given to the Kefauver Committee, testimony that was quotable, telegenic, and almost damning enough. When the Apalachin Meeting was busted, yet other investigations moved into gear.

The good news was the same as the bad news: Congress was our agent of governmental accountability. The government had to ask government agents to testify about government agency. Agents did outrageous things, many of them unknown to the vast majority of the audience. The questions abound, not only ethical and political, but also psychological. The richest account of the 1950s drug projects of the CIA is the testimony of the Church Committee hearings, only convened in 1974. The United States Senate Select Committee to Study Governmental Operations with Respect to Intelligence Activities heard wild testimony from the special agents that had cruised about with CIA and Federal Bureau of Narcotics credentials: White, Siragusa, Williams, the whole gang. In 1977, Senator Edward Kennedy once more probed the activities of the CIA drug projects and their covert experiments, this time before the Subcommittee on Health and Scientific Research. All of these committees entertained, along with expert testimony, expert forgetting, expert inability to recall, expert failure to recollect. Dr. John Blank silences in response to the senators' questions.

Over and above the questions of what kind of mind or personality can enter a disguise and stay in it for months or years operating among strangers and enemies, and what are the mental and psychological effects of living and working that way, others remain: Why, when the senators asked the very special agents years later what they had known and what they had done, why couldn't they remember? Does being an undercover agent produce amnesia? No, they remembered, but they still thought their operations were good ideas tested in the service of defending the greatest country on earth. They were just afraid the committee, or the television audience, might not see it the same way. Years later, the former agents still imagined that they had the prerogative to decide what was good and what was true, and when the national defense required a few fictions, even way after the fact.

43 CHASING THE GHOSTWRITERS

In 1953, the big banner year that led from the postwar years to the 1960s, Harry coauthored his first book, *The Traffic in Narcotics*, a dry "anatomy" of various narcotics and the history of policy, law, and enforcement efforts that derived in large part from testimony given in the Kefauver hearings a couple of years earlier. William F. Tompkins, Harry's coauthor, was a prominent New Jersey Republican who had chaired the Legislative Commission to Study Narcotics. He went on to become assistant attorney general under Eisenhower and then to head up a new internal security division in the Justice Department that was focused on countering "subversive" activities. One of Tompkins's Cold War battles ended in the vanquishing of the Soviet spy Rudolf Ivanovich Abel, and he prosecuted many other Communist infiltrators.[1] He was an early subscriber to Anslinger's theories about organized crime, had mobster Albert Anastasia denaturalized, and brought down many more racketeers throughout the 1950s.

The collaboration of Anslinger and Tompkins proceeds along familiar lines—the poppy throughout human history; the impassioned decrying of sensational media tactics butting up against the sensational rendering of youth in peril; the dangers of doctors;[2] the evil of dealers; the Communist threat; disintegration in the cities; treaties of the twentieth century; legislative victories touted overtly, covert tactics between the lines; the massaging of statistics amounting to misconstruction of the facts, known in philosophy as falsehood, elsewhere as fiction. Leading narcotics historian David Courtwright points out that Anslinger and Tompkins's claims about decreases in the number of addicts in the country are taken from incomparable sets of data collected many years apart and complete with their own methodological problems. Had Anslinger and Tompkins not exaggerated the numbers "they would have been closer to the truth."[3]

John A. Williams, *The Angry Ones* (Ace Books, 1960), cover. Original from the Henry W. and Albert A. Berg Collection of English and Literature, New York Public Library. Reproduced by permission from Penguin Random House.

Untruths may have been the gateway genre; by 1963, Harry was working with a professional fiction writer. *The Murderers: The Shocking Story of the Narcotic Gangs* was published around the time that Harry resigned the commissionership. *The Murderers* was a collection of narratives about gangsters and gangs and their very wily ways that Harry coauthored with Will Oursler, writer of dozens of detective and mystery novels.[4] Oursler had begun his career as a journalist: his *Father Flanagan of Boys Town* served as the basis for the character played by Spencer Tracy in *Boys Town*, in which a local priest leads a gang of boys to capture crooks and save their town. In 1951, Oursler edited a collection of mystery writing; he was an expert in the genre.

Writing with his wife under the pseudonym Gale Gallagher, Oursler developed a "female" detective who was an early departure from the two stock types who had prevailed until then. Neither the two-hundred-plus-pound, hard-drinking cussing female dick of the past nor the genteel retiree deceptively delicately inquiring into domestic murders in the English branch of the genre, Oursler's Gale Gallagher was a comely young woman—"gal" in every word, twice the girl. Gale Gallagher was an attractive urbane "skip tracer," locating missing persons who did not want to be found.

Now I am the skip tracer, Harry the elusive object. It's not just that he's dead. It is hard to know who Harry was when he was alive. It is hard to know who Harry was when Martha was bedridden for the last year of her life following heart failure. They lived at 612 Pine Street, Hollidaysburg, at the other end of the interurban streetcar line from Altoona, the house he built for their retirement and their deaths, first hers, and then sixteen years later, his. The story draws to a close, in which Harry's character is immortalized by the inventor of *Father Flanagan*, as a leader among men, a hero, a captain of good guys out to get the crooks.

Harry's third book, also coauthored, also memoiristic, was published in 1964 and has more than a bit of nostalgia and glory days about it: *The Protectors: The Heroic Story of the Narcotics Agents, Citizens and Officials in Their Unending, Unsung Battles against Organized Crime in America.*[5] As the protectors, Anslinger and his coauthor "J. Dennis Gregory" begin their first-person account of the former at the moment that Harry leaves Pennsylvania, no Altoona about it. Recall the opening scene of Harry's persona, which he begins by singing the origin story of his heroism, and that of others like him:

> **I began my government career as a member of the efficiency board of the Ordnance Division, War Department, in Washington in 1917.**[6]

Sing in him, O fictitious J. Dennis, of the story of the heroic warrior's battle against the demon narcotic, locating the origin of the hero's hero's heroism in the first moment of government employ, specifically in war administration. *The Protectors* is chock-full of pulp, yellowy, not just with age, and hard-boiled, and purple, pages of bruised prose telling of its time and its passage.

If Tompkins had a tolerance for untruths, and Oursler had a habit of outright fiction, Harry's third coauthor disguised his own identity. J. Dennis Gregory is a pseudonym for John A. Williams, a writer who had, three years before working with Harry, published *The Angry Ones*, a fictionalized account of his own experience of racism as an educated Black professional. By 1964, when *The Protectors* was published, Williams had also written novels called *Sissie* and *Night Song*, and edited an anthology called *The Angry Black*, "a brutal and shocking look at how 18,000,000 Americans think, live, and feel."[7] Most of what Williams wrote in his long career was for and/or about African Americans, a good deal of it politically motivated, and he also wrote for the popular African American press, including *Jet* and *Ebony*.

How can we understand the encounter between Harry J. Anslinger and John A. Williams? At first, the relation is contractual:

> **Anslinger wanted to do this book, but he couldn't write. I could, and I needed money, as usual.**[8]

The hookup was brokered through a publisher who brought together the most paradigmatic assortment of white oddball bedfellows the late midcentury had to offer. Williams remembers:

> **At this time I was still one of Roger Straus's authors at Farrar, Straus and Cudahy. Roger tended to weld his authors together in**

> a big family, which is the way I met James Purdy, Isaac Bashevis Singer, Susan Sontag, and Harry J. Anslinger, former Federal Commissioner of Narcotics.[9]

I like to think of Harry in the room with that gang of cultural capitalists. Williams was a consummate professional who had encountered people like Harry before, as *The Angry Ones* attests. In a series of martini lunches, Harry enjoyed a captive audience for the same old stories:

> I'd never worked with any kind of cop before, but I found Harry to be very cooperative with his files and chats. He was also fun to be with, since he drank a good martini and told lots of stories. His bodyguard-chauffeur, however, didn't much like me. When Harry wasn't looking, he gave me those cop glances and grimaces. According to Harry, the old narcotics bureau was rather like the gang that couldn't shoot straight. Also, his was the first report I heard about cooperation between the Mafia and the government during WWII, when the feds sought help to prevent pilfering and sabotage on the New York and New Jersey docks.[10]

Wink wink nudge nudge. Harry's "muscle" sends a certain message to Williams in coded body language while Harry brings Williams in on the joke: there really has been organized crime for decades in the United States. Harry may have been paranoid but he was, in this case, also right. If Williams truly found Harry fun to be with, he was not alone. Abe Cobus of Altoona, Harry's lawyer and poker partner at Blairmont Country Club, concurred, remembering the off-duty, retired Harry as a "compassionate and generous man with a wonderful sense of humor."[11] Yet Williams did not sign his real name to *The Protectors*. Lends new, or rather old, meaning to "cover."

"The poppy, the symbol of sleep and death, is age-old in the lore of antiquity."[12] And even older in the lore of modernity. In the lore of Harry J. Anslinger, he was reaching his own antiquity. He gave over the descriving, in imitable style, to being descrived. In Harry Edward Neal's never-published novel (archived in Harry J. Anslinger's bureau), the former Secret Service agent with the heavy writing habit seems to have got Harry J. Anslinger's voice down, practically verbatim. Here is an extract from Neal's manuscript *The Treasury Musketeers*, from the second chapter titled "The Narcotic Bureau—Men against Demons":

> **The origin of marihuana . . . is shrouded in the mists of antiquity. For centuries it has been a problem in many parts of the world. Homer was its prophet, Marco Polo its advance courier. . . . In underworld argot it has colloquial colorful names such as reefers, muggles, hay and tea. Marihuana destroys mental fabric; insanity frequently results from its continued use.**

First Harry gave up the ghostwriters, then he gave up the ghost. Harry wrote a lot, but he was no prose stylist. If he was persuasive, it was not because of his powers of suasion. Rather, he leaned heavily on coauthor, as on crutches, and he carried a big stick. Perhaps he should have taken a page from his own book. Maybe his prose would have benefited if Harry had heeded the advice he lodged in his curriculum on undercover work, his training manual for Federal Bureau of Narcotics agents, instructions to the aspiring spy,

> **Take only necessary notes and write in such a way that information would be unintelligible to anyone else.**[13]

I know I have.

44 EVERY INCH A MAN

Harry J. Anslinger left the commissionership in 1962, at age seventy, after over thirty years in office. There he was up the fat middle of the twentieth century in a job for which his qualifications were largely bureaucratic savoir faire and ideological commitment. With the expertise that had accrued to him distributing, collecting, and improving forms and procedures for the interdiction of smuggled alcohol during Prohibition, Harry leveraged his small budget and staff into a stable, even stubborn institutional presence in the Treasury Department. Scrapping to maintain and grow both, Harry's political gifts emerged in his publicity campaigns, his nose for the Mafia, his alliances with powerful friends. He survived many a scandal.

For a single individual, Harry had a fair amount of authority and political power, which he garnered, consolidated, and applied to lawmaking during the 1930s. Harry began the 1940s with his star high in the sky. He got the country through a potential morphine shortfall by stockpiling it for use during the war, and he rode the wave of the wartime downturn in drug trafficking and use. From 1945 to 1960, Harry played a significant role domestically, elaborating his preoccupation with the covert, nailing doctors and pushers, dabbling in truth sera and statistical discourses, and pushing diehard prohibitionist legislation. His power should not be overestimated. His power should not be underestimated. He was a persistent cog in a wheel he persistently stabilized, persistently hammered and held to its axles or alliances inside and outside of the Department of the Treasury, during the Depression, the Second World War, and the cold one; repeatedly he was reappointed; successfully he created the figure of his own authority.

What accounted for Anslinger's endurance in a demanding job, his skill at out-toughing toughies from a desk at headquarters, as well as

Anslinger's last home, Hollidaysburg, PA. Images by Kayla Reopelle, with thanks to Jay and Mary Fornwalt.

his justifying to Congress every year a budget for a problem that had to be put on the map in the first place? How did he endure through five presidencies, administrations both Democratic and Republican? Why did so many people believe what Harry J. Anslinger had to say about drug traffic, drug traffickers, drug use, drug users, drug policy, drug law enforcement, when he had no medical or scientific background, no legal education, and no experience in law enforcement? How did his authority persist in the face of constant failure at interdiction and wildly fluctuating statistical accounts of narcotics imported and exported, numbers of addicts, commission of drug-related crime, and so on. Anslinger came to the game at just the point when a new discourse would be forged on the crucible of Prohibition. Alcohol would no longer monopolize the slang or the black market; drugs would fill the void. The phrasing was his to coin. He was positioned and poised to corner the discursive market, and so he did, albeit with already-tired xenophobic bumper sticker-isms, carefully crafting media representations as he went.

Thank you, Mr. Anslinger, for your remarkably effective work.

His legacy—effects of misinformation and propaganda, stigmatization and criminalization, support for or ignorance of government misdeeds, intensification and improvement of covert procedures, untold suffering by people convicted of violations of the Harrison Act and other instruments, their suffering in the forms of harsh penalties, mandatory sentencing, and lack of services, and the suffering of their loved ones, their communities, and the establishment and reestablishment of systematic disadvantage through unjust application of those harsh narcotics laws—his legacy lingers long after he left town, long after he laid his hammer down, long after he had his last lunch at Lusardi's Luncheonette.

Lost is the luster of yesterchapter in which Harry had been the child of immigrants, and of the standardization of time and labor; that was his youth. No longer did Harry grow to assimilate nation to the corporation in his bloodstream; that was the early diplomacy. Harry worked hard, like a bumblebee, buzzing from one arena to another, the floor of Congress, the law enforcement conventions, the social clubs and ladies' events, his top men, his contacts in the press, bringing information and other vital elements to and fro, publishing them liberally. Hushed conversations with world-class agents. Furthering the ends of prohibition. The ends of good. The end of evil. For decades. Other agency heads increasingly preferred not to have to work very closely with Harry. His colleagues waited for him to retire, and waited, and then the wait was over. Robert F. Kennedy had no great respect for Harry. After retirement, Anslinger's policy role focused on international stages. He had always loved a treaty and was at ease with the formal procedures of the UN.

But Harry J. Anslinger's career headlines still shone bright as he headed northwest from Washington back home to Horseshoe Bend:

The Marijuana Tax Act of 1937—Harry got it passed!
The stockpiling of morphine for domestic use
    during World War II—HJA's foresight!
His anti-communism—Harry held the line.
Harry's precocious identification of syndicated
    crime—he beat Hoover to it.[1]

These are Harry's own headlines; he is pleased with his performance, proud to recap it on any given occasion. Statistical claims about the reduction of manufacture, traffic, addiction, and abuse, their accuracy notwithstanding. And damned if here it doesn't come again as the bell curve of life lowers him back down in the Juniata Valley of Blair County. Same old sewer system. Damned if that isn't the tympanic echo of the inaugural moves of the career of the covert-loving commissioner. Damn if there's not another car on that train there behind the 1920 revelation of Third International action in Amsterdam—isn't that the old "Kaiser Wilhelm" saw? Why, yes it is. Remarks at a retirement dinner of 1962 review that red-letter day: *For the first time I am able to tell you about an achievement of his during the first World War which had it been known at the time would have been sensational.* Only then *he could reveal the secret of the fake armistice of November 7, 1918 but I doubt if we could pry it out of him.*[2] Though by then the intelligence had long gone cold. Harry J. Anslinger never ever backed down. But he did back out, and back to Altoona, whose population was on the way down from its peak the year Harry became commissioner. *Biff bang crack.*

At the Remington Medal dinner in New York, December 1962, under the Tiffany chandeliers and the Arthur Crisp murals of Cinderella, Harry was roasted by Henry Giordano, the inside man who succeeded him as commissioner. Guy Lombardo no longer played at the Grill but echoes of "Auld Lang Syne" could still be heard, and with them a rags-to-riches story hovering in the background and featuring the son of immigrants made good, Madison and Vanderbilt Avenues humming with traffic outside the walls of the hotel. Giordano's remarks were

90 percent roast to 10 percent toast. Having worked with Anslinger for thirty years on his way up through the ranks, and even now on the phone with him constantly, of similar political stripe, Giordano seemed to think that Harry had a law degree, that Harry's despised stepson Joe was in fact his biological son. Giordano knew less about Harry J. Anslinger than you do after reading this book, and he had nothing to say that was any funnier than this: "Commissioner is the world's greatest authority on dope (long pause)—and if you want to infer that that's because he's a dope—the inference is yours, not mine."[3] His successor makes a joke about Harry's laundry. Seriously though, folks, Giordano did refer to Harry's legacy, a laundry list not unlike the one we have assembled here: stockpiling, naming and fighting the Mafia, and so forth.

Thank you, Mr. Anslinger, for your remarkably effective work.

Summing up his former boss, Giordano toasted that Harry was known as an officer of law enforcement, an investigator, and a boss, but that he was *loved* and *enshrined* in Henry's heart, and those of their colleagues, "as every inch a MAN."[4] And every inch counts. Harry's wife Martha would die in 1961, following her long and painful illness. They were barreling toward it, he and she, round and round the sun, 'til they rounded the corner and the Cuban Missile Crisis faded into the background, barreling as ever. Back to Hollidaysburg.

And there those trains still run, as they did around the Horseshoe Bend of Harry's youth, now that all six feet of him lie six feet under them, and still will from rust to dust. There he lies in the Presbyterian Cemetery from here to eternity in Hollidaysburg, in the company of Martha and her family, his work be done.

Thank you, Mr. Anslinger, for your remarkably effective work but . . .

The closer he got to the end, the more he spiraled back, like any other ordinary human, timeline looping back around, full circle on the railroad roundtrip of life.

45 OUT WITH A WHIMPER

On August 8, 1962, Altoona observed Harry Anslinger Day, which was attended by several members of the local community, senior members of the Federal Bureau of Narcotics, and a number of congressmen. Perhaps the most senior governmental official to attend was Nicholas Katzenbach, then deputy US attorney general. But it was Katzenbach's boss, the ascendant attorney general, Robert F. Kennedy, who would preside over the White House Conference on Narcotics in Washington the very next month on September 27 and 28. As Harry retired, the new ruling clan in Washington was already changing the direction of drug policy.

Hollidaysburg Presbyterian Cemetery, Plot Sec. C, Lot 320. Image by Cathy Lee Crane.

Two weeks before the conference, Harry received an acknowledgment of his acceptance of the president's invitation to participate. The enclosed materials included his registration card, information about the conference site, and a list of hotels, as though Harry might not be excruciatingly familiar with the Roger Smith, the Willard, and the other hotels that lined Pennsylvania Avenue. The week before, Ted Kennedy had just won the Democratic primary for the Massachusetts Senate seat vacated by his brother when the latter was elected president; Teddy would win the special election to the Senate in November. The week of the conference, he graced the cover of *Time* magazine. Now his brother Robert F. Kennedy masterminded and headlined the September conference, whose speakers included his other brother, the president; Governor Pat Brown of California; and Mayor Wagner of New York.

Harry greatly admired Robert Kennedy, confident in the latter's willingness to recognize, and intention to eradicate, organized crime. Nevertheless, Harry was surprised that President Kennedy had reappointed him in 1961. But it was just a year before Harry would reach the mandatory retirement age of seventy. Indeed the inevitable came to pass—and together the Kennedy brothers oversaw a sea change that included an ultimately slight and arguably temporary but important shift in public policy on narcotics.

Having been invited by the Kennedys, Harry came back out of his extremely recent retirement to speak on the sole panel concerning "law enforcement and controls." Having been replaced by Henry L. Giordano as commissioner, Anslinger was listed according to one of his continuing, though increasingly attenuated, functions: "U.S. Member, Narcotics Drug Commission of the U.N." Though it may have been a function of President Kennedy's need to support Pat Brown against Richard Nixon in the upcoming gubernatorial race in California, the conference's timing could not have been better synchronized with the change of personnel, regime, agenda. Absent from the host committee, Harry must have felt his decentering at the conference.

Attorney General Bobby Kennedy began his speech there with an extended encomium for the life's work of an outstanding individual, detailing his many contributions to the field of narcotics over the many decades, extolling his extreme dedication, and finally presenting an award for long years of dedicated service—to Dr. Harris Isbell, director of the National Institute of Mental Health's Addiction Research Center in Lexington, Kentucky. Though the Federal Bureau of Narcotics had relied on some of Isbell's research earlier on, the researcher had gone on to submit a paper to Congress for the Boggs Act hearings testifying that marijuana was not addictive—but the insult to that injury was made explicit several laudatory paragraphs later. In plain talk, RFK redefined narcotics as a "socially spawned" problem, noting how little credible research had been done in the past, opening the investigation to academics, and inviting psychologists, economists, criminologists, and even doctors to question the assumption that "the narcotics problem is so intensely dangerous and vicious that the solution is principally punitive."[1] In so saying, RFK contravened a core tenet of Anslinger's approach and overturned a cornerstone of official policy for decades.

The attorney general did go on to thank Anslinger for "remarkably effective" work, for reducing traffic and sending racketeers to prison. And then the White House mouthpiece put him in his place: "But law enforcement is only one aspect. The root of the problem remains." The Kennedys then reframed narcotics as a public health issue, calling for research that put the care of the addict at the center of programmatic action, and according more time on the conference program to the problem of addiction than to that of law enforcement. The idea of rehabilitation was dusted off. Perhaps the greatest shift in values came under the rubric of "civil commitment" to the former violator, the former fiend, the weak link in the march of our species and our national defense. Now the addict needed treatment in addition to a prison term, "with an intensive period of institutional care followed by closely supervised parole and aftercare." It is easy to see, from the perspective of the twenty-first century, how current practice represents a nightmarish elaboration of these very principles. But at the time, it marked a significant change in values for the attorney general to say, "There is no federal program for civil commitment at present, but the Administration supports extensive experimentation with the principle."[2]

By this time, Harry was hanging his hat at 612 Pine Street in Hollidaysburg. He still served on the UN committee and he was still well remembered. But not for his scintillating speeches, which had showed, throughout the 1950s, progressively more modest ambition, more resting on laurels, likelier recourse to claims to authority, than his sensational fire-and-brimstone speechifying of years past. By 1962, Harry had two or three points he liked to make, repeatedly, and his remarks at the White House conference that year were unexceptional. The United States has promoted nine treaties and protocols. Here were seven of them: 1912, 1925, 1931, 1936, 1948, 1953, 1961. His passion now lit on two "objectionable features" in the 1961 "Single Convention" that the United States would seek to have eliminated. Onto his typescript of his remarks—more of a chronicle of protocols, really—Harry added, in his own hand, a forgotten 1946 protocol, the letters a bit wobbly at the top of the second page.[3]

Gone was the fierce rhetoric, the ideological appeal, the hysteria, the guts and glory, a personal sense of mission. As though the lifeblood had been drained out of the formerly animated narrative, there is not much left in Harry's presentation, just bones, the bare bones of a formerly juicy story. There are simply dates and conventions, beginning with "Since 1909 the United States has promoted nine treaties and protocols to suppress the abuse of narcotic drugs."[4] Dry, very dry, likely less sexy than the panels later that day on civil commitment and probation, and current and experimental methodologies. Then again, Harry had been asked to address "international narcotic control," as befit his new post with the UN, and he had merely fulfilled his assignment.

A cryptic note-to-self appears on the first page, in that increasingly wobbly penmanship: "statistical control." The Kennedys stood at the podium bemoaning the dearth of research and the inadequacy of existing statistics. Anslinger's statistics were no longer merely woefully incomplete or wrong; they were fully obsolete.

> **In spite of excellent cooperation from the Bureau of Narcotics and others with whom the Panel has consulted, we have been unable to obtain an accurate assessment of the extent of current drug abuse, either in terms of the number of persons involved or in terms of the**

> amount of economic damage which these practices wreak on the
> community at large. The discrepancies between Federal, State and
> local enforcement agencies are so great in some instances (more
> than 100%) that the Panel prefers not to make numerical estimates
> at this time.[5]

Thank you, Mr. Anslinger, for your remarkably effective work, but . . .

Harry's remarks concluded with a minor statistical claim that redounded to his own glory if not his credibility: "By international action, and Federal and State legislation to carry out treaty obligations, drug addiction in the United States has decreased from one in 400 to one in 4,000, a 90-percent reduction." Later in 1962, Harry did indeed receive a medal—the Remington Medal for service to American pharmacy—and at that convention of lesser lights Harry would repeat these statistics. There, Harry contextualized the claim by placing it in the fifty-year period that follows the 1909 treaty and coincides with his tenure at the bureau, but ends with a "current wave of addiction" (for which he blamed not the loyal and cooperative pharmacists). But not three months earlier, he had delivered to the august company at the White House a more cheerful conclusion to his long career: Overmanufacture of morphine and heroin and cocaine had stopped. Synthetic drugs were under complete control. Opiate and cocaine addiction were all but nonexistent. And barbiturates didn't count because there was no illicit international traffic in them. Which left marijuana to worry about . . . its traffic and abuse increasing . . . "Little or no progress has been made in control of this drug."[6] Harry's claims about the rates of addiction and the success of legislation and law enforcement still depended on context.

The week leading up to the White House conference, Bobby Kennedy spent some tense time on the phone to Mississippi governor Barnett, persistently insisting that James Meredith must be allowed to register at the University of Mississippi, must show up to class, would integrate the university—or the latter would be shut down. Kennedy asked Barnett over and over to try to prevent violence. Meredith made history. W. D. "Doppelganger" Chasin coauthored the Current Concepts in Therapy column with the piece "New Treatment of Epistaxis" in the

New England Journal of Medicine released that week.[7] Right and Left, like Anslinger and Kennedy, agreed gangsters should pay their taxes. They would not agree on much else.

As the new commissioner, Henry L. Giordano carried on Harry's positions and policies fairly unadapted for the next six years until the bureau ceased to exist. Because—O historical heresy!—if it hadn't been Harry it would have been someone else, like Henry. There were other candidates to replace Harry besides Henry, but in the end, appointing an Italian American had political utility in the face of waves of arrests of Italian and Italian Americans, arrests that Harry had been gunning for for years. Giordano was a safe compromise but transitional, as was his office. He held on, with frequent calls to Harry in Hollidaysburg, but the times they were a-changin'. In 1968, the bureau merged with the FDA's Bureau of Dangerous Drugs to become the Bureau of Narcotics and Dangerous Drugs.

There would have been another James Meredith. Ole Miss was going to be integrated. Meredith and Anslinger, unique genetic recombinants, no doubt loved by those who loved them, stand in for big action, though they were humans among humans. Meredith would go on to deplore civil rights and work for Senator Jesse Helms. Anslinger would procure morphine for Joseph McCarthy. History leaves them a page, a heading, a headstone, any number of documents attesting to their courage, their pathbreaking acts, the moments of change that seemed to swirl around their epicentric figures. Of course Anslinger's story is not the same as Meredith's. Meredith willy-nilly did good, while Harry's idea of good was bad.

So is that it? Harry J. Anslinger was a chimerical functionary of being in the right place and the right time to be himself in history? No different ontogenetically than any of us reproducing reproductions. Every bit as made as self-making. If Anslinger was made for the Federal Bureau of Narcotics, he was made for it in the nursery, the classrooms, the backyards, and the shops of Altoona, each one bearing the tracks of the Pennsylvania Railroad, but he made himself the kind of guy who could keep the trains of prohibition running efficiently.

And then he died, in 1975, following the onset of literal blindness, the loss of function, the angina that called for morphine, the morphine that almost rose to irony but the humor was lost in the rotations, the revolutions, the longitudes and latitudes crisscrossing in space, denoting the restful place where Harry once and future lies at the crossroads of the Alleghenies, Altoona their footnote.

Epilogue

46 CHASING THE GHOST

When Harry retired, half the questions that animate this study retired as well: the question of what made him who he was; the question of which strands of cultural history he picked up at home and school in Altoona, at the Pennsylvania Railroad Company, as a diplomat; the question of what he created in turn, by way of culture, practice, and ideological and legal narratives. After Harry's retirement, the war on drugs continued to occupy the same channels: law, policy, enforcement, statistics, facts. From presidents to stoolies, the same cast of characters remained in play, along with the occasional flamboyant flouter, like Timothy Leary. As president, Nixon ramped things

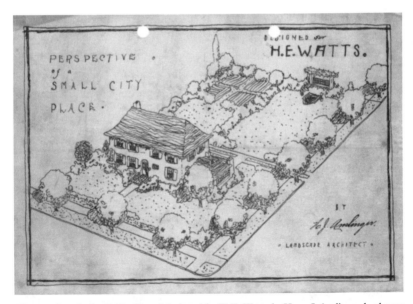

"Perspective of a Small City Place," designed for H. E. Watts, by Harry J. Anslinger, landscape architect. Harry J. Anslinger Papers, Special Collections Library, The Pennsylvania State University Libraries.

up with his War on Drugs and more than tenfolded the drug enforcement budget in his five years in office, growing it from $65 million to $719 million. Harry hung out in Hollidaysburg in the 1960s and 1970s—his seventies and eighties—and thought it was good. Conspiracies abounded; Marxist terrorists and drug traffickers continued in cahoots; but on this side of the Iron Curtain, what Harry feared most was hippies, whom he saw on TV.[1]

Then, like all biographical subjects, all historical personages, and the rest of us nonfictional subjects, like everyone everywhere, Harry died. The war on drugs went on without him. Drug cartels reached levels of elaboration and organization that rivaled government itself, partly as a result of increased enforcement in the 1970s, as well as provisional political alliances that would provisionally benefit traffickers. New drugs have been synthesized and derived. And the rest of the questions that animate this study are still being born: people adversely affected by Harry's work.

To review the course of the war on drugs since Harry's death is to confront the human consequences of the strategy of suppression. Jail time, genocidal levels of incarceration and the concomitant disenfranchisement, minimum levels of humane treatment in the criminal justice system, mandatory minimum cycles of poverty, addiction without recourse, entrenchment of racial inequality and ethnic hatred are sequelae of Harry's work. The usual suspects have been subject to a rage for order that finds expression in rectilinearity of thought, grafts social difference onto social values, punishes difference, and calls forth, in the name of progressive perfection, ever more differentiated administrative measures, measurements, and measurers, which blossom as bureaucratized institutions engineered to process the measured, those people who have been hurt—we number in the millions—by the materialization of prohibitionist values in drug policy and law, and their enforcement in the United States for the last one hundred years.

As though conservation of energy were a social law, Anslinger's energy has been transferred to those he trained and supervised, those he scared and convinced, those who heard the addresses and read those articles, those who were convicted or exonerated under the words, those arrested and processed in the criminal justice system and their families and friends and neighbors and coworkers, those unable to seek medical help, those unable to offer medical relief. Harry Anslinger did a great deal of damage to those whos, and that damage is ongoing. The mass carceral system in the United States is a function of the laws Harry championed.

Drug prohibition has been so durable in part because it serves a social control function; thus, in retrospect, it turns out that drug prohibition has been the perfect legal mechanism for disenfranchising the social groups that have been associated with both criminality and drugs since before drugs were illegal. Locking up so many people serves certain political and economic interests. And it destroys communities, families, and individuals. One of the consequences of current policies that result in the mass incarceration of human beings (including drug offenders) is

> **the creation of a huge class of individuals who see themselves as different from "normal" people. The development of this "us" versus "them" distinction worsens the very problems that social policies are supposedly designed to resolve.**[2]

I believe the creation of a distinct criminal class, disenfranchised, largely of color, was achieved by a slightly more complex process than a bunch of white guys sitting down at the table to control everything and everyone, even if one of the guys was William Randolph Hearst: there is an oscillation between beliefs and attitudes (like xenophobia and temperance, for example) and laws, as well as other institutionalized performatives—and historical happenings. The table itself oscillates.

Among those guys at that table that doesn't really exist (because it doesn't have to), Harry J. Anslinger occupied a position of unparalleled power with respect to the discursive and legal control of the meaning of drugs in the United States in the twentieth century. His lasting legacy has produced similar results to those seen during his lifetime. In June 2011, the Global Commission on Drug Policy declared:

> **The global war on drugs has failed, with devastating consequences for individuals and societies around the world. Fifty years af-**

ter the initiation of the UN Single Convention on Narcotic Drugs, and years after President Nixon launched the US government's war on drugs, fundamental reforms in national and global drug control policies are urgently needed.[3]

47 TOWARD A POETICS OF DRUG POLICY

The abovementioned 2011 report, *The War on Drugs*, was issued by Martha, the last of the passenger pigeons, our penultimate Martha, who died on September 1, 1914, three months before the passage of the Harrison Act found Harry learning how to push paper in Harrisburg. Martha flies in the face of time and reason, straight lines and realism. A little steam-tug put out from the land; she was an object of thrilling interest; she would climb to the summit of a billow, reel drunkenly there a moment, dim and gray in the driving storm of spindrift, then make a plunge like a diver and remain out of sight until one had given her up, then up she would dart again, on a steep slant toward the sky.[1] Like the other Marthas, she takes the facts and drops them again elsewhere, seeding a new way to tell the story. A new heroine. She tells the truth but tells it slant, sans statistics. Zigzagging through time and place puts a new spin on an old war.

Ever since Benjamin Rush wrote *An Inquiry into the Effects of Spirituous Liquors on the Human Body and Mind* in 1785, flip and shrub, gaming and peevishness, hospital and poorhouse. Stealing and swindling. Apoplexy, palsy, prison for life. Ever since 1785, hallooing, imitating the noises of brute animals, dancing naked, black eyes and rags. Rumbuds. Puking of bile and discharging of frothy and viscous phlegm. Perjury and dropsy. And gallows. Ever since Patrick Swindall, Republican Rep. from Georgia, lied to a grand jury about his plans to turn drug-dirtied money into a brand-new siren-song never-been-built luxury home, stealing and swindling, to the tune of $850,000, singing perjury and dropsy, while a DEA agent in Miami boarded a plane bound for Boston with sixty-two pounds of cocaine in the hold stuffed in stuffed bears and stuffed into the hollow centers of bamboo and stuffed into balloons he swallowed and stuffed into his anus and stuffed into the camel's anus and stuffed into his tampon holders until was he bust-

A passenger pigeon on a perch. Part of a group of pigeons that lived in captivity in the aviary of Professor C. O. Whitman, professor of zoology at the University of Chicago. Image by J. G. Hubbard, 1914. From the Wisconsin Historical Society, WHS-32610.

ed?[2] You bet he was. Would Harry have been proud of the bust—you bet he would. There was a man proud of busting Billie Holiday. Sad man lived to see Nixon resign in ignominy, no longer really a man, but a malignant essence informing a cadaverous human shape, the opium addict of 1880 as he appeared in the shadows of the *New York Times*. He must lie on a filthy pallet in a miserable, nasty den crowded in there with all kinds of creature . . . every town on the coast where there is a Chinaman.[3]

Zigzagging through time and space let the Supreme Court let Timothy Leary off his conviction for smuggling marijuana from Mexico into Texas in 1969, three months before a three-minute inspection check at the border was put into effect for every vehicle. Decade after decade, nine million containers entered the country, and in them, batteries, mannequins, sneakers, surfboards, fence posts, boa constrictors, racehorses, all with drugs inside. Nothing new under the hood until the Senate Caucus on International Drug Control suspects Peru of intercropping marijuana with corn, camouflaging the former, the corn as beard, making it harder for the authorities to locate the drug. Now we know "instead of war on poverty / they got a war on drugs so police can bother me." So sang Tupac in the year of the 1998 Brownsville Agreement requiring US and Mexican drug enforcement agents to communicate with each other, while those that work drug cases know that you can't work the case if you follow all those rules. Remember the golden days of that marvelous moment in Marseilles when the jig was finally up. We were winning, every time there was a Republican president, interdiction seemed imminent, and in the miserable intervals, we watched hopelessly on the border the tide coming in and the tide coming out.[4] Carrie Nation raising up her hatchet rises up to testify before the Kefauver Committee blaming it all on the Muslim, the Sunni, the Shiite, the Druze, people from Damascus, Juniyah, and Sidon, the Gemayel and Franjiyeh clans; under the oath, she's seen narco-terrorists in the Bekka Valley programming Detroit into the flight plan to trade the shit for guns, taking off and landing by dint of the otherway look of Marxist lackeys on narrow swaths of tarmac high in the mountains of Colombia, Ecuador, Afghanistan. Carrie Nation raises up her right hand and swears it's like a water balloon: we squeeze one side it goes out the other. It's like hitting mercury with a hammer. It's like carrying water with a sieve—that's why it's so important to get more sieves and run faster, said Ronald Reagan. Moonrock, parachute, paraquat, speedballs right by us on the Shining Path. What the FARC?

Abraham Lincoln stood next to testify. Head high, voice quavery after all these years, he made his play: Prohibition will work great injury to the cause of temperance. It is a species of intemperance within itself, for it goes beyond the bounds of reason in that it attempts to control a man's appetite by legislation, and makes a crime out of things that are not crimes. A prohibition law strikes a blow at the very principle upon which our government was founded. He said the bag held his "cooking kit." In it he kept the glass pipe, a cylinder-shaped glass vial that was about three inches in length, a small container of baking soda, cotton, a pair of pliers, a razor, a thin metal stick, a bottle of 151-proof rum, a copper scouring pad, and a lighter. He laid out the contents as if preparing for surgery. Then he began. Slightly at an angle waving the torch, the vial in a circular motion, twirling, the solution began to boil. Ignoring my irritation, he began to gently blow on the white glob, which began to harden immediately. Just as the rock began to melt, he put the pipe to his lips and took a long slow hit. As he inhaled, small clouds of white smoke began to twirl around inside the glass pipe. That night I learned how. It was the best feeling I'd ever had in my life. Think of the happiest, most joyful, blissful moment of your life. Now multiply that feeling by a hundred.[5]

"Chasing the ghost" is the perpetual and perpetually failing attempt to recapture the feeling of that one and only first high. Drug addicts are said to be chasing the ghost. Pursuing Harry, a pursuit more memo than memory, has been a lot like chasing a ghost. Harry spent his life chasing a host of villains: barracudas, Mafiosi, drug dealers, doctors, Communists, and other troublemakers. He was hooked on simple moral equations, but who among us is not hooked on some story or other. Fernando Arenas, for example, pilot for the CEO of a Colombian drug cartel, explains the pull of the dealer's high-risk vocation, the compulsive draw of the chase and the narrow escape:

> Then, after a while, if you go back to your regular life, you miss that craziness. I have seen many people that go back to the drug business, not because of the money, but because of the excitement that is behind that. We are humanly absolutely nutcases. And we feel a different kind of excitement during that kind of a trip flying and knowing that somebody could be down there and they're going to catch you—that you're going to spend the rest of your life in prison or you can be killed by somebody.[6]

Martha Nieves Ochoa, cousin to the brothers who ran the massively profitable Medellín cocaine operation, was kidnapped in 1981 by the

DEPARTMENT OF THE TREASURY
U.S. CUSTOMS SERVICE
BOSTON, MASS.

June 7, 1985   REFER TO

(Civil) District Case No. 85-0401-30122

Alex Chasin
5 Ashland Street
Somerville, MA 02144

Dear Alex Chasin:

This is to inform you that under the provisions of section 145.59(a)(b), title
19, Code of Federal Regulations, United States Customs authorities seized the
following described merchandise, addressed to you, which is prohibited and contrary
to law.

6 - grams of Hashish

The above-described merchandise has now been destroyed by Customs Enforcement
Officers.

The case is now closed on the records of this office.

Sincerly Yours,

JOHN V. LINDE
DISTRICT DIRECTOR OF CUSTOMS

By: Constance C. Lewis
      Fines, Penalties & Forfeitures Officer

REPLY TO: DISTRICT DIRECTOR OF CUSTOMS, U.S. CUSTOMHOUSE, BOSTON, MASSACHUSETTS 02109

A letter received by author Alexandra Chasin from the US Department of the Treasury. Used
with permission from the author.

M-19, which caused the cartel to organize murder sprees of a proto-
paramilitary kind. The M-19 released Martha unharmed the following year, though she still makes hash of the chronology, zigzag-like.
Everybody is chasing some ghost or other. Here Marthas turn the
tide. Seeing from a vantage point, slightly off center, not dead center in the gun sight of the law, Marthas can tell us what's missing
from official accounts. Martha says even though the social differences between us are multiple and massive, I must imagine Fernando
Arenas, though I have only these words of his. I don't know him. For
the same reasons, I must imagine Harry, like a fictive technique, like
an ongoing question.

What are the ghosts that drive me to chase down Harry? They are
political and personal issues, nothing special among Americans of
my generation. One of my parents was addicted to alcohol. Another

dependent on pills. I tried everything else except heroin in my prolonged youth. Because I am a white person with class privilege, my
experiences with the police and customs were mercifully brief. I have
smoked a lot of pot. Fear and shame have been less merciful and
brief—my privilege makes these private matters, not matters of state
interest. But everything from the internal monologue to the latest UN
convention, all of it is an unnecessary fiction in the service of social
division. What kind of narrative might disserve division, and serve,
instead, justice, equality, compassion, and curiosity? If the narrative
makes room for Marthas, maybe the Lotus Eaters would send word
back, at last.

48 LOTUS EATERS

Charadrius Dubius

Turn the rhetorical tables, and with them the tides. Lotus Eaters can speak right through the blank parts in Book IX of the *Odyssey*, where they are mentioned in passing, seeming to say nothing themselves. Harry wrote the book on drug prohibition, the several books. Harry had his discipline and punish. Odysseus, his odyssey. Lotus Eaters know better than anyone the stakes of language. Sea change: the Lotus Eaters speak:

Three stalwarts show up out of the clear blue sky. Hardly bend a knee they do. Turns out they lost their way—they never meant to come here. Fools are trying to get back to someplace sounds like "home." And they can take it with them when they go.

Three men land ho out of the clear blue sky and ask what manner of man I am. No manner of man, friend. Three sailors each with a little saltpeter in the hold. Party of keg and conger. Three saltwaters all with pockets empty but for powder fools like us might mistake for sand.

Three blank white men from over the waves they say. What manner of this and that they say pulping the bushes, pointing to birds. Sit down and shut up offers my sister perching by me and our other one proffers them the leaf, which they take. Now they are less afraid but more thirsty.

They will need fresh water to carry on their journey home. Sure they will go, though to listen to those little ringed plovers right now, you'd think they'd stay forever. *Charadrius dubius*. They will as surely go home as they have war in their hearts and a captain lurking nearby. They will find it another nonce. We need not show the way.

Three men arrive. As in, a stranger comes to town. Except the people in the town are stranger than the strangers. And it's not a town, it's more of a tropical jungle. So this is the other kind of narrative: this one's a trip.

Whosoever may lose their way.

Three people have come from the sea. They seek to know us. They wish to understand what we eat. There is a superabundance of the lotus in these parts and we offer some to them. "Chrono notes," sounds like they say over and over, making strange gestures with their hands. It looks like this is the first time they have eaten the lotus.

If ever a stranger should come, and that stranger assume our same form, we will take him and her to market. We have saved traffic for such a time, supposing leafs could be bought and sold, though we would prefer not to sell them. If a stranger came and were many and moved to squash us like bugs, we would squeak bloody murder, we agree.

We are half-wrasse half-human, he-some she-some, we slim dusky perch, we swim with the garfish at night, walk upright fish-free, foot-ed, by day. Leaf of shade afford us dusky perch. Fear only congers who travel in threes by the water-greened moon, and greedy moray who make late-morning land and come looking, innocent-like, for something of a meal.

When a stranger comes, we will change into beetle, triton, and plump turtledove. We will litter the path with lotus leaf leading right up to our tree, so strangers wishing to peace with us may do. For others, the leaf is invisible so the path will lead them on past our tree and into the village where they will see others like themselves, villagers strolling and stopping to look into shops, their pockets throbbing with letters from Marthas.

Three figures, three whats, three *beings*, emerge from cerulean curli-cues, yellow and orange emanating from the luxuriant hair cascad-ing down their shoulders. They are he and she—so are we—and they stride toward us, that azure slowly sinking down our evening, bluing six friendly faces. All three of us wax curious about all three of them and vice versa. We do not need forever, but surely we could pass a single hot damn night without a thought to the rest of the world. Never mind the lotus or the spear.

Other hot dark nights, my true love arrives on the other boat, the one bringing the changes. He and she is half-human, half-wrasse. When my true love flops on the dry beach before dawn, he and she becomes a beetle, a triton, a plump turtledove. A wing, aloft. And then. My love becomes a leaf. When my love arrives by air, my love is already a leaf.

I lose my way, nine, ten years, nine, ten times, you could say I'm lost. Say, after the storm, I wash up on shore in a place of short palms, put the leaky sun at my back, and follow a couple of vines into the thicket looking around for what to eat, and where and how to shelter, when I stumble onto some locals, who share a leaf unspeakably sweet with me. Say, where I lived when I lost my way was like a war zone, my neighborhood a battleground between beating up and being beaten up, my prospects for some clean sky and a job, null. Here in the land of the date, palm, jujube, clover, lotus, if I don't move much, it is not too hot.

What you see in the steely gray sea is the story beyond your control. Sometimes nothing happens for long, long, long periods of time. Sometimes time is irrelevant. Other times, a ship appears on the horizon. In the ship, crates of commodities with false bottoms, contraband, booty, and dope packed into hollowed-out walnut shells, and suspended in capsules in less viscous liquids inside oil cans inside cardboard boxes piled on wooden pallets or packed in metal containers, loaded at large port cities onto and off of trains or trucks bound for roads, tunnels, and bridges, and over and through them, to successively smaller and smaller towns, that way lighting up all the land with love.

Humans come and humans go; I may neither care nor know. To this splinter of beach, my shipment comes in, the leaf with the sunwink of magic. In the Martha of my mind, I've never needed nothing.

Pain is for the suckers athwart the benches, tied fast in endless ropes by that motherfucker captain. Ropeburn for those members of the corps who stopped awhile to jaw but failed to send back word. My love can change the changes fools like us might mistake for love, and changes me. I become in a sliver a filmy fish and shoot shotfast straightaway from land waterwards evading the oar with which his more stalwart men smite the gray sea.

Ball gowns on mannequins in *Las Marthas* (2014), directed by Cristina Ibarra.

From William Goodyear, *The Grammar of the Lotus*, 1891, p. 267. Courtesy of the Internet Archive (at archive.org) with funding from the Microsoft Corporation.

ACKNOWLEDGMENTS

Acknowledgments. I hereby humbly acknowledge that the research and writing were long and hard, and that I had a great deal of inspiration, assistance, and company along the way.

Institutional Support. I am enormously grateful for the gift of time and support from the Leon Levy Center for Biography at CUNY, where I spent the 2013–2014 year in residence as a fellow. The collection of Harry J. Anslinger Papers in the Special Collections Library at Pennsylvania State University is an unparalleled resource. Thanks for the friendly cooperation, and contributions of time, information, and/or artifacts, from Michael Sherbon, Pennsylvania State Archives; Crystal Miles, Bancroft Library, University of California, Berkeley; Paula Forman and the Altoona Area School District; Edward Copenhagen, Gutman Library, Harvard University; Rachel Greer, Fales Collection, Bobst Library, New York University; Scott D. Seligman, author of *Three Tough Chinamen*; Cristina Ibarra, director of *Las Marthas*; E. J. Fleming, author of *Wallace Reid: Life and Death of a Hollywood Idol*; May and Jay Fornwalt Jr., Hollidaysburg; Rebecca Baker, University of Washington Library; Tad Bennicoff, Smithsonian Institution; Wes Schwenk, Lebanon County Historical Society; and Jack Crispin, Crispin's Drug Store Museum.

Research Support. Lindsay Silver Cohen and Jodie Nicotra performed a first wave of research in the Anslinger archive at Penn State. Teresa Iacobelli, Dilara O'Neill, Robin Graven-Milne, and Renata Ngaiza provided crucial assistance. And Kayla Reopelle tracked down every last image here, shot some herself, secured permissions and scans, and kept the associated chaos meticulously organized. Kayla's mad skill set—technological and design acumen, archival research abilities, people handling, and indefatigability, along with her sheer intelligence—is certainly only very briefly housed in the person of a research assistant; the book was lucky to catch her at the start of her career.

Sine Qua Nons. Malaga Baldi, inscrutable agent of few words, brings it. Malaga rocks. Why say more. A dweller on the imaginary border between fact and fiction, Tim Mennel exercises editorial vision at the level of genre, true-believing in hybrid forms. Also firmly in the hybrid camp, James Goodman, pathbreaker in genre-busting work of scholarly importance and real beauty, dropped in from Heaven, or somewhere else in the tristate area, to support this work. Lucia Gill Case's close attention to eliminating cheap shots at Harry helped balance the book. Any remaining snarkiness is not her fault. And David Jauss saw this book from muddled thought to its present state, perhaps no very great distance, but any yardage at all derives from his acuity in reading tons of crude drafts.

BACKLIT BY

Company. I derive great comfort, along with great ideas, from my writing group: Margo Jefferson, Elizabeth Kendall, and Wendy S. Walters, my brilliant friends, my esteemed and cherished comrades. I enjoy all kinds of interchange, intellectual, creative and otherwise that feeds the work from ongoing, if occasional, conversation with Albert Mobilio, Andrew Meier, Dan Waterman, Dana Chasin, Davis Schneiderman, Deb Kennedy, Debra Di Blasi, Debra Minkoff, Elizabeth Graver, James Greco, Jane Kamensky, Jennifer Firestone, Jessica Case, Jill Schneiderman, Laura Chasin, Laura Tanner, Mary Jean Corbett, Matthew Case, Michael Leong, Nina Manasan Greenberg, Olga Rodríguez-Ulloa, Olivia Cueva, Peter Gill Case, Richard Chasin, Robert Lopez, Savannah Bundy, Sue Schardt, Suzanne Engler Case, Taylor Davis, Zina Goodall, Zishan Ugurlu.

Backlit By. I am unutterably lucky to have my children, Zoa Madlena Vasquez Chasin and Graham Sansom-Chasin, making every day simply amazing, and complexly too. Judith Butler and Ira Livingston make it make sense. As for Cathy Lee Crane, for outrageous encouragement—love and everything!—great big thanks.

Inspiration. The gratitude of the flounder writing fan mail for Edmund Morris, whose *Dutch* is a brave beacon of formal ingenuity and persuasive prose standing on an awesome foundation of research, and for Isaac Julien, whose *Looking for Langston* opened the door to, and blew the roof off of, lyrical and speculative biography and history.

Marthas. I am driven in no small part by the idea of what I call Marthas, eccentric characters who offer to complicate stories narrated by their own principal characters, who play with serious material, who muckrake. Marthas hold the mirrors. Marthas multiply the minoritarian perspectives from which it is possible to review and revise those stories, reveling in the inevitability of performing imaginative twists while rewriting history. Marthas make the kaleidoscope. Lotus Eaters turn it.

NOTES

CHAPTER 1

1. The case has been made again and again, relatively recently and utterly persuasively by Michelle Alexander in *The New Jim Crow: Mass Incarceration in the Age of Colorblindness* (New York: The New Press, 2010). Alexander's book is notable but hardly alone in the field.

2. Statistics abound. NAACP, "Criminal Justice Fact Sheet," accessed October 26, 2015, http://www.naacp.org/pages/criminal-justice-fact-sheet.

3. The Anslinger biography of standard is John C. McWilliams, *The Protectors: Harry J. Anslinger and the Federal Bureau of Narcotics, 1930–1962* (Newark: University of Delaware Press, 1990).

CHAPTER 2

1. The Authority of the Medical Colleges and Societies, *The Pharmacopoeia of the United States of America* (Boston: Wells & Lilly, 1820), 272.

2. [Advertisement], *Hartford Courant*, December 10, 1844. "Those who inhale the Gas once, are always anxious to inhale it the second time. There is not an exception to this rule. No language can describe the delightful sensation produced" (ibid.).

3. Ibid.

4. Alexander Wood, "New Method of Treating Neuralgia by the Direct Application of Opiates to the Painful Points," *Edinburgh Medical and Surgical Journal* 82 (April 1855): 265–81.

CHAPTER 3

1. Charles B. Clark, *A History of Blair County, Pennsylvania* . . . (Altoona, PA: Charles B. Clark, Esq, of the Blair County Bar, 1896), 69–70.

2. U. J. Jones, *History of the Early Settlement of the Juniata Valley* . . . (Philadelphia: Henry B. Ashmead, 1856), 311.

3. Clarence E. Weaver, *The Story of Altoona, the Mountain City: Railroad, Industrial and Commercial Center* (Altoona, PA: The Eddy Press Corporation, 1911), n.p.

4. Clark, *History of Blair County*, 69.

5. Ibid. A perch is a square rod, or 16.5 by 16.5 feet.

6. Department of the Interior, National Park Service, National Register of Historic Places, nomination form for Horseshoe Curve, 1978, Washington, DC, http://pdfhost.focus.nps.gov/docs/NHLS/Text/66000647.pdf.

CHAPTER 4

1. Sources differ. Ancestry.com identifies Morat as Robert Anslinger's birthplace (http://www.ancestry.com/genealogy/records/robert-john-anslinger_55594273, accessed October 26, 2016), but McWilliams has it in Bern (*The Protectors*, 195).

CHAPTER 5

1. Albert F. Blaisdell, *The Child's Book of Health*, rev. ed. (Boston: Ginn & Company, 1897), 1.

2. William Bender Wilson, *History of the Pennsylvania Railroad Company: With Plan of*

Organization, Portrait of Officials, and Biographical Sketches (Philadelphia: Henry T. Coates & Company, 1895), 1:115–16.

3. Robert N. Bellah, Richard Madsen, William M. Sullivan, Ann Swidler, and Steven M. Tipton, *Habits of the Heart: Individualism and Commitment in American Life* (Berkeley: University of California Press, 1985), 42.

4. American Association of Passenger Traffic Officers, *The Official Railway Guide: North American Freight Service Edition* (Philadelphia: National Railway Publication Company, 1879), 91.

5. "PHILADELPHIA, Penn., Nov. 18—There was a good deal of interest manifested at the railroad stations and other places to-day in the change of time that went into effect at noon. A curious assemblage gathered in front of Independence Hall to witness the operation of setting the hands forward, and the intent expression with which the spectators gazed at the dial deepened into one of bewilderment when, after half an hour's watch, no change was apparent on the face of Philadelphia's principal clock. The delicate operation of adjusting the monster mechanism in the belfry of Independence Hall was performed by William E. Harpur, and occupied just 10 minutes. At the Broad-street station of the Pennsylvania Railroad several amusing incidents occurred among anxious individuals who did not have a clear idea of the change that was about to take place. By the new standard Philadelphia is 36 seconds faster than before" ("The Change Elsewhere," *New York Times*, November 19, 1883).

6. Clark Blaise, *Time Lord: Sir Sandford Fleming and the Creation of Standard Time* (New York: First Vintage Books, 2002), 75.

7. Waldon Fawcett, "Distribution of Time Signals," *The Technical World*, March 1905, 22.

CHAPTER 6

1. H. H. Kane, *Opium Smoking in America and China* (New York: G. P. Putnam's Sons, 1881), 1. "Men and women, young girls,—virtuous or just commencing a downward career—hardened prostitutes, representatives of the 'hoodlum' element, young clerks and errand-boys who could ill afford the waste of time and money, and young men who had no work to do, were to be found smoking together in the back rooms of laundries in the low, pestilential dens of Chinatown, reeking with filth and overrun with vermin, in the cellars of drinking-saloons and in houses of prostitution" (ibid., 2). "Many females are so excited sexually by the smoking of opium during the first few weeks, that old smokers with the sole object of ruining them have taught them to smoke. Many innocent and over-curious girls have thus been seduced" (ibid., 8).

2. California State Supreme Court, 1887, 73 Cal. 142, 145 14 Pac. 405.

3. US Congress, House of Representatives, *Executive Document No. 79: C. S. Fairchild to Mr. Carlisle*, 50th Cong., 1st sess., January 12, 1888, quoted in Charles Edward Terry and Mildred Pellens, *The Opium Problem* (New York: Bureau of Social Hygiene, 1928), 747.

4. *Encyclopaedia Brittanica*, 3rd ed., s.v. "syringe."

CHAPTER 7

1. The sewage work had been seeded earlier, in 1872. "About the same time Eleventh and Eighth avenues were macadamized." Jesse C. Sell, *Twentieth Century History of Altoona and Blair County, Pennsylvania, and Representative Citizens* (Chicago: Richmond-Arnold Publishing, 1911), 289.

2. Charles B. Clark, *History of Blair County*, 27.

3. *Altoona Mirror*, May 20, 1892, 3. All subsequent references are to the same Friday evening edition.

CHAPTER 8

1. Pennsylvania Railroad Company, "General Rules," in *Rules and Regulations for the Government of the Transportation Department of the Pennsylvania Railroad* (Harrisburg, PA: Theo. F. Schefer, 1857).

2. Ibid.

3. *Rules and Regulations for the Government of the Public Schools of the City of Altoona, to Which Is Attached a Graded Course of Instruction* (Altoona, PA: Dern & Pitcairn, Printers, 1894), 8. Also printed in *Report of the Public Schools of Altoona, PA, 1902–03* (Altoona, PA: Board of Directors), 32.

CHAPTER 9

1. Blaisdell, *Child's Book of Health* (1897), 30. In the book's "Contents," this chapter is listed as "A Few Facts about Alcoholic Drinks." The remainder of the figures in this chapter are from Albert F. Blaisdell, *The Child's Book of Health*, rev. ed. (Boston: Ginn & Company, 1905), 39, 47, 1, 43, and 48, respectively. All were taken from the HaithiTrust, digitized by Google, original from Harvard University. The snippet taken from page 47 was edited from the original version to move up the final line.

2. Blaisdell, *Child's Book of Health* (1905), 39.

3. Albert F. Blaisdell, *Our Bodies and How We Live* (New York: Ginn & Company, 1893), 95.

4. Ibid., 95.

CHAPTER 10

1. James Oliver Robertson, *American Myth, American Reality* (New York: Hill and Wang, 1980), 177.

2. These several cases had arisen after Congress passed the Pacific Railway Act of 1862: "An Act to aid in the Construction of a Railroad and Telegraph Line from the Missouri River to the Pacific Ocean, and to secure to the Government the Use of the same for Postal, Military, and Other Purposes." "Subsequently, by the act of March 3, 1871, Congress incorporated the Texas Pacific Railroad Company, with power to construct and maintain a continuous railroad and telegraph line from Marshall, in the state of Texas, to a point at or near El Paso, thence through New Mexico and Arizona to San Diego, pursuing, as near as might be, the thirty-second parallel of latitude." Santa Clara County v. Southern Pacific Railroad Company, 118 U.S. 394 (1886).

3. *Santa Clara County*, 118 U.S.

4. Blaisdell, *Child's Book of Health* (1905), 48.

5. *Rules and Regulations for the Government of the Public Schools of the City of Altoona*, 8.

6. Harry J. Anslinger and Will Oursler, *The Murderers: The Shocking Story of the Narcotics Gangs* (New York: Farrar, Straus and Cudahy, 1961), 8.

7. Blaisdell, *Child's Book of Health* (1897), vii–viii.

8. Blaisdell, *Our Bodies*, 98, 99.

9. Franz Kafka, *Letters to Felice* (New York: Schocken Books, 1973), 1. Kafka wrote this in a letter in 1904, though it was not published until much later.

CHAPTER 11

1. Multiple translations of the *Odyssey* are represented in this collage: *The Odyssey of Homer*, trans. S. H. Butcher and A. Lang (New York: P. F. Collier & Son Company, 1909), 122; *The Odyssey, Translated into English Prose for the Use of Those Who Cannot Read the Original by Samuel Butler* (London: A. C. Fifield, 1900), 110; *The Odyssey of Homer, Rendered into English Verse*, trans. G. A. Schomberg (London: John Murray, 1879–1882), 235–37; *The Odyssey of Homer, Translated into English Blank Verse by William Cullen Bryant* (Boston: James R. Osgood, 1871), 214–15.

2. *Homer: Odyssey, Books I–XII, with Introduction, Notes, Etc.*, trans. and ed. W. W. Merry (Oxford: Clarendon Press, 1899), 103n84.

3. William Goodyear, *The Grammar of the Lotus: A New History of Classic Ornament as a Development of Sun Worship* (London: Sampson Low, Marston & Company, 1891), 49.

4. "In ancient times the fruits were an important article of food among the poor; whence 'lotophagi' or lotus-eaters." *Encyclopaedia Britannica*, 11th ed., s.v. "lotus."

5. Ibid.

6. P. Champault, *Phéniciens et Grecs en Italie d'après l'Odyssée*, p. 400, note 2, and Victor Bérard, *Les Phéniciens et l'Odyssée*, 1902–1903, vol. 2, p. 102, quoted in *Encyclopedia Britannica*, 11th ed., s.v. "lotus."

7. R. M. Henry, *Classical Review*, December 1906, p. 435, quoted in *Encyclopedia Britannica*, 11th ed., s.v. "lotus."

8. "To breakfast at Alkinoos's on the eighth of September, in the land of the Lotos-eaters on the sixteenth, and in the realm of Aiolos on the twenty-fifth! βάλε δὴ βάλε κηρ ὐλος εἴην. Nothing more tempting has ever crossed the vision of the lover of the Odyssey. But by the time these lines see the light, the wonderful trip, conducted by M. VICTOR BERARD, the famous author of *Les Phéniciens et l'Odyssée* will be over, and the scholar who is chained to his desk must console himself as scholars have been wont to console themselves since the time of Ecclesiastes, and before, with doubt and disillusionment." "Brief Mention," *American Journal of Philology* 27, no. 3 (1906): 360.

9. *Homer*, trans. and ed. Merry, 103n84.

10. "Lotus-Eaters (Gr. Λωτοφαγοι), a Libyan tribe known to the Greeks as early as the time of Homer. Herodotus (iv. 177) describes their country as in the Libyan district bordering on the Syrtes, and says that a caravan route led from it to Egypt. Victor Bérard identifies it with the modern Jerba. When Odysseus reached the country of the Lotophagi, many of his sailors after eating the lotus lost all wish to return home. Both Greeks and Romans used the expression to eat the lotus to denote forgetfulness (cf. Tennyson's poem 'The Lotus Eaters')." *Encyclopedia Britannica*, 11th ed., s.v. "lotus." The earliest mention of the appellation on English soil may have been Tennyson's eponymous poem of 1832. The *Oxford English Dictionary* defines "lotus-eater" as, "One of the Lotophagi," or "one who gives himself up to dreamy and luxurious ease." Lotus Eaters have, by definition, an eccentric relation to labor: "A summer like that of 1893 may be all very well for the lotus-eater, but is a calamity to people who have to get their living out of English land." "1893," *The Times*, December 30, 1893, quoted in *Oxford English Dictionary*, 2nd ed., s.v. "lotus-eater."

CHAPTER 12

1. Job application, 1918, Harry J. Anslinger Papers, HCLA 1875, Special Collections Library, The Pennsylvania State University Libraries (hereafter cited as Anslinger Papers).

2. Peter Galison, *Einstein's Clocks and Poincaré's Maps: Empires of Time* (New York: W. W. Norton, 2003), 30, 244, 245, 247.

3. Ibid., 29.

4. Ibid., 37–38.

5. Ibid., 143.

CHAPTER 13

1. Richard Davenport-Hines, *The Pursuit of Oblivion: A Global History of Narcotics* (New York: W. W. Norton, 2004), 205.

2. Charles Henry Brent, memo of 1904, quoted in Davenport-Hines, *Pursuit of Oblivion*, 204.

3. Hamilton Kemp Wright, "Report on the International Opium Commission and on the Opium Problem as Seen within the United States," [in *Report of the International Opium Commission, Shanghai, China, February 1 to February 26, 1909*, 2 vols. (Shanghai: North-China Daily News and Herald, 1909)], quoted in David F. Musto, ed., *Drugs in America: A Documentary History* (New York: New York University Press, 2002), 373–74.

4. Ibid., 374.

5. Ibid., 373.

6. Ibid., 375.

7. Ibid.

8. Ibid., 372.

9. Ibid., 378.

10. Ibid., 371.

11. Harry's impairment prevented both induction and enlistment during World War I, a fact that may have influenced his choice to go to work for Ordnance during the war, according to McWilliams, *The Protectors*, 28.

12. Weaver, *Story of Altoona*, s.vv., "A. F. Shomberg," "E. J. W. Keagy."

CHAPTER 14

1. Henry J. Finger to Hamilton Kemp Wright, July 2, 1911, "Records of United States Delegations to the International Opium Commission and Conferences, 1909-1913," Papers of Dr. Hamilton Wright, RG 43, National Archives, quoted in David F. Musto, *American Disease: Origins of Narcotic Control* (New York: Oxford University Press, 1999), 218.

2. Ibid.

3. Davenport-Hines, *Pursuit of Oblivion*, 211.

4. Frederick Winslow Taylor, *The Principles of Scientific Management* (New York: W. W. Norton, 1911), 40, 37-38.

5. Ibid., 44-46.

6. Ibid.

7. Ibid., 21, 5.

8. Ibid., 5.

9. Ibid., 3.

10. Weaver, *Story of Altoona*, s.v., "The Altoona Shops."

CHAPTER 15

1. Clark, *History of Blair County*, 73.

2. The case is related in McWilliams, *The Protectors*, 26.

3. Collage of Albert Einstein, *The World as I See It* (Amsterdam: Querido Verlag, 1934); and Einstein to Robert S. Marcus, New York, February 12, 1950, in Albert Einstein Archives, Hebrew University of Jerusalem, available in Nancy Rosenbaum, "Einstein Sleuthing," *On Being* (blog), November 12, 2009, accessed January 15, 2016, http://www.onbeing.org/blog/einstein-sleuthing/3637.

4. Anslinger and Oursler, *The Murderers*, 9-10.

5. Ibid.

6. Ibid., 9.

7. Taylor, *Principles of Scientific Management*, 51-52.

8. Albert Einstein, "Autobiographical Notes," in *Albert Einstein: Philosopher-Scientist*, trans. and ed. Paul Arthur Schilpp (LaSalle, IL: Open Court, 1949), 5, 7.

CHAPTER 16

1. From the vantage point of the historical epoch where the already-industrialized prison system has been saturated with private capital, the curtailment of medical authority by the courts in the 1910s and 1920s seems to foreshadow the same as exerted by the private insurance industry presently.

2. "Mental Sequellae of the Harrison Law," *New York Medical Journal* 102 (May 15, 1915): 1014.

3. Ibid.

4. "Editorial Comment," *American Medicine*, o.s., 21, n.s., 10 (November 1915): 799-800.

5. Ibid.

CHAPTER 17

1. Job application, 1918, Anslinger Papers.

2. Harry J. Anslinger, *The Protectors: The Heroic Story of the Narcotics Agents, Citizens and Officials in Their Unending, Unsung Battles against Organized Crime in America*, with J. Dennis Gregory (New York: Farrar, Straus and Company, 1964), 3.

3. Job application, 1918, Anslinger Papers.

4. Ibid.

5. Office Order No. 147 (Efficiency Boards), February 1918, Anslinger Papers.

6. Anslinger, *The Protectors*, 3.

CHAPTER 18

1. Louis Beck suggests that, in the spirit of Christian charity, "several charitable and wealthy persons became interested in the youthful student, among them Mrs. George Washington Reed, and her husband (who was at one time publisher of the *Brooklyn Daily Eagle*), residing on Berkeley Place, that city." Louis Joseph Beck, *New York's Chinatown: An Historical Presentation of Its People and Places* (New York: Bohemia Publishing Company, 1898), 267–68.

2. "Country Flooded with Counterfeit Pennies," *New York Times*, February 10, 1901.

3. Beck, *New York's Chinatown*, 266–69.

4. Ibid., 269.

5. Ibid., 266.

6. Musto, *American Disease*, 129.

7. U.S. v. Jin Fuey Moy, 241 U.S. 394 (1916).

8. Ibid.

9. *Houdini*, 1953 film directed by George Marshall, starring Tony Curtis as the escapologist.

CHAPTER 19

1. All quotations in this chapter are from Harry's unpublished diary in the Anslinger Papers.

CHAPTER 20

1. "In order that these facts may have their true color, it should also be stated that within a period of eleven months Goldbaum purchased from wholesalers in Memphis, thirty times as much morphine as was bought by the average retail druggist doing a larger general business, and he sold narcotic drugs in 6,500 instances; that Webb regularly charged fifty cents for each so-called prescription, and within the period had furnished, and Goldbaum had filed, over 4,000 such prescriptions." Webb v. U.S., 249 U.S. 96 (1919).

2. The text of *Webb* reads like a vaudeville skit or an avant-garde prose-poem:

> If question one is answered in the negative, or question two in the affirmative, no answer to question three will be necessary; and if question three is answered in the affirmative, questions one and two become immaterial. Upon these facts the Circuit Court of Appeals propounds to this court three questions:
>
> 1. Does the first sentence of §2 of the Harrison Act prohibit retail sales of morphine by druggists to persons who have no physician's prescription, who have no order blank therefor and cannot obtain an order blank because not of the class to which such blanks are allowed to be issued?
>
> 2. If the answer to question one is in the affirmative, does this construction make unconstitutional the prohibition of such sale?
>
> 3. If a practicing and registered physician issues an order for morphine to an habitual user thereof, the order not being issued by him in the course of professional treatment in the attempted cure of the habit, but being issued for the purpose of providing the user with morphine sufficient to keep him comfortable by maintaining his customary use, is such order a physician's prescription under exception(b) of §2? (*Webb* 249 U.S.)

3. Ibid.

4. Jin Fuey Moy v. U.S., 254 U.S. 189 (1920).

5. Diary entry, March 4, 1919, Anslinger Papers.

6. U.S. v. Doremus, 249 U.S. 86 (1919).

7. Ibid.

CHAPTER 21

1. Unless otherwise noted, all quotations in this chapter are from Harry's unpublished diary in the Anslinger Papers.

2. McWilliams, *The Protectors*, 29.

CHAPTER 22

1. McWilliams, *The Protectors*, 30. See "Statement of Training and Experience," 1929, Anslinger Papers.

2. Treasury Department, *Traffic in Narcotic Drugs: Report of Special Committee of Investigation Appointed March 25, 1918, by the Secretary of the Treasury* (Washington, DC: Government Printing Office, 1919), 9.

3. Sarah E. Igo, *The Averaged American: Surveys, Citizens, and the Making of a Mass Public* (Cambridge, MA: Harvard University Press, 2007), 9. "Architects of the technocratic state of the 1920s, with its managerial charge and emphasis on planning, took a further step, seizing upon social statistics as objective, seemingly nonpolitical instruments for decision making. . . . In President Herbert Hoover's two ambitious information-collecting projects of the late 1920s and early 1930s, the Committee on Recent Economic Changes and the Committee on Social Trends, official statistics were elevated as ends in themselves, tools for expressing facts about the population and capable of giving shape to the nation" (ibid.).

4. Treasury Department, *Traffic in Narcotic Drugs*, 3.

5. Ibid., 17.

6. Ibid., 20. "These estimates must, however, be looked upon as mere guesses in most cases because of the fact that there have been no means available for reaching an accurate estimate in the past" (ibid.).

7. Ibid., 24.

8. Ibid., 20.

9. Bishop Brent to Theodore Roosevelt, Manila, July 24, 1906, in H.R. Doc. No. 380, at vii (1923), quoted in Peter D. Lowes, *The Genesis of International Narcotics Control* (Geneva: Librarie Droz), 108.

10. Igo, *Averaged American*, 102. "The *Journal of the American Statistical Association* judged the technique of the Middletown studies to be 'far beyond that of the sociological novel' but not yet 'concerned with the problem of generalizing illuminating incidents, anecdotes, and case studies into a system of principles or laws.'" Robert Lynd, "Problem of Being Objective in Studying Our Own Culture" (lecture, Princeton University, Princeton, NJ, December 9, 1938), quoted in Igo, *Averaged American*, 65.

11. Treasury Department, *Traffic in Narcotic Drugs*, 28.

CHAPTER 23

1. As though telepathically, and yet too literally, the *Bridgeport Standard Telegram* commended *Valley of the Giants* for "the red-blooded stuff that fans adore." *Bridgeport Standard Telegram*, November 1, 1919, quoted in David W. Menefee, *Wally: The True Wallace Reid Story* (Albany, GA: BearManor Media, 2011), 425.

2. "Had Dope for Sale," *Variety*, November 19, 1920, 39.

3. E. J. Fleming, *Wallace Reid: The Life and Death of a Hollywood Idol* (Jefferson, NC: McFarland, 2007), 164.

4. Dorothy Davenport, "Part Three: Drug Demon's Debut in Wallace Reid Home Described," *Los Angeles Herald*, December 21, 1922.

5. "World-Wide Condemnation of Pictures as Aftermath of Arbuckle Affair," *Variety*, September 23, 1921, 46.

6. Fleming, *Wallace Reid*, 218.

7. "The Hell Diggers," *Variety*, August 26, 1921, 36.

8. "Wallace Reid: 30 Days," *Indianapolis Star*, January 1, 1923.

9. Mae Tinée, "Wally Stars as Breaker of Ghosts," *Chicago Daily Tribune*, November 8, 1922.

10. "Ghost Breaker," *Variety*, September 15, 1922, 42.

11. Fleming, *Wallace Reid*, 145.

12. *Picture Show Magazine*, May 3, 1919, 101, quoted in Fleming, *Wallace Reid*, 146.

13. U.S. v. Behrman, 258 U.S. 280 (1922).

14. Rufus King, *The Drug Hang-Up, America's Fifty-Year Folly* (New York: W. W. Norton & Co., 1972), 44.

15. Menefee, *Wally*, 187.

16. Fleming, *Wallace Reid*, 222.

17. Dorothy Davenport, "Wife Pens Dramatic Story of Wallace Reid's Drug Ruin," *San Francisco Examiner*, December 31, 1923.

18. Fleming, *Wallace Reid*, 232.

19. Ibid., 81.

20. *Progress*, April 1, 1921, quoted in Fleming, *Wallace Reid*, 456.

21. *Fayetteville Daily Democrat*, September 19, 1921, quoted in Fleming, *Wallace Reid,* 167.

22. *Los Angeles Evening Herald*, July 18, 1923, quoted in Fleming, *Wallace Reid*, 232.

23. *Behrman*, 258 U.S.

CHAPTER 24

1. Language from James Joyce, *Ulysses* (London: Bodley Head, 1937), episode 5; and Mark Twain, *Following the Equator: A Journey around the World* (Hartford: American Pub. Co., 1897), ch. 37.

2. Joyce, *Ulysses*, 76.

3. Unattributed Treasury Department memo in Anslinger Papers. The order referenced is Executive Order 3180 of November 25, 1919: "E. O. [2837] of Apr. 11, 1918, revoking certain powers relative to enemy alien trademarks and copyrights vested in the Treasury Sec'y under the Trading with the Enemy Act, rescinded and said powers revested in said Sec'y." Quoted in Clifford L. Lord, *Presidential Executive Orders Compiled by the W.P.A. Historical Records Survey* (New York: Hastings House, 1944), 270.

4. Hugh H. Corkum, *On Both Sides of the Law* (Hantsport, NS: Lancelot Press, 1989), 15, 27 (first quotation), front cover (second quotation).

5. Ibid., 34, 99, 9.

6. Memorandum from H. T. Nugent to the Division of Foreign Control, June 24, 1927, Anslinger Papers.

7. Corkum, *On Both Sides*, 94.

8. Consular memo, Anslinger Papers. Harry's was not the only move to a sandier clime from a European post: "Winthrop A. Scott is shifted from Paris to Cape Haitien. We can almost experience his emotions when leaving the Ville Lumiere to drop down into the Haitian town of darksome population. . . . And thus the list continues juggling men from tropics to artics [*sic*] from wilderness to metropolis, from savage lands to civilization and back again. Yes, it's the life" (ibid.).

9. Anonymous, "The Lure of La Guaïra," Anslinger Papers.

10. "The Assignment, or Infinite Echoes," 1916, Anslinger Papers.

11. McWilliams, *The Protectors*, 31, 30.

12. Twain, *Following the Equator*, 336.

13. H. J. Anslinger, "The La Guaïra–Caracas Railroad," *American Consular Bulletin* 6, no. 9 (September 1924): 319.

14. Ibid.

15. Ibid.

16. Corkum, *On Both Sides*, 9.

17. Twain, *Following the Equator*, 339.

18. McWilliams, *The Protectors*, 30.

19. David Kahn, "Heterogeneous Impulses," chap. 18 in *The Code Breakers: The Story of Secret Writing*, abr. ed. (New York: Macmillan, 1967).

20. McWilliams, *The Protectors*, 31.

21. Ibid.

22. Corkum, *On Both Sides*, 28.

23. Memo of the Division of Foreign Control, Anslinger Papers.

24. Corkum, *On Both Sides*, 72.

25. Ibid., 96.

26. Ibid., 71.

27. Re: Consolidated Exporters Corporation, Ltd., of Vancouver, B.C. [unpublished memorandum], 1930, p. 8, Anslinger Papers.

28. Corkum, *On Both Sides*, 18.

29. Ibid., 25.

30. Memo of the Division of Foreign Control, Anslinger Papers.

31. Corkum, *On Both Sides*, 58, 50.

32. No. 1126. Canton, China "Importation of Chinese Medicinal Wines," April 26, 1928, Anslinger Papers.

33. To Consul General R. C. Tredwell, Esq., Hong Kong, November 8, 1926, Anslinger Papers.

34. Untitled manuscript, Anslinger Papers.

35. Corkum, *On Both Sides*, 23.

CHAPTER 25

1. Bertrand Russell, "Truth and Falsehood," in *The Problems of Philosophy* (London: Williams and Norgate, 1912), 88.

2. John G. Lake, "A Lecture on Divine Healing," *Spokesman Review*, March 17, 1918.

3. Motion to quash search warrant, Linder v. U.S., 268 U.S. 5 (1925), quoted in Rufus King, "The Narcotics Bureau and the Harrison Act," *Yale Law Journal* 62 (1953): 784–87.

4. Linder v. U.S., 268 U.S. 5 (1925).

5. Ibid.

6. Ibid.

7. Ibid.

8. Russell, "Truth and Falsehood."

CHAPTER 26

1. Twain, *Following the Equator*, 339, 340.

2. Joyce, *Ulysses*, 66.

3. "The Assignment, or Infinite Echoes," 1916, Anslinger Papers.

4. All text images in this chapter are from "The Assignment, or Infinite Echoes," 1916. Harry J. Anslinger Papers, Special Collections Library, The Pennsylvania State University Libraries.

5. Ibid.

6. H. J. Anslinger, "The Tiger of the Sea," *Saturday Evening Post*, June 12, 1926.

7. "Shark Fins," pp. 3, 6, Anslinger Papers.

8. Ibid.

9. "Tiger of the Sea" [draft], Anslinger Papers.

10. "Shark Attacks Boy Bather," *Canberra Times*, January 14, 1929. The Anslinger Papers include the indignant responses of readers who felt that Harry's piece in the *Saturday Evening Post* might mislead swimmers into a false sense of safety around sharks, and thus might be dangerous. There were direct letters to Harry, as well as references in other publications, such as this one.

11. "Says Drug Addicts Number 1,000,000: Captain Hobson Charges Health Service Suppressed Report on American Victims. Doctors Dispute Figures," *New York Times*, July 7, 1926.

12. Treasury Department, Bureau of Narcotics, Federal Narcotics Control Board, *Traffic in Opium and Other Dangerous Drugs for the Year Ended December 31, 1925* (Washington, DC: Government Printing Office, 1926).

13. McWilliams, *The Protectors*, 34.

14. Fred D. Pasley, *Al Capone: The Biography of a Self-Made Man* (New York: Ives Washburn, 1930), 39.

15. Ibid., 40.

CHAPTER 27

1. Also located in the Treasury, the Narcotics Division was headed by Colonel L. G. Nutt. The lawyer for Lugnut's division was Alfred L. Tennyson, denotative doppelganger of the author of "The Lotos-eaters," in which "dark faces" feed some storm-tossed sailors "that enchanted stem / Laden with flower and fruit," which brings on a drowsiness. In another nutty doppelgang, one George Bush was the supervisor of the North Atlantic Zone—George P. Bush. But that is another chapter.

2. Memo of the Division of Foreign Control, Anslinger Papers.

3. Jay Richard Kennedy, "One World against Dope," *Sunday Star*, March 7, 1948.

4. Yet by 1964, Harry had a more realistic appraisal of Prohibition, as it related to alcohol:

> Prohibition, conceived as a moral attempt to improve the American way of life, would ultimately cast the nation into a turmoil. One cannot help but think in retrospect that Prohibition, by depriving Americans of their 'vices,' only created the avenues through which organized crime gained its firm foothold. (Anslinger, *The Protectors*, 10)

The clarity with which he saw it in hindsight is remarkable mainly for its myopia. How could he have written the preceding sentences and yet still maintained the belief that prohibitionist drug policy was practicable, socially beneficial, economically sensible, or morally defensible, as he did, unwaveringly, for the entire thirty-one years of his tenure as commissioner?

5. Department of Justice, Office of the Attorney General, National Commission on Law Observance and Enforcement, *Report on the Enforcement of the Prohibition Laws of the United States*, National Commission on Law Observance and Enforcement Reports no. 2 (Washington, DC: Government Printing Office, January 7, 1931). This commission and its report will be hereafter referred to using the popular name, Wickersham, after Attorney General George W. Wickersham who presided over this committee. It will be discussed in greater depth in chapter 29.

6. Wickersham Commission, *Report on the Cost of Crime*, National Commission on Law Observance and Enforcement Reports no. 12 (Washington, DC: Government Printing Office, June 24, 1931), 74.

7. McWilliams, *The Protectors*, 37.

CHAPTER 28

1. Anslinger's vanquishing of horse dopers will be covered in chapter 33.

2. Outline of speech before the International Association of Chiefs of Police at St. Petersburg, FL, October 13, 1913, Anslinger Papers.

3. "In faraway India and in some of Britain's Eastern possessions, opium, under state mo-

nopolies, is grown, cured and smoked. . . . A net profit, during the year 1933, of $2,800,000 from two government factories in British India alone was reported. . . . The government of British India anticipates that it will end its distasteful but profitable export business in the sinister drug by 1935." "Bulgaria 'Dope' Plants Smuggled into France; Opium Still Growing," Anslinger Papers.

4. State Department, press release, Stuart Fuller, February 25, 1936, Anslinger Papers. The following references come from the same source.

5. Opium Board memo, Anslinger Papers.

6. H. J. Anslinger, "Address," International Association of the Chiefs of Police, *The Police Yearbook* (1931): 81.

7. A. E. Fossier, "The Menace of Marihuana," *New Orleans Medical and Surgical Journal* 84 (May 1931); Eugene Stanley, "Marijuana as a Developer of Criminals," *American Journal of Police Science* 2 (May–June 1931): 256.

8. An editorial appeared nationally in Hearst newspapers on September 11, 1935:

> Much of the opposition to the Uniform State Narcotic Law must be imputed to the selfish and often unscrupulous opposition of racketeering interests.
>
> But more than half the states have now acted favorably, and Commissioner Anslinger has announced that an intensified drive will be made at once to bring the rest into line.
>
> One thing that the indolent legislatures should be made to understand is that the "dope" traffic does not stand still.
>
> Of recent years the insidious and insanity producing marihuana has become among the worst of the narcotic banes, invading even the schoolhouses of the country, and the Uniform State Narcotic Law is THE ONLY LEGISLATION yet devised to deal effectively with its horrid menace. ("State Narcotic Control," *New York American*, September 11, 1935)

9. A 1937 resolution of a narcotics conference of lawyers, judges, and civic leaders commended William Randolph Hearst and his papers for "pioneering the national fight against dope." *Washington Herald*, February 20, 1937, quoted in Richard J. Bonnie and Charles H. Whitebread, *The Marijuana Conviction* (Charlottesville: University of Virginia Press, 1974), 101.

10. Circular Letter No. 324 from H. J. Anslinger, December 4, 1934, box 19, file OF 21-X, Franklin D. Roosevelt Presidential Library, quoted in McWilliams, *The Protectors*, 84.

11. "Walker Admits Dope Charge Propaganda," *San Francisco News*, November 11, 1933.

12. Women's Narcotic Defense Association Special Meeting in the Offices of the Chief Justice of the Court of Special Sessions in New York City, January 25, 1933, Anslinger Papers.

13. Anslinger, "La Guaïra–Caracas Railroad."

14. H. J. Anslinger, "Address," International Association of the Chiefs of Police, Proceedings, Milwaukee, WI, September 12, 1940.

15. Anonymous unpublished report, Anslinger Papers.

CHAPTER 29

1. "Tidal shorelines were measured in 1939–40 with a recording instrument on the largest-scale charts and maps then available." US Department of Commerce, National Oceanic and Atmospheric Administration, *The Coastline of the United States*, NOAA/PA 71046, rev. ed. (Washington, DC: Government Printing Office, 1975). The shore was remeasured in 1961, and though the 1915 measurement of Alaska's coast was retained, there was an increase in the Florida shoreline due to "a new approach to measurement" in the Keys. The same measurements were supplied to "Members" and "Committees of Congress" taking up border security and immigration issues at least as recently as 2006. Janice Cheryl Beaver, "U.S. International Borders: Brief Facts" (US Library of Congress, Congressional Research Service Report for Congress RS21729, 2006).

2. Quoted in Edward Behr, *Prohibition: Thirteen Years That Changed America* (New York: Arcade, 1996), 86.

3. Wickersham Commission, *Enforcement of the Prohibition Laws*, 280.

4. Franklin P. Adams, "The Conning Tower," *New York World*, January 22, 1931.

5. Wickersham Commission, *Enforcement of the Prohibition Laws*, 271.

6. Wickersham Commission, *Cost of Crime*, 2.

7. U.S. v. One Book Called "Ulysses," Random House, Inc., 110 F. Supp., 5–6 (S.D.N.Y. December 6, 1933).

8. Ibid., 6–7, 8 (quotations at 6 and 8). Another precedent cited in Judge Woolsey's judgment is *U.S. v. One Book Entitled "Married Love"* (ibid., 7).

9. Morris L. Ernst, introduction to *Ulysses*, by James Joyce (New York: Vintage, 1961), vi.

10. Ibid., v.

11. *"Ulysses,"* 110 F. Supp. at 8.

12. Ibid.

13. Ibid.

14. Ibid.

15. Joyce, *Ulysses* (1937), 31.

CHAPTER 30

1. H. J. Anslinger and Courtney Ryley Cooper, "Marijuana: Assassin of Youth," *American Magazine* 124, no. 1 (July 1937), 18ff.

2. Ibid.

3. Files on Marijuana Related Arrests, Anslinger Papers. These files will hereafter be referred to as the Gore Files.

4. Ibid.

5. Northrup Frye, *A Secular Scripture: A Study of the Structure of Romance* (Cambridge, MA: Harvard University Press, 1976), 117.

6. H. J. Anslinger, "The Psychiatric Aspects of Marijuana Intoxication," *Journal of the American Medical Association* 121, no. 3 (January 16, 1943): 312.

7. H. J. Anslinger, "Opening Statement Containing Review of Proceedings of Sub-Committee on Cannabis of Advisory Committee on Traffic in Opium, League of Nations" (lecture, Marihuana Conference, United States Bureau of Internal Revenue, Washington, DC, December 5, 1938).

8. *Cincinnati Enquirer*, March 1, 1937, Gore Files, Anslinger Papers.

9. Gore Files, Anslinger Papers.

10. Ibid.

11. Ibid.

12. Ibid.

13. Anslinger and Oursler, *The Murderers*, 38.

14. Anslinger and Cooper, "Assassin of Youth."

15. Ibid.

16. Ibid.

17. Ibid.

18. Though numerous stories appeared with a female marijuana-smoking window-jumper in magazines, journals, and books from 1938 on, some of which locate her in Chicago, this 1937 piece by Anslinger is not only the first; it is also unsubstantiated by newspaper reportage 1931–1937. A Norma de Marco jumped from a twelfth-story window in New York in 1938, but her story was not in the Federal Bureau of Narcotics' Gore Files. Antique Cannabis Museum, *Antique Cannabis Book*, 3rd ed. (2014), under "Harry Anslinger's Gore File Illinois: Girls Jumping Out of Windows" (http://antiquecannabisbook.com/chap04/Illinois/IL_RMWindow.htm, accessed February 22, 2016).

19. Gore Files, Anslinger Papers.

20. Anslinger and Cooper, "Assassin of Youth."

21. Anslinger and Ourseler, *The Murderers*, 38.

22. Department of State, Office of Language Services, Translating Division, *Narcotic Drugs: Their Legal and Social Status from a National and International Standpoint*, by Reshat Saka (Istanbul: Cumhuriyet Printing House, 1948), 21.

23. "Dean Acheson Has Lighter Side," *Portland Sunday Telegram and Sunday Press*; Drew Pearson "Acheson's Philosophical Calm Helps Him Weather Criticism," *Paris News*; Drew Pearson, "Humor Helps Secretary to Weather Criticism," *Ogden Standard-Examiner*; Drew Pearson, "Acheson Develops Own Philosophy," *Spartanburg Herald-Journal*. All are from October 8, 1950.

CHAPTER 31

1. Anslinger and Cooper, "Assassin of Youth."

2. Ibid.

3. Musto, *American Disease*, 220.

4. US Congress, House of Representatives, Committee on Immigration and Naturalization, *Deportation of Aliens Convicted of Violation of Narcotic and Prohibition Acts on H.R. 11118 (Amended forms of H.R. 10075 and H.R. 10058)*, 67th Cong., 2nd sess., March 29, 1922, 544 (statistics), 554 (quotations). In response to which a Mr. Siegel remarked, "I will venture to say, Brother Jones, you will find what you are saying right now will be very inaccurate and precarious" (ibid., 554).

5. Gore Files, Anslinger Papers.

6. McWilliams, *The Protectors*, 58.

7. Department of the Treasury, Federal Bureau of Narcotics, *Report by the Government of the United States of America for the Calendar Year Ended December 31, 1931; on The Traffic in Opium and Other Dangerous Drugs* (Washington, DC: Government Printing Office, 1932), 51.

8. Frederic M. Thrasher, "Social Attitudes of Superior Boys in an Interstitial Community," in *Social Attitudes*, ed. Kimball Young (New York: Henry Holt, 1931), 236–64.

9. Ibid.

10. May Case Marsh, "The Life and Work of the Churches in an Interstitial Area" (PhD diss., New York University, 1932), 421–22.

11. Margaret Campbell Tilley, "The Boy Scout Movement in East Harlem," (PhD diss., New York University, 1935), 199.

12. Dorothy Reed, "Leisure Time of Girls in a 'Little Italy' " (PhD diss., Columbia University, Portland, OR, 1932), quoted in Philippe Bourgois, *In Search of Respect: Selling Crack in El Barrio* (New York: Cambridge University Press, 1996), 67.

13. Nels Anderson, "The Social Antecedents of a Slum: A Developmental Study of East Harlem Area of Manhattan Island, New York City" (PhD diss., New York University, 1930); Mary J. Concistre, "A Study of a Decade in the Life and Education of Adult Immigrant Community in East Harlem" (PhD diss., New York University, 1943); Irving V. Sollins, "A Socio-Statistical Analysis of Boys' Club Membership" (PhD diss., New York University, 1936); Tilley, "Boy Scout Movement"; Frederic M. Thrasher, "Final Report of the Jefferson Branch of the Boys' Club of New York" (typewritten, submitted to the Bureau of Social Hygiene, 1935).

14. Frederic M. Thrasher, "The Boys' Club and Juvenile Delinquency," *American Journal of Sociology* 42 (July 1936): 74, quoted in Bourgois, *In Search of Respect*, 59.

15. "National Affairs: Veto Vito?" *Time*, November 4, 1946, 24–25, quoted in Bourgois, *In Search of Respect*, 61.

16. See Noel Ignatiev, *How the Irish Became White* (New York: Routledge, 1995); and Karem Brodkin, *How Jews Became White Folks & What That Says about Race in America* (New Brunswick, NJ: Rutgers University Press, 1998).

17. "Mafia's Code in New-York: Italians Who Avenge Their Own Grievances in Blood," *New York Times*, May 16, 1893, 9, quoted in Bourgois, *In Search of Respect*, 58.

CHAPTER 32

1. H. J. Anslinger memo, Anslinger Papers.

2. Anslinger and Cooper, "Assassin of Youth."

3. US Congress, House of Representatives, Committee on Ways and Means, *Hearing on Taxation of Marihuana*, 75th Cong., 1st sess., April 27–30, May 4, 1937.

4. Ibid. The *JAMA* editorial, "Opium Traffic in the United States," is from January 23, 1937, and the *Washington Herald* editorial, "The Narcotic Invasion of America," is from April 10, 1937. Copies of both were entered into the record as part of Woodward's testimony. The quotation here is from the *Washington Herald* editorial, and Woodward also quoted it in his statement before the committee.

5. Ibid. (Woodward's statement).

6. Ibid. (quoted in the *Washington Herald* editorial).

7. Musto, *Drugs in America*, 438.

8. Committee on Ways and Means, *Taxation of Marihuana*.

9. H. J. Anslinger memo, April 30, 1937, Anslinger Papers.

10. James A. Swartz, *Substance Abuse in America: A Documentary and Reference Guide* (Santa Barbara, CA: Greenwood, 2012), 75.

CHAPTER 33

1. W. C. Vreeland, "No Evidence of Doping at Tropical Park," *Brooklyn Daily Eagle*, January 11, 1934.

2. Frank G. Menke, "Hopping Horses," *Esquire*, April 1, 1936. 57ff.

3. G. F. T. Ryall, "A New Year of Racing," *Polo*, January 1934, 13–14.

4. Ibid.

5. Bradford Wells, "A Landis for Racing?," *Post Time*, June 1935, 5.

6. Bradford Wells, "Combatting the Dope Evil," *Post Time*, July 1935, 6–7, 39.

7. Ryall, "New Year of Racing," 13.

8. Menke, "Hopping Horses."

9. Ibid.

10. Ibid.

11. Ibid.

12. Ibid.

13. Mayor's Committee on Marijuana, *The Marijuana Problem in the City of New York* (New York: New York Academy of Medicine, 1944), 213. This is commonly known as the La Guardia report.

14. Ibid, 214.

CHAPTER 34

1. Gerard Jones, *Men of Tomorrow: Geeks, Gangsters and the Birth of the Comic Book* (New York: BasicBooks, 2004), 1.

2. *Doppelganger* means, among other things: "a person who has the same name as another."

3. H. J. Anslinger's biographer McWilliams notes that Anslinger listed "on some of his résumés that he earned an L.L.D. from the University of Maryland Law School. However, an extensive check by the registrar of that institution's records failed to produce any evidence that Anslinger was ever enrolled there, or that he was conferred with an honorary degree." McWilliams, *The Protectors*, 192.

4. Jones, *Men of Tomorrow*, 41.

5. Ibid., 20, 21, 1.

6. Ibid., 2.

7. McWilliams, *The Protectors*, 64.

8. Floyd R. Baskette, City Editor, *Alamos Daily Courier*, September 4, 1936.

9. Woody Guthrie, "Pretty Boy Floyd" (1939).

10. "Floyd Flushed," *Time*, October 22, 1934.

11. Guthrie, "Pretty Boy Floyd."

12. Others tell you 'bout a stranger
    That come to beg a meal,
    Underneath his napkin
    Left a thousand dollar bill.

13. "The Case of the Cincinnati Narcotics Ring" [recording], *Gang Busters*, Blue Network, September 25, 1948.

14. Ibid.

CHAPTER 35

1. George Wilkes, *Project of a National Railroad from the Atlantic to the Pacific Ocean for the Purpose of Obtaining a Short Route to Oregon and the Indies* (New York: Burgess, Stringer & Co., 1845), 15.

2. Ibid., 23.

3. The excerpts in this section were pulled from the following sources. The bracketed numbers identify excerpts. [1, 6, 11, 14-17, 21-22, 25-28, 46, 49-50, 54-55, 58, 60, 64] "Smash Reno's Narcotic Ring! By a Federal Narcotic Agent Who Worked on the Case, as Told to Patrick O'Hara," *Official Detective Stories* 4, no. 6 (August 1, 1937); [2] *Grand Forks Herald*, March 19, 1939; [3, 9] "Inferiority Complex Is Usual Basis for Taking of 'Dope'; Lack of Belief in Selves Makes Easy Victim of Men and Women," Anslinger Papers; [4, 10, 13, 19, 29-30, 32-33, 35, 37, 39, 41, 57] James W. Booth, "New Orleans' Dope Secret," *Startling Detective Adventures* 21, no. 122 (September 1938), 34ff; [5, 8, 12, 52] Philip R. Rand, "Kansas City's Drug Mob and the Secret Sleuth," *Startling Detective Adventures* 23 (January 1940); [7] "'Dope' Makes Strange Creatures of Beautiful Women," Anslinger Papers; [18, 31, 36] Frederick Collins, "One Woman against the Narcotic Ring," *Liberty*, February 26, 1938, 43; [20, 24, 38] "White Girl Trap," Anslinger Papers (printed column cut for an album, captions in print: "Dope Den Romeo" and "Oriental Stronghold"); [23] sourceless clipping, Anslinger Papers; [34, 48, 51, 53, 59] George Courson, "The Dope Mob—and the Revolution and the Sunken Clues," *Master Detective*, September 1939, 30; [40, 45, 47] Courtney Ryley Cooper, "Double Dealers in Dope," *American Magazine* 125, no. 5 (May 1938), 74; [42-44] "Find the Girl in the Prowler's Hat! By Detective John Whitman, Homicide Squad, Detroit Police Department, as told to Francis V. Roberts," Anslinger Papers; [56, 61-62] "One World—against Dope," *Washington (DC) Sunday Star This Week Magazine*, March 7, 1948, 4ff; [63] Anslinger and Cooper, "Assassin of Youth," 42.

4. Harry J. Anslinger and William F. Tompkins, *The Traffic in Narcotics* (New York: Funk and Wagnalls, 1953), 214.

5. Anslinger and Tompkins, *Traffic in Narcotics*, 213.

6. Ibid., 218.

7. Ibid., 216.

8. Anslinger and Tompkins, *Traffic in Narcotics*, 213.

9. Ibid., 218.

10. Wilkes, *National Railroad*, 15.

CHAPTER 36

1. "Dangerous Rendezvous with Opium Smugglers Is Bared," *Modesto Bee*, February 9, 1943.

2. Stanley P. Lovell, *Of Spies and Stratagems* (New York: Pocket Books 1963), 122.

3. Toni Howard, "Dope Is His Business," *Saturday Evening Post*, May 7, 1957.

4. Ibid.

5. Ibid.

6. Federal Bureau of Narcotics Training School curriculum, "Undercover Work," Anslinger Papers.

7. XXIV. Physician Presenting Prescription to the Pharmacist and Taking Drugs with Him:
1. Should be looked upon with suspicion.
2. Not considered as an ethical standard.
(Federal Bureau of Narcotics Training School curriculum, Anslinger Papers)

8. William J. Spillard and Pence James, *Needle in a Haystack* (Columbus, OH: McGraw Hill, Whittlesey House, 1945), 146.

9. Rand, "Kansas City's Drug Mob," 50.

10. Much more on George White in the chapter after next.

11. Harry Edward Neal, "The Narcotic Bureau—Men against Demons," chap. 2 in *The Treasury Musketeers* (unpub. ms.), p. 18, Anslinger Papers.

12. Ibid.

CHAPTER 37

1. Alexander Cockburn and Jeffrey St. Clair, *Whiteout: The CIA, Drugs and the Press* (New York; Verso, 1998), 145, 151. The experimental subjects did reveal one truth: they hated their captors.

2. Ibid., 154.

3. As just one example of the ease of using certain social groups in certain experimental contexts, in 1939, University of Iowa Professor Wendell Johnson began an experiment with childhood stuttering at the Soldiers and Sailors Orphans' Home in Davenport, Iowa.

4. Harriet A. Washington, *Medical Apartheid: The Dark History of Medical Experimentation on Black Americans from Colonial Times to the Present* (New York: Anchor, 2007). From 1951 to 1974, for one example, University of Pennsylvania Dr. Albert Kligman performed skin experiments on hundreds of prisoners at Holmesburg Prison; when he first visited the prison he famously exclaimed, "All I saw before me were acres of skin," the captive people naturalized as earth, as natural resource, the whole prison population laid out before him like one big body of experiment. Ian Urbina, "Panel Suggests Using Inmates in Drug Trials," *New York Times*, August 13, 2006.

5. H. L. Andrews, "Cortical Effects of Demerol," *Journal of Pharmacology and Experimental Therapeutics* 76, no.1 (September 1942): 89, 90–93.

6. Ibid.

7. Herbert Wieder, "Addiction to Meperidine Hydrochloride (Demerol Hydrochloride): Report of Three Cases," *Journal of the American Medical Association* 132, no. 17 (December 28, 1946): 1067.

8. Ibid., 1066.

9. Ibid.

10. Clipping, Anslinger Papers.

11. Ibid.

12. Ibid.

13. Harris Isbell et. al., "Tolerance and Addiction Liability of 6-Dimethylamino-4-4-Diphenylheptanone-3 (Methadon)," *Journal of the American Medical Association* 135, no. 14 (December 6, 1947): 889.

14. Ibid.

15. Ibid.

16. Ibid., 883.

17. Ibid., 894.

18. Norman Carlisle and Madelyn Carlisle, "Thrill Pills Can Ruin You—Barbiturates," *Colliers*, April 23, 1949, 20.

19. Clippings, Anslinger Papers.

20. Carlisle and Carlisle, "Thrill Pills," 60.

21. Ibid.

22. Howard Whitman, "One Up on Narcotics," *Collier's*, December 15, 1945, 88.

23. Ibid.

24. Clipping, Anslinger Papers.

25. "Marihuana Research" by Dr. H. J. Anslinger, United States Commissioner of Narcotics, reprinted from the *1938 Convention Book of the Association of Medical Students*, Anslinger Papers.

26. "Anticipated Need for Opium, Critical and Strategic Material," Anslinger Papers.

27. McWilliams, *The Protectors*, 96.

28. Clipping, Anslinger Papers.

29. U.S. Congress, *Traffic in, and Control of, Narcotics, Barbiturates, and Amphetamines*, 84th Cong., 2nd sess., 1955–56, 412–14.

CHAPTER 38

1. "This suggests that behavior of any kind might fruitfully be studied developmentally, in terms of changes in meanings and concepts, their organizations and reorganization, and the way they channel behavior, making some acts possible while excluding others." Howard S. Becker, "Becoming a Marijuana User," *American Journal of Sociology* 59, 3 (November 1953): 242.

2. Anslinger and Tompkins, *Traffic in Narcotics*, 296–97.

3. US Congress, *Illicit Narcotics Traffic: Hearings before the Subcommittee on Improvements in the Federal Criminal Code of the Committee on the Judiciary*, 84th Cong., 1st sess., 1955–56, 16.

4. Gerald G. Gross, "U.S. Narcotics Chief for Stern Penalties," *Washington Post*, November 11, 1939.

5. Eli Marcovitz and Henry J. Meyers, "Army Study of Marijuana Smokers Points to Better Ways of Treatment," *Newsweek*, January 15, 1945, 72.

6. Warren Weaver Jr., "U.S. Aide for Death in Narcotics Sales," *New York Times*, September 8, 1951.

7. "The trouble with the death penalty would be that juries would acquit guilty people." Congressional Record, "Appendix," March 23, 1953, A1545.

8. "Inferiority Complex Is Usual Basis for Taking of 'Dope'; Lack of Belief in Selves Makes Easy Victim of Men and Women," Anslinger Papers, for example.

9. Wieder, "Addiction to Meperidine," 1067.

10. Urbina, "Panel Suggests Using Inmates."

11. Jonathan D. Moreno, *Undue Risk: Secret State Experiments on Humans* (New York: Routledge, 2001), 251.

12. Cockburn and St. Clair, *Whiteout*, 195, 202–3.

13. Soon thereafter, Hayes died from an overdose of previously seized heroin. Douglas Valentine, *The Strength of the Wolf: The Secret History of America's War on Drugs* (New York: Verso Books, 2004), 135.

14. Cockburn and St. Clair, *Whiteout*, 207.

15. Valentine, *Strength of the Wolf*, 235.

CHAPTER 39

1. *Bangor Daily News*, August 1, 1942, Anslinger Papers.

2. Ibid.

3. Office Memorandum: U.S. Government to Commissioner of Narcotics from District #14, November 15, 1951, Anslinger Papers. The attached clipping was taken from the article "Help Wanted in Washington," 127.

4. Clipping, Anslinger Papers.

5. Ben F. Widger, "Who's Who and Why," Anslinger Papers.

6. "World Authority," *Bangor Daily News*, [date unknown], and "Man for the Place," *Bangor Daily News*, June 22, 1946, [clippings], Anslinger Papers.

7. "Marihuana Research" by Dr. H. J. Anslinger.

8. H. J. Anslinger, "The Psychiatric Aspects of Marihuana Intoxication," *Journal of the American Medical Association* 121, no. 3 (January 16, 1943): 212–13.

9. "Merry Go Round," *Bangor Daily News*, October 8, 1951.

10. Ray Tucker, "National Whirligig: News Behind the News," *Telegraph*, September 17, 1948. Robert Mitchum was arrested on September 1, 1948. His subsequent conviction was overturned in 1951.

11. "Help Wanted in Washington," Anslinger Papers.

CHAPTER 40

1. Gerald R. Scott, "How Opium, a Jap Weapon, Perils the World," *Sunday Mirror Magazine*, August 12, 1945.

2. Hendrik De Leeuw, "Japan Continues Narcotic Traffic in World Trade," *Toledo Times*, November 25, 1945.

3. Untitled, undated, unpublished retirement speech about Harry J. Anslinger, possibly self-authored, in Anslinger Papers.

4. "Red China Waging Drug War," *Akron Beacon Journal*, April 26, 1952.

5. Ibid.

6. Edward S. Sullivan, "Smashing Red China's Fifth Column," *Master Detective*, December 1954, 8ff.

7. United Nations, "Red Chinese Accused of Drug War on GIs," Anslinger Papers.

8. Ibid.

9. The Federal Bureau of Narcotics reported a steady climb in seizures of narcotics from 1945 to 1948, and then a significant jump in 1951. Accurate numbers are hard to come by, but reports of the increase contributed to the development of legislation in the 1950s; this will be discussed in chapter 42.

10. Gore Files, Anslinger Papers.

11. Sullivan, "Smashing Red China's Fifth Column."

CHAPTER 41

1. William Burroughs and Allen Ginsberg, *The Yage Letters Redux*, ed. Oliver Harris (1963; repr., San Francisco: City Lights Books, 2006).

2. R. H. Boll, "Lotus Eater," *The Word and Work* 47, no. 12 (December 1953), 275.

3. Ibid.

4. Gwendolyn Brooks, *Maud Martha* (New York: Harper & Row, 1953; Chicago: Third World Press, 1993) 104–5. Citations refer to the Third World Press edition.

5. Burroughs and Ginsberg, *Yage Letters Redux*, 22.

6. Brooks, *Maud Martha*, 9.

7. Boll, "Lotus Eaters," 276.

8. Burroughs and Ginsberg, *Yage Letters Redux*, 124. The misspelling of Tangier is Ginsberg's in the original.

9. Ibid.

10. Franz Boas, "The Methods of Ethnology," *American Anthropologist* 22, 4 (October–December 1920), in *Ethnographic Fieldwork: An Anthropological Reader*, ed. Antonius C. G. M. Robben and Jeffrey A. Skula. (Malden, MA: Blackwell Publishing, 2007), 42.

11. Aldous Huxley, *The Doors of Perception* (London: Chatto & Windus, 1956), 63.

12. Brooks, *Maud Martha*, 101.

13. Boas, "Methods of Ethnology," 42.

14. Martha Gellhorn to Bernard Benson, September 17, 1953, in *Selected Letters of Martha Gellhorn* (New York: Holt, 2007), 243.

15. Huxley, *Doors of Perception*, 31.

16. Anslinger and Tompkins, *Traffic in Narcotics*, 1.

17. Ibid.

18. Brooks, *Maud Martha*, 146.

19. H. P. Albarelli Jr., *A Terrible Mistake: The Murder of Frank Olson and the CIA's Secret Cold War Experiments* (Walterville, OR: Trine Day, 2009), 246, 412.

20. Brooks, *Maud Martha*, 45.

21. US Congress, Senate, Select Committee on Intelligence and the Subcommittee on Health and Scientific Research of the Committee on Human Resources, *Project MKULTRA, The CIA's Program of Research in Behavioral Modification*, 95th Cong., 1st sess., August 3, 1977, 5 (statement of Stansfield Turner).

22. Philip Bagby, "Culture and the Causes of Culture," *American Anthropologist* 55, no. 4 (October 1953): 535–54.

23. Bronislaw Malinowski, "Method and Scope of Anthropological Fieldwork," in *Argonauts of the Western Pacific: An Account of Native Enterprise and Adventure in the Archipelagoes of Melanesian New Guinea* (1922; repr., Prospect Heights, IL: Waveland Press, 1984), in Robben and Skula, *Ethnographic Fieldwork*, 56.

24. Burroughs and Ginsberg, *Yage Letters Redux*, 28.

25. Brooks, *Maud Martha*, 113.

26. Ibid., 68.

27. Boll, "Lotus Eaters," 276.

28. Burroughs and Ginsberg, *Yage Letters Redux*, 26–27.

29. Ruth Benedict, *Patterns of Culture* (1934; repr., New York: Houghton Mifflin, 2005), 3.

30. Boll, "Lotus Eaters," 276.

31. Huxley, *Doors of Perception*, 64.

32. Ibid, 2.

33. Brooks, *Maud Martha*, 26–27.

34. Ibid.

35. Huxley, *Doors of Perception*, 7.

36. Burroughs and Ginsburg, *Yage Letters Redux*, 70.

37. Barry Miles, *Call Me Burroughs: A Life* (New York: Twelve, 2013), 128.

38. Anslinger and Tompkins, *Traffic in Narcotics*, 1.

39. Burroughs and Ginsburg, *Yage Letters Redux*, 36.

40. Albarelli, *Terrible Mistake*, 412.

41. Malinowski, "Scope of Anthropological Fieldwork," 51.

42. Boll, "Lotus Eaters," 275.

43. Brooks, *Maud Martha*, 132.

44. George White to Sidney Gottlieb, 1996, quoted in Cockburn and St. Clair, *Whiteout*, 209.

45. E. E. Evans-Pritchard, foreword to *The People of the Sierra*, by J. A. Pitt-Rivers (New York: Criterion Books, 1945), ix.

46. Burroughs and Ginsburg, *Yage Letters Redux*, 25–26.

47. Select Committee on Intelligence and Committee on Human Resources, *Project MKULTRA*, 6 (statement of Stansfield Turner).

48. William Burroughs, *Junky* (New York: Penguin, 1977), 133. First published in 1953 by Abe Books.

49. Brooks, *Maud Martha*, 178–79.

50. Gellhorn to Benson, September 17, 1953, in *Selected Letters*, 243.

51. Huxley, *Doors of Perception*, 7.

52. Boll, "Lotus Eaters," 276.

53. Anslinger and Tompkins, *Traffic in Narcotics*, 2.

54. Ibid. Odd phrasing in the original.

55. Huxley, *Doors of Perception*, 55.

56. Anslinger and Tompkins, *Traffic in Narcotics*, 2.

57. William Burroughs, "In the Interests of National Security," in *The Adding Machine* (New York: Seaver Books, 1986), 155.

58. Boll, "Lotus Eaters," 275.

59. Anslinger, *Protectors*, 171-72.

60. Gellhorn to Benson, September 17, 1953, in *Selected Letters*, 244.

61. Brooks, *Maud Martha*, 113.

62. Tony Bennett, "Stranger to Paradise" (1953).

63. Boll, "Lotus Eaters," 276.

64. Erich Hesse, *Narcotics and Drug Addiction* (New York: Philosophical Library, Inc., 1946), 22.

65. Burroughs and Ginsburg, *Yage Letters Redux*, 70.

66. Collage of Boll, "Lotus Eaters," 276; Brooks, *Maud Martha*, 105; and Burroughs and Ginsberg, *Yage Letters Redux*, 29.

67. Boll, "Lotus Eaters," 276.

68. Collage of Burroughs and Ginsberg, *Yage Letters Redux*, 28-29; Gellhorn, *Selected Letters*, 316; and Hesse, *Narcotics*, 22.

69. Burroughs and Ginsberg, *Yage Letters Redux*, 70.

70. Bennett, "Stranger to Paradise."

71. Boll, "Lotus Eaters," 275.

72. Bennett, "Stranger in Paradise."

73. Brooks, *Maud Martha*, 180.

CHAPTER 42

1. McWilliams, *The Protectors*, 114.

2. "Masterly Service, Cynical Reward" *Christian Science Monitor*, January 9, 1953, 22.

3. Department of the Treasury, Bureau of Narcotics, Advisory Committee to the Federal Bureau of Narcotics, "Interim Report of the Joint Committee of the American Bar Association and the American Medical Association on Narcotic Drugs" (New York, 1958).

4. Ibid.

5. Department of the Treasury, Bureau of Narcotics, Advisory Committee to the Federal Bureau of Narcotics, "Comments on the Interim Report of the Joint Committee of the American Bar Association and the American Medical Association on Narcotic Drugs" (1958), 170.

6. Anslinger to Hon. Morris Ploscowe, New York, March 4, 1958, quoted in Advisory Committee, "Comments on Interim Report," vii.

7. Federal Bureau of Narcotics Training School curriculum, Anslinger Papers.

8. Carlisle and Carlisle, "Thrill Pills."

9. McWilliams, *The Protectors*, 99.

CHAPTER 43

1. "William Tompkins, Ex-Prosecutor, 76; Fought Subversives," *New York Times*, July 8, 1989.

2. "However the Bureau is not completely powerless to prevent a physician who is misusing narcotic drugs from obtaining them even though they may not revoke his license. The case of Ratigan v. Commissioner of Narcotics is authority for the proposition that the Bureau of Narcotics may properly request registered drug manufacturers and dealers to refrain from filling narcotic orders for a particular physician." Anslinger and Tompkins, *Traffic in Narcotics*, 135. In the early 1930s, Dr. Ratigan ran a clinic he called the Public Health Institute in Seattle. He was committed to responding to addicts and he gave injections on-site only, and when prosecuted by the Federal Bureau of Narcotics, he was subsequently represented in court by the renowned John F. Dore, former mayor of Seattle. According to Anslinger, Ratigan was "unregenerate" (ibid.). Rufus King, a lawyer and author of one of the most detailed, credible, and influential chronicles of the history of the drug war, saw it differently: "If this were a work of fiction, I would present Dr. Ratigan very much as he played his part in real life—only I would substitute a victorious ending. I believe he was right and had he emerged as a conqueror instead

a near-forgotten martyr, America might well have been turned back toward dictates of common sense in the 1930's, avoiding most of the errors and excesses of the three succeeding decades." King, *The Drug Hang-Up*, 49.

3. David T. Courtwright, *Dark Paradise: A History of Opiate Addiction in America* (Cambridge, MA: Harvard University Press, 2001), 120.

4. Anslinger and Oursler, *The Murderers*.

5. Anslinger, *The Protectors*.

6. Ibid., 3.

7. John A. Williams, ed., *The Angry Black* (New York: Lancer Books, 1962), front cover.

8. "Case Eight: The Protectors (1964)," in *John A. Williams: Writings of Consequence* [online exhibition], Department of Rare Books and Special Collections, University of Rochester, accessed 2013, http://rbscp.lib.rochester.edu/2987.

9. Ibid.

10. Ibid.

11. Abe Cobus, interview by John C. McWilliams, January 16, 1985, Altoona, PA, quoted in McWilliams, *The Protectors*, 187.

12. Anslinger and Tompkins, *Traffic in Narcotics*, 1.

13. "Incognito Operations" (33-7), in Federal Bureau of Narcotics Training School curriculum, "Undercover Work," Anslinger Papers.

CHAPTER 44

1. "Closed Far Eastern Opium Monopolies," "Destruction of World-Wide Narcotic Drug Rings," "Tied Up Ships Engaged in Smuggling," "Anti-Communist Investigations," Anslinger Papers.

2. Unattributed retirement speech, Anslinger Papers.

3. Address of Henry L. Giordano, commissioner, Federal Bureau of Narcotics, 1962 Remington Medal dinner, December 4, 1962.

4. Ibid.

CHAPTER 45

1. Robert F. Kennedy, address at the White House Conference on Narcotic and Drug Abuse, September 28, 1962, p. 2. Typescript available at http://www.justice.gov/sites/default/files/ag/legacy/2011/01/20/09-28-1962.pdf (accessed February 17, 2016).

2. Ibid.

3. H. J. Anslinger, United States representative on the United Nations Commission on Narcotic Drugs, "International Narcotic Control" [draft], statement before the White House Conference on Narcotic and Drug Abuse, September 27 and 28, 1962, pp. 2, 4 (quotations), Anslinger Papers.

4. Ibid., 1.

5. "The attached document is a progress report of an ad hoc panel convened at the request of the president by his Scientific Advisor, Sept 7, 1962" [unpublished typescript document issued by the White House in advance of the White House Conference on Narcotics], Anslinger Papers.

6. Anslinger, "International Narcotic Control," 4.

7. Werner D. Chasin and David L. Pierce, "Treatment of Epistaxis," *New England Journal of Medicine* 267, no. 13 (September 27, 1962): 660–61.

CHAPTER 46

1. Carol Parks, "Harry Jacob Anslinger: Distinguished Citizen," *Town and Gown*, September 1968, 47, quoted in McWilliams, *The Protectors*, 186.

2. Chuck Terry, *Overcoming Prison and Addiction* (Boston: Cengage Learning, 2002), 34.

3. Global Commission on Drug Policy, *War on Drugs*, June 2011, p. 24, accessed Octo-

ber 16, 2015, http://www.globalcommissionondrugs.org/wp-content/themes/gcdp_v1/pdf/
Global_Commission_Report_English.pdf.

CHAPTER 47

1. Twain, *Following the Equator*, 312. This chapter is a collage. Additional sources noted throughout.

2. Rachel Ehrenfeld, *Narco-terrorism* (New York: Basic Books, 1990), 166. In 1989, a highly decorated DEA agent, Edward K. O'Brien, admitted to carrying cocaine from Florida to Boston on two occasions for $147,000. On the second trip, he was arrested with sixty-two pounds of cocaine in his possession.

3. "Topics in the Sagebrush," *New York Times*, February 21, 1881, 1–2, quoted in Charles Edward Terry and Mildred Pellens, *The Opium Problem* (New York: Bureau of Social Hygiene, 1928), 33.

4. John E. Hensley, interview, *Frontline: Drug Wars*, PBS, October 10, 2000, http://www.pbs.org/wgbh/pages/frontline/shows/drugs/interviews/hensley.html.

5. Cupcake Brown, *A Piece of Cake: A Memoir* (New York: Three Rivers Press, 2007), 204–5.

6. Fernando Arenas, interview, *Frontline: Drug Wars*, PBS, October 10, 2000, http://www.pbs.org/wgbh/pages/frontline/shows/drugs/interviews/arenas.html.